The second section of *The Georgia Catalog* is a complete, updated listing of nearly four hundred sites in the Historic American Buildings Survey. Each entry gives the precise location of the site; a brief description of the structure; the date of construction and the name of the architect, if known; changes in name, structure, or location of the building; its present condition; any facts of historical significance; and the number and dates of drawings, photographs, and data sheets in the HABS collection at the Library of Congress.

To add to its value as a guide, the volume also includes a glossary of architectural terms and a list of Georgia properties that are included in the National Register of Historic Places, have been designated National Landmarks, or are part of the Historic American Engineering Record.

front cover marked up as of 1/26/10

W.H.S. / NERL-HQ

The Georgia Catalog

Historic American Buildings Survey

This book was published with

the generous assistance of

THE WORMSLOE FOUNDATION

and is volume fifteen in their

publication series.

JOHN LINLEY

The Georgia Catalog

Historic American Buildings Survey

A Guide to the Architecture of the State

The University of Georgia Press Athens, Georgia

Historic American Buildings Survey
National Park Service
Department of the Interior
Washington, D.C.

Part I. A History of the Architecture of the State, copyright © 1982
by the University of Georgia Press, Athens, Georgia 30602

Printed in the United States of America

Set in Trump Medieval types

Library of Congress Cataloging in Publication Data
Linley, John.
    The Georgia catalog, Historic American Buildings
Survey.
    (Publications / The Wormsloe Foundation; v. 15)
    Bibliography: p.
    Includes index.
    1. Architecture—Georgia—History. 2. Historic
buildings—Georgia—Catalogs. I. Historic American
Buildings Survey. II. Title. III. Series:
Publications (Wormsloe Foundation); v. 15.
NA730.G4L564   720'.9758   81-19856
ISBN 0-8203-0613-4   AACR2
ISBN 0-8203-0614-2 (pbk.)

Contents

Acknowledgments

The author wishes to express his gratitude to the many organizations and individuals who have contributed to this book: to those who graciously gave him entree into their historic homes, to those who furnished needed information and data, and to those who contributed photographs taken to the exacting requirements of the Historic American Buildings Survey. Such helpful individuals and organizations are too numerous to acknowledge each by name, but the list would include the initial editor, Iris Hill, whose enthusiasm for the original manuscript was a major factor leading to its publication. Exceedingly helpful were Mr. Coy Ballard, Mrs. Janice Biggers, Miss Lurleen Collier, Mr. William Cawthon, Mrs. Patricia Cooper, Mr. Charles Doyle, Mrs. Carolyn Humphreys, Dr. Albert I. Ike, Mrs. Elizabeth Lyons, Mr. James Marshall, Mr. John McKay, Dr. Ernest Melvin, Mrs. Mary L. Morrison, Mr. Ed Neal, Mr. W. L. Sheftall, Miss Dee Shelander, Mr. David Sherman, Mr. Kenneth Thomas, and Mr. Fred Wilencheck.

The staffs of the Georgia Room and the Rare Books Room of the University of Georgia Libraries were unfailingly helpful as were those of the Georgia Historical Society Library and the Historic Preservation Section of the Georgia Department of Natural Resources. The Institute of Community and Area Development of the University of Georgia provided funds to help procure photographs and drawings not otherwise available. Robert Gamble, who is preparing a similar catalog for the state of Alabama, and Allen Chambers, Jr., of the staff of the Historical American Buildings Survey, helped in innumerable ways including editing the manuscript and offering valuable suggestions as the work progressed.

My special thanks to David Lunde, campus architect, who taught my classes for a term so that I would be free to work on the book, to William Hudson, director of campus planning, who allotted him time to do so, and to Dr. S. Eugene Younts, vice-president for services, and to Dr. Robert C. Anderson, vice-president for research, who arranged for the leave of absence.

J. L.

Sponsors for HABS Photographs

The Magazine *Antiques*
Athens Historical Society
Atlanta Arts Alliance
Atlanta Historical Society
Baldwin County Historical Society
Mr. William N. Banks, Georgia Trust for
  Historic Preservation
The Descendants of Lamartine T.
  Hardman, M.D.
Historic Augusta Incorporated
Historic Columbus Foundation

Laurens County Historical Society
McDuffie County Historical Society
Old Campbell County Historical Society
Old Clinton Historical Society
Putnam County Historical Society
Mr. Phinizy Spalding
University of Georgia Institute of Com-
  munity and Area Development
Washington-Wilkes Historical Society
Mr. H. Fred Wilencheck

Foreword

During my twenty-one years in Georgia, I became aware of the wealth of historic architecture within the state. Having been raised in Massachusetts I felt I had an inside track on architectural excellence and historic preservation, but I soon discovered that Georgia held its own on both counts. And then to have had the Historic American Buildings Survey as one of my responsibilities was a real honor and pleasure. The survey, or HABS as it is affectionately known in the preservation community, is among the oldest of the federal government's many efforts to document America's architectural and historical resources. Established in 1933 as a program of the National Park Service, the survey has amassed a wealth of archival material in the form of architectural measured drawings, written data, and photographs during its forty-eight-year existence. From 1978 to 1981 HABS operated within the Interior Department's Heritage Conservation and Recreation Service (HCRS); it is now back within the organizational framework of the National Park Service. Under the aegis of both HABS has expanded its horizons in recent years from a strictly documentary approach to act as a catalyst in the actual preservation and reuse of the buildings and areas it records. In Georgia, as much as in any state, this new approach is manifest. In the summer of 1979, HABS field teams recorded both Atlanta's Sweet Auburn and Savannah's Victorian historic districts. In Atlanta, the survey team not only produced accurate drawings of the structures of Auburn Avenue as they now exist, but prepared drawings and models of what a revitalized avenue, with compatible new construction, could become. Records made by the Savannah team are being used in the renovations of now dilapidated structures, to insure that these renovations will be accomplished without destroying significant original fabric. Also in 1979, an inventory team identified important buildings which will be affected by the construction of the Richard B. Russell Dam and Reservoir in Elbert County. These buildings were further documented in 1980, and the HABS drawings will insure an accurate and authentic reconstruction of those identified as of paramount importance. These and other such projects are undertaken by HABS in concert with local, state, and federal agencies whose responsibilities and interests include the preservation arena.

With the increase in records which

these and other projects have produced, the survey has a keen interest in seeing that its collections are publicized and used. The publication of the HABS Georgia catalog, one in a series of state catalogs, is undertaken with this aim in mind. In 1957 Frederick D. Nichols wrote in his introduction to *The Early Architecture of Georgia* that "in spite of the stature of the architecture of Georgia, little has been written about it." Fortunately, during the interim a number of articulate scholars have taken up his editorial gauntlet, and a formidable corpus of works dealing with the architecture of the state now exists. HABS feels fortunate to have secured the services of John Linley to compile its Georgia catalog, and to have as a part of this book his architectural history of the state.

We anticipate that many more recording projects will be undertaken in Georgia in the future, and we look forward to them. Much has been done, as we hope this catalog will demonstrate, but much more remains. Meanwhile, Georgia is most definitely on our minds.

Hope T. Moore
Former Associate Director
  for Cultural Programs
Heritage Conservation and
  Recreation Service
United States Department
  of the Interior

Preface

The Historic American Buildings Survey (HABS) was founded in 1933 during the depression years as a part of the Civil Works Program, to produce accurate records of significant American architecture and to provide work for architects, draftsmen, and photographers. In 1934 the survey was made a continuing program under the National Park Service in the United States Department of the Interior. In 1935 the Library of Congress and the American Institute of Architects agreed to help administer the program. The records, including photographs and drawings, were filed at the Library of Congress, which issued copies on request. A comprehensive catalog of the HABS buildings was published in 1941, and a supplement in 1959.

The records, including those of many buildings that have since been destroyed, have proven of inestimable and ever-increasing value, particularly to architects and architectural historians. Over the years, buildings have been added to the survey, and use of the records has proliferated. To accommodate the expanded survey and to facilitate its use, catalogs for states or groups of states are being, or have been, prepared.

The catalog for Georgia is divided into two principal parts: the first is a history of and a guide to the architecture of the state; the second, a revised record of the data for each of the HABS buildings in Georgia. To add to its value as a guide, *The Georgia Catalog* also includes a list of Georgia properties that are included in the National Register of Historic Places, have been designated National Landmarks, or are part of the Historic American Engineering Record.

The major portion of the survey was assembled in the 1930s, and in retrospect there are noticeable omissions, particularly of buildings constructed after the Civil War. To rectify this in part, representative examples of omitted types are also included here. Because the Historic American Buildings Survey is a continuing program, it is anticipated that more examples will be included in the near future and that underrepresented areas will be expanded as funds permit.

The data in the catalog are given in standard HABS format, listed according to the nearest town or city, with the name of the county and the county's HABS number, the name and HABS number of the building, its precise location, a brief description, the date of construction if ascertainable, the name of the architect if known, changes in the structure or location of the building, its present condition, and the number and dates of any drawings (sheets), photographs, and data pages.

The author or a qualified representative has visited each site. Care has been taken to assure the accuracy of the information given here, but in a project of this scope there are bound to be some errors. Persons finding errors or having more accurate data are asked to report such information to HABS so that corrections can be made in later catalogs.

Copies of the photographs, drawings, and data pages listed here are available at moderate prices from the Division of Prints and Photographs, Library of Congress, Washington, D.C. 20450.

The author is a practicing architect and a teacher. His primary interest lies in the rationale and logic that produced the architecture, in the effect that past architecture has had on modern architecture, and in the lessons that the past has for present and future architects. This study reflects those factors. It also emphasizes the influence of climate, ecology, landscape, and city planning on both historic and contemporary architecture. Though the emphases may differ, it is hoped that this history of Georgia architecture will be seen as complementary to, rather than in conflict with, more conventional architectural histories.

Part I
A History of the Architecture
of the State

The symbol ⋆ following the name of a site or building indicates that the site or building is included in the Georgia Catalog of the Historic American Buildings Survey. See Part II for individual listings.

Chapter One

Out of the Clouded Past

Few relics from the past could be found that would lend more credence to the popular theory that early monuments were built as signals to gods, or to men from outer space,[1] than two ancient effigy mounds in Putnam County. Built of rocks and shaped like birds with outspread wings, the true forms of the effigies are not recognizable from the ground, but appear to be emblazoned on the hills when seen from above. One of the mounds, known as Rock Eagle★, located at the Rock Eagle 4-H Center near Eatonton, is accessible and has been provided with a viewing tower, where its powerful stylized form can be appreciated by today's visitors. The effigy measures 120 feet from wingtip to wingtip, and 102 feet from head to tail. The other effigy is the same length, but has a wider wingspread and is oriented differently.

Monumental and enigmatic, they are awe-inspiring examples of Georgia's prehistoric architecture. Because no original artifacts have been found within them, no precise dates can be assigned to these ancient memorials, though comparisons have been made between these and the effigy earth mounds found in other sections of the country. It is generally agreed that such mounds date from the Woodland period (roughly 1000 B.C. to A.D. 700 or 1000). Some archaeologists, however, have asserted that the rock eagles, as they are called, were built much earlier.

Equally old or older are the shellfish-eater mounds (8000 to 1000 B.C.) scattered along the coast and up the rivers of Georgia. A number of these are in the form of perfect circles and measure up to 300 feet in diameter. They seem to have been primarily refuse heaps, though some were converted to burial mounds or used as bases for later earth mounds.

In Georgia, earth mounds were usually either burial or temple mounds, the ones called temple mounds having been built as platforms for temples or chiefs' houses. The mounds might be oval or rectangular, but all had steeply sloping sides. Access was by ramps, usually on the eastern side and ascending in a straight line, but sometimes spiraling like an ancient ziggurat. Though smaller ones were being built as late as DeSoto's time,[2] and the Kolomoki Mounds near Blakely are thought to be earlier, most of the great mounds were built between A.D. 1000 and 1300. The largest mound in Georgia is one of the Kolomoki group. This rectangular mound measures 325 feet at its base and stands 56 feet high.

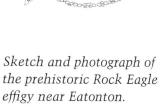

Sketch and photograph of the prehistoric Rock Eagle effigy near Eatonton.

The Ocmulgee Mounds near Macon are of special interest because the original layout of the village has been indicated and some of the buildings have been accurately restored on the site. The foundation, seats, firepit, and platform (all of clay) of the winter council chamber were found intact, and enough of the charred remains of its timber roof were found so that the earth-covered room could be reconstructed. The platform is in the shape of an eagle, a recurring motif in American Indian art.

The Etowah Mounds near Cartersville cover forty acres and are rich in artifacts that have much in common with pre-Columbian Mexican art.

A lone mound on the grounds of the Nichols-Hardman House★ in Nacoochee Valley rises abruptly from the level floor of the valley, and for the past hundred years has been whimsically capped with a Victorian gazebo. William Bartram, who visited the site in 1773, described the mound as being forty or fifty feet high, with a still-visible spiral track leading to its summit.[3] About one hundred years later, Charles C. Jones, Jr., wrote of it, "Within the recollection of the oldest inhabitants, it has lost much of its original dimensions."[4] Unfortunately, most of the earth mounds have lost their original dimensions, while others have disappeared completely.

According to Spanish records, Indian villages of the sixteenth century in Georgia were handsomely constructed and rich in treasures. Garcilaso de la Vega, who wrote one of the early accounts of DeSoto's expedition, described an Indian town named Talomico, thought to have been in the vicinity of Augusta.

Ocmulgee Mounds Council Chamber, Macon vicinity, A.D. 900–1100.

Talomico is described as a town of some five hundred houses situated on an eminence overlooking the gorge of a river and containing the most impressive examples of native architecture witnessed by DeSoto's expedition. The principal building was a temple which served as a sepulcher for notables. According to the description, it was more than a hundred feet in length, forty in width, and was proportionately high. The roof was covered with several layers of mats which were made of reeds and of slender canes split in half. The mats were said to have been similar to those made by the Moors, and the roofs built of them to be impervious to sun and rain, and to be beautiful when seen from the exterior or the interior. Over the roof of the temple, many large and small shells had been arranged, placed with the inside out so as to display their luster. Between them had been placed large strands of pearls "half a fathom in length, which hung in a graduated manner so that some left where others began. . . . They made a splendid sight in the brilliance of the sun."

Inside, and close to the doorway, were six pairs of giant, ferocious-appearing statues bearing various types of arms and seeming to guard the entrance. The first two bore massive clubs, the upper fourth of which were "spiked with diamonds" (rock crystal?), and were said to have borne a remarkable likeness to those seen in paintings of Hercules.

The other statues are also described, as are the coffins and chests of valuables (there was no gold), and the ceiling of the temple, which was adorned with "strands of pearls and seed pearls which were stretched so as to adhere to and follow the contour of the roof. Among these decorations were great headdresses of different colors of feathers such as those made for wear, and in addition to the pearls stretched along the ceiling and the feathers nailed to it, there were many others which had been suspended by some thin, soft-colored strings that could not be seen distinctly. Thus both pearls and feathers seemed to have been placed in the air at different levels so that they would appear to be falling from the roof. In this manner the ceiling of the temple was adorned from the walls upward, and it was an agreeable sight to behold."[5]

Twentieth-century excavations of the Etowah Mounds have uncovered some of the valuables that were customarily interred with the notables. These included pearls, necklaces, carved shell and copper ornaments, mica ornaments, embossed copper plates, stone weapons, decorated pottery, and, perhaps most interesting, a pair of marble statues, male and female. The figure of the male is 22½

Mound with gazebo on the grounds of the Nichols-Hardman House in Nacoochee Valley.

inches high, that of the female 15¾. Both are represented in squatting positions and have traces of white, red, black, and a greenish-black paint. The primitive, stylized quality of the sculpture imbues the statues with a power and an apparent size greater than the actual dimensions. These and other artifacts are exhibited at the Etowah Mounds Museum near Cartersville.

Though the custom of erecting mounds had apparently ceased in Georgia before the English colonists arrived, important buildings in some villages were still being placed on older preexisting mounds during the years just before the American Revolution, and the Indians generally adhered to the original basic plan for their villages, a plan that consisted of a great open plaza surrounded by public buildings and houses. Large settlements might have two or more such plazas. All the villages were surrounded by palisades. Bartram wrote that the "plazas were well built and maintained . . . and the households neatly arranged in rectangular blocks with wide streets leading to the square."[6]

During colonial times, numerous descriptions and drawings were made of the houses, not all of them consistent. The Creeks and Cherokees had separate summer and winter houses, with auxiliary buildings for storage. The summer houses were rectangular, usually with gabled or arched roofs covered with thatch or bark. The sides were partly open, partly covered with split clapboards. Occasionally the only opening would be a small doorway. Most were whitewashed, inside and out, with pulverized oyster shell or white clay.[7]

The winter houses were small, tight, and heavily insulated. Those of the Cherokees were rectangular in plan; those of the Creeks and Chickasaws, round. Roofs were plastered inside and out with six or seven inches of clay mixed with dried grass or Spanish moss and covered with thatch or bark shingles. An English traveler who lived among the Carolina Indians in the early eighteenth century wrote of such houses:

These savages live in wigwams or cabins built of bark which are made round like an oven, to prevent any damage by gales or wind. They make the fire in the middle of the house and have a hole in the top of the roof right above

the stoves, to let out the smoke. These dwellings are as hot as stoves, where the Indians sleep and sweat all night. . . . I have never felt any ill unsavory smell in their cabins, whereas should we live as they do, we should be poisoned with our own nastiness; which confirms the Indians to be, as they really are, some of the sweetest people in the world.[8]

The houses varied in detail from time to time and from place to place. A Creek chief, Inomatuhata, one of the fourteen who signed the 1783 Augusta treaty known as the Wofford Settlement, lived in what was described as a "picturesque house made of the branches of hickory trees, carefully intertwined and neatly plastered both inside and out, with a light, brick-colored mortar. . . . The roof was of moss, evidently taken from the swamps a few miles to the south, and growing, soon became impervious to water."[9] This house was located on Pea Ridge, north of the present town of Winder.

During the nineteenth century, the Indians, their culture, and their architecture were overwhelmed by the white settlers. The Cherokees endured for a while by adapting to the settlers' culture. In 1821 one of their number, Sequoya, devised a Cherokee alphabet and taught the chiefs to read. The newly acquired knowledge spread; by 1828 the *Cherokee Phoenix*, a weekly newspaper in Cherokee and English, was being published in New Echota in Gordon County. New Echota was the capital of the Cherokee nation, and its

Vann House, Spring Place, 1805.

public and private buildings are now being reconstructed. Houses of the nineteenth-century Cherokees varied from the ancient types to log cabins (a type of construction borrowed from the settlers), to frame or brick dwellings. Some, such as Carter's Quarters★ at Carters, and the Vann House★ at Spring Place were equal in size and style to the finest of the settlers' homes.[10]

The name of their newspaper was prophetic. The subsequent history of the Cherokees was to be a series of shattering defeats and phoenixlike recoveries: their forced removal to the Oklahoma Territory in 1838, their renewed prosperity in that territory, the loss of their slaves and the destruction of their property during the Civil War, their recovery during and after the Reconstruction years, and then the forced sale of much of their land in 1892 and the remainder in 1902.

Except for descendants of mixed blood and for a few small groups who are mostly

Carter's Quarters at Carters, built in the early nineteenth century.

of Creek extraction and live in isolated communities, only relics remain in Georgia of those Indian nations that successively occupied the region. Relics include the ancient mounds and monuments, innumerable arrowheads and artifacts whose dates span the millennia, and the last mementos, houses that survived because their basic design was so similar to that desired by the invading settlers that they were taken and maintained by them for their own use.

Chapter Two   The Colonial Period

When Oglethorpe selected a high bluff overlooking the Savannah River as the site for the first English settlement in Georgia, it was occupied by the Yamacraw Indians, an outlawed tribe of the Creek Nation. They proved friendly and welcomed the settlers; their aged chief Tomochichi and Oglethorpe became close friends. The settlers arrived February 12, 1733, and consisted mostly of "sober, industrious and moral persons"; few if any were released debtors.[1] At first they camped out in tents, but in less than two weeks they had two clapboard houses built and the framing for three more in place. A drawing of Savannah by Peter Gordon dated March 29, 1734 shows about eighty houses, a number of small public buildings and utilities, and some beautiful sailboats. The houses were apparently identical. They were built of wood, frame with clapboarding, 24 feet by 16 feet, with a center doorway flanked by a window on each side, and with a gabled roof.[2] The houses were set next to the street, with the side and rear yards enclosed by high fences. Unlike most of the later houses in Savannah, they were built close to the ground.

Inside, the houses consisted of a principal room with a fireplace on one side and two small rooms on the other, and a sleeping loft overhead.[3] It is interesting to note that the layout is the same as that advocated by William Penn for houses in colonial Philadelphia, though the dimensions in Penn's plans were 30 feet by 18 feet.[4] The Savannah plan was also markedly similar to later coastal slave cottages described by Fanny Kemble, Sir Charles Lyell, and Frederick Law Olmsted.[5]

The first group of settlers was followed by a company of Sephardic and Ashkenazic Jews who came from London that same year, 1733. Despite the express disapproval of the trustees in England, they were welcomed by Oglethorpe and the settlers. In 1734 the first of several groups of German Protestants who had been expelled from their home in the Archbishopric of Salzburg arrived. They were initially located in a settlement called Ebenezer, but shortly removed to a more healthful location which they named New Ebenezer. The Salzburgers were followed by Lutherans from Switzerland, and by a group of Moravians who remained only a few years, but who introduced a type of construction similar to European half-timbered structures. This they adapted to local conditions by using the Indian wattle-and-daub com-

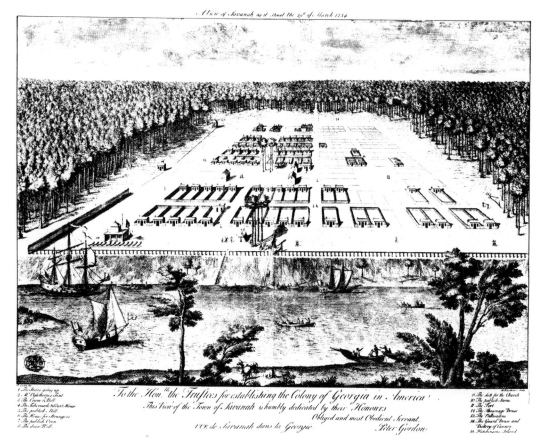

Peter Gordon's 1734 drawing of Savannah.

bination of sticks and clay instead of stuccoed masonry between the timbers. The first building for Christ Church,★ Savannah, described as being of "wattle work," was probably of this type, as was Mary Musgrove's house on Sapelo Island.[6]

At Frederica, a military town laid out by Oglethorpe in 1736, the settlers likewise adapted construction techniques from the Indians. Instead of erecting tents like the first settlers, they made bowers of palmetto leaves for temporary shelters. According to a 1736 visitor, "These pal-

metto bowers were very convenient shelters, being tight in the hardest rains; they were about twenty foot long, and fourteen foot wide, and in regular rows, looked very pretty."[7] The permanent houses built shortly thereafter were more varied, and included some that must have been finer than any in Savannah. By November 1736 the first two houses at Frederica, built of brick and two-and-a-half or three stories high, were nearly complete. Within a few years, the streets were lined with houses: some of brick,

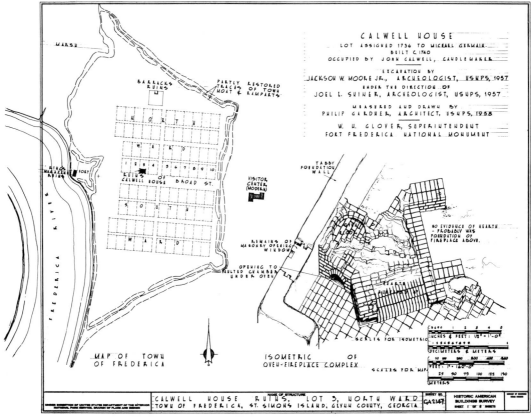

Top of page: *A restoration drawing of the Hawkins-Davison House (1736–38).*
Below: *Drawings from the excavation of the Calwell House (ca. 1740). Both
structures were part of the Town of Frederica on St. Simons Island.*

some of wood, and some of tabby.[8] The prosperous little town was short lived. By 1749 the regiment of British soldiers stationed there was disbanded, and with its principal source of income cut off, Frederica was abandoned. In 1945, when the National Park Service acquired the site, the only visible remains of the settlement were a small section of the fort and part of a powder magazine. Excavations since that time have revealed the foundations of the fort, the barracks, two large warehouses, and many of the dwellings and shops. Most of these are included in the Historic American Buildings Survey.

Architecturally, Frederica's greatest contribution must have been the development of construction methods for using tabby, a type of concrete made of shells, lime, and sand. It was not a new material. The Indians had developed its use for mortar, and the Spanish may have

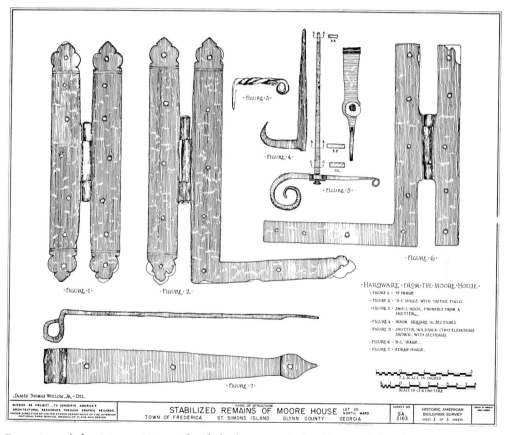

Remains of the Moore House (built before 1743), St. Simons Island, Town of Frederica.

used it in Saint Augustine. Tabby had been used for minor buildings in South Carolina, and in 1732 the fort at Port Royal was constructed of it.[9] Its use there probably influenced Oglethorpe in his choice of tabby for Fort Frederica, where it was also used for parts of the powder magazine, a large military warehouse, and for dwellings and various other buildings throughout the town.

New Ebenezer and Frederica were two of several early settlements. Most were near Savannah, but some were as far inland as Augusta. Within half a dozen years after the founding of Savannah, the colony could number among its settlers Piedmontese, Swiss, Salzburgers, Moravians, Jews, Germans, Scots Highlanders, Welsh, and English.[10] Though not encouraged by the trustees' policy favoring displaced Europeans, there were also settlers from other colonies, particularly from South Carolina, whose influence on architecture may have been disproportionate to their number. The first Savannah houses were constructed under the supervision of William Bull, who came from South Carolina with four of his slaves to lend assistance to the new colony.[11]

But if South Carolina influenced Georgia's architecture, the Spanish colonies had no such effect. Though their missions had dotted the Georgia coast and extended up the rivers, the Spaniards had withdrawn from settlements north of the Saint Marys River before the eighteenth century. Intermittent warfare between the English and the Spanish colonists in Florida obstructed architectural interchange thereafter. Aside from a few foundations, nothing seems to remain of those Spanish settlements. A number of picturesque tabby ruins, at least one with graceful arches and classic details (Thicket Sugar Mill and Rum Distillery,★ Darien Vicinity), were once thought to have been of Spanish origin, and were so designated in early HABS data sheets. These were later documented to be early nineteenth-century sugar mills or other plantation outbuildings.[12]

Little other than remnants of the fort and buildings★ at Frederica, the ruins of Fort Wimberly★ on the Isle of Hope, and the tabby walls of the Horton House★ on Jekyll Island remains from the first two decades of English colonization. The Horton House (built before 1742) was

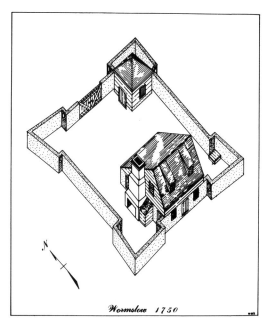

A conjectural reconstruction of Fort Wimberly.

The remains of Fort Wimberly on the Isle of Hope.

two stories high and evidently had a two-tiered porch across the south side. Fort Wimberly (ca. 1740–44) was a fortified house; both house and fortifications were of tabby. Fortifications were in the form of a small (approximately 70 feet by 80 feet) rectangular fort with bastions at the corners. Part of the south wall doubled as a wall for the house, which was likewise rectangular (24 feet by 36 feet). The downstairs consisted of one large corner room with a fireplace, and four smaller ones. According to conjectural drawings,[13] the house was a story and a half high, and had shed-type dormer windows.

A part of the defensive walls of Fort Wimberly remains, and archaeological excavations have revealed the foundations of the missing portion, as well as those of the house and of the first-story rooms. Similar work has been carried out at Frederica, so that in both places the layout of the structures can be seen.

Contemporary descriptions and drawings give us an idea of what some of the other buildings were like. The Orphan House, built in 1741 at Bethesda, near Savannah, was probably the most imposing building of the period. It was two-and-a-half stories high, had a wide, unobstructed central hall, and generous porches completely around it.[14] Except for the fact that it was set near the ground, it was well related to the climate, and its architecture seems closer to that of early- and mid-nineteenth-century plantation houses than to contemporaneous buildings.

The philanthropic and paternalistic rule of a colony intended to be a haven for the unfortunate, administered by trustees in accordance with a charter granted by the Crown, was expensive and not very successful in its idealistic goals. The initial prohibition against rum was dropped after it was found to be impossible to enforce; a prohibition against slavery followed suit. By 1750 about four thousand people had come to Georgia, but of these a number had left for other colonies. Discouraged, the trustees surrendered their charter to King George II, and in 1754 Georgia became a royal colony. The population of the colony then increased rapidly, and by the outbreak of the Revolution numbered between forty and fifty thousand, about half of whom were slaves.[15] The immigrants included large numbers from Germany and some from Ireland, but the majority were from the Carolinas and Virginia. A visitor wrote of Savannah in 1762: "At present there are about two hundred houses in the city. Of these, I have seen but three built of brick. The rest are wood and are painted in shades of blue and red."[16]

Most of the colonial buildings seem originally to have had gabled roofs or variations thereof, though some had hipped roofs and records also mention flat and gambrel roofs.[17] Predominating were the New England salt-box type, and

Christian Camphor House, Savannah. The house was built between 1760 and 1767, but raised on its high foundation in 1871.

a southern version which for want of a better name will be called a spraddle roof. A salt-box house is one with a plain gabled roof that is integral with a shed roof on the rear. The pitch of the shed roof is frequently flatter than that of the main roof. The Christian Camphor House★ in Savannah has such a roof. It was built in the 1760s, but was raised and placed on a high foundation during the nineteenth century. The spraddle roof type is similar to the salt-box type, except that it has shed roofs front and back. With a spraddle roof, one or both of the shed roofs must be flatter than the main part of the roof. Occasionally such a shed roof is carried around the house, either as a shed roof against the gable, or as a double-pitched hipped roof. Variations of the spraddle roof are found in unrelated areas around the world. They had been used earlier in other colonies, particularly the southern ones, and in the West Indies and the French and Spanish colonies in Louisiana.

Wild Heron★ (1752–57), probably the oldest house in Georgia that has not undergone radical changes, and the Button Gwinnett House (1765?) on St. Catherines Island both have spraddle roofs. Just as the Orphan House in Savannah had most of the features of the fully developed antebellum mansion, so Wild Heron, with its spraddle roof and porches front and back, is a type of cottage which was to become ubiquitous in antebellum Georgia. Along the coast and in the sand hills, the finer ones would generally be raised a story above the ground, like Wild Heron.

Of public buildings dating from the colonial period, Jerusalem Church★ (1769)

Jerusalem Church, Rincon vicinity, 1767–69.

near Rincon appears to be the only one remaining. It was built of brick, English bond, with an entrance on both the short and the long side. Evidently the entrance on the short side was the principal one, though the entrance to the earliest Protestant churches was generally on the long side. At Jerusalem Church the entrance on the short side was emphasized by a gable on that end of the roof (the other end being hipped), and by the inte-

Wild Heron Plantation, Savannah vicinity, 1756.

rior arrangement and the presence of a tower over that end.[18] Primarily a meetinghouse type, the severity of the early Protestant architecture is relieved by segmental arches over the openings, and by the pronounced tilt of the flared eaves.

The Old Jail★ in Augusta was a two-story brick building with a sloped parapet and a pierced brick ventilator at one gable end. It was reputed to have been built before the Revolution, but has since been demolished.

Toward the end of the colonial period, a distinctive regional architecture began to develop in Georgia. Previously most of the settlers had come from England or

Cochran House, near Braselton, built in the late eighteenth century.

Old Jail, Augusta, ca. 1740.

Europe, and like most first settlers tended to follow the building patterns of their native land, though there were exceptions such as the adaptation of Indian bowers for the temporary shelters at Frederica and the development of tabby construction. Despite extensive forests, log structures were uncommon in the first decades of the colony, being considered an expensive form of construction at the time. Logs were used for the construction of jails, however, because it was difficult to break out of a log building.[19]

After Georgia became a royal colony and settlers skilled in that type of construction began to arrive in large numbers, log houses became the most common type in newly opened areas. As had been the case in older colonies, there was an abundance of timber and a scarcity of nails and other manufactured goods. The first house of these new settlers was usually a

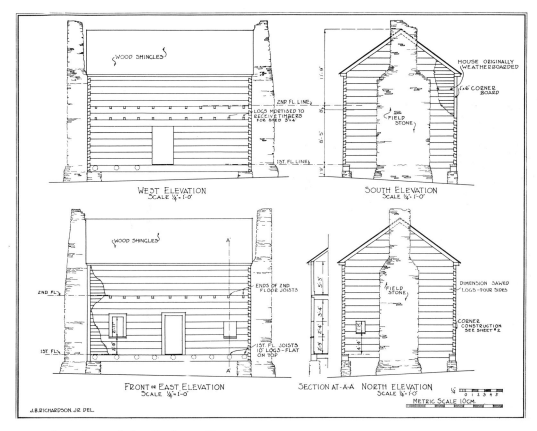

HABS elevations of the Cochran House.

one-room log cabin, the walls frequently carried above the ceiling level to permit an attic room overhead. The floors of the downstairs rooms were often "puncheon," a term that in Georgia meant "split logs with the face a little smoother."[20] Logs in the walls were sometimes left round, with the axe-cut ends projecting irregularly beyond the joints, which had a tendency to hold moisture and rot the wood. The more industrious settlers built their homes of hewn logs, the joints carefully shaped to shed water, and the ends cut smooth. Spaces between logs were often left open in the summer to admit breezes, but chinked with a mixture of clay and dried grass or moss during the winter. In the earlier cabins, chimneys were built of stones laid in clay, or sometimes of clay held in place by small logs. Stones piled on top of each other served as piers; roofs were of hand-split shingles.

In the Valdosta area, which remained forested until the late nineteenth century, a number of log houses and out-buildings remain, some of which have been removed to the Agrirama near Tifton, where a late nineteenth-century village has been reconstructed. Log houses are not uncommon in the Georgia mountains, where the craft of building with logs is now being revived. Occasional log structures, particularly barns and smokehouses, can be found throughout the state.

When the family outgrew its one-room house, a porch might be added, or another room. There was no set order for the additions, but a fairly typical expansion would be the addition of another room, a mirror image of the first, but with a space between the two which could be roofed and floored, and thus serve as a pleasant outdoor room in mild or hot weather. This room became the center of life for pets as well as people; it seems to have been a favorite haunt for the pack of dogs that most pioneers kept, and thus earned its name, the "dog trot." Weatherwise builders oriented their cab-

Jordan Cabin, Davisboro vicinity, built in the late eighteenth century.

ins so that the dog trot would catch the prevailing summer breezes and as much shade in summer and sun in winter as possible. The next addition might well be porches front and back. These usually extended the full width of the house, were covered with shed roofs, and frequently had small rooms at one or both ends. By the time these rooms were added, sawed lumber was more plentiful, and rooms under the porch were for the most part of frame construction. The gabled roof of

Top of page: *The kitchen hearth at Refuge Plantation.* Below: *Refuge Plantation, near Woodbine, was built ca. 1775.*

the cabin and the added shed roofs on each side formed a spraddle roof. As originally constructed on the old cottages, this type of roof blended with the landscape. If the terrain were flat, the low-sloping shed roofs seemed to hover over the land, picturesquely rising to a steeper pitch at the center. If the topography were hilly, the various slopes of the roof repeated the slopes of the surrounding hills, and the house became one with the landscape. As the settlements grew and sawmills were brought in, sawed or hewn framing with clapboard siding was used instead of log construction, but the form of such houses, referred to hereafter as "plantation type cottages," remained the same.

Another basic type is generally known as the "plantation plain style" house. The term was apparently coined by Frederick Doveton Nichols to describe early Georgia houses that were "of wood covered with weatherboard, topped with a single gable, and had masonry or clay chimneys."[21] In the intervening years the term has been adapted to describe the typical two-story, one-room-deep, plain plantation house, with a one-story porch and a shed roof across the front. The type was common throughout the settled areas of the state during the late eighteenth and the entire nineteenth century. It is in the latter, now widely accepted, sense that the term is used here. Such houses usually had a one-story lean-to across the back which could be completely enclosed, or which might be similar to the porch in front. Both front and back porches frequently had rooms on

one or both ends, these often arranged so that, except for the central hall or dog trot, all rooms could have windows on three sides.

Apparently no plantation plain style houses remain from colonial Georgia; in fact the only surviving two-story houses seem to be the Horton House★ ruins on Jekyll Island and the remodeled Pink House★ in Savannah. Both were one room deep, but the Horton House had a two-story porch, and the porch of the Pink House was changed or added during the early part of the nineteenth century. One-story porches on Wild Heron★ near Savannah and as shown on drawings of the Orphan House at Bethesda would indicate that their use was not unusual.[22] On the basis of those examples and the popularity of plantation plain style houses in Georgia in the years immediately following the American Revolution, also on the fact that the style was common in South Carolina, it seems logical to assume that plantation plain style houses were also built earlier, in colonial Georgia. Later examples would include Carter's Quarters★ at Carters, the Gachet House★ near Barnesville, Travelers Rest★ near Toccoa, the Jackson House★ near Toomsboro, and the Stage Coach Inn★ near Marshallville.

Both plantation type cottages and plantation plain style houses are found in warm climates in widely separated areas. In some cases they seem to have evolved naturally from local conditions; in other cases they were influenced by earlier houses from older regions. Middleburg, a plantation plain style house near Pompion Hill, South Carolina, was built in the seventeenth century.[23] Supposedly, its pattern was adapted from even older houses in the West Indies. Whatever their origin, the forms of the plantation cottage type and the plantation plain style house evolved from considerations of use, climate, available materials, and methods of construction which were common to Georgia, and so are considered indigenous to the state. The suit-ability of this indigenous architecture is confirmed by its widespread use from colonial times until the Civil War and occasionally thereafter and by its adaptability to the Federal, Greek Revival, and Victorian styles.

Not all the early houses were so suitable. Settlers generally tried to reproduce homes they remembered, and those from colder areas tended to build snug houses close to the ground, with minimal porches

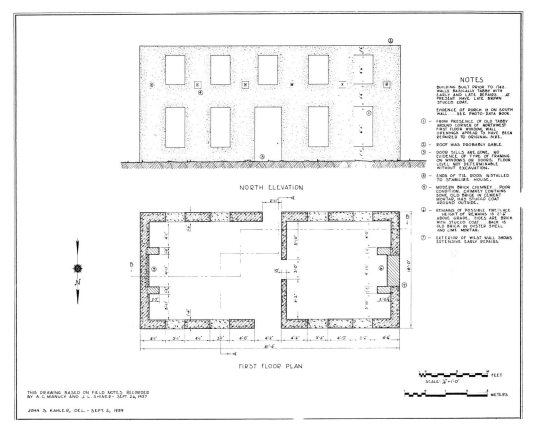

HABS drawings of the remains of the Horton House (built before 1742) on Jekyll Island.

and little consideration for Georgia's long, hot summers. Such mistakes were usually rectified in part by adding or enlarging porches, and sometimes by replacing small windows with floor-length ones, adding blinds, or installing latticed or louvered sunscreens on parts of the porches.

Aspects of colonial architecture too often ignored are the fences and planting.

Peter Gordon's 1734 drawing of Savannah shows even those first cottages set in lots surrounded by high wooden fences, the fences apparently considered an indispensable adjunct to the houses. They enclosed the side and rear yards, since the houses were set too close to the streets to have front yards. From that time until the end of the nineteenth century, no house was considered complete without

HABS elevations of the Gachet House, near Barnesville.

a proper enclosure. If the house was set back from the street, the front as well as the side and rear yards were enclosed. Fences were, of course, a necessity in a day when livestock was allowed to roam freely and when wild animals were a menace.

The fences shown in the early drawings were probably made of split boards. Later they would be more ornamental,

wooden picket fences being the most common, but brick or tabby walls were often built by those who could afford them. Rail fences were used extensively in rural areas, but even there, picket fences or fences built of split saplings were preferred near the house.

None of the gardens have survived from colonial times. The earliest gardens were doubtless planted for food and med-

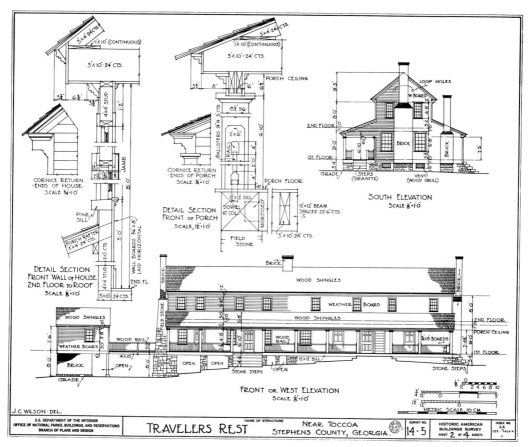

HABS drawings of Travelers Rest, near Toccoa. The original structure was built between 1816 and 1825 and enlarged ca. 1835.

icine; except for a few treasured plants, there would have been little time for growing flowers. The vegetable and herb gardens, which might include some flowers, were doubtless laid out in geometric designs, for both convenience and neat appearance.

A public garden of ten acres called the Trustees' Garden was included in the plan of Savannah. Here, useful plants were tested, grown, and propagated for the benefit of the settlers. Among the plants included were mulberry trees for silkworm culture, apple, pear, fig, olive, and orange trees, pomegranate bushes, grapevines, and cotton. The garden was abandoned about the time Georgia became a royal colony, and the site was later converted to a residential area.

Toward the end of the colonial period, gardens laid out in patterns and devoted exclusively to ornamental plants began to make their appearance. Like those of a later period, the gardens within the small enclosed lots of Savannah must have been especially charming, with vine-covered fences, brick or sand walks, an open area for sitting or working, and beds of fragrant herbs, flowers, and vegetables as well as a few flowering shrubs and trees.

More lasting than the buildings or the gardens were the early city plans, particularly Savannah's. John Reps, one of America's foremost city planners, wrote that it, along with the revised plan for Williamsburg in Virginia, was "the most successful essay in community layout in colonial America."[24]

Designed partly for defense, partly for convenience, and obviously for beauty and delight, this eighteenth-century plan imparts to twentieth-century Savannah the verdure of a park combined with an efficient and viable traffic plan. The basis of the plan is a series of wards (superblocks) laid out in a gridiron pattern. The wards are subdivided into nine smaller blocks consisting of an open square in the center, four blocks for residences, and four small blocks (called trustee lots) for public buildings. The squares are flanked on the east and west (ESE, WNW) by the trustee lots, two on each side, with a street between them, that street being on axis with the center of the square. North and south (NNE, SSW) of the square and of the trustee lots are the blocks for houses, two blocks on the north side and two on the south, the street between them also being on axis with the center of the square. There are ten lots within each of these blocks, arranged back-to-back with an alley between; so five of the houses within the block face outward toward one of the peripheral streets, and five face inward toward the square or toward one of the trustee lots. This arrangement permits either the front or the garden side to have the desirable SSW orientation which admits maximum winter sun, and, if proper overhangs are provided, no summer sun; it also admits the prevailing southwest summer breezes.[25] The alleys at the rear obviate the need for individual driveways, and permit the development of row houses that stand continuous for a whole block.

Since the streets between the trustee lots and between the blocks for houses

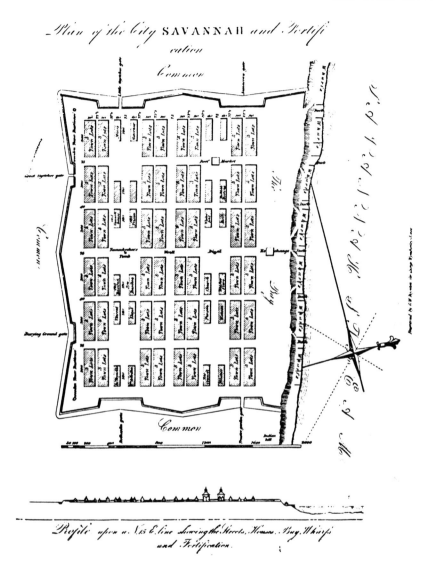

De Brahm's 1757 plan of the city of Savannah.

are interrupted by squares, traffic within the superblocks moves at a leisurely rate. The streets that border the wards have minimal interruptions, the plan thus permitting an ideal combination of slow-moving traffic within the wards and fast-moving traffic outside them. The alleys in various ways alleviate twentieth-century parking problems. Few modern city plans ameliorate the liabilities or exploit the advantages of the automobile so successfully.

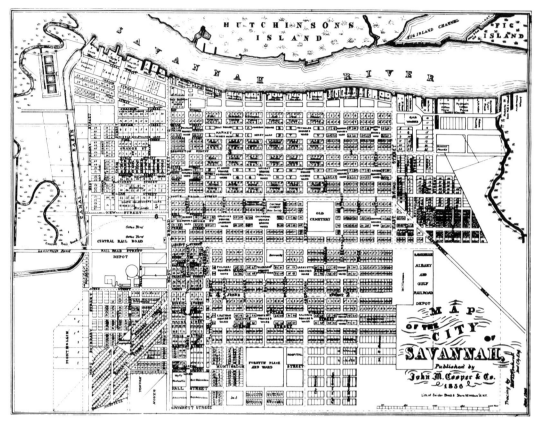

Savannah city plan, 1856.

As the plan developed, some of the major streets were built wide enough to permit medians with trees; in addition most of the streets are also bordered with trees. These, combined with the flora of the private yards and the public squares, give much of Savannah the appearance of a large and beautiful garden.

As remarkable as the plan itself, was its successful implementation, which may have been due to the fact that land for Savannah's early expansion was municipally owned and controlled, and therefore not subject to the vagaries of real estate speculation. Oglethorpe's foresight in providing for municipal control of the land and in planning for traffic, climate, row houses, and a public garden suggest that he envisioned a utopian city in many ways similar to that described in Sir Thomas More's *Utopia*:

The streets are laid out both for traffic and for protection against the winds. The buildings, which are far from mean, are set together in a long row, continuous through the block and faced by a corresponding one. The house fronts of the respective blocks are divided by an avenue twenty feet broad. On the rear of the houses, through the whole length of the block, lies a broad garden enclosed on all sides by the backs of the blocks. . . . The Utopians are very fond of their gardens. In them they have vines, fruits, herbs, flowers, so well kept and flourishing that I never saw anything more fruitful and more tasteful anywhere. Certainly you cannot readily find anything in the whole city more productive of profit and pleasure to the citizens. There is nothing which their founder seems to have cared so much for as these gardens.

In fact, they report that the whole plan of the city had been sketched at the very beginning by Utopus himself. He left to posterity, however, to add the adornment and other improvements for which he saw one lifetime would hardly suffice. Their annals, embracing the history of 1760 years, are preserved carefully and conscientiously in writing. Here they find stated that at first the houses were low, mere cabins and huts, . . . but now all the homes are of handsome appearance with three stories. The exposed faces of the walls are made of stone or cement or brick.[26]

The Savannah plan, with minor variations, was used at Darien and New Ebenezer. New Ebenezer has long since disappeared, and only Jerusalem Church★ and the cemetery mark its site. Darien is

provocatively interesting in that parts of the village adhered to the plan and part did not. The areas that developed naturally, with curving streets, seem to be more in harmony with the predominately rural landscape than the grid of the planned areas. This suggests that until there were enough buildings to dominate the landscape, Savannah may not have appeared to be a well-planned city. The plans of Highgate and Hampstead, both laid out before 1736, were radial, with diagonal streets.[27] These towns no longer exist.

Augusta was established by Oglethorpe in 1735, primarily as a trading post and fort. Apparently no copy of the original plan exists, but it seems to have been laid out in broad, straight streets at right angles, with the lots for public buildings facing a large open square, like a military encampment.[28] As in Savannah, the principal streets were roughly parallel to the river, and oriented so that either the front or the rear of the buildings would face ssw. The original plan determined the width and direction of the principal streets and the location of some of the public buildings; otherwise the plan of Augusta evolved from later developments.

All the towns of colonial Georgia seem to have been carefully planned, with generous amounts of open space. In view of the haphazard planning and gross misuse of land since that time, the careful planning of those early towns is impressive, particularly when one remembers that most of Georgia was then a wilderness, and land seemingly endless.

Chapter Three

The Federal Period

The Federal period of architecture is usually considered to cover the years from the end of the American Revolution until about 1820 to 1825, after which it was gradually superseded by the Greek Revival. The term *Federal architecture* is, however, ambiguous, because late Federal architecture bears little resemblance to early Federal and there were marked divergencies throughout the period.

In his authoritative book, *American Buildings and Their Architects*, William Pierson has more logically used the designation *neoclassical* for most of the architecture of the period, employing the term *Federal* only in connection with the early Adam-inspired architecture which he included as part of the background of the neoclassical style. This style he subdivided into four phases: (1) the traditional phase, (2) the idealistic phase, (3) the rationalist phase, and (4) the nationalist phase. The first three phases fall into the category generally called Federal, but the fourth is more often termed Greek Revival. Pierson's classifications are apt, but in Georgia the term *Federal* (with modifications for particular variations) has become too well established to discard, and in most cases the line between Adam type architecture and the traditional phase of the neoclassic is so nebulous that different terms are used here: traditional Federal to cover both the Adam type and the traditional phase of neoclassic architecture; Jeffersonian Federal instead of the idealistic phase; rational or transitional Federal instead of the rationalist phase; and Greek Revival (despite frequent use of Roman orders) instead of the nationalistic phase. In those cases where the Adam influence is particularly strong, it is mentioned; also in those cases wherein the vigor or simplicity of the design is paramount.

Traditional Federal, Post-Colonial, and Indigenous Architecture

Within the traditional phase, there were distinct trends: one toward Adamesque Federal, a delicate rococo type architecture; another, more American in spirit and usually of a slightly later date, toward simplification, and toward the end of the period, a heavier, more classical version, presaging the Greek Revival.

The inspiration for Adamesque Federal architecture originated in England, particularly in the work of Robert Adam and his brothers. Adam architecture, like that which preceded it, was based on Palladian and classical principles, but was handled with a lightness of scale and freedom of planning that were new. Robert Adam was especially intrigued with the newly discovered examples of Roman domestic architecture of Pompeii and Herculaneum, and wrote of this architecture: "With regard to the decoration of their private and bathing apartments, they [the Ancients] were all delicacy, gaiety, grace and beauty."[1] No more apt description could be made of Adam decoration.

Adamesque Federal architecture tended to be a simplified version of such English architecture, but with a free substitution of the building materials available in America, especially wood, for those used in England. It differed from American Colonial in a number of ways. Roof pitches were usually flatter, the roof often partly hidden by parapets or balustrades. Smooth wall surfaces were preferred, brick was sometimes stuccoed and wood siding sometimes applied flush, particularly when protected by porch roofs. Columns were attenuated, and entablatures correspondingly lightened. Entrance porches might be bowed or given special shapes to deemphasize their structural qualities and to accentuate their lightness. Classical elements were handled freely, triglyphs often being represented by grooves only, and modillions given more decorative shapes. Graceful fanlights over entrance doors replaced the heavy pediments of the preceding era; Palladian windows and windows set in recessed wall arches often repeated the arches of the fanlights. In general, windows and windowpanes became progressively larger, but in the newer areas of the state the small 8-inch by 10-inch windowpanes of colonial times were still being used at the end of the period. Wrought-iron railings with delicate medallions and scrollwork were particularly popular in Savannah. Exterior brickwork was usually left natural, but wood and stucco were likely to be painted shades of tan, beige, or gray, presumably to match stone prototypes in England.

Floor plans were generally axial, but planning became less formal and rooms were arranged for use and convenience rather than strict symmetry. Major rooms were likely to be interrelated with openings which might have folding or sliding doors or columns in antis, or which might be spanned by elliptical arches. Shapes of the rooms became more varied, and included shapes ranging from rectangular to round to oval; there were also combinations such as rectangular with rounded ends or with bay windows.

Stairways were lighter and more graceful; circular stairways were generally preferred by those who could afford them. Delicate plaster cornices and ceiling medallions with classical motifs were used in the principal rooms of the finer houses.

Adamesque mantels usually had slender fluted colonettes or pilasters and finely detailed moldings. They might be further ornamented with dentils, gouge work, sunbursts, or carvings of fruit and flowers. Important door and window frames were sometimes similarly treated.

Interior colors were generally shades of gray or pure white, Americans of this early period usually avoiding the sparkling range of colors used by the Adam brothers.[2]

The Independent Presbyterian Church★ in Savannah, built in 1818, burned in 1889, and rebuilt according to the original design, is a superb example of the style. Like many churches of the period, it has a Gibbes-type steeple that is reminiscent of an earlier era.

The most Adamlike building in Georgia was probably the Bank of the State of

Bank of the State of Georgia, Savannah, 1819.

Georgia (demolished) built in Savannah in 1819. For a public building, it was intimate in scale, with an entrance porch that was lightened and refined by being concave at the corners. Its slender paired Corinthian columns, small modillions and dentils, its delicately carved moldings and exquisite wrought-iron railings—all were characteristic of Adam architecture, as were the doors and windows, with their graceful fanlights of leaded glass and their reeded or fluted trim.

Another example is the Ware-Sibley-Clark House★ in Augusta. Adamesque features included the delicate bow-front tiered porch with flanking bay windows and the rococo effect of the pilasters, ornamental panels, triglyphs, and medallions. Except for an enormous fanlight over the sliding doors between two parlors, the comparatively simple interiors

Independent Presbyterian Church, Savannah. The church was built in 1819, burned in 1889, and rebuilt according to the original design in 1890.

Ware-Sibley-Clark House, Augusta, 1818.

have a restrained elegance more typical of mid-Federal architecture than of the earlier Adam type.

The Belcher-Hunter House★ and the Houston-Screven House★, both in Savannah, Mount Nebo★ near Milledgeville, and the Richmond County Courthouse★ in Augusta were built in this style but have been destroyed. The rare Adamesque mantels and other wood and plaster work of the Belcher-Hunter House were photographed by HABS shortly before the house was demolished. The center panel

of one mantel features a pastoral scene in relief with sheep and a shepherd boy piping. The Houston-Screven House had a groined vaulted ceiling, evidently a simplified version of one in Derby House, London, designed by Robert Adam. Victorian wallpaper and picture moldings, added before the HABS photographs were made, overwhelmed the original design.

Other Federal buildings that reflect the Adam influence include St. Paul's Church★ in Augusta, the Oliver Sturges House★ in Savannah, the Terrell House★

Steps and fanlight doorway, Ware-Sibley-Clark House.

Richmond County Courthouse, Augusta, ca. 1811.

in Sparta, Mount Nebo★ (destroyed) near Milledgeville, and Lowther Hall★ (destroyed) in Clinton. The Davenport House★ in Savannah is a treasury of Federal ornamentation, being embellished with a plethora of decorative woodwork, plaster work, and marble, possibly because the owner-architect-builder wished to display the broad range of work his construction firm could produce.

The sophisticated Federal style of architecture did not prevail in all areas of the state. Throughout Georgia, diverse influences caused an amazing variety of building types, styles, and substyles dur-

ing the Federal period. In 1807 the state legislature met in the new state capitol building (Old State Capitol★) at Milledgeville, a building designed in the avant-garde Gothic style. At the same time, the governor and his family moved into the double log cabin which served as the governor's mansion.[3] Most of the state was still being settled, and in the western part, large areas were Indian territory. In such frontier settlements there was often a time-lag of as much as a generation before newer styles were accepted. Typical was the Harris-Pearson-Walker House★ in Augusta, which for years was assumed

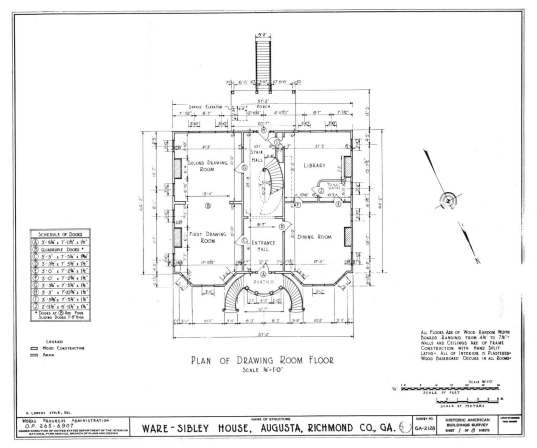

Floor plan of the Ware-Sibley-Clark House in Augusta.

by experts to be Colonial, but which has since been documented as having been built during the Federal period, probably in the late 1790s, and can best be described as post-Colonial.

The architecture of the Harris-Pearson-Walker House★ is confusing not only because of its Colonial appearance, but because it reflects the diverse origins of the settlers of the area. Two stories, one room deep (except for the end rooms on the porches), with a central hall and double-

tiered piazzas front and back, the plan is typical of many southern plantation houses. It has the favored NNE—SSW orientation, the rear porches to the south with end rooms which help funnel the breezes through the hall. Other features, however, betray a complex background. The gambrel roof is generally associated with the Dutch settlers of New York or the Huguenot settlers of New Jersey, though the post-Colonial Arnold House★ and the Hampton-Lillibridge Houses★ in

Front door and balcony, Belcher-Hunter House, Savannah, 1797–1803.

Detail of mantel, Belcher-Hunter House.

Alcove, adjacent doorway, and cornice, Belcher-Hunter House.

Savannah likewise had gambrel roofs, as did some houses in the other southern colonies. It was noted in the previous chapter that the houses of colonial Savannah were painted in shades of red and blue; so was the Harris-Pearson-Walker House★, which has been restored to its original blue-gray color with dull red trim. The entrance, very tall, with fluted pilasters and a pulvinated frieze, and with arched lights in the top of double doors, was typical of those used in Mas-

sachusetts and Connecticut during the mid-eighteenth century. An unusual feature is the arched ceiling of the hall. Though built during that period, the architecture of the Harris-Pearson-Walker House★, with its many Colonial features, can hardly be called Federal. Neither could Midway Congregational Church★, which was built in 1792 at Midway, but which is strikingly similar to early New England meetinghouses; the roof and the position of the steeple are also similar to

Front hall of the Houston-Screven House, Savannah, 1784–96.

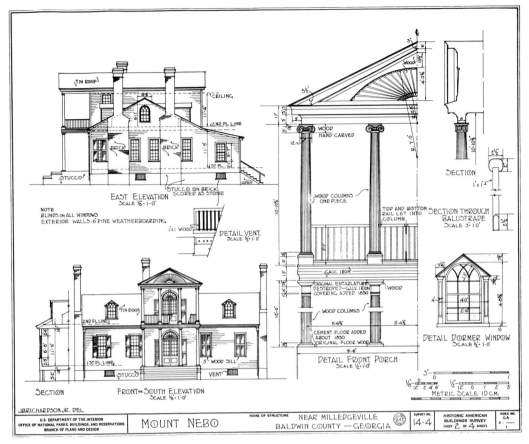

HABS drawing of Mount Nebo near Milledgeville.

those of the Colonial Jerusalem Church★ near Rincon. Much architecture of the early Federal period in Georgia had more in common with the Colonial than with the Federal style, and is categorized here as post-Colonial.

In general, characteristics of post-Colonial architecture were comparatively steep roofs (necessary with wood shingle roofs), plain verge boards instead of eaves on the gable ends, boxed eaves on the drip side, with end closures cut from a single board to the profile of the eave, and beaded clapboard siding. When protected, as it was under porch roofs, the siding was often applied flush. Many of the houses, like the restored Hampton-Lillibridge Houses★, were built without porches; in such cases porches were frequently added within a few years.

Entrance doors were usually the six-panel type, though variations with extra

Mount Nebo, Milledgeville vicinity, 1823.

panels, as at Meadow Garden★ in Augusta, are occasionally found; elaborate doors with glass panels like those of the Harris-Pearson-Walker House★ were rare. Plain transoms were often used over the entrance door. Glass panes in the transoms and in the windows were small, nearly always 8 inches by 10 inches.

Floor plans most often included a central hall, but there were variations, the most common of which was an enlarged version of the first Savannah houses: a large room on one side with two smaller rooms on the other, and, usually, an enclosed staircase. The plan seems to have had various origins. Many of the settlers of the Piedmont came there via the Carolinas and Virginia; prototypes exist along the route, and the origin of these can be traced back to Pennsylvania.

A few of the post-Colonial houses had paneled walls; more often the walls were finished with boards or had a paneled wainscot with plaster above. The older

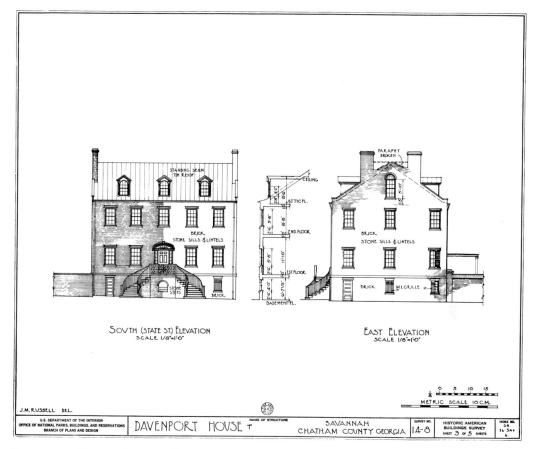

Davenport House, Savannah, 1820.

section of Meadow Garden★, an indigenous house with some Colonial and some Federal features, has a paneled wainscot with plaster above, and a projecting chimney that is paneled in the Colonial manner. Silhouetted against the paneling is an exceptionally graceful mantel with bolection moldings and a pulvinated frieze, likewise in the Colonial manner.

Mantels of the plainer houses were simpler, usually with bolection moldings surrounding the opening, a plain or paneled frieze over, and a shelf supported by moldings at the top. Interior doors were most often the six-panel type, the panels raised on one side, the raised part about ⅞ inch thick; stiles were about 1 ⅛ inch thick. Stiles of modern doors are heavier, and panels usually lighter. Batten doors were sometimes used, particularly in minor rooms.

Along the frontier, the architecture was primarily indigenous, but both post-Colonial and Federal influences were

Old State Capitol, Milledgeville. The center portion was built in 1807, the corner towers in 1833, and the porticoes in 1850.

Harris-Pearson-Walker House, Augusta, ca. 1797.

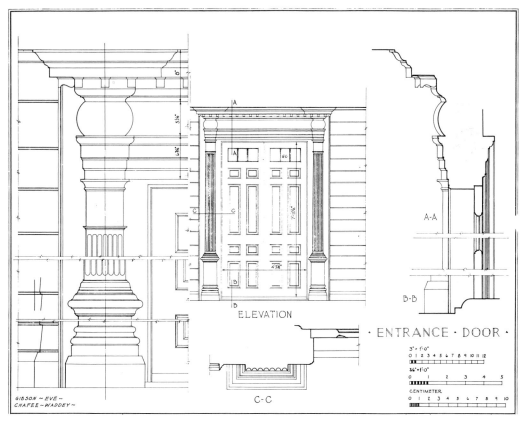

Details of the Harris-Pearson-Walker House.

often apparent. As applied to architecture, the term *indigenous* implies that such architecture evolved from the requirements for use, climate control, site conditions, available building materials, and local methods of construction. Log cabins, timber barns, covered bridges, and old water mills are typical. So were the houses that were built of local materials, usually of lumber and logs cut and finished on the site. In such houses, the rafters and joists were frequently exposed, doors were the batten type, and batten shutters served as windows. Chimneys were built of clay reinforced with small logs, or of local stone, or of handmade brick. Gable eaves were likely to be wide, sometimes extending well beyond the end chimneys as if to protect the clay or soft brick of those chimneys. Logs placed on end, or stone piers (often appearing to be precariously stacked but

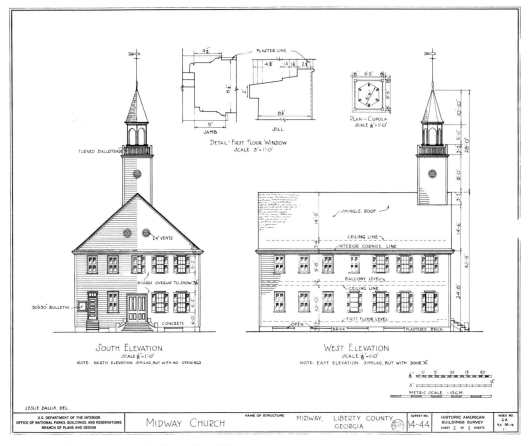

Midway Congregational Church, Midway, 1792.

remaining in place for a century or more), usually served as the foundation. Clapboards might be rough or planed; log houses were often covered with board and batten siding. Buildings were generally left unpainted, and because of the superior quality of the lumber, they weathered to mellow tones without undue deterioration. Some were whitewashed, a method that produced a particularly fresh and sparkling surface, but one that had to be renewed at frequent intervals. Interior walls were usually either exposed logs or boarded, non-load-bearing partitions often being only one board thick. Boards, clapboards, and timbers frequently had a bead on exposed corners, softening the sharp outline and providing a pleasant contrast to the rugged hand-hewn timbers and the hand-planed boards. Puncheon floors, described in the previous chapter, were the

Stairs at High Gate, Augusta, ca. 1810.

Front door of Meadow Garden, Augusta. The house was built in the late eighteenth century.

most common type. Mantels were usually built in place, and consisted of narrow boards that covered the joint between masonry and wood, and of a plain board shelf. In the smaller houses, ladders sometimes gave access to attic rooms. Stairways were nearly always enclosed, presumably to keep heat from escaping to the upstairs.

Few completely indigenous houses remain. Of those that were built, glass windows were usually installed within a few years, brick or stone later replaced clay chimneys, and other improvements were made over the years. Descriptions of the houses by travelers and other contemporaries abound. Still standing and in use are many of the plantation type cottages and plantation plain style houses. Their basic form is indigenous, but the features reflect, in varying degrees, concurrent styles of architecture.

Since parts of Georgia were still on the frontier throughout the Federal period, indigenous architecture with Colonial or Federal details was built from the beginning to the end of the period, and for a decade thereafter. The Harrison House★

Mantel at Meadow Garden.

Meadow Garden.

Stage Coach Inn, near Marshallville, 1810.

Kolb House, Kennesaw Mountain, 1836.

Rice Mill, Wormsloe, Isle of Hope.

Jackson House, Toomsboro, built in the early nineteenth century.

near Warthen was originally a two-story, dog-trot log house, but the open trot has since been enclosed, and the logs covered with asbestos siding. It has a two-tiered porch with hand-hewn posts and railings, which because of their delicate proportions, and reliance on simplicity and repetition for effect, are Federal in spirit.

The Mitchell-Barron House★ in Clinton has a two-tiered porch like the Harrison House★, but is more sophisticated, with classical columns and a Federal entablature. It also has the beaded siding and narrow verge boards typical of Colonial and post-Colonial architecture, and is illustrative of the next step in the transition from indigenous to Federal architecture.

An interesting variation which might better be called vernacular Federal is the Thomas Cheely House★ in Hancock County (Shoals vicinity). It is one of the

Harrison House, near Warthen, built probably in the early nineteenth century.

few two-story houses that still has the dog trot, though this has been semi-enclosed at the rear by the installation of louvered blinds. It has separate stairways for the sons and daughters of the family; the one leading to the boys' quarters is outside, on the porch, and the one leading to the girls' rooms is accessible only by way of the master bedroom. Equally interesting is the interpretation of some of the classical details. Ionic capitals of the second-story porch are carved out of a thick board cut to the silhouette of Ionic scrolls, and affixed to the front side of the columns. The cornice is embellished with a board decorated with repetitive holes and scallops, lightly conveying the idea of a classic fret with dentils. Unlike most indigenous architecture, ornamental details were applied to this house to gain the visual effect of Federal architecture.

Top left: *Porch details, Mitchell-Barron House.* Bottom left: *Front porches, Mitchell-Barron House, Clinton, 1822.* Top right: *Porch post and beam, Harrison House.*

As the era progressed, Federal architecture tended to become simpler and less delicate; there seems at times to have been a deliberate search for a plainer, more structurally expressive architecture. The flatter roofs, smooth exterior walls, arched fanlights, and curving stairways remained, but elegance was sought through simplicity instead of intricacy. There were exceptions. Cast- and wrought-iron work of the period was fre-

Thomas Cheely House, near Shoals,
ca. 1825.

Proto-Ionic capital, Neandria, Greece,
sixth century B.C. Note the similarity to
the Cheely capital.

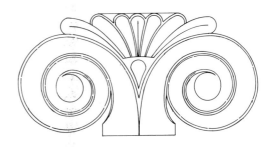

Dog trot and stairway, Thomas Cheely House.

Porch column and plate, Thomas Cheely House.

quently fanciful and delicate. Wood and plaster work of the interiors occasionally bordered on the ornate.

As has been noted previously, simplification in architecture was an American trait that dates back to colonial times and that is also typical of indigenous architecture. In this case, the trend was led by England and France, with their Regency and Empire styles. It is, however, frequently difficult to tell whether specific examples of mid-Federal architecture are based on native, Regency, or Empire styles.

At its most simplistic, Federal architecture anticipated by more than a century Mies van der Rohe's dictum that less is more, eschewing all applied ornament or imitative classicism, and relying on pure geometric form, plain walls, studied proportions, frank structural expression, and quality craftsmanship for distinction. Surviving examples of such purist architecture are rare, but there are a few in Georgia, including the James C. Daniel House★ near Washington. This house is outstanding for the clean-cut geometry of its mass and for the precise workmanship of its plain brick walls, unornamented except for an arched entrance in front, an arched window in the rear, and such structural features as splayed lintels. Within, the square openwell stairway is Miesian in its simplicity and superb craftsmanship. So is the stairway in Carter's Quarters★ (ca. 1800) in Carters.

The Lufburrow House★ in Savannah is a fine example of urban architecture that attains elegance primarily through sim-

James C. Daniel House, Washington vicinity, ca. 1815.

plicity and restraint. Built of oversize brick on a nonsymmetrical plan, its only concession to ornament is a brick dentil cornice and a small fanlight over the recessed entrance door. Weathered stone lintels, old brick, louvered blinds, and the simplest of wrought-iron step railings give this house a distinction no amount of ornament could equal.

The architecture of the Hamilton-Johnson House★ in Clinton and the Tenement Houses★ in Savannah appears to have been similarly restrained, but these houses have been destroyed. Demosthenian Hall★ at the University of Georgia in Athens is likewise notable for the grace and simplicity of its architecture, though it has a Palladian window with a frame intricately carved in the earlier manner. Inside, the principal room has a coved ceiling with Adamesque decorative plaster.

Stairway of the James C. Daniel House, photographed from the top floor.

Lufburrow House, Savannah, ca. 1830.

Stairway, Carter's Quarters.

College Hill★, a house in Augusta, has a double tiered porch across the front with elliptical arches between square columns. The frieze and architrave are without ornamentation. Balusters are plain rectangular pickets, those of the first floor in an alternating vertical and x design, those of the second floor in the sheaf-of-wheat design. The double entrance doors have sidelights with rectangular panes, but the square-head transom has muntins radiating like a fan from a semi-elliptical block at the base. College Hill imparts an effect of unity and serenity attained by the repetition of a few major themes: the verticals of the columns and of some of the balusters, the arches, the lattice motif found in the balustrade and the lattice underpinning, also

Demosthenian Hall, University of Georgia campus, Athens, 1824.

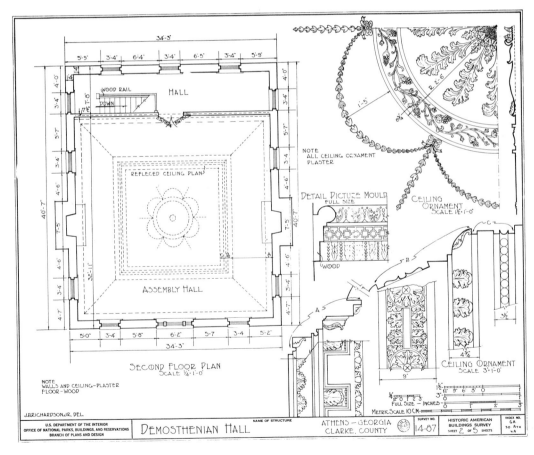

College Hill, Augusta, 1818.

in the latticelike effect of the small paned windows and the muntins of the entrance sidelights and transom. The arches are, of course, nonstructural, and though there is no applied ornament, the pattern of the plain porch balusters is deliberately decorative. Inside, the plain rectangular pickets of the railing emphasize the grace of a curving stairway without distracting details. A mantel, illustrated in the HABS photographs, has reeded pilasters, fluted frieze, and carved sunbursts

that have a crisp vitality that is distinctly Federal, though not simplistic.

A unique group of houses, mostly in the vicinity of Milledgeville and sometimes designated as Milledgeville-Federal in style, have comparatively narrow two-story porches with slightly attenuated, full-length columns that appear to be transitional, though early New England examples might be cited as prototypes. Several of the houses are attributed to Daniel Pratt, a native of New Hampshire,

The Cedars, Milledgeville, ca. 1825.

and in those the New England influence is apparent. All had exquisite Federal details, most of them adapted from Asher Benjamin. These included semicircular or elliptical fanlights, curving stairways, and wood and plaster work, much of which was reminiscent of the Adam-Federal period. Frequently the woodwork was grained, some was marbleized, and details might be gilded or touched with gold.

HABS houses in the group include the Cedars★, the John Williams House★, the Boykin House★, and Westover★, the lat-

Entrance to the John Williams House (ca. 1830) in Milledgeville.

ter (since destroyed) having had a portico with four instead of the usual two columns. The Gordon-Banks House★, formerly near Haddock, now near Newnan, is probably the most sophisticated of those remaining, and has been meticulously restored. The Homestead★ in Milledgeville and the John Davidson House★ in the Whitesville community have similar porches, but were not designed by Pratt. The Brown-Sanford★ House in Milledgeville has a unique two-story Palladian porch and interiors similar to those of the Pratt houses. Symbolic of the national pride of that era is the lead figure of an American eagle at the pivotal center of the fanlight over the second-story entrance. The house has been restored to its original colors, and the interior may be considered fairly representative of the more luxurious houses of the period. It is of frame construction, with clapboard siding, and is painted a deep buff. Inside, the walls are light, but the woodwork is either grained or painted in dark muted colors touched with gold.

Despite the tendency toward simplification, ornament continued to be used to some extent in most of the work. As in the early Adamesque architecture, later ornament was usually based on classical motifs, but in general was simpler, bolder, and more highly stylized; frequently it was closer to the classic original than was the Adam type. Toward the end of the period, eaves brackets and occasional heavy or ornate details, which suggested approaching changes in style, began to appear.

The Adam type mantels with pilasters

Boykin House, Milledgeville vicinity, ca. 1830.

or colonnettes on each side of the opening continued in favor, but the designs became bolder, exhibiting a crispness and a verve that were new. In the finer houses of Savannah, marble mantels were not uncommon. These were heavier in style than the wood mantels, and usually had engaged columns on each side of the opening. Occasionally atlantes or caryatids substituted for the columns. Walls were sometimes papered, a particularly fine example having been that in the Hamilton-Johnson House★ (destroyed) in Clinton. The wallpaper, which can be seen in the HABS photographs, was the rare 1821 edition of Zuber and Company's "Le Jardin Francaise" multicolor.[4]

Where buildings were in close proximity to each other, as they were in Savannah and parts of Broad Street in Augusta, they were usually of brick or of stucco over brick, because of the ever-

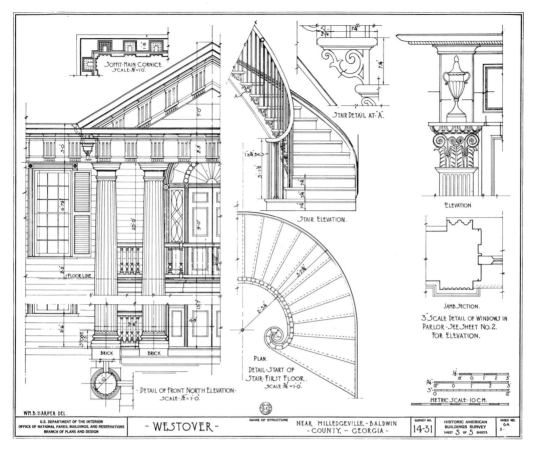

Westover, Milledgeville vicinity, ca. 1822.

present danger of fire. In smaller towns and in the country, they were more likely to be of frame construction with clapboard siding. Brick houses, in general, seem to have been trimmed in white and to have had white or dark green blinds. Favorite colors for painted exterior walls were shades of gray, buff, and brown. A conscious attempt was often made to match the color of painted stucco to various kinds of stone.

In addition to those already mentioned, HABS examples of traditional Federal architecture include the Broad Street Stores★, 700 block, south side, Augusta; the Old Government House★, Augusta; the Court House★, Dahlonega; the Brown-Sanford House★, Milledgeville; and the Clark House★ and Gibbons Block★ in Savannah. Traces of a brick dentil cornice and elliptical arches, typical of elegant Federal architecture, can

Gordon-Banks House, Newnan, 1828.

still be seen in the ruins of the Thicket Sugar Mill and Rum Distillery★ near Darien.

An anomaly is the Vann House★ at Spring Place. Erected in 1805 by Chief James Clement Vann, who was known alike for his wealth and violence,[5] it was probably the finest house in the Cherokee territory. Built of brick, two stories high and one room deep, it has details that could be described variously as Georgian, traditional Federal, post-Colonial, and Cherokee. Stucco pilaster strips, which may have been added later, could reflect Jeffersonian influence.

Jeffersonian Architecture

In Washington, D.C., and in Virginia, new architectural forms were emerging, largely under the influence of Thomas Jefferson, who was consciously seeking a nobler architecture to express the

View from the entrance hall of the Gordon-Banks House.

Arch and stairway, Gordon-Banks House.

Parlor mantel with flanking alcoves, Gordon-Banks House.

The Homestead, Milledgeville, 1818.

saw it on a visit to southern France. Part of his esteem for Roman architecture stemmed from his admiration for the ancient Roman Republic, though the buildings he so much admired were built during the reign of the Caesars.

The ensuing Jeffersonian architecture exhibited an extensive use of the Roman orders and a return to classic proportions, but with a practicality and a stateliness that was new and distinctly American. The Cowles-Sams House★ in Macon is an example, though in Georgia his influence is usually more apparent in Greek Revival than in Federal architecture. The two-story columns of some of the Federal

Brown-Sanford House, Milledgeville, ca. 1820.

ideals of the new republic. Appointed minister to France, Jefferson lived there from 1784 to 1789, traveling and avidly studying European architecture when he could get away from his official duties. He was impressed with the current neoclassical architecture of Paris, both because of its practicality and because of its gracious dignity. Having long been steeped in the architectural philosophy of Palladio, which is based on Roman principles, Jefferson was awed by the grandeur of Roman architecture when he first

Mantel at Casulon, High Shoals, 1821. Note the marbleizing.

Wallpaper, Hamilton-Johnson House, Clinton, ca. 1824.

Thicket Sugar Mill and Rum Distillery, near Darien, ca. 1816.

Mantel, Vann House, Spring Place, 1805. See p. 8 for exterior of the house.

style houses may have been inspired by examples of Jefferson's work. These would include those of the Homestead★ (1818) in Milledgeville and subsequently those of houses in the group described as Milledgeville Federal; of Jefferson Hall (1830) in Crawfordville; and of several houses designed by Collin Rodgers located in or near La Grange, among them the Boddie House★ (1836) and the Edwards House★ (1835–40). The columns of the portico at the Magnolias★ (1833) in La Grange, also designed by Collin Rodgers, are only one story high, but their proportions are closer to classical than to Federal prototypes, and may reflect Jefferson's influence.

Jeffersonian Greek Revival buildings include the Hermitage★ (ca. 1840, demolished) near Savannah, which had a Corinthian porch with an arcaded loggia beneath, wings with diagonal corners, and an inconspicuous stairway in a side corridor; it also had an air of classic serenity that was reminiscent of Monticello. The architect of the Hermitage is thought to have been Charles B. Cluskey, who designed the Governor's Mansion★ (1838) in Milledgeville. The plan of the latter, which has a central rotunda and dome, and its principal stairway in a side corridor, can be traced back to the Villa Rotonda by Palladio. It is strikingly similar to plans drawn by Jefferson (but not executed) for the governor's house in Richmond and for the president's house in Washington. The Governor's Mansion in Milledgeville is probably the finest Jefferson-inspired design outside of Virginia.[6]

Other Greek Revival buildings that

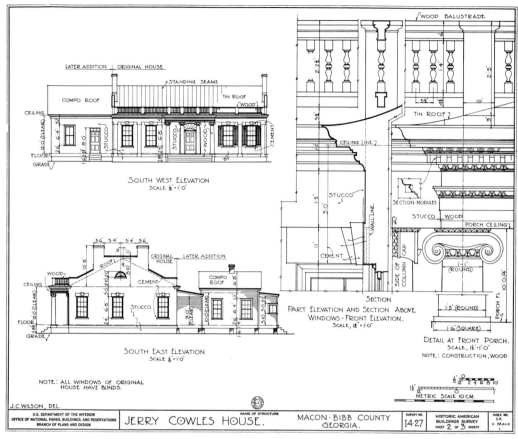

Cowles-Sams House, Macon, ca. 1830.

seem to reflect his influence include Bulloch Hall★ (1840) and Mimosa Hall★ (1847), both in Roswell, and both designed by Willis Ball, an architect from Connecticut. With their plain, unfluted columns and their temple forms, they have the monumental unity and the deliberate simplicity characteristic of much of Jefferson's architecture. At Bulloch Hall★, the bottom of the entablature is flush with the ceiling of the portico, as it is at Monticello.

Though the relationship to Jeffersonian architecture is tenuous, many of the Greek Revival cottages, particularly those derived from such indigenous prototypes as the plantation type cottages and changed slightly to conform more closely to classical principles, may best represent Thomas Jefferson's ideals of simplicity, democracy, and dignity.

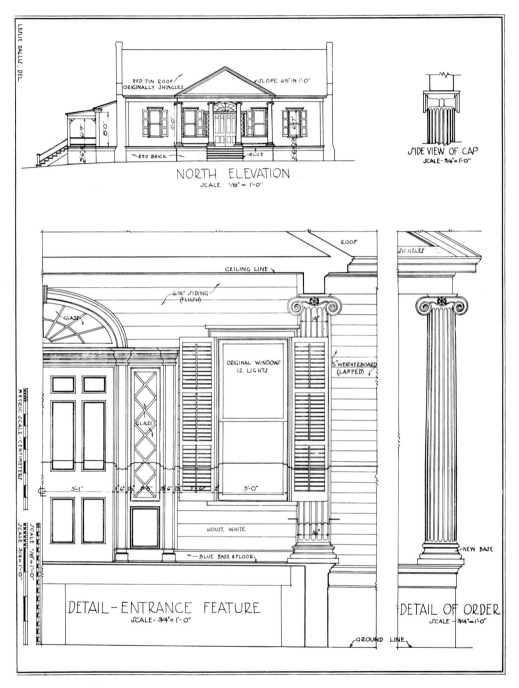

LESLIE DALLS, DEL.

RED TIN ROOF
ORIGINALLY SHINGLES
SLOPE 6½" IN 1'-0"

RED BRICK   BLUE

NORTH ELEVATION
SCALE ⅛" = 1'-0"

SIDE VIEW OF CAP.
SCALE - ¾"= 1'-0"

ROOF

SHINGLES

CEILING LINE

6½" SIDING
(FLUSH)

GLASS

ORIGINAL WINDOWS
12 LIGHTS

5" WEATHERBOARD
(LAPPED)

GLASS

14"

METRIC SCALE - CENTIMETERS

SCALE ⅛"=1'-0"

SCALE ¾"=1'-0"

3'-1"   3'-0"

HOUSE WHITE

16"

BLUE BASE & FLOOR

NEW BASE

DETAIL - ENTRANCE FEATURE
SCALE - ¾"= 1'-0"

DETAIL OF ORDER
SCALE - ¾"= 1'-0"

GROUND LINE

The Magnolias, La Grange, ca. 1833.

Portico of the Boddie House, near La Grange.

Detail of column capital of the Boddie House. The house was built between 1833 and 1836.

The Hermitage, Savannah vicinity, ca. 1830.

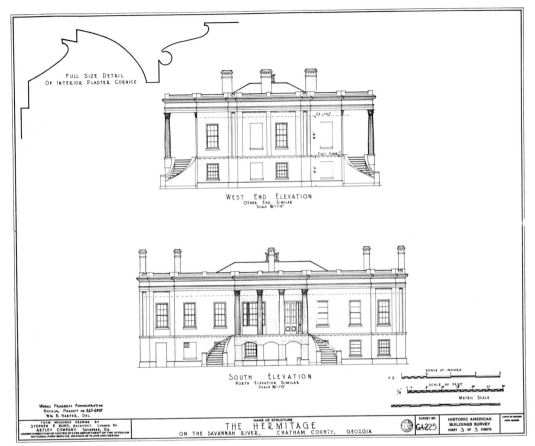

FULL SIZE DETAIL
OF INTERIOR PLASTER CORNICE

WEST END ELEVATION
OTHER END SIMILAR
SCALE ⅛"·1'0"

SOUTH ELEVATION
NORTH ELEVATION SIMILAR
SCALE ⅛"·1'0"

THE HERMITAGE
ON THE SAVANNAH RIVER, CHATHAM COUNTY, GEORGIA

HABS elevations of the Hermitage.

The Transitional or Rationalist Phase

Younger than Jefferson, but working closely with him, were Benjamin Latrobe and Robert Mills, architects who led the transition in this country from a comparatively small scale architecture based on Roman orders, to a large scale architecture usually based on Greek orders.

A native of England, Latrobe came to this country in 1796, imbued with the philosophy of a new generation of English and European architects who were espousing radically new concepts of design. Expanding on the theory that interior arrangements should derive from functional requirements, and that the resulting interior and structure should be expressed on the exterior, the rationalists subordinated or eliminated ornament to emphasize the space, mass, structure,

Polhill-Baugh House, Milledgeville vicinity, ca. 1840.

and geometry of their buildings. The resulting structures were usually combined with classic Greek orders, producing a dichotomy that was resolved only because the Greek orders were handled with great freedom and were modified to complement the new architectural forms.

Robert Mills received his training in part under both Jefferson and Latrobe. His work reflected Jefferson's practicality, but his architectural philosophy was

closer to that of Latrobe and the new generation of architects. He stated it well in a paper that was found among his effects after his death. Excerpts from it are ". . . that beauty is founded upon order; and that convenience and utility are constituent parts. . . . His considerations when designing a building were first, the object of the building; second, the means appropriate for its construction; third, the situation it was to occupy; these served as guides in forming the outline of his plan."[7] In more modern parlance, the requirements of function, structure, and site, combined with the logic of Greek architecture (order) should determine the form of the building.

For their more important buildings, both Mills and Latrobe usually relied on an arcuate structural system consisting of arches, vaults, and domes. This Roman type structure they combined with the post and beam structure of the Greek orders. The two structural systems were antithetical, but because of the skill of the architects, the resulting designs were simultaneously viable and serene.

In France, Étienne-Louis Boulée and Claude-Nicholas Ledoux envisioned an architecture in which the pure geometric forms would emerge free of all applied ornament. They consistently emphasized the functional (the functionalism was liable to be more symbolic than actual) and structural elements of their designs, and deemphasized the elements based on classical precedent. In their published drawings, both architects included designs of buildings whose powerful geometric forms were free of imitative classicism and of ornament. Apparently their clients were unenthusiastic and none of that type was built, though their philosophy was vindicated with the completion in this country of the Washington Monument (1836–84), years after they and Robert Mills, the architect of the monument, had died. The irony is compounded because the monument, universally acknowledged for its beauty, achieved its purity of form over the protest of the ar-

chitect. As originally designed, the great obelisk rose from a circular Greek Doric colonnaded building. Primarily for economic reasons, and to the chagrin of the architect, only the obelisk, its proportions slightly changed, was built. The simple beauty of its unadorned geometric form indicates the direction architecture might have taken had American architects likewise discarded the traditional appendages. It is probably just as well that they did not. The use of the classic orders gave whole cities, Washington in particular, a harmony that would have been most difficult to attain without their use.

The Nathanael Greene Monument★ in Savannah was designed by William Strickland, and the cornerstone laid by Lafayette in 1825. It is an obelisk also, mounted on a pedestal and similar except in scale to Mills's drawings for the Washington Monument. In both cases the pyramidal caps were flatter than that of the completed Washington Monument, and bases were an integral part of the designs, the proposed building to be the base for the Washington Monument. The flattened cap and pedestal seem right for the much smaller scale of the Greene Monument, as does the subtle refinement of the shaft's being less thick than it is wide; the proportions are such that the composition of pedestal, shaft, and cap is one of admirable unity.

The old Chatham County Courthouse (demolished) in Savannah was often attributed to Mills on the basis of an entry in his diary to the effect that he had finished designs for the courthouse in Savan-

The First Presbyterian Church★ in Augusta was designed by Robert Mills in the traditional Federal style, but was remodeled to the Romanesque style in 1892. The remodeling was accomplished with so few major changes that it suggests that the preliminary design might have been submitted in both the classical and Gothic styles. This was not an uncommon practice; Latrobe submitted drawings in both styles for the Baltimore Cathedral, and Mills occasionally designed in the Gothic manner. The original working drawings, which have been preserved by the church, show conventional square-head windows with lunettes at some distance above, these unified by being framed within blind

Nathanael Greene Monument, Savannah, 1825–30.

nah.[8] The entry included rough sketches of his design which were similar to the courthouse as built, differences being easily accounted for by the fact that Mills frequently changed his designs as work progressed. The drawings, however, were evidently entries in a competition, as the *Augusta Herald* of June 9, 1830 stated that the premium of one hundred dollars offered for plans for the new courthouse to be built in Savannah had been awarded to the firm of Russell Warren, Tallman, and Buckling of Rhode Island.

First Presbyterian Church, Augusta, 1809–12.

Richardson-Owens-Thomas House (rear view), Savannah, 1816–19.

arches. The spire, on an otherwise Gibbes type steeple, was shown as conical. Except for the spire, the drawings indicate little to suggest that Mills was the architect.

In Georgia, the transitional phase of Federal architecture is best represented by the work of William Jay, a native of Bath, England. Like Latrobe, he was evidently influenced by the work of Sir John Soane, and maintained a practice in London before coming to this country. His work in England included the drawings for the Richardson-Owens-Thomas House★ to be built in Savannah. Still in his early twenties, he arrived in Savan-

nah in 1817, and practiced there and in Charleston until 1824. The evolution from the traditional Federal (or Regency equivalent), to the transitional or rationalist phase of Federal architecture, to the Greek Revival can be traced in Jay's work of these few years.

The Richardson-Owens-Thomas House★ (1818) was built on one of the trustee lots formerly reserved for public buildings. These lots were oriented east and west, an orientation that created problems the architect coped with in several ways, including interior wall openings for ventilation. As previously mentioned, the plans were drawn in England,

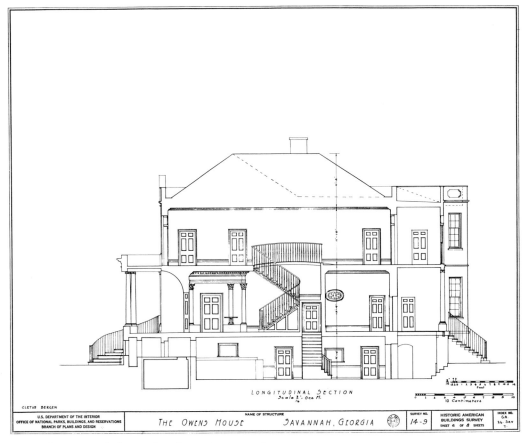

LONGITUDINAL SECTION
Scale ⅛" One Ft.

CLETUS BERGEN

| U.S. DEPARTMENT OF THE INTERIOR OFFICE OF NATIONAL PARKS, BUILDINGS, AND RESERVATIONS BRANCH OF PLANS AND DESIGN | NAME OF STRUCTURE THE OWENS HOUSE JAVANNAH, GEORGIA | SURVEY NO. 14-9 | HISTORIC AMERICAN BUILDINGS SURVEY SHEET 6 OF 8 SHEETS | INDEX NO. GA 1L. SAV 7. |

HABS drawing of the Richardson-Owens-Thomas House.

so the house is designated as Regency, though it could also be included within traditional Federal architecture. Unlike architecture of the rationalist phase, structural elements were deemphasized, subordinated to the lyrical movement of the curves and countercurves of blind arches, stair railings, and the undulating entrance porch. The attenuated Roman Ionic columns, the fanlighted doorway over the porch, the nonstructural disposition of the pilasters, and its domestic scale place this house in Jay's earlier style.

In contrast to the graceful elegance of the Richardson-Owens-Thomas House★ is the monumentality of the Scarbrough House★ (1819), representative of the transitional and rationalist phase. Here the dichotomy, so typical of that style, is exploited to its utmost. The majestic repetition of Roman arches of various sizes and for various uses is counterbalanced so precisely that the building is outstand-

Scarbrough House, Savannah, 1819. The third floor was added in the late nineteenth century, but removed during restoration in 1975–76.

ing both for its vitality and for its serenity. Inside, the atriumlike reception room is two stories high, surrounded by a balcony supported on four classic Greek Doric columns, and lighted from a clerestory and from the Diocletian window over the entrance. Frederick Doveton Nichols wrote that "this noble room was one of the grandest spatial compositions in American domestic architecture."[9]

The branch of the United States Bank★ (destroyed) built in Savannah in 1820 represents the final nationalist or Greek Revival phase. Here, too, Roman arches are used, but they are completely dominated

by a Greek hexastyle porch and ponderous roof parapets. Despite the arches, the building is Greek Revival, the first of that style in Georgia. Perhaps for that reason it was, at the time, the most admired of Jay's buildings. Views of the building were featured on china and in books of the day.[10]

While the Scarbrough House was under construction, President James Monroe visited Savannah, and Jay designed a pavilion for the occasion. In a letter to his wife, William Scarbrough described it: "Mr. Jay is fixing up a temporary Pavilion on the Church Square opposite to

Entrance hall of the Scarbrough House.

Telfair Academy, Savannah. The structure was built in 1820, the attic story added ca. 1880, and the statues sometime thereafter.

Andrew Low offices for the Ball and Supper Rooms. It is lined with red Maize or flannel with festoons and pilasters of white muslin. It is most tastefully and elegantly done—and by candle light will look most superbly."[11] Jay also designed the Savannah Theater, since greatly altered. The pavilion and the theater might well have been his most exciting works. In all of Jay's work, there is something of the theater, a dramatic quality that would have burgeoned in the design of an actual theater or of a pavilion, which was basically a stage set.

Other works that have been attributed to Jay include the Bulloch House (destroyed), the City Hotel (possibly the building at 23 Bay Street), the Wayne-Gordon House★, the Telfair Academy★, and the Cranston House (since destroyed), all in Savannah.

Despite differences in style, buildings designed by Jay had many features in common. Front façades were symmetrical with a central entrance porch; walls were of brick with stucco scored; roofs were low pitched with parapets with incised panels; windows were frequently set in wall arches and were themselves sometimes arched; the classic orders were freely used, changed, or modified to emphasize or deemphasize various parts

United States Bank, Savannah, 1818.

Balcony of the Richardson-Owens-Thomas House.

of the buildings. Surviving houses by Jay all have raised basements with strongly banded rustication, and string courses at the second story, the latter frequently in the form of a modified entablature. Most of them had cast-iron or cast- and wrought-iron balconies, some with the columns slotted, apparently for louvers. Rooms were laid out on either side of a central hallway, the more lived-in rooms usually to the south. Instead of an axial hall with a view to the rear, central halls or reception rooms were clearly defined spaces with an upward view to either a clerestory or an imposing flight of stairs. The arrangement was apparently not as well adapted to hot climates as was the

Richardson-Owens-Thomas House stairway.

Mantel, Telfair Academy, Savannah.

open-ended central hall, though the clere-stories originally may have been combined with a natural ventilating system.

Curved end walls and imported marble mantels, some the work of well-known sculptors, were features of the more important rooms of the finer houses. Tall base moldings with classic profiles were used instead of the wainscot of an earlier era. Decorative plasterwork was used with restraint and verve; the motifs were classical, usually Greek but used in new and original ways. The oversize egg-and-dart crown molding in the entrance hall, the palmette cresting in the dining room, and the corner fans in the drawing room of the Richardson-Owens-Thomas House★ are outstanding examples, though these are Regency in style. Palmette friezes were likewise used in some of the rooms of the Scarbrough House, but a Greek entablature with minor modifications was used over the columns of the entrance hall.

Characteristic of most of the architecture of the rationalist phase was the unorthodox use of Greek orders based on the post and lintel sytem in combination with arches, the synthesis of porches with Greek columns and entrances with fanlights being the most common example. Classical orders were freely modified or changed to suit conditions, the design approach being rational, not archaeological.

Buildings of the period were nearly always of masonry, usually stucco over brick, wood not being in character with the durable effect desired. The scale of the buildings and of their parts was larger than in previous styles; wall openings were emphasized while the details within the openings were deemphasized. Windows and doors were frequently recessed; the tracery of fanlight was unimportant in comparison with the effect of the arched openings. Window muntins became narrow, and were often painted in dark colors to minimize their effect. As in the preceding phases of neoclassical architecture, exterior walls were usually painted in light brown shades, similar to

Top of page: *Rockwell, Milledgeville, 1834.* Below: *First African Baptist Church, Savannah, ca. 1860.*

the color of some favored type of stone. In general, the architecture was characterized by simplicity, restraint, and monumentality.

Before the addition of a steeple with a projecting base, the First African Baptist Church★ in Savannah was a pseudo-temple form structure with a classical pediment and an entablature modified for brick and (apparently) molded brick.[12] Three entrances on the front and the windows on the sides were placed within wall arches; the arches had raised brick archivolts that extended down the sides of the wall piers, emphasizing the arcuate structure and giving the effect of a peripteral arcade. Though built in 1859, the

combination of arches and restrained classicism would place the architecture of the church as originally built within the rationalist phase of neoclassicism.

At Eldorado★ in Columbus, a magnificent house with a heroic porch on three sides, the entablature was reduced to little more than a light architrave, expressive of its wooden structure. Porch and roof balustrades, and the crystalline pattern of a cast-iron balcony provide a vibrant contrast to the powerful Tuscan columns, arched doorways, deepset windows, and smooth stucco walls.

Other examples include the Wayne-Gordon House★, Telfair Academy★, and the Gibbons Servants' and Car-

Top of page: *Eldorado, Columbus, 1828–33.* Below: *Balcony over the entrance to Eldorado.*

Gibbons Servants' and Carriage House, Savannah, ca. 1830.

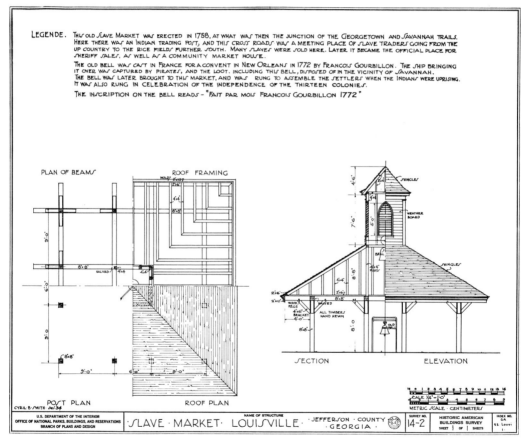

LEGENDE. This old Slave Market was erected in 1758, at what was then the junction of the Georgetown and Savannah trails. Here there was an Indian trading post, and this cross roads was a meeting place of slave traders going from the up country to the rice fields further south. Many slaves were sold here. Later it became the official place for sheriff sales, as well as a community market house.

The old bell was cast in France for a convent in New Orleans in 1772 by Francois Gourbillon. The ship bringing it over was captured by pirates, and the loot, including this bell, disposed of in the vicinity of Savannah. The bell was later brought to this market, and was rung to assemble the settlers when the Indians were uprising. It was also rung in celebration of the Independence of the Thirteen Colonies.

The inscription on the bell reads - "Fait par mois Francois Gourbillon 1772"

PLAN OF BEAMS   ROOF FRAMING

SECTION   ELEVATION

POST PLAN   ROOF PLAN

CYRIL B. SMITH 06/34

| U.S. DEPARTMENT OF THE INTERIOR OFFICE OF NATIONAL PARKS, BUILDINGS, AND RESERVATIONS BRANCH OF PLANS AND DESIGN | NAME OF STRUCTURE SLAVE · MARKET · LOUISVILLE · JEFFERSON · COUNTY · GEORGIA · | SURVEY NO. 14-2 | HISTORIC AMERICAN BUILDINGS SURVEY SHEET 1 OF 1 SHEETS | INDEX NO. GA 52 Louis 1 |

HABS drawing sheet of the Slave Market at Louisville.

Slave Market, Louisville.

riage House★, in Savannah; and the Phinizy House★ and some of the buildings of the United States Arsenal★ in Augusta. South End House (ca. 1810, demolished ca. 1912 and replaced by a modified replica) on Sapelo Island was a very early and sophisticated example of the style.

Miscellaneous Structures

Unique buildings of the period include the Slave Market★ (ca. 1795) in Louisville, which was built at the juncture of primary Indian trails and used as a trading post and for all kinds of public sales. It is an open shelter with a pyramidal roof supported by heavy hand-hewn timbers, all exposed. The Roe-Harper House (ca. 1800) about two miles northwest of

Devereux in Hancock County, is a half-timber house, apparently the only one of its type left in Georgia, and particularly curious because of the late date of its construction. The Old Rock House★ (ca. 1784) was built in the long defunct Wrightsborough Quaker Community about three miles northwest of Thomson in McDuffie County. It is built of fieldstone, with two-foot-thick walls. This type of construction was common in the vicinity of Freehold, New Jersey, where Thomas Ansley, the builder, was born. The house is one story over a raised basement and has a full attic. In appearance it is fortresslike, reminiscent of seventeenth-century New England frontier houses, which served to protect their residents from the Indians.

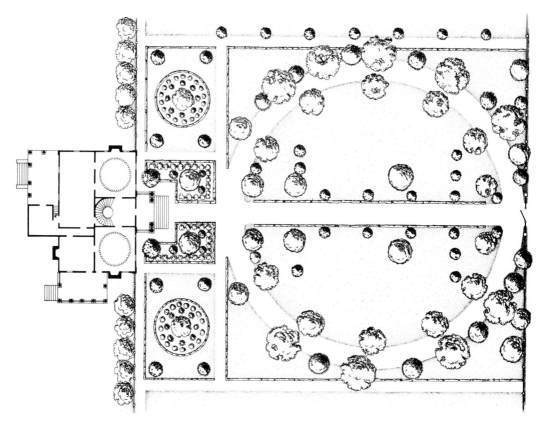

Top of page: *Plan of the principal floor and adjoining gardens at Westover, near Milledgeville. The house was built ca. 1822.* Bottom: *Garden of the Carnes House, Augusta, 1784.*

The Landscape

Travelers and others of the Federal period frequently mentioned the parks of Savannah and the tree-lined streets of Georgia towns, but beyond the disparaging remarks made by visitors to the backwoods, there are few contemporaneous descriptions of the grounds and gardens of that period. There are a number of gardens and traces of gardens connected with the Federal period houses, but it is difficult to tell which parts date back to the time of the house. Interest in gardening probably reached its peak in the mid-nineteenth century, and most of the old gardens still in existence were planted or greatly embellished at that time.

Tree-lined driveways leading to plantation houses are an exception; many of these were planted during, or even before, the Federal period. Avenues of live oaks seem to have been favored in the coastal regions, elms and cedars elsewhere.

It is generally thought that grass was little used in Georgia at the time, since hardy varieties did not flourish in the shade, nor were they evergreen. The squares of Savannah, however, were planted with Bermuda grass,[13] and it is unlikely that this was the only example, though parterre gardens with boxwood (or other evergreen) borders were usually substituted for lawns. From a distance the evergreen borders appeared cooler and greener than grass; close up, the flowers within were an added delight. If the garden were in front of the house, the axis of the central walk would usually be continued as the axis of the central hall within, and possibly extended through to another garden at the rear, thus strongly integrating the house and the grounds. The boxwood borders of the garden in front of the Homestead★ in Milledgeville are typical, and are said to date back to about the time of the construction of the house.

The grounds of many of the houses, particularly of the simpler ones, had swept sand or clay yards, with only trees and shrubs for verdure. Incidentally, until the twentieth century, shrubs were usually planted away from the house and were rarely used as continuous founda-tion plantings. The principal reason for the preference for swept yards was the difficulty of maintaining grass lawns, a difficulty aggravated if children were allowed to play there. For them the swept yards offered special delights: ants to be observed, doodle bugs to be teased, and jacks (ferocious-looking worms with pincers on their heads) to be caught by lowering weed stems into their holes. In addition, there was drawing on the ground with a stick, and by the same token, hopscotch, tick tack toe, and marbles.

Snakes were a problem in some areas and were thought to be attracted by grass and repelled by bare earth; also, in a verdant countryside and with the green of the trees above, the white swept yards were often a pleasant contrast.

As in colonial times, the grounds were enclosed with fences or walls, frequently with additional enclosures for special gardens. In small gardens, the flower beds might be separated by brick walks, or bordered with brick or tile and small plants. The herb garden was still essential, but occupied a less prominent place than in colonial times. Grape or scuppernong arbors, the latter a requisite in the following period, are mentioned in some accounts, including that of a garden behind the Richardson-Owens-Thomas House★.[14] Though little if any original planting remains, an idea of the appearance of the small city gardens can be obtained from such accounts and from remaining structural elements. The small front garden of the Richardson-Owens-Thomas House★ is enclosed by a balustraded wall, and most of the enclosed

Lowther Hall, Clinton, 1822. Note the surrounding fence.

area is paved with cut flagstone. Planting here was probably originally held to a minimum, as it was at the townhouses of Bath and London, though at one time pomegranates, oleanders, and crepe myrtles grew there.[15] A large part of the rear garden was occupied by a paved carriage turn-around and walks. The remaining space was planted with flowering shrubs, figs, citrus trees, and an herb garden.[16]

Despite its run-down condition, the courtyard of the center unit of the Broad Street Stores★, 582–90 Broad Street in Augusta, is pleasant with a galleried porch, old brick walls, small brick service buildings, remnants of brick paving, weeds, and vines. Originally it was doubtless used for service as well as leisure, and most of the area was paved with brick.

There are many records of the plants used at that time, but space does not permit their inclusion. Some of the now exotic fruit trees that were successfully grown in the warmer areas should be mentioned, including oranges, nectarines, olives, and pomegranates.

Portion of the wall enclosing the grounds of the Richardson-Owens-Thomas House in Savannah.

Towns and Cities

In his book *Town Planning in Frontier America* John Reps wrote: "One of the great misfortunes of American town planning was that the Savannah plan seemingly exercised no influence on the layout of towns outside Georgia. Even there, only Brunswick, planned in 1770, followed the novel and effective neighborhood pattern."[17] Actually, Brunswick failed to follow the plan as the town expanded, so that only the oldest part of the city enjoys its advantages.

Though fairly generous areas were usually set aside for parks, most of the cities founded during the Federal period lack the detailed planning that gave Savannah its series of public squares, different types of streets for different types of traffic, and residential lots oriented (whether deliberately or fortuitously) so that all houses could have the benefits of a southerly exposure.

In 1794 Louisville was established as the new capital of the state, laid out in the gridiron manner around a central square "after the style of the streets of Philadelphia."[18] All too typically, the planners ignored superior examples within the state to copy stylish examples from afar. In this case it made little difference; by 1803 Louisville was considered too far east, and plans were made to move the capital to the center of the state. In 1804 Milledgeville was established as the capital. It was situated near the Oconee River and laid out on the gridiron plan with four large public squares, each square the equivalent of four blocks, or about twenty acres. One square was called the State House Square and reserved for the capitol building (Old State Capitol★) and for churches; one was called Governour Square, though the governor's house (Old Governor's Mansion★) was later built within one of the regular city blocks; one was Penitentiary Square, now part of the campus of the Georgia College at Milledgeville; and one square was reserved for public use but was shortly thereafter set aside as a cemetery. Regardless of usage, the squares remain green and pleasant places, invaluable assets to the city.

Macon, founded in 1821 on the south-

Broad Street Stores between Fifth and Sixth Streets in Augusta. The stores were built in the early nineteenth century.

west side of the Ocmulgee River, was likewise laid out on the gridiron plan, with each block bisected both ways by alleys. Building lots were arranged with the desirable SSW by NNE orientation. One block was reserved for the courthouse, one for churches, and one for an academy; there was also a large open area at the intersection of Mulberry and Fifth streets. Originally the town was bound on the north and west sides by open commons. Unfortunately this land was later absorbed by the growing city.

Columbus was laid out on the east side of the Chattahoochee River in 1826, in a grid of rectangular blocks. Unlike most of the other planned cities, the building lots faced east and west. Separate squares were reserved for male and female academies, and others for the courthouse and churches. There was a promenade along the picturesque river front, and a median with trees down the center of Broad Street, the principal street. The town was originally bound by commons on the north, east, and south sides; these, like those of Macon, were later absorbed by the growing city.[19]

Smaller towns generally adopted the gridiron plan, with the courthouse square in the center. Many of the county seats in rural areas consisted solely of the courthouse square (Crawford County Courthouse★ in Knoxville) with one or two stores and residences, but no town plan as such.

The original layout of Augusta (1735) determined the direction of the principal streets and influenced their widths, but colonial expansion from the small nucleus was haphazard. In 1780, during the American Revolution, five commissioners were appointed to enlarge the limits of the town, to lay out vacant land in lots of one acre each, to arrange the new streets to conform with existing streets, and to straighten streets that had been encroached upon.[20] Because of the fighting in and around Augusta, the plans were not carried out until 1783, when another board of commissioners was appointed. By the beginning of the nineteenth century the downtown part of Augusta was established. The combination of natural growth and varying plans led to a unique layout consisting of a grid of rectangular blocks of varying sizes, arranged so that most of the buildings received the desired ssw by NNE orientation. Instead of a series of parks, as in Savannah, the two principal streets, Broad and Greene, were so wide that they became, in a sense, continuous parks, parks of widely differing character.

An 1801 description asserts that "the principal street, called Broad Street, running nearly east and west is a handsome well-built street, one hundred and sixty-five feet wide, and has a row of trees for nearly a mile on each side."[21] The section between Fifth and Ninth streets was primarily commercial. During the first half of the nineteenth century, this meant that it was composed mostly of houses, the first floors of which were workshops, taverns, or stores (Broad Street Stores★). The public market, one "haunted pillar" of which remains, was also in this area.

Many of the finer residences were concentrated on Greene Street, which likewise had its rows of fine trees, but without the bustle and confusion of the commercial section of Broad Street.

As previously mentioned, the Savannah plan exercised little influence on the plans of succeeding towns and cities. One reason may have been that it was not until the nineteenth century, nearly a hundred years after the founding of Savannah, that the visual advantages of its plan became apparent. As the blocks surrounding the squares were built up, the open space of the squares, which formerly merged with that of the streets and of the vacant lots, became defined. About 1810 the squares were enclosed with cedar posts painted white and with chains between them, thus effectively separating the squares from vehicular traffic. Trees and Bermuda grass were planted within, and paved footpaths bisected them in both directions.[22]

Visitors of the time often noted that Savannah, with its grassy squares and tree-lined streets, seemed more like a collection of villages than a large city. A meticulously executed view of Savannah painted by Joseph L. F. Cerveaux in 1837 attests to its pastoral air. Cantering horses and various horse-drawn vehicles fail to

View of Savannah painted by Joseph L. F. Cerveaux in 1837.

disturb the children playing or the cows resting in the deep sand of the wide, unpaved streets.

It was also during this period that the now-familiar Savannah row house (e.g., the John Hunter House★) became typical. Built with common side walls, which were extended to become garden walls between the back yards, they were raised a story off the ground. The entrance was usually approached by side steps, and the living porch was placed on the rear overlooking the garden. A carriage house and servants' quarters could be placed at the rear of the lot, accessible to the alley behind. This general plan was continued throughout the nineteenth century, and is still viable, though the carriage houses may have been converted to garages, and the servants' quarters to modern apartments.

The striking difference between Savan-nah's elegant row houses and Charleston's equally elegant detached houses has often been noted, the contrast being particularly interesting because of the proximity of the two cities and because of the similarity of climate and of social conditions. The differences may well be the result of differences in their city plans. In Charleston, the streets were multidirectional. Few of the lots were serviced by alleys, so driveways were a necessity if privies were to be cleaned and if horses and carriages were to be kept. Space being at a premium, the drives were usually incorporated into a small garden on the side, and the typical house—high, deep, and narrow, with tiered porches preferably facing south or southwest—opened to the garden at the side instead of to the street or to the rear. In Savannah, residential lots were arranged so that either the front or the back of the house would

receive the desired southern orientation, and the alleys eliminated the need for driveways; so the more traditional and practical row house was easily adapted in that city to the local climate and conditions.

Exceptions were some of the great houses, such as the Richardson-Owens-Thomas House★, which were built on lots that originally were set aside for public buildings, and which faced east or west. In such cases, more and larger windows were usually placed on the south side than the north; balconies or extra porches were also likely to be placed on the southerly side. In nearly all cases, however, the established Savannah custom of placing the principal porches on the rear, overlooking a garden, was followed.

Top of page: *William Taylor Store, Savannah. The store was built in 1818, partially destroyed by fire in 1885, and rebuilt that same year.* Bottom: *Interior of the William Taylor Store.*

Chapter Four   The Antebellum Period

After 1840 the dominant form of architecture in antebellum Georgia was Greek Revival, but it was by no means the only style of the period. Indigenous structures continued to be built throughout the state, as did numerous buildings so conservative that they had no marked stylistic features. Outside the south, Gothic, Romanesque, and Italianate, plus a variety of styles loosely classified as mid-Victorian, were, at mid-century, fast replacing Greek Revival as the favorite style, and were slowly becoming accepted in Georgia. There seems to have been a nebulous correlation between the growth of industry and commerce and the acceptance of the new styles. It is interesting to note that the Gothic style Green-Meldrim House★ in Savannah and the Italianate Johnston-Hay House★ in Macon, both more lavish than any of the Greek Revival plantation houses, were built by businessmen. Judging by these and other homes of Georgia entrepreneurs, the larger fortunes of the 1850s were being made in commerce and industry, not agriculture.

Georgia's first textile mill began operation in Athens in 1829; the state's first railroad was chartered in 1833. By 1860 railroads connected all the major cities, and the growth of industry, particularly in the field of textiles, earned for Georgia the nickname of "the New England of the South." The industrial and commercial buildings were assuming new and unique forms dictated by new and unprecedented requirements; stylistic features were necessarily relegated to details, which might be of classical, Gothic, or Romanesque inspiration. Nevertheless, the bulk of the economy was still based on agriculture, and even at the end of the period, Georgia was predominately rural. The architecture was predominately neoclassical, indigenous, or a combination of the two.

In Savannah, neoclassical porticoes with heroic columns were largely reserved for churches and important civic buildings, but Greek Revival houses, with columned porches and wide cool halls (frigid in winter), proliferated in the suburbs of most of the cities, and particularly in the small towns and in the countryside of the Georgia sand hills and piedmont. In those areas, many of the planters had two houses: one in a nearby village or town where their families lived most of the year and where their children went to school, and another, much simpler and sometimes crude, on the plantation. Here the family summered, and the planter could stay as he was needed in other seasons.

Nearer the coast the process was reversed. Families left the hot, humid plantation areas in spring and did not return until fall or winter, when danger from malaria was over.

Climate was a major factor in the design of most antebellum dwellings, and whatever the style, regional characteristics were usually apparent. This was generally true whether the house was an indigenous cottage built according to local traditions, or a sophisticated residence like the Low House★ in Savannah or Barrington Hall★ in Roswell, both of which were designed by architects from the North. Many of the architectural books of the time featured houses designed especially for the South, designs that usually incorporated generous porches, detached kitchens, and other features that were peculiarly suited to the region.

Greek Revival Architecture, the National Phase of Neoclassicism

The first Greek Revival building in Georgia was apparently the United States Bank★ in Savannah, built circa 1820 and described in the previous chapter. Though it had some Federal features, the Greek portico dominated the design. The Greek Doric order possesses an aesthetic logic that is not easily assimilated into other styles; unless modified, it either dominates the entire design or conflicts with other parts. The lordly architecture on which the Greek Revival was based was primarily that of the marble temples remaining from the Periclean period (450–400 B.C.) on the Acropolis at Athens. Their design and aesthetically perfect proportions had been developed over a period of centuries, and their beauty and majesty were reflected in much nineteenth-century Greek Revival architecture.

Though the classical temples were built centuries after the early ones, which were of wood, many of the features of wood construction were maintained as decorative details for the later marble temples. The triglyphs of the Doric frieze represented the exposed ends of wooden beams, and the sloping mutules, wooden rafters.

The early wooden temples were built in the archaic manner with immense timbers (witness the size of the triglyphs) which were out of proportion to the much smaller structural elements of the nineteenth-century buildings. The disparity in scale between the real structure and the simulated Greek structure intensified the dichotomy arising from the use of temple architecture for more mundane purposes.

Despite that dichotomy, few if any periods of American history have produced an architecture so suited to the needs of the people, to the climate (at least in the South), and to the building technology of the time; nor one so visually appealing. Of this architecture, Talbot Hamlin wrote: "Never before or since, I believe, has there been a period when the general

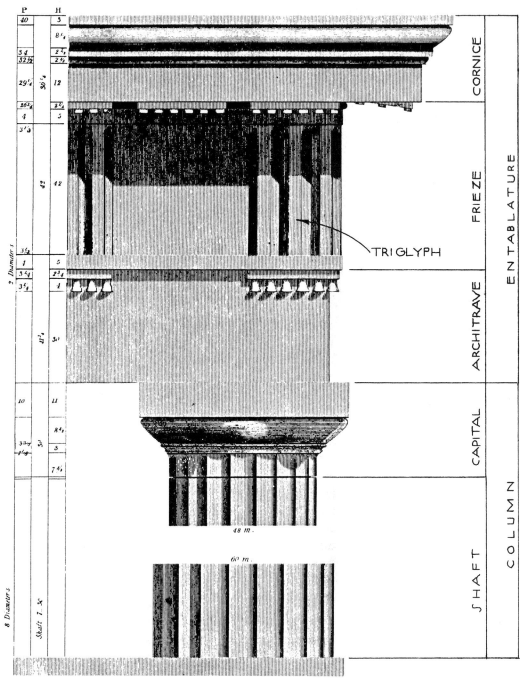

Greek Doric Order from Asher Benjamin. Nomenclature added.

THE ANTEBELLUM PERIOD 99

level of excellence was so high in American architecture, when the ideal was so constant, and its varying expressions so harmonious, when the towns and villages, large and small, had in them so much unostentatious beauty and loveliness as during the forty years from 1820 to the Civil War."[1]

The truth of his statement is brought home to anyone traveling through Georgia who comes upon one of those rare old towns where a group of Greek Revival buildings and gardens remain.

Numerous books of the time, including those of Peter Nicholson, Minard Lafever, and Edward Shaw, as well as the later ones of Asher Benjamin, illustrated the ancient orders, with the preferred proportions and details. Mantels, stairways, moldings, and other elements that were designed to be in keeping with the Greek architecture, but for which there were no prototypes, were also illustrated. Though the period is called Greek Revival, the books presented both Greek and Roman orders.

The authors of most of the books emphasized the fact that the proportions and details varied from temple to temple and that there was no rigid set of criteria to follow. They also recognized that nineteenth-century conditions were not the same as those of the ancient world, and they usually simplified or modified the orders illustrated, sometimes juxtaposing elements from different orders. In practice, further modifications occurred. Many builders gained their knowledge of architecture solely from built examples, and their buildings often reflected only

the more obvious of the classic characteristics; heavier columns and stock millwork in the Greek Revival style were sometimes the only features that distinguished a Greek Revival building from an indigenous one.

The most familiar feature of Greek Revival architecture is, of course, the columned portico. This might be elegant with tall Corinthian columns like Twelve Oaks in *Gone with the Wind* or the President's House★ at the University of Georgia in Athens, or it might be a vernacular version like Margaret Mitchell's Tara, or the Johnson House★ in Jefferson. It might be only one story high, and it might be small or large; the building might even have no front porch, like the Old Emory Church★ in Oxford.

As in ancient times, the most popular of the Greek orders was the simplest, the Doric order. The Tuscan order, a variation described by the Roman historian Vitruvius, and unknown to the Greeks, was even simpler, and, as used in Georgia, was frequently a hybrid of both orders.

A very practical difficulty with the use of unmodified orders resulted from the depth of the classic entablature, which, instead of being a simple beam over the columns, was composed of an architrave and frieze in addition to the cornice. If the Greek Doric proportions were followed, the combined depth of architrave and frieze would be more than a fourth the height of the columns. Though not too objectionable so far as porches were concerned, this posed immediate problems if the complete entablature were

President's House, University of Georgia, Athens, 1857–58.

Johnson House, Jefferson, ca. 1836.

Huntley House, La Grange, mid nineteenth century.

Old Emory Church, Oxford, 1841.

White Hall, West Point, 1857–58.

T. R. R. Cobb House, Athens, showing entablature rising above roof.

carried around the body of the building, since the tops of windows would cut into the entablature, or the windows would have to be lowered several feet. There were various solutions, none of them altogether satisfactory to both academic and practical architects. One method was to use the full entablature over the porch but to omit the architrave and frieze elsewhere, as was done at White Hall★ in West Point. Another was to treat the entablature as a parapet that rose above the

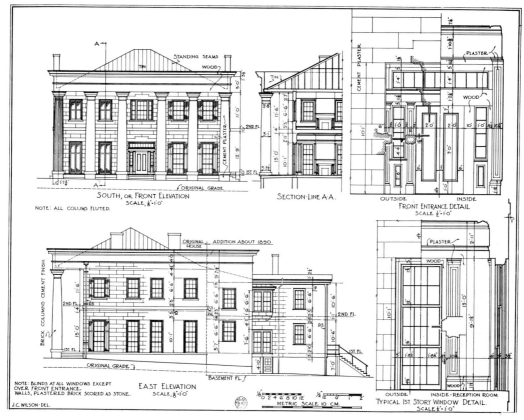

HABS drawings of the Dr. Marcus A. Franklin House, Athens, 1847.

roof, a solution that belied its structural function and that presented problems with roof drainage. An expensive alternative was to raise the whole roof as at the Old Governor's Mansion★ in Milledgeville, but this created excess space in the attic unless the space were used for additional rooms as at Montrose★ in Augusta, where small windows were incorporated into the frieze. The practical solution was to ignore the canons and to reduce the architrave and frieze to more sensible proportions, as was done at Bulloch Hall★ in Roswell. Occasionally an academically correct porch was added to an ordinary house without modifications to either; in such cases the scale of the porch was likely to be so powerful that the rest of the house appeared to be dangling from it. An example is the Abbot-Toombs House★ in Washington. A frontal view of the magnificent porch is most impressive; the side view is interesting but disconcerting because of the difference in

Old Governor's Mansion in Milledgeville, built in 1838.

scale between the porch and the house, also because the porch cornice is higher than that of the house. Such combinations are not untypical, the porch of Andrew Jackson's mansion, the Hermitage in Nashville, Tennessee, probably being the most famous example. Such naive juxtapositions, almost embarrassing to early twentieth-century classicists, are now considered particularly interesting features and illustrate a fascinating aspect of Victorian manners: that of seeing only what one is supposed to see. Chairs of the period were frequently upholstered with fine material except for the backs, which might be of plain cloth. The Victorian version of Louis XV chairs usually had cabriole legs in front but plainer legs sticking out behind (or, as Mark Twain supposedly put it, "they have Queen Anne fronts and Mary Anne behinds").

The variations were endless, the more unorthodox being the more numerous, and perhaps the more interesting. Brackets were often substituted for the traditional members of the frieze, a practice

Montrose, Augusta, 1849.

that permitted very wide eaves without their seeming disproportionate. Columns, too, were subject to modification. They might be square, round, fluted, or unfluted; occasionally they were multisided, the many flat faces giving the impression of flutes, as on the columns of Casulon★ at High Shoals. The capitals of the columns there are also unusual in that they have a series of small brackets that substitute for the acanthus leaves of the orthodox Corinthian capital; they seem much more in keeping with the carpentry of the rest of the house than would the classic version.

The scrolls of Ionic capitals were frequently carefully carved on the front and back, but a simple turned member between the faces might suffice for the sides. Occasionally, as at the Straus–Le Vert Memorial Hall★ in Talbotton, a flat board cut to the silhouette of a scroll answered for the faces of Ionic capitals. The variations on Tuscan and Doric orders were less obvious and far too numerous to describe. Though sometimes awkward, the changes more often than not helped unify the design.

Some of the more successful variations relied least on archaeological precedent. At White Hall★ near Montrose, the square columns that rest in front of the porch acknowledge their relation to Greek architecture only by their studied propor-

Bulloch Hall, Roswell, 1840.

tions, heavier and more stately than those of earlier periods. The house is a hybrid, combining the easy practicality of indigenous architecture with the dignity and clarity of the Greek; it is close to the ideal Jefferson sought several decades earlier, i.e., an architecture that would embody the simplicity and the majesty symbolic of the new republic. Its relation to Greek architecture is one of spirit rather than detail, and is not unlike that expressed by Sir Edwin Lutyens when he wrote: "That time-worn Doric order—a lovely thing—I have the cheek to adopt it. To be right you have to take and design it . . . you cannot copy." On the other hand, "You cannot play originality with the Orders. They have to be so well digested that there is nothing but essence left. When they are right, they are curiously lovely."[2]

The straightforward simplicity of the design of White Hall★, the sheltering porch, the repetition of the well-proportioned columns, make it representative of the best of a number of similar houses and buildings of the period which are peculiarly right, peculiarly Greek, and peculiarly American. Among them are the cottage behind the President's House★, University of Georgia in Athens, the Davis-Edwards House★ in Monroe,

Abbot-Toombs House, Washington. The house was built ca. 1796; the portico and west wing added ca. 1837.

Fair Oaks (the Mitchell House) in Thomasville, the Polhill-Baugh House★ near Milledgeville, the Pendergrass Store★ in Jefferson, the Neal-McCormick House★ in Covington, and Fruitlands★ in Augusta. Fruitlands, now the clubhouse for the Augusta National Golf Course, was expressly designed to meet the requirements of local climatic conditions, available structural materials, and the functions of a plantation house.[3] The resulting form was an outgrowth of those requirements, style hardly being taken into consideration, and appears to be the product of a deliberate search for simplicity which was strangely at odds with

Rear view of the Abbot-Toombs House.

Top of page: *Casulon, High Shoals. The house was built in 1822, the porch in the mid nineteenth century.* Below: *Few Literary Society Hall, Oxford, 1852.*

the prevailing taste in more fashionable areas.

Certain features were common to most of the Greek Revival houses. Walls under porch roofs were frequently treated as though the porch were an interior room. If the house were brick, those walls might have a plaster finish; if the house were clapboard, walls there would likely be of boards laid flush for a smooth surface or, occasionally, of plaster.

Porch floors were usually supported by brick piers, the space between the piers either left open or filled in with latticed brick or wood lattice. The Taylor-Grady House★ in Athens has elliptical, arched openings, covered with exceptionally del-

Maxwell House, Talbotton, mid nineteenth century.

icate lattice work, between the piers.

The back porches, usually one story or a series of tiered porches, were in many cases more important than the front. In pleasant weather, meals might be eaten here, and many of the household chores were performed in their shade. In Savannah, and occasionally in other cities, the only large porch was generally placed on the back, with a stoop or small entrance porch at the front leading to a Greek Revival doorway. The doors of the ancient Greek temples were too large to copy for domestic buildings, but their design was reflected to some extent in those of the Greek Revival period, as at the Low House★ in Savannah with its pedimented

sandstone entrance with Corinthian columns, behind which is the elaborate doorway with sidelights and transom. The double doors are heavily studded like the bronze doors of the ancient temples. Painted white, however, the studding appears decorative, merges with the carving of the door frame, and is more reminiscent of the lacy white collars worn by ladies of the period than of the heavy doors of a Greek temple. Most of the entrance doors had sidelights and straight-top transoms, the transoms replacing the fanlights of the previous era

White Hall, Montrose vicinity, ca. 1820.

Cottage behind the President's House, University of Georgia, Athens.

on the grounds that the Greeks rarely used arches. Glass in the sidelights and transoms was frequently frosted, or a combination of frosted and stained glass. Doors with four panels, or two vertical panels, or one large panel were more popular than the traditional six-panel door. Occasionally, there would be two sets of doors, an outer set (sometimes louvered) that fit into the jambs of the door when not in use, and an inner set made of glass,

Davis-Edwards House, Monroe, ca. 1835.

as at the Kerr House★ or the Customs House★, both in Savannah.

Windows were large, with larger panes than before. They frequently came down to the floor, particularly under porches or on balconies, where they could be used as doors. Occasionally, as at the Low House★, double-hung windows had extrawide center muntins to give the appearance of casement windows or French doors.

Nearly all the houses had louvered blinds, which before the advent of screened windows were in constant use.

The large windows and doors, usually wide open during the summer months, made the interior seem a part of the outdoors, an interrelation that was apparently appreciated and often mentioned in writings of the time. An instance is found in a letter written by Mary Jones to her five-year-old granddaughter: "The doors and windows stand open now, and the bright sunshine peeps in, and the cool breezes, filled with perfume from the tea-scented olive and the sweet roses and flowers of the garden, come freely through the entry and halls."[4] For the warm sea-

Top of page: *Nichols House, Griffin, mid nineteenth century.* Below: *Neal-McCormick House, Covington, 1852.*

sons, draperies and rugs were customarily removed. Bare floors or rush mattings, white curtains, and linen or chintz covers for furniture imparted an air of coolness almost as refreshing as the breezes.

Charles Cluskey, probably Georgia's most prominent architect of the period, sought other solutions, but the central-hall plan, relict of dog-trot cabins, was most often used. Breezes were funneled through it, and in summer it was likely to be the coolest area in the house. Axial landscaping often accentuated the interrelation of the hall with the outdoors. On small city lots, the hall was frequently on one side only, and the house was built several stories high to obtain the necessary number of rooms. Rooms were usu-

ally high ceilinged, square or rectangular, and spacious. Folding or sliding doors were nearly always used between parlors, and often between other rooms.

For most interior work there were few Greek prototypes to follow, though mantels and openings between rooms sometimes had Greek columns and entablatures. Ornament, sparingly used, was based on Greek motifs, among them the Greek frets and keys, the anthemion motif (a stylized representation of the honeysuckle vine), and laurel wreaths. Moldings and door and window casings were large, simple, and vigorous, as were the Greek ones. Stairways were generally wide with straight runs, and with heavier balusters than in the preceding eras; the handrails were frequently curved at the

Top of page: *Orange Hall, St. Marys, ca. 1850.* Below: *Fruitlands, Augusta, 1854–56.*

Orange Hall, St. Marys, ca. 1850.

*Back porch of the Clanton House,
Augusta, mid nineteenth century.*

Back porch of Orange Hall, St. Marys.

turns, ending with a heavy newel post.
Interior doors usually had four panels,
two short ones at the bottom and longer
ones above; sometimes they had only
two vertical panels. Plaster moldings as
well as ceiling medallions were generally
broad and comparatively simple, though
occasionally decorated with Greek frets.
Mantels, with or without columns, were
heavy and simple; black marble was a favorite material for them.

Furniture was likewise large and massive, relying more on beautiful patterns
of matched veneers, frequently of rosewood, than on ornament for interest. An
exception to the above was the widespread use of other styles with the Greek.
Both Gothic and Italianate styles were
also popular, and inspired fanciful designs that can only be called Victorian.
Ornate marble mantels, usually with
arched openings and cast-iron grates, and
with amazingly realistic floral motifs, as
well as plaster medallions and moldings
with leaf, grape, and floral designs, pro-

vided a delicate contrast to the Greek-
inspired background, as did the rococo
Belter and other versions of Louis XV
furniture.

Ivory, cream, white, off-white, and gray
were the favored interior colors, but ornate wallpaper, influenced by Italianate
or Gothic styles, was sometimes used.

A dubious legacy remaining with us
from this period is the idea that the exterior of all houses should be painted white.
The notion is thought to have arisen
from the assumption that, because they
were built of marble, all classic temples
were white. At any rate, during this period, most of the houses that were built
of wood were painted white and had green
blinds. Those that were stucco were often left natural as was the Cowles-Bond
House★ in Macon, or painted a rich color
and allowed to mellow, as was the Champion-McAlpin House★ in Savannah. The
Old Governor's Mansion★ in Milledgeville was painted a muted pink, described
at the time as "mellow rose, the color of

Entrance to the Low House, Savannah, 1849.

Front door of the Chew House, Augusta, mid nineteenth century.

Entrance to the Old Governor's Mansion in Milledgeville.

a lovely pink-tinged sunset just deepening into crimson."[5]

Examples of Greek Revival architecture, so right for the Georgia climate and for the customs of the times, can still be found in most areas of the state, including the southwestern part, which was strangely underrepresented in the original Historic American Buildings Survey. Among the area's outstanding buildings are those designed by the English architect John Wind in and around Thomasville. These include the Thomas County Courthouse★ and Greenwood, a magnificent plantation house. Though Greek Revival pediments were generally left plain except for needed windows or louvers (or

occasionally a frieze under the raking cornice) the pediment of the portico at Greenwood was ornamented with a carved magnolia blossom, flanked by swags. Wind also designed Susina Plantation, Fair Oaks, and the Hansell House, all in or near Thomasville.

Other Greek Revival buildings with unique features or qualities include the columned brick houses built as summer retreats in the Etowah Valley region; the buildings of old Mercer University at Penfield in Greene County; the Customs House★ in Savannah, with its monolithic granite columns and geometric marble stairway; the Old Governor's Mansion★ in Milledgeville, with its central rotunda

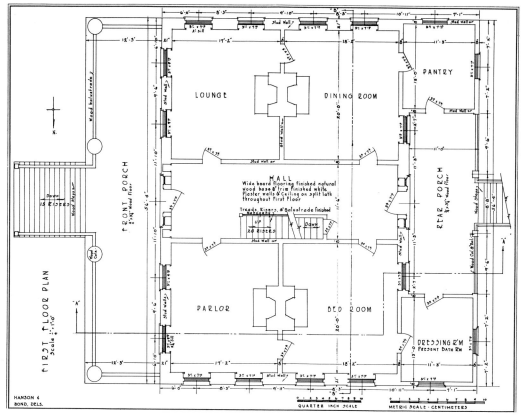

Floor plan for Orange Hall, St. Marys.

and dome; and the Billings House★ in Columbus, with its T-shape plan. Boxwood★, in Madison, has a parlor still furnished with the draperies, carpet, gold-leaf mirrors, and furniture installed when the house was built; its formal gardens, of approximately the same date, retain the original pattern of the boxwood flower-beds. The Low House★ in Savannah, so obviously suited to the climate, has balconies on its south side and a tiered porch with louvers protecting it from the sun on the west side. The President's House★, University of Georgia, in Athens, White Hall★ near Montrose, and the Hermitage★ (demolished), near Savannah, have, for sheer grace, rarely been surpassed.

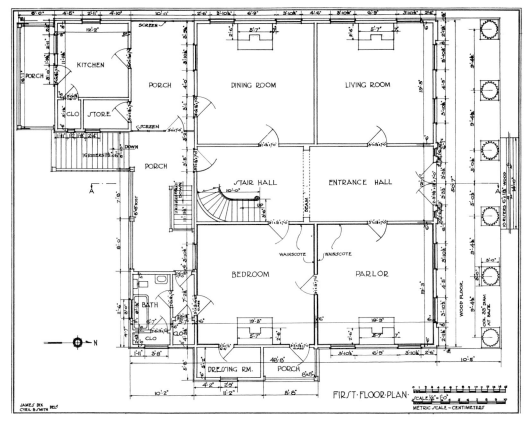

Floor plan for the Oaks, La Grange, ca. 1840.

Antebellum Gothic and Romanesque Revivals

Gothic architecture was the architecture of the late Middle Ages in Europe and in England. Houses and smaller buildings were usually of stone or half-timber, the latter consisting of heavy framing members, the spaces between filled in with plaster or masonry, called nogging. Other characteristics were steep roofs, casement windows, prominent chimneys,

and a general informal picturesque quality.

Castles and ecclesiastical buildings were usually of stone, precisely cut and fitted. Castles were likely to be heavily fortified with moats, walls, and bastions; the tops of defensive walls were castellated, that is with alternating indentations (embrasures) and raised portions (merlons). Defenders could shoot through the embrasures while using the merlons as shields.

Gothic churches and cathedrals were

*Interior view of the entrance to the Old
Governor's Mansion in Milledgeville.*

triumphs of engineering, with lofty
vaults whose thrusts were countered by a
complicated system of buttressing. Most
obvious characteristics were the pointed
arches, the buttresses, the spires and
finials, and the glory of the medieval
stained glass.

Random elements of Gothic architecture can be traced from the earliest years
of Georgia's colonization. The Salzburgers brought with them the tradition
of half-timber construction, which they
modified by adapting elements of the
Indians' wattle-and-daub technique of
building. None of these has survived, but
the Roe-Harper House (ca. 1800), a re-

markably late example of half-timber
construction with brick nogging, remains
near Devereux in Hancock County.

The Thornton House, originally built
at Union Point in Greene County and
since moved to Stone Mountain Park
near Atlanta, has paired medieval type
chimneys, the outer wall continuous between them, and with a pent roof over
the recess thus formed. The upper part of
the recess was utilized for cupboards; the
lower part provided an exterior entrance
to the basement. This great double chimney with broad weatherings, independent
shafts, and ingle recess seems more medieval than eighteenth century. So does
the diaper work that is found on the chimneys of a number of houses throughout
Georgia, including the Cabaniss-Hunt
House, ca. 1810, in Jones County, the
Joseph Rucker House (early nineteenth
century) in Elbert County, and the Richardson House (1832) in Nacoochee Valley, White County.

More viable, in that it provided a continuing linkage between true Gothic and
Gothic Revival architecture, was the use
of castellated walls on the Barracks★
(1741–42) at Fort Frederica and their repeated use a few decades thereafter on
the Old State Capitol★ (1805–7) at Milledgeville. In neither case were they built
for defense; instead the battlements were
a traditional and symbolic form of decoration; as such they were later used on
innumerable Gothic Revival buildings.

Despite continued sporadic use of some
of its elements (mostly in remote areas)
Gothic architecture had fallen into dis-
repute with the advent of the Renais-

Mantel in the Sayre-Shivers House, Sparta, 1829–39.

sance and the concomitant preference for classical architecture; the very word *Gothic* was a term of disparagement, meaning barbaric, as the early Goths were assumed to have been. During the mid-eighteenth century, however, European and English savants began to view the work of their medieval forbears with fascination instead of antipathy. For poets and other writers, the Middle Ages and its architecture became the symbol of a past more mysterious and in some ways more intriguing than that of Greece and Rome; for painters, Gothic ruins became correlated with romantic landscapes and were popular subjects. Ironically, the first widely accepted use (or reuse) of the style began with a few En-

The Parsonage, Milledgeville, mid nineteenth century.

Mantel in the east front room of the Green-Meldrim House, Savannah.

glish landscape designers who destroyed scores of venerable formal gardens and replaced them with naturalistic panoramas. To this day, historians alternately curse those designers for wanton destruction and praise them for the inspiring beauty of their work. These were the designers who founded the English school of naturalistic landscape, a revolutionary approach to landscape gardening.

Instead of laying out geometric beds and clipped hedges, they sought to restore the natural landscape, but improving on the original, much as the landscape painters had done when they rearranged elements on their canvases to produce more picturesque effects. Thus roads and drives were changed to create a series of vistas; streams were altered, lakes added, existing trees removed, and new clumps of trees planted. If a crumbling castle or Gothic ruin was on the estate, it would be emphasized, because it was the kind of feature that could lend an element of romance to the picturesque effect being sought. If there were no existing ruins, the situation could be remedied; landscape gardeners were quite capable of building a new Gothic "ruin" as picturesque as a genuine one. Whether real or fake, many of the extensive gardens boasted Gothic ruins, and Gothic architecture, long disparaged, became a model for high fashion. Batty Langley, the son of a Twickenham gardener, published *Gothick Architecture Restored and Improved*, to be followed by similar works which increased interest in the subject. In 1753 Sir Horace Walpole started construction of his house Strawberry Hill,

The parlor at Boxwood. The house was built in Madison between 1845 and 1851.

built in the "Gothick manner," that is, with turrets, roof crenellations, pointed arches, and an emphasis on the vertical elements. The style was adapted in this country for occasional carriage houses and minor buildings shortly thereafter. Decorative details derived from Gothic motifs were often used in buildings that were otherwise classical; a HABS photograph of a mantel in the Belcher-Hunter House★ (ca. 1800, destroyed) shows a delicately classical mantel with a series of miniature Gothic arches on each side of a center panel featuring a pastoral scene in relief.

The Old Medical College, Augusta, 1835.

Remains of the Barracks, St. Simons Island, Town of Frederica, 1741–42.

The Old State Capitol in Milledgeville (oblique view). The center portion was built in 1807, the corner towers in 1833, and the porticoes in 1850.

The gates to the Old State Capitol were constructed ca. 1865.

Apparently Sedgely (1799, destroyed) in Philadelphia was the first house in this country to be built in the revived style. Still standing are St. Mary's Chapel★ (1807) in Baltimore, Maryland, and the Old State Capitol★ in Milledgeville. The capitol building was begun in 1805 and in use in 1807, though work continued on the structure until 1811.[6] Of major buildings in this style, these two appear to be the oldest ones remaining in the United States. Like all very early Gothic Revival buildings, the Old State Capitol was basically a classic building with Gothic details. Conventionally symmetrical, it had cross-axial corridors, but also had pointed arched windows, crenellated parapets, and a Gothic-style tower. Later additions, built between 1828 and 1837, included corner towers and Gothic porches which emphasized the picturesque aspects; the gateway built about 1865 by Col. W. B. Frobel of the Federal occupying forces completed the ensemble.

Because the Gothic elements of the early work often tended to be superficial, applied as decoration with little regard for archaeological accuracy or for structural or functional meaning, many historians make a distinction between this phase of the Gothic style (sometimes labeling it "Gothick" as in the eighteenth century) and the more archaeologically correct Gothic Revival architecture that followed.

Superficial though the beginnings were, the interest created thereby led to the restoration of a number of original Gothic structures and fostered more profound studies which led to a better understanding of the aesthetic and engineering (and eventually of the intellectual and theological) premises upon which the architecture was based. Also revealing were the studies of Romanesque architecture, the precursor to Gothic architecture. Simpler and heavier than Gothic, Romanesque architecture was characterized by round arches, massive piers, and thick walls with flat buttresses. Windows were smaller and walls more manifest than in Gothic architecture. Stone was the primary material of both types of architecture, and both were expressive of their function, climate, site, and structure.

Interest in Gothic and Romanesque architecture grew with increasing knowledge of the subject. Not only architects, but poets, novelists, historians, and especially high-church ecclesiastics became ardent advocates of the medieval styles. The Ecclesiological Society of New York published plans for small Gothic-style churches, plans that were widely adapted throughout the south.

Although the Old State Capitol★ in Milledgeville was among the earliest of the "Gothick Style" buildings, the Gothic Revival never acquired quite the favor in Georgia that the Greek Revival did. Exceptions were the churches, most of which were built in variations of the Gothic or Romanesque styles from the mid-nineteenth century until after the turn of the twentieth.

The small churches built of wood with comparatively light framing members were among the more successful. The unorthodox combination of medieval design with nineteenth-century building methods and materials sometimes forced the architects into using new and original forms, Gothic in spirit, but expressive of contemporary construction. A particularly felicitous example is the Episcopal Church (1867) in Greensboro, with board and batten siding, delicately flared eaves, and square head windows. Zion Episcopal Church★ (ca. 1850) in Talbotton is finished outside and in with vertical boards, applied flush. Those on the outside have been painted brown, but originally may have been left unpainted or been stained; those on the inside have been left natural. The Gothic elements are as naive as any of those of the earlier "Gothick Style" buildings, and relieve what would otherwise be a severely simple but architecturally sophisticated building. As the Old State Capitol★ was basically a classical building with Gothic details, so Zion Church seems basically of the modern West Coast tradition, lightly teased and enriched with Gothic Revival details.

More academically correct is St. John's Episcopal Church★ in Savannah, which is built of brick with stucco, and which has a hammerbeam ceiling and structural buttresses. Similarly academic is Mickve Israel Synagogue★, likewise in Savannah and likewise brick with stucco and with functional buttresses. The synagogue, which was built after the Civil War, has a clerestory with round windows and a belfry with an octagonal onion dome that has a distinctly Eastern character when compared to the Gothic Revival architecture of the rest of the church.

Gothic and Romanesque styles were not, however, limited to churches. They were freely adapted to residential, commercial, and industrial buildings, and to monuments, furnishings, and bric-a-brac. Proselytes for the styles included the architects Richard Upjohn and Alexander Jackson Davis, and the landscape architects Calvert Vaux and Andrew Jackson Downing, the latter seemingly the period's arbiter of style. All wrote popular books with logical arguments in favor of the medieval styles, particularly as compared with the Greek. Because of its light appearance and its emphasis on the vertical, Gothic architecture was more expressive of contemporaneous structural methods than the Greek. The materials used—brick, wood, or stone—could be frankly expressed, whereas in Greek architecture they were expected to resemble marble. Furthermore, a house or cottage designed in the Gothic style looked like a house or cottage, not like a Greek temple. Because the plan of a Gothic building did not have to be restricted to squares and rectangles, there could be projections and recesses; the plan could even be irregular, thus permitting a more efficient and pleasing arrangement of rooms (herein lies the seed of Richardsonian and Wrightian planning). In addition, a Gothic building could be designed to interrelate more harmoniously with rugged landscapes than the Greek could. There were other arguments in favor of the Gothic style, and of course there were counterarguments.

Aside from the practical considerations, there were historic and sentimental rea-

Zion Episcopal Church, Talbotton, ca. 1850.

St. John's Episcopal Church, Savannah, 1852–53.

sons for its popularity. In his book *Cottage Residences* Downing wrote that "the sight of an old English villa will call up in the mind of one familiar with the history of architecture, the times of the Tudors, or of 'Merry England' in the days of Elizabeth."[7] He described the houses illustrated in terms of "picturesque Gothic villas" and "old English style cottages" which "nestle in the trees," and within have "oaken wainscot" and "pleasant nooks," "shadowy recesses" and "cheerful firesides."

Characteristics of the style included steep roofs with wide eaves and gables with carved or fancifully sawed barge boards, or, conversely, flat roofs with crenellated parapets. Further characteristics included elaborate chimneys, frequently with the separate flues indicated at the top, turrets, bay and oriel windows, windows and doors with pointed arches or hooded trim, and porches with carved or sawed wooden tracery between the columns. Generally, columns were slender, their shafts taking a variety of shapes, frequently octagonal, and occasionally in odd shapes representing clustered columns. Sometimes the columns and tracery were of cast iron, painted and "sanded"[8] to resemble stone. Gothic moldings were intricate in design and deeply cut, the concave and convex facets often more than half round. Ornament was usually based on architectural, religious, or naturalistic motifs: Tudor and Gothic arches, trefoils and quatrefoils; stems, leaves, and fruit. The latter were stylized yet expressive, and appeared viable and naturalistic.

Fashionable exterior colors were generally muted. Downing recommended neutral tints such as fawn, drab, gray, and brown; he also gave specific directions for mixing the colors, and some of his books included color samples. Interior colors varied, depending on the use of the room: "a cool and sober tone of color for the hall . . . the drawing room lighter, more cheerful and gay . . . white, ashes of roses, pale apple green . . . the dining room rich and warm . . . the library quiet and comfortably grave in color." Generally he recommended the use of fine woods such as oak or walnut, but he also recommended graining in imitation of these woods, or, in the cheapest cottages, staining for the same effect.[9] Most of the recommended colors were general, and applied equally to Romanesque or other styles featured in his books. In Georgia, however, interior walls were apt to be left the white of unpainted plaster walls, or to be painted white.

Like most American architects, Downing handled Gothic and Romanesque designs with unabashed freedom, varying from the prototypal architecture as needed to adapt to climate, function, and practical building methods.

Though many of the Gothic Revival buildings in Georgia were adapted from books such as Downing's, the finer ones were usually individually designed by trained architects. John S. Norris of New York was the architect for the sumptuous Green-Meldrim House★ in Savannah. Unlike most Gothic Revival houses, the main block of the house is rectangular, has a flat roof, is almost symmetrical,

and has regularly spaced windows. Crenellated roof parapets, oriel windows, and a wealth of Gothic-inspired detail fit it into the Gothic revival. William Howard Russell, a Civil War correspondent for the London *Times*, described it in 1861 as among the best of a number of Savannah houses that had a "New York Fifth Avenue character."[10] With its floor-length windows, filigreed iron porches around three sides, and wide central hall, it seems today to be altogether southern.

Plans for the Redd House★ (destroyed) in Columbus were said to have been adapted from illustrations in *Godey's Lady's Book*. Apparently it was a close likeness to one designed by A. J. Davis and illustrated in A. J. Downing's *Archi-

Top of page: *Green-Meldrim House, Savannah, 1853–61.* Below: *Sketch by William Waud of the interior of the house while it was being used as General Sherman's headquarters in December 1864.*

Redd House, Columbus. Construction was begun on the house in 1858 and completed after the Civil War.

tecture of Country Houses as "a Villa in the Pointed Style."[11] The Redd House had a small open veranda in front of the entrance porch, and there were minor differences at the sides, but basically it was the same as that in the illustration. It was a house of many gables and of many Gothic Revival elements, including oriel and bay windows, roof crenellations, turrets, clustered chimney tops, and verandas with simulated Gothic tracery. Though symmetrical, the overall effect was picturesque. Downing estimated that if it were set on the Hudson and built of brick with sandstone trim, it would cost ten thousand dollars.

Augusta's Academy of Richmond County★ was finished in 1802, but its Gothic Revival features apparently date from mid-nineteenth-century remodeling.

A building that merits further study is the Old Jail in Greensboro. It was built of huge fitted stones and has battlements

Academy of Richmond County, Augusta. The academy was built in 1802 and renovated between 1856 and 1857.

that could be used for defense, as well as dungeonlike rooms and a gallows. Far from superficial, its architecture is grimly Gothic throughout. Conflicting data give 1807 and ca. 1837[12] as the year of its completion.

Novel styles were popular for summer homes, and Clarkesville and many of the Georgia mountain resort areas are rich in Gothic Revival architecture and its variations. Gothic design was also used extensively for minor architectural elements, such as the wrought- and cast-iron Harbor Beacon★ in Emmett Park in Savannah. Older parks and cemeteries through-

out the state abound in Gothic Revival fences, gates, and monuments; some of the monuments, like the Taylor Monument★ in Athens, are most impressive.

Most of the antebellum Romanesque Revival architecture was based on the English Romanesque, frequently called Norman, because it was introduced to England by invaders from Normandy. The Romanesque Revival relied primarily on the bold expression of masonry, particularly of powerful arch forms, for effect. Carving, if used, was deliberately crude and vigorous. Decoration was generally concentrated on the principal door-

Taylor Monument, Athens, ca. 1860.

ways and at the top of masonry walls, where it was liable to be closely related to structure, taking the form of masonry corbels, brackets, and dentils. Masonry corbel tables with miniature blind arches were frequently used. The play of light and shadow on this intricate masonry gave an air of richness and dignity to the structures. Because of its pronounced lithic character, the Romanesque style was rarely, if ever, used with wood construction. Houses were occasionally built in the Romanesque style, but the best examples in Georgia are to be found in bridges, industrial and commercial buildings, and in churches. It was an enduring style, used to some extent throughout the remainder of the nineteenth century, though eclipsed by the Richardsonian Romanesque after the mid seventies.

The First Presbyterian Church★ in Macon was designed in the Romanesque and the First Presbyterian Church★ in Augusta was remodeled into that style, though not until 1892.

Because of the practicality of its construction—rows of arched windows for illumination, easily built corbelled brick cornices, and simple but impressive bell towers from which to sound the working hours—the Romanesque Revival style was used for many of the textile mills built in Georgia from about 1860 to 1900. Segmental arches, however, were usually substituted for the semicircular Romanesque arch, and Gothic details often combined freely with the Romanesque.

To the nineteenth-century French architect Eugene Viollet le Duc, engineering was the essence of Gothic and Ro-

First Presbyterian Church, Macon, 1858.

manesque architecture, and in true Gothic spirit, he advocated an analogous and frank use of such contemporary building materials as cast iron. The new materials were to be used to the maximum advantage of their structural qualities, which were to be expressed visually. Such rational principles were set forth in his *Dictionnaire raisonné de l'architecture* and became fundamental precepts of twentieth-century "modern" architec-

Central of Georgia Railroad Bridge, Savannah, 1852.

ture. Frank Lloyd Wright repeatedly acknowledged the influence of le Duc's books on his own philosophy and work.[13]

The antebellum structures in Savannah for the Central of Georgia Railroad (most of which are listed in the HABS catalog) include several that were designed in the spirit advocated by Viollet le Duc. So were those for the Confederate States Powder Works★ in Augusta, though only the majestic chimney remains.

The Central of Georgia Train Shed★ has magnificent Romanesque arched masonry walls, clerestory lighting, and heavy wooden trusses whose tensile members are plain iron rods; all materi-

als are frankly exposed, and each is expressive of its structural function. The combination smokestack, water tower, and privies for the shop is spectacular. The round chimney, 123 feet high, is surrounded at its base by a series of brick arches behind which are the privies for the workmen. Resting on the arches is a polygonal cast-iron water tank, the iron plates reinforced with embossed motifs of Gothic design. The unlikely combination of disparate components such as a chimney, water tank, and privies into one unified element is logical if startling, and in line with the tenets of Wright as well as with Gothic practices such as the con-

Interior of train shed, Central of Georgia Railroad Station, Savannah, 1861.

solidation of roof drains and gargoyles with flying buttresses.

Though utilitarian structures such as the train shed and the chimneys were generally excluded from attack, the Gothic Revival, like the Greek Revival, has been much criticized, and often for similar reasons. Both were said to be escapist styles; both styles often featured imitations of heavy, ancient construction methods, erected with lighter, more modern materials. Unlike Greek Revival architecture, Gothic Revival architecture was not particularly suitable for the hot climate of most of Georgia. The complicated roofs designed for picturesque

effects were difficult to construct, expensive to maintain, and often leaked. Wooden finials and trim exposed above the roof quickly deteriorated. And, despite avowals of honesty in architecture, iron, wood, and stucco were often disguised as stone. Nevertheless, the Gothic and Romanesque styles opened the eyes of architects to new theories of architectural design, theories that were to affect future architecture throughout the Western world.

Combination smokestack, water tower, and privy, Central of Georgia Railroad, Savannah, ca. 1850.

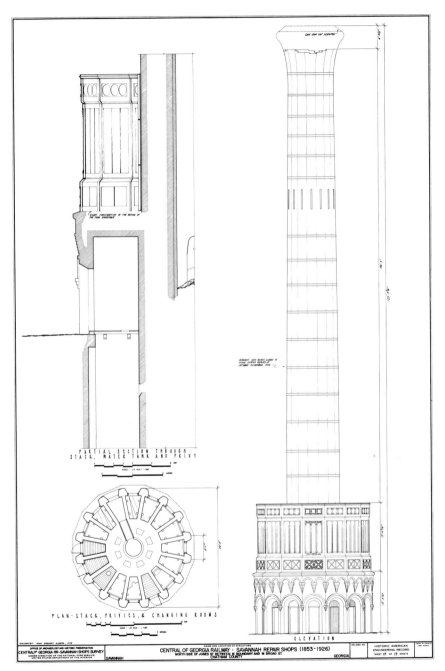

HAER drawing sheet for Central of Georgia Railroad smokestack, water tower, and privy.

The Italianate Style

As was true of most eighteenth- and nineteenth-century styles, the Italianate style was introduced to this country via England, but its roots could be traced back to Renaissance Italy and thence to ancient Rome. In Georgia the style was fashionable chiefly in the decade before the Civil War. Though details were of classical inspiration, the style like that of the Gothic Revival permitted irregular plans, symmetrical or asymmetrical façades, and a freedom of design that was appealing to those classicists who felt that the Greek Revival precepts were too restrictive.

With the Italianate style came a penchant for the word *villa*, and Italianate houses with towers were generally designated as villas in the plan books of the time. Those with irregular plans and a projecting tower at the front or side were usually labeled Italian villas; those which were symmetrical and had a tower in the center of the roof as Tuscan. The irregular Italian villa was considered particularly adaptable to rugged terrain and picturesque settings, the Tuscan type to more conventional surroundings. The central towers of Tuscan villas could facilitate ventilation in summer, which made it a desirable feature in Georgia.

Italianate architecture was characterized by low slope roofs, ample but not overwhelming verandas, arches, and Renaissance detail. Porch columns were smaller than those of the Greek Revival style, rarely over one story high, and might be square, chamfered, or round.

Roof brackets were almost invariably used, permitting wider eaves than did the classical cornice; the wider eaves were an advantage in Georgia with its fierce rains and fiercer sun. Arches were almost a symbol of the style—arched doors, arched windows, arcaded porches, and arched panels. Four-panel doors, the two upper panels arched and frequently of glass, were particularly popular. Though semicircular arches were more common, elliptical, segmental, stilted, and pseudo arches were also used.

Heavy, turned balusters and elaborate door and window frames were typical of the style. Entrance doorways frequently had arched transoms with wood tracery, but not with the radiating muntins of previous eras. Glass in sidelights and transoms was often the frosted type, and occasionally stained or a combination of stained and frosted glass. Windowpanes were larger than during preceding periods, also larger than those used with other contemporaneous styles. Windows of principal rooms were usually floor length, particularly when they opened onto porches or balconies. Fanciful cast-iron balconies, railings, and window guards were often used with Italianate buildings, as were cast-iron urns, bird baths, fountains, and fences. Whimsical delights were an integral part of the architecture and included such features as quirky and intriguing tower stairs, tower rooms high above the roof, and romantic balconies that invited theatricals and serenades.

High ceilings and ornate moldings, cornices, and ceiling medallions marked the

Mercer-Wilder House, Savannah. Construction was begun on the house in 1860 and finished in 1866.

interiors. Heavy, turned stair railings were also characteristic. Marble mantels, sometimes in rare colors and with arched openings with cast-iron grates, were not unusual. Rococo gold-leaf pier and overmantel mirrors and matching window cornices added to the rich effect of the interiors.

The style was expensive, but otherwise had most of the advantages of the Greek Revival, and permitted a freedom of design not usually associated with classical architecture. It seems to have been a favorite of the prestigious architect Samuel Sloan, particularly for urban buildings, judging by the designs appearing in his books. Sloan was versatile, however, and most of the current styles, including Oriental, were featured in his books. Downing, normally prone to Gothic styles, felt that Italianate was the appropriate style for the South, based as it was on villas designed for a similar climate.[14] Outstanding examples in Georgia include the Mercer-Wilder House★ in Savannah, the Johnston-Hay House★ and the Emerson-Holmes Building★ in Macon, and Dinglewood★ in Columbus. The Nichols-Hardman House★ in Nacoochee Valley was built in the Italianate style a decade after the Civil War. The Cowles-Bond House★ in Macon was built in the Greek

Johnston-Hay House, Macon, 1855–60.

Interior of the Johnston-Hay House.

Revival style, but Italianate wings were added and the entrance and balcony changed to conform with the wings. Picturesque ruins of an "Italian villa" set in the midst of overgrown formal gardens are the relics of an estate in Bartow County that was once the showplace of north Georgia, first named Woodlands and later called Barnsley Gardens.

Ornamental and Structural Cast Iron

As early as 1819 William Jay was using cast-iron columns and ornament in a balcony on the Richardson-Owens-Thomas House★ in Savannah. It was almost mid-century, however, before the extensive use of cast iron became a vital force in design. First limited to balconies, railings, and incidental features which contrasted with the architecture of the edi-

Emerson-Holmes Building, Macon, 1856.

sible wood beams were used instead. The appearance of the roof was nearly always lightened by making it flat or by making the slope concave. An unfortunate twentieth-century practice has been the substitution of fragile appearing ironwork for the wooden columns of some antebellum houses; the ironwork supports often appear ridiculously weak in comparison with the heavy classic entablatures.

Galleries of the Barclay-Wetter House★ in Savannah completely dominated the Italianate architecture of the stuccoed brick structure. The cast-iron galleries had pointed, three-centered, and round arches, all with fanciful cast-iron tracery. Railings had cast-iron medallions with portraits of famous poets and statesmen. These were widely scattered when the house was demolished, but some were salvaged for fences in the city and can be seen outside the Savannah Port Authority Building at 42 East Bay Street and outside the Atlantic Mutual Fire Insurance Company Building at 17 McDonough Street.

The Rankin House★ in Columbus has a cast-iron veranda across the front with a cast-iron balcony over, as well as cast-iron roof cresting, attic ventilators, bird baths, and fence. The Pease House★ in Columbus (since destroyed) had heavy classic entablatures over delicate cast-iron columns, indicating that the cast-iron work may have replaced earlier classic columns. Other buildings with cast-iron porches include the Greek Revival Camak House★, the Lucy Cobb Institute★, the James Sledge House★, and the Phinizy House★, in Athens; the Old Govern-

fice, its use proliferated until it became the major design element of many antebellum buildings. From its earliest use with the balcony of the Richardson-Owens-Thomas House★, antebellum architects recognized its deceptively fragile appearance and designed the roof structure accordingly. With rare exceptions, heavy entablatures were eliminated, and delicate cast-iron friezes or the smallest pos-

Dinglewood, Columbus, 1859.

Interior of Dinglewood.

ment House★ and the Platt House★ in Augusta; the Greek Revival Andrews House★ (since destroyed) and the Chapman House★ in Macon; and the Green-Meldrim House★ in Savannah.

Buildings with notable cast-iron balconies or railings include Eldorado★ in Columbus; the Emerson-Holmes Building★ in Macon; Rockwell★ in Milledgeville; Gordon Row★, the Low House★, and the Mercer-Wilder House★ in Savannah. Though not cast iron, the twisted wire railing at the Taylor-Grady House★ in Athens should be mentioned because its extreme delicacy contrasts so effectively with the heavy Greek Revival columns.

Decorative iron fences surrounded the front yards of most of the finer antebellum houses of Savannah and other cities. Some, like those at the Green-Meldrim House★ and the Abram Minis House★ in Savannah, were designed to relate directly to the ironwork of the houses. Lockerly★ in Milledgeville and the University of Georgia in Athens have particularly fine cast-iron fences from the period; both were cast within the state. Some of the loveliest fencing can be found in old cemeteries throughout the state.

The cast- and wrought-iron Harbor Beacon★ in Emmett Park and the cast-iron fountain in Forsyth Park, both in Savannah, are outstanding. One of the few

Paschal-Sammons House, Eatonton. The house was built in the mid nineteenth century and remodeled ca. 1860.

Barclay-Wetter House, Savannah. The house was built ca. 1822 and the ironwork and porches added in 1857.

remaining mid-century cast-iron commercial buildings is the Bank of Columbus★ in Columbus. It is in the Renaissance Revival style (closely akin to the Italianate) and has three tiers of Corinthian columns and arched windows.

Heterogeneous Mid-Victorian Architecture

New machinery and methods of production permitted the mass manufacture of fanciful scroll-saw work and of slender turned columns in new and nonclassic forms. Also during the antebellum period, the balloon method of construction, permitting lighter framing members, was introduced. Admirably expressing both the lightness of the new construction and the machine-made decorations, a variety of styles—light, fanciful, and novel—emerged. The Ethridge House (1853) in Sparta, with its scroll-saw filigree is a good example. So is the Epping House★ near Darien, which has scroll-saw brackets and scroll-saw balusters, though this "gingerbread" may have been added after the Civil War. The use of similar ornamentation would continue

Rankin House, Columbus, mid nineteenth century.

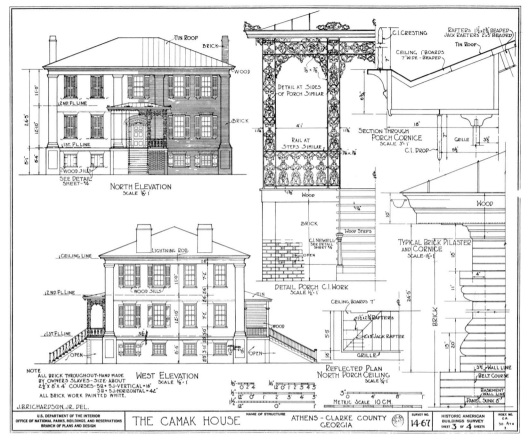

Camak House, Athens, 1834–35.

until the turn of the century. Though primarily an American development, the lacelike ornamentation is generally, at least by Americans, called Victorian.

The John A. Cobb House★ and the Lampkin-Mell House★ (since destroyed), both in Athens, had two-story-high porches with very slender quatrefoil columns, delicate wooden versions of Gothic clustered columns. The John A. Cobb House★ has a light entablature and

pseudo arches with wooden tracery between the columns. The columns are beautifully expressive of wood construction, the details are Victorian Gothic, and the overall effect classic.

The Lampkin-Mell House★, with similar columns, had a heavy classic entablature with roof brackets. There were also brackets between the columns: console brackets near the top, and below these, brackets with ogee curves meeting those

Lucy Cobb Institute, Athens, 1858–59.

of the adjacent columns. The juncture of the columns was emphasized by a flat pendant. The overall effect was flamboyantly Victorian.

The porch of the Rossiter-Little House★ in Sparta was added or remodeled, probably about the middle of the nineteenth century. Columns and friezes are inset with lattice work. The railing, which was removed before the HABS photograph was made, was probably the sheaf-of-wheat design, a lattice design in the form of an X, with an extra vertical member in the center and a mortised block at the crossing. This design was frequently used in

antebellum architecture, and was a favorite for the railings of balconies that were protected by porches, such as that of the Crane House★ (Sigma Alpha Epsilon Chapter House) in Athens.

A curious fad that may be resurrected for the energy crisis was that of building houses in the shape of an octagon. It was promoted on the thesis that the shape produced a maximum of interior space with a minimum of outside wall surface, yet was compatible with current construction methods. The octagon shape not only reduced the amount of expensive exterior walls to be constructed, it

Porch of the James Sledge House, Athens, 1860. Note the curved rafters in the porch ceiling. See p. 155 for view of house.

Entrance and front steps, Gordon Row, Savannah, 1853.

Fountain in Forsyth Park, Savannah, 1858.

also reduced heat loss, thus saving fuel.

May's Folly★ in Columbus was completed in the form of a double octagon, thus losing most of the economic advantages, but it was doubtless a sensation at the time, with its stylish shape, scroll-saw porch work, ornate doorway, and cast-iron cresting. The Raines House★ in Macon has an octagonal core with four projecting wings. These wings increase the ratio of outside wall surface to floor area, but permit ventilation on three sides of the major rooms, a more important consideration in the Columbus area than heat loss.

The indigenous plantation cottage and plantation plain style houses remained in favor throughout the antebellum period. Minor elements were sometimes varied to conform to current styles: columns were enlarged for the Greek Revival, scroll-saw brackets and railings were added, or columns with lattice insets were used in the more delicate Victorian modes. The simple indigenous prototypes, however, were more common; functional blinds and picket fences relieved their austerity.

There were other styles and substyles; only the more significant have been covered here. A remarkable quality of antebellum architecure was that, either by contrast, similarity, or a combination of both, the various styles seemed always to be in harmony with each other.

Bank of Columbus, 1860.

Outbuildings and Dependencies

Along with wooden fences, antebellum outbuildings and dependencies have mostly disappeared. Kitchens of the period were generally in separate buildings, except when space was limited, in which case they were likely to be in raised or semi-raised basements. For all but the most modern houses there were privies, frequently sociable affairs with accommodations for several. There were also servants' houses, well houses, and stables.

The servants' and slaves' quarters varied from owner to owner, and from those for house servants to those for field hands. The ones in towns and cities, many of which have been converted to modern apartments, appear to have been attractive, if crowded. Numerous examples remain in Savannah and in the older cities. Though rarely included in the photographs, the quarters still exist behind many of the HABS houses, including the Low House★ and the Richardson-Owens-Thomas House★, both in Savannah, and

Ethridge House, Sparta, ca. 1853.

the Cannon Ball House★ in Macon. A wing, now used for a rectory, of the Green-Meldrim House★ in Savannah was built as a combination carriage house and servants' quarters. The Gibbons Servants' and Carriage House★ (since destroyed) in Savannah, and the kitchen and servants' house for the Carnes House★ in Augusta were photographed for the survey. So were several of the plantation slave cabins, including the Negro Cabin★ (since destroyed) near Darien, the Slave Cabins★ at the Old Bass Plantation (since destroyed) near Columbus, the Slave Cabin at Wormsloe Plantation★ on the Isle of Hope, those at the Hermitage★ near Savannah, the Hamilton Plantation Slave Cabin★ on St. Simons Island, and those shown in the photographs of Liberty Hall★ in Crawfordville. It is difficult to judge the condition of the houses at the time they were occupied by slaves. Most of those remaining in town have been remodeled, as was the Hamilton Plantation Slave Cabin★, while most of those on plantations had deteriorated badly during the seventy-odd years between the end of the

James Sledge House, Athens, 1860.

Civil War and the time the photographs were taken. Contemporary descriptions vary widely. Of those on her husband's Georgia plantation, Fanny Kemble wrote in 1839:

> These cabins consist of one room about twelve feet by fifteen, with a couple of closets smaller and closer than the staterooms of a ship, divided from the main room and each other by rough wooden partitions, in which the inhabitants sleep. They have almost all of them a rude bedstead, with the gray moss of the forests for mattress, and filthy, pestilential-looking blankets for covering. Two families (sometimes eight and ten in number) reside in one of these huts, which are mere wooden frames, pinned as it were to the earth by a brick chimney outside, whose enormous aperture within pours down a flood of air, but little counteracted by the miserable spark of fire, which hardly sends an attenuated thread of lingering smoke up its huge throat.[15]

John A. Cobb House, Athens, mid nineteenth century.

Lampkin-Mell House, Athens, ca. 1840.

Rossiter-Little House, Sparta. The house was built in the late eighteenth or early nineteenth century; the porch and wings were added in the mid nineteenth century.

Sir Charles Lyell visited the same plantation in 1846, and wrote: "The negro houses were neat and whitewashed, all floored with wood, each with an apartment called a hall, two sleeping rooms, and a loft for the children."[16]

Of the quarters on another Georgia coastal plantation, Frederick Law Olmsted wrote:

There was a street, or common, two hundred feet wide on which the cabins of the negroes fronted. Each cabin was a frame building, the walls boarded and whitewashed on the outside, lathed and plastered within, the roof shingled; forty-two feet long, twenty-one feet wide, divided into two family tenements, each twenty-one by twenty-one; each tenement divided into three

Top of page: *May's Folly, Columbus. The house was built between 1829 and 1830 and remodeled ca. 1860.* Below: *Raines House, Macon, 1848.*

rooms—one the common household apartment, twenty-one by ten; each of the others (bedrooms) ten by ten. There was a brick fireplace in the middle of the long side of each living room, the chimneys rising in one, in the middle of the roof. Besides these rooms, each tenement had a cock-loft, entered by steps from the household room. Each tenement is occupied, on an average, by five persons. There were in them closets, with locks and keys, a varying quantity of rude furniture. Each cabin stood two hundred feet from the next. . . . Each cabin has a front and back door, each room a window, closed by

Stairway in the Raines House.

a wooden shutter, swinging outward, on hinges. Between each tenement and the next house, is a small piece of ground, enclosed with palings, in which are coops of fowl, with chickens, hovels for nests, and for sows with pigs. . . . In the rear of the yards were gardens—a half acre to each family.[17]

Other than the tradition in a few coastal areas of painting doorways and window frames blue, there seems to have been little or no carryover of African traditions in the design of the slave quarters. The carving of figures by newly imported slaves seems to have been re-

garded as heathenish, and the same may have been true of African methods of construction and decoration. When James Hamilton Couper learned that one of his slaves was building an African-style dwelling, he had him tear it down. From the quarters to the hospital to the great house, the Couper Plantation was a model, and according to the ex-slave from Altama★ who related the incident, Mr. Couper wanted no African-style house on his land.[18] Couper had moved from the adjoining Hopeton Plantation to

Woodrow Wilson's Boyhood Home, Augusta, ca. 1840.

Altama in 1857, and it is likely that the incident occurred at Hopeton. Lack of appreciation of the exotic forms of African art was widespread and, as with other aspects of slavery, has proven costly; Georgia's art and architectural heritage would have been enriched immeasurably had such work been encouraged.

Wage Earners' Houses

In rural areas log cabins were still being built at the time of the Civil War; some were occupied by well-to-do planters, rich in land and slaves, if not always in cash. Throughout most of the state, however, frame houses were more economical to build and most of the more mod-

Outbuilding of the Taylor-Grady House, Athens, 1845.

est houses were of that type. In small towns and villages, houses of wage earners were usually similar to those of the plantation cottage, though the front porch roof was likely to be distinct from that of the house, starting just below the eave line, and continuing with a much flatter slope. The porches also tended to be smaller, rarely the full width of the house. In general this resulted in less subtle roof lines and some loss of unity. Similar houses, most of them identical with their neighbors' and differing from the plantation cottage in that they were apt to be drab and graceless, were built by many of the textile mills to rent to their employees.

In larger towns and cities, where land

Kitchen and servants' quarters, mid nineteenth century, Carnes House, Augusta.

Well house of the Marsh House, Lafayette, ca. 1836.

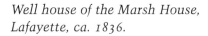

Mid-nineteenth-century Negro cabin near Darien.

Interior of a slave cabin at Wormsloe on the Isle of Hope.

Slave quarters (ca. 1830) at the Hermitage near Savannah.

was at a premium and lots very narrow, houses were more likely to be built shotgun fashion, that is, one room wide and several rooms deep. Sometimes there was a corridor to one side so that the rooms at the back could be reached without going through those in between. Numerous examples still exist in the older cities, among the more interesting being the one-story cottages on Front Street in Columbus. They appear to have been built at various times from the middle to the end of the nineteenth century. To avoid monotony, the builders concentrated their ingenuity on the design of the façades and front porches. Brackets, spindles, scroll-saw work and ornate front doors abound. Many have been re-

stored and painted in authentic period colors; they present a fascinating panorama of fanciful Victorian architecture. W. H. Russell, a London correspondent during the early war years, wrote of similar houses in Savannah, "The streets were composed of the most odd, quaint, green-windowed, many coloured little houses I have ever beheld."[19] The Timothy Bonticou Double House★ in Savannah may have been one of these.

The double octagonal cottage in Columbus appropriately named May's Folly★ was enlarged and given its unique shape by the owner, a cabinetmaker, in the early 1860s. The difficulty of categorizing housing in Georgia according to the trade of the owners is illustrated by the fact that

Timothy Bonticou Double House, Savannah, 1854–61.

this cottage, in the days when it was a much smaller and plainer house, had been the home of Alfred Iverson, a young Princeton-educated lawyer and future United States Senator.

Judging from the individualistic woodwork with which it was decorated, the house at 261 Watkins Street★ in Augusta likewise belonged to a cabinetmaker or to a carpenter. Tenements of the time were less picturesque, usually two stories high and of frame construction. The Denis Houses★ (since destroyed) in Savannah, though apparently of higher quality than most of those rented by wage earners, were not untypical. The Tenement Houses★ (since destroyed), likewise in Savannah, were of an older period but apparently were built for tenants with comparatively low incomes.

Two-story brick tenements, begun in 1839 and now known as the Old Bricks, were erected for the Roswell Manufacturing Company in Roswell. One has been converted into a library, but others are still used as apartments. Similar tenements modeled on those at Lowell, Massachusetts, were built in the late 1840s and rented to employees of the Augusta Manufacturing Company in Augusta.

House at 261 Watkins Street in Augusta, probably built in the mid nineteenth century.

Both companies were manufacturers of textiles.

The Landscape

A century after the informal school of landscape gardening had been accepted in England, a few leading landscape designers were still trying to get people of this country to accept the "new" concept of landscape gardening. In sections of New England and along the Hudson River the naturalistic style was adopted as eagerly as it had been in England; Georgians, however, seem to have been loath to forsake the old-fashioned gardens. Of twenty-five plans of antebellum gardens illustrated in *The Garden History of Georgia, 1733–1933*, only Barnsley Gardens, home of the Englishman Godfrey Barnsley, was in the informal style. The part nearest the house was formal, relating to the architecture, but there were also serpentine walks, wooded glades, and a bog garden. *The Garden History* states that at Bulloch Hall★ in Roswell there was an "informal planting of flowers and shrubs"[20] that dated back to the 1830s, but it is questionable whether this was deliberately planted in the naturalistic manner. The plans for the houses and the layout of most of the towns as well as of the vegetable gardens, orchards, and barnyards which were near the houses were generally rectangular; geometric shapes for the ornamental areas must have seemed most appropriate, especially at a time when much of the state was still wilderness and there was almost a surfeit of inimitable natural and pastoral scenery.

When houses were sited in existing groves, as many were, it is difficult to tell whether naturalism was accidental, or whether it was the result of studied artistry on the part of a landscape gardener. In many cases where the grounds were extensive, the original layout of drives and walks was functional, determined primarily by convenience and topography, and with changes as dictated by use over the years. The grounds usually included a fenced-in garden for flowers, and some were elaborately landscaped like the President's House★ in Athens. A few of the gardens boasted fountains and statues; marble statues of wood nymphs "embowered in greenery" seem to have been favorites.

The variations are too numerous to describe, but there were features that were common to most. There were no fence laws at the time, livestock was allowed to roam, and the grounds of homes and even fields were of necessity enclosed by some form of barricade. Around the fields and at a distance from the house, there were usually rail fences. Natural growth within the angles of the fences formed miles of colorful hedgerows which provided provender and cover for songbirds and for an abundance of small game, which at the time was an important source of food. Cherokee and Macartney roses were often planted along the fences or as independent hedges. Closer to the house, criss-cross, horizontal board, or picket fences were used, as they had been in previous eras. Barrington Hall★ in

Fence at Casulon, High Shoals. The house was built in 1822 and remodeled in the mid nineteenth century.

Roswell, the President's House★ in Athens, and the First Presbyterian Church★ in Augusta are among the few antebellum places that have maintained their picket fences intact. Houses were generally raised above the ground for ventilation, and the foundations, which were frequently of lattice work, were rarely concealed by foundation planting. One or two flowering shrubs might be planted against the house, but most shrubs were planted within the gardens, or as specimens on the lawns, or along the borders of the grounds. Vines were used extensively, on porches, on trellises built against the house, or on the delicate gazebos so popular in antebellum days. Most of the gazebos have long since disappeared, but a particularly fanciful one still remains on the grounds of the Cowles-Bond House★ in Macon; there is another atop the Indian mound in front of the Nichols-Hardman House★ in Nacoochee Valley, though this was built a few years after the Civil War.

The central halls of the houses, having established an axis within, were often interrelated with the grounds by having the axis continued in the form of walks, front and back, for at least a short dis-

Gazebo at the Cowles-Bond House in Macon.

tance. Sometimes, as at Mimosa Hall★ in Roswell, the drive itself is on axis with the hall, providing a most impressive entrance.

As in previous eras, the grounds in front of the houses might be of swept earth, grass, or evergreen parterres. Examples of the parterre arrangement can still be seen at Boxwood★ in Madison and at the President's House★ in Athens. More secluded gardens were usually placed to one side of the house, some of them with "walls" of glossy euonymus, so high that gates were cut through them as they were in English yew. Unfortunately, this versatile plant fell victim to blight, and such hedges are a thing of the past.

Many of the town and row houses were set adjacent to the street; those that were not were enclosed with picket or ornamental iron fences, or with stone, brick, or stucco walls. Small gardens between the fence and the house were laid out in patterns and bordered variously with boxwood or with stone, brick, or tile in combination with various edging plants. Brick borders were sometimes laid sawtooth fashion, that is, diagonally and partly underground, so that the visible part appeared serrated. In small cottage gardens, empty bottles were sometimes used, likewise laid in a sawtooth pattern. The patterns of the gardens at the Battersby House★ in Savannah, of Boxwood★ in Madison, and of the President's House★ in Athens have been retained.

Among the favorite shrubs were boxwood, winter honeysuckle, forsythia, flowering quince, and crepe myrtle. In the warmer areas gardenias and camellias

Parterre garden at Boxwood (1845–51) in Madison.

were planted; old prints of the Green-Meldrim House★ in Savannah show plantings of banana trees. Lilacs, rosemary, and lavender were popular, but could not always survive the extremes of Georgia weather. Azaleas were not as widely grown as today; roses were the great favorite and provided a spectacular show in the spring. A correspondent of the *Southern Cultivator* wrote of a visit to Savannah in April 1856: "The whole city was a perfect Rosary—every wall and trellis, pillar and garden nook, being covered and glorified with all the finest varieties of the 'Queen of Flowers' and the whole air redolent as the 'spicy gales of Araby.' We thought we had never seen Roses so luxuriant and perfect before, but we have since learned that the duration of bloom is quite brief."[21]

Besides roses, scuppernong vines and arbors were found on the grounds of nearly every plantation and town house. Other favored vines were wisteria, yellow jessamine, star (confederate) jasmine,

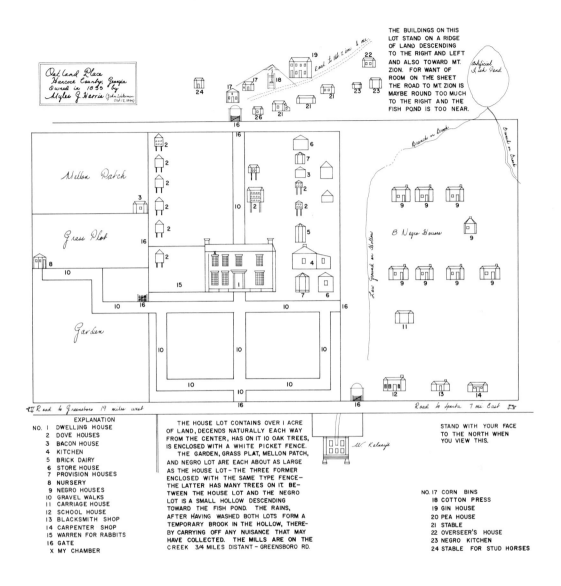

Plan of the Harris-Rives Plantation near Sparta. The original drawing was done by John Waterman and dated October 12, 1835.

scarlet honeysuckle, clematis, English ivy, and smilax. Native dogwood and red-bud trees were planted extensively; mimosa, rain trees, and Pride of India or Chinaberry trees, because they came from the Orient and were considered exotic, were also fashionable. Where the planting has not been destroyed, antebellum homesites can often be spotted from a distance by the pleasant contrast of pale green elm leaves against the dark evergreen foliage of English ivy and ancient cedar and magnolia trees.

Upkeep of the grounds, in antebellum times as today, frequently fell to the mistress of the house. The Reverend C. C. Jones gave the following account of his wife's activities in a letter written in 1854 to his son who was then at Harvard.

She rises about six in the morning, or now half-past five; takes her bath, reads, and is ready for morning worship about seven; she breakfasts with a moderate appetite and enjoys a cup of good tea. Breakfast concluded and the cups, etc., washed up and dinner ordered, Little Jack gathers up his "weepons," as he calls them—the flower trowel, the trimming saw, the nippers and pruning shears and two garden hoes—and follows his mistress, with her sunbonnet on and her large India-rubber-cloth working gloves into the flower and vegetable gardens. In these places she spends sometimes near two hours hoeing, planting, pruning, etc., Little Jack and frequently Beck and several other little fellows and Gilbert in the bargain all kept busy as bees about her—one sweeping, another watering, another weeding, another planting and trimming, and another carrying off the limbs and trash.[22]

Plantation Crafts and Industries

Despite a growing tendency to specialize in cotton at the expense of other crops, most well-run antebellum plantations were basically self-supporting, with provisions for curing meat, tanning hides, distilling spirits, for spinning, weaving, and quilting, for basketry and caning, and for blacksmithing, cabinetmaking, carpentry, and masonry. Large plantations had their own cotton presses and gins; some even had their own rice and grist mills. For a number of reasons, these crafts and small industries declined or were discontinued after the Civil War. In comparing the prewar and postwar economies, the value of their total production has too often been ignored.

Plantation crafts and industries flourished primarily because of the seasonal nature of farming and because of the large labor forces needed for planting and harvesting. During cotton-planting time or the time for harvesting grain, most of the slaves, including some of the craftsmen, worked in the field, at times from before sunrise until after sunset. In the months between and on rainy days, plantation owners often had difficulty finding enough work to keep all the slaves reasonably well occupied. The crafts and small industries helped fill the void and flourished on plantations long after they had become uneconomic elsewhere.

Though especially skilled artisans might be brought in to supervise or to help with the more important structures, most plantation buildings were constructed and maintained by the slaves on the plantation. The building process started with felling and sawing the timber and curing the lumber. On many plantations even the bricks were made from clay on the site. Much of the hardware was hand forged, and beautiful examples of strap and H and L hinges can still be found in some of the buildings.

Of particular interest to collectors are the quilts and coverlets, and the plantation-made furniture. The chairs were usually the slat back type, made of hardwood with woven white oak splint seats, the splints similar to those used for making fish traps and the rugged baskets used in gathering cotton.

Some of the chairs and most of the other plantation-made furniture were of pine. Generally the furniture had clean, simple lines reminiscent of that made by the Shakers, though much of it had a vigorous, primitive quality that was strictly original. Quality of workmanship varied according to the skill of the cabinetmaker and according to the use for which the furniture was intended. Some was meticulously made with mortise-and-tenon joints, and with no exposed nail heads. Other pieces were more casually constructed, the rose-head pattern of the nails becoming part of the design. Hunt boards, cupboards, small tables, blanket chests, and chairs seem to have survived in the greatest number, though types of most ordinary articles of furniture and of farm equipment were made.

Pine furniture was often painted, a dark blue-green known as teal blue having been the most popular color with red a close second. Pigments for the paint were probably natural and obtained on the plantation, but the formulas apparently have been lost.

Fanny Kemble described the work of the slave artisans in one of the few passages of her journal that was not totally critical of plantation life.

There are here a gang (for that is the honorable term) of coopers, of blacksmiths, of bricklayers, of carpenters, all well acquainted with their peculiar trades. The latter constructed the wash-hand stands, clothespresses, sofas, tables, etc., with which our house is furnished, and they are very neat pieces of workmanship—neither veneered or polished indeed, nor of very costly materials, but of the white pinewood planed as smooth as marble—a species of furniture not very luxurious perhaps, but all the better adapted therefore to the house itself, which is certainly rather more devoid of the conveniences and adornments of modern existence than anything I ever took up my abode in before.[23]

Her reference to the meager plantation house of the wealthy Pierce Butler is likewise revealing. Though there were many magnificent plantation houses in antebellum Georgia, they were vastly outnumbered by simple cottages and

Pigeon house (probably mid nineteenth century) on the Cox-Steward Farm near Lexington.

The outbuildings at Peacewood in Washington are primarily antebellum but some apparently are postbellum.

plain style houses. These were furnished at least in part with plantation-made furniture similar to that described by Kemble, as, in fact, were the porches and the more utilitarian rooms of many of the mansions.

Westville near Lumpkin in Stewart County is being developed as a living history center, displaying houses and appurtenances as well as the small industrial, commercial, and craft enterprises of the mid-nineteenth century. Buildings of the period, mostly from within the county, have been moved to the area and positioned to form a typical mid-nineteenth-century village. Included in the array of crafts demonstrated are carpentry, brick-making, shingle riving, basketry, weaving, quilting, and pottery.

Towns and Cities

The quarter century just before the Civil War saw a number of revolutionary innovations that must have seemed in strange contrast to the primitive roads and frontier vestiges of the newly settled areas. Telegraph lines and railways traversed the state; water and gas systems were installed in the larger cities; manufacturing plants of unprecedented size and complexity were constructed. Textile mills predominated, but there were also iron foundries, woodworking manufacturers, machine shops, a factory for making railroad cars in Atlanta, and a paper mill in Columbus.

Villages, usually beginning with a station, a hotel, and a few commercial buildings and residences strung along one or both sides of the tracks, developed around railroad stops. Some of them grew into sizable towns, usually bisected by tracks which resulted in visual and traffic problems.

Four major railroads met at a location appropriately called Terminus in the piedmont area of northwest Georgia. Shacks and shops burgeoned; mechanics, frontiersmen, farmers, and traders moved in; the railroad crossing became a raw and boisterous village incongruously renamed Marthasville, a hybrid that grew without benefit of plan or design into a city named Atlanta.

In Augusta a canal was built connecting various areas downtown with the Savannah River; it also furnished water power for the industries that sprang up along its banks. An incidental but extremely popular use for the canal was as a recreational facility. Excursion boats ran on a regular schedule, and picnicking on the banks of the canal was a favorite pastime. Low-lying Augusta was hot

Ackworth at the time of General Sherman's Campaign, 1864.

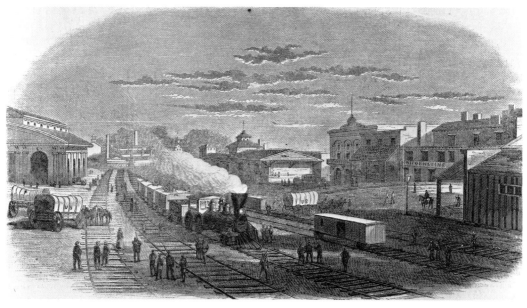

Atlanta in 1864.

Augusta cotton factory of the mid nineteenth century.

and humid in summer, and plagued with mosquitoes. In the late eighteenth century, Augustans had begun to build summer homes in the nearby sand hills, the favorite location being about two miles west of Augusta, where the resort village of Summerville developed. By the 1830s the homes were lived in throughout the year, and the village became a fashionable suburb, bringing to Augusta much earlier than to most cities the advantages and the problems of suburban living, with its attendant flight of the wealthier citizens from the core of the city.

Savannah, already famed for the beauty of its squares and tree-lined streets, expanded in orderly fashion until the last of its municipally owned land was developed shortly before the Civil War. Oglethorpe's plan was varied to permit the development of a whole ward into Forsyth Park. It was during this time that the successful combination of warehouses facing the river with offices toward Bay Street was developed. Built on the river, at the base of the bluff on which Savannah was established, the buildings were several stories high. Lower stories, opening onto the river and facing north, were for warehousing; upper stories, facing south toward the park along Bay Street, were for offices and commercial purposes. Iron footbridges spanned the space between the bluff and the buildings, connecting them to Factors' Walk, which was parallel to and projected from the buildings at about the same level as the park. The principal offices opened onto Factors' Walk, with auxiliary offices above and warehouses below. East of the row of

Antebellum buildings on Factors' Walk, showing connection to adjoining park and Bay Street in Savannah.

buildings nothing interfered with the view of the river from Emmett Park. City traffic, office buildings, trees, park, warehouses, wharves, river, and ships were integrated into an exciting architecture, at once viable and serene.

The mid-nineteenth century was a period of elaborate monuments to the dead, a period in which the design of cemeteries was of paramount importance. Bonaventure Cemetery was located near Savannah on the site of one of the early plantations. The natural beauty of the grounds had been augmented with terraced gardens and avenues of trees, but the house had burned years before the site was converted to a cemetery. A visitor to "The Evergreen Cemetery of Bonaventure" described it in 1856: "This most charming of all resting places . . . blends and mingles in memory with all that is solemn and most grandly beautiful in nature. . . . Could we have done so, we would have lingered long and happily amid its 'groined arches' of evergreen oak and its hoary drapery of festooned mosses."[24] Since that time, azaleas have been planted throughout the cemetery, their glowing colors in the spring intensifying the beauty of the grounds.

Macon, 1857.

Rose Hill Cemetery in Macon was designed in the 1840s by Simri Rose, editor of a local newspaper. It is one of the few antebellum landscape designs in Georgia that can be authenticated as having been planned in the informal manner. Located on a hilly site overlooking the Ocmulgee River, its winding drives reveal ever-changing vistas of open and wooded areas, of hills and valleys, and of the river. A small lake within one of the valleys has recently been filled to make room for more graves. Most of the hills are so steep that high retaining walls have been built to enclose the plots, which ascend the hills like so many terraces. The overall effect of the hills, walls, and markers is strikingly picturesque, like the ruins of ancient Italian hill towns.

To the west the primeval landscape which for centuries had been respected by the Indians began to vanish after their removal in 1838 and was replaced by farms, plantations, villages, and towns. In the mountains the gold rush of the 1830s was superseded by the California rush, but opened the way for summer visitors who came from the cities and lowlands to enjoy the cool mountain air, the health-giving waters of well-advertised springs, and the social life of increasingly fashionable resorts.

Two interesting town plans of the era were those of Oxford (1837) and Roswell (ca. 1838). Oxford was planned as a university community by Edward Lloyd Thomas. Like the classic plans that evolved from Roman camps, it was based on a grid with a large open area, in this case the campus, located at one end. The plan differed in that four of the streets, two on each side of the axial north-south

Fort Pulaski, near Savannah, 1829–47. Note the inverted-arch foundation.

street, changed direction as they neared the campus so as to converge diagonally toward it. Roswell was laid out in an irregular, rectilinear pattern as a small residential community. Evidently it was deliberately designed so that streets would terminate at the entrances to the grounds of several of the more important homes, thus giving the effect of a long avenue approaching the house and integrating the residential landscape with that of the village. One of these streets, Bulloch Avenue, ends in a cul-de-sac.

Most of the newer towns were primarily centers of agricultural communities, and usually consisted of a courthouse square with a few shops and offices surrounding it; if planned as a larger town, the extensions usually followed a conventional grid system.

Despite canals, railroads, and new industries, agriculture was still the mainstay of most Georgians in 1860 and the most potent force economically and politically. Cotton was still king, picturesque gristmills still ground corn, comfortable indigenous houses and unfashionable Greek Revival mansions were still being built, but even in Georgia the industrial revolution had begun, and in the offing was the most devastating war that either Georgia or the nation had known.

Chapter Five

The Civil War to the End of the Century

Except for construction related to the war effort, there was little building in Georgia during the Civil War. In Georgia the war was primarily destructive, and by the time it was over, most of the mills within the state had been destroyed, three-fourths of the wealth had vanished, cities and countryside had been laid waste, innumerable homes had burned, and forty thousand citizens were missing.[1] Atlanta had been a battleground, its inhabitants living in underground shelters, and the greater part of the city destroyed.

In the country there was ever-present danger and bleak desolation. The largely self-sustaining antebellum plantation system was dead; farming operations had to begin under new and difficult conditions. Postwar plantations were seldom self-sustaining. Necessities as well as luxuries had to be bought, and crop failures meant genuine deprivation or ever-increasing indebtedness. Plantation owners coped in various ways. Many sold out and moved to the towns and cities to find other ways of making a living. For those who remained it was an uphill battle, particularly in the years immediately following the war.

A few were successful, among whom were two women of outstanding ability.

Emma Le Conte Furman wrote a diary when she was sixteen, vividly describing the burning of Columbia, South Carolina, and published years later under the title *When the World Ended*. After the death of her husband, Mrs. Furman successfully managed their plantation at Scottsboro. Frances Butler Leigh was the daughter of Fanny Kemble, but loved the plantation at Butler's Island as much as her mother hated aspects of it. She moved there shortly after the war, and with her English clergyman husband ran the plantation "despotically but with benevolence and some material success." Like her mother, she kept a diary that was later published.[2]

The exodus from the farms brought about the creation of new towns and the expansion of existing towns and cities. Combined with the destruction wrought by war, it also created an urgent demand for new buildings. Makeshift though many of them were, innumerable buildings were begun in the postwar period. Atlanta, hardest hit of all Georgia cities, rebounded with stubborn vigor.

In Atlanta, Augusta, Columbus, and other cities where wartime industries had attracted large forces of skilled workers, the mills were rebuilt, and in many cases

Atlanta in ruins, November 1864.

were made larger and more efficient than in previous years. If agriculture suffered, industry eventually emerged stronger than it had been in antebellum days.

Cut off from the rest of the world during the war, the South had become dependent on her own industries, which were expanded or built from scratch with incredible rapidity. An example of a new factory was the Confederate States Powder Works★ in Augusta, which was begun in September 1861 and by April 1862 was in operation and producing powder. More than thirteen hundred tons of gunpowder were manufactured there between April 10, 1862 and April 18, 1865.[3] The buildings were brick with Romanesque and Gothic details; the great chimney still stands, a landmark in Augusta. Mills for the manufacture of ordnance were also established, and manufacturers of textile goods and other necessities increased production to meet the unprecedented demand.

Railroads, too, were improved to meet wartime demands. Previously, transportation was impeded by the fact that the railroad systems, many of which consisted only of short lines, operated independently of each other. Each had its own station, frequently at some distance from its competitors, and little attempt was made to correlate schedules. Changing trains was time-consuming and expensive; freight shipped long distances had to be loaded and unloaded continually. Rapid transit of war materiel was impossible, and the various railroad companies were therefore compelled to connect their tracks and to cooperate in ship-

Refinery of the Confederate States Powder Works, Augusta, 1861–62.

ping. The improved service proved to be a boon to the railroads during the postwar era, when they prospered as never before.

Architecturally, postwar industrial buildings differed little from their predecessors. Most of the textile mills were at least two stories high, had rows of straight topped or segmental arched windows, a bell tower, and some Gothic or Romanesque inspired details. Muscogee Mills★ in Columbus salvaged remnants and material from the older buildings which had been burned; doubtless others did too.

Numerous churches were built by the newly freed slaves who withdrew from established white-dominated churches after the war. Severe budget limitations restricted the design of most, but many

of these had a primitive quality that was at once powerful and picturesque.

Apparently not cramped by such budgetary considerations, the design of the steeple that was added to the First African Baptist Church★ in Savannah in 1888 and partially destroyed by a hurricane in the early twentieth century was both unique and intriguing. It bore a vague resemblance to an Oriental pagoda.

Postwar commercial buildings were frequently brick with glass and cast-iron fronts on the first floor, and with living quarters with false fronts over. Windows in the living quarters usually had segmental arches or pressed metal cornices over them; the false fronts had corbel brick or pressed metal cornices, often combined with intricate brick dentils

Confederate States Powder Works Chimney.

Top of page: *Sibley Mills, Augusta, 1880.* Below: *Muscogee Mills, Columbus. The one-story section was built in 1867; the five-story unit in 1882. Minor additions and other units shown were undertaken between 1867 and 1900.*

and sawtooth or other masonry motifs.

Because of financial conditions, many postwar houses were built of whatever materials could be scrounged locally, and in some respects were similar to pioneer dwellings. This was particularly true in areas of south Georgia where timbering was the main industry and where dog-trot cabins and log buildings were still being constructed late in the century. A number of these houses, along with stores and other village buildings of that era, have been moved to the Georgia Agrirama near Tifton, where a typical south Georgia late-nineteenth-century village has been reconstructed.

Of those who could afford to build quality homes, a few built nostalgically, using antebellum designs like that of the Italianate Nichols-Hardman House★ (ca. 1872) in Nacoochee Valley. The Old Campbell County Courthouse★ (1871) in Fairburn was built in the Greek Revival style. Churches, in particular, usually adhered to the older styles, but in general, the war-weary populace was frantically eager for the new. The most popular style of the late sixties and early seventies is known as the Second Empire style. The style was based on contemporaneous Parisian architecture and was dramatically new to most Georgians.

First African Baptist Church, Savannah, 1859–61. The high steeple (which was later destroyed) was added in 1888.

The Second Empire Style

Napoleon III, whose reign from 1852 to 1870 is known as the Second Empire, rebuilt large sections of Paris. Most of the new buildings had mansard roofs, which

Nichols-Hardman House, Nacoochee Valley, ca. 1873.

Gazebo on the grounds of the Nichols-Hardman House.

Old Campbell County Courthouse, Fairburn, 1871.

have two pitches: the upper part is flat or with a slight pitch, the lower part has a very steep pitch. In the case of the Second Empire style, the lower part frequently was flared at the base and so steep it practically became a wall for the top story. Heavy curbs, sometimes with cast-iron cresting, usually marked the transition from the flat to the steep pitch. Dormer windows, often round or arched, were a feature of the style, as were elab-orate bracketed cornices, quoins, and prominent chimneys with corbel tops.

As built in America, details of Second Empire architecture were similar in many ways to those of the Italianate architecture of the preceding era, particularly the use of arched windows and doors, and of a projecting tower on the front. Houses built in the style were often irregular in plan, but public buildings were nearly always symmetrical.

Crescent Hill Baptist Church, Nacoochee Valley, ca. 1872.

Brick with marble trim was the favored material, though cast iron or pressed metal was sometimes substituted for marble, and stuccoed brick and wood construction were also used. Whatever the material, it was generally of high quality—hard-burned, precisely manufactured brick laid with machinelike precision, slate roofs frequently applied in varicolored patterns, marble or granite steps, hardwood doors and interior trim, large window panes of extra heavy glass. It was an urban architecture, and the houses looked best in a group of similar houses, all high and narrow, with ornamental iron fences, gravel walks, and clipped grass lawns. The lawns frequently were inset with one or more round flower beds having precise rings of plants whose foliage or blooms contrasted with those in the adjoining circles. Previous styles generally blended with each other and

*Mickve Israel Synagogue, Savannah,
1876–78.*

were harmonious with the landscape, but
the Second Empire style stood out like a
prima donna. In rural settings the elegantly fashionable architecture was likely
to seem out of place, like an overdressed
lady on a picnic.

Inside, the houses had high ceilings,
heavy and ornate cornices, heavily paneled doors, and heavy stairways with
elaborate newels and turned balusters,
usually of hardwood. Marble mantels
with arched openings and ornate cast-
iron grates were popular, as were hardwood mantels with mirrors and shelves.

Many of the finer houses had interior
blinds that folded into the window jambs.
Woodwork was often stained and highly
varnished.

Probably no other American style has
so distinct a personality, a style that is
more easily described in personal terms
than in architectural. In the 1870s it was
a haughty style, with the haughtiness of
an ostentatious parvenu. The style was
dropped abruptly in the 1880s, and for
succeeding years became increasingly an
object of scorn.

In old age, the powerful personality of
the style began to be reappreciated. No
longer bright and shiny, more often than
not begrimed and dirty, the elegant style
persisted, nowhere better revealed than
in the painting *House by the Railroad* by
Edward Hopper. Charles Addams drew
similar houses for his weird and wonder-
ful cartoon characters; the style had gone
full circle, from parvenu to decadent
aristocrat.

Examples in Georgia include the Hancock County Courthouse★ in Sparta, the
Zachary Daniels House★ in Augusta,
the Samuel P. Hamilton House★ in Savannah, and the Augusta Hotel, shown
in the photograph of the Broad Street
Stores★, 600 Block, South Side, Augusta.
Late nineteenth-century photographs of
Peachtree Street in Atlanta indicate that
most of the houses in that fashionable
area were in the Second Empire style.

Hancock County Courthouse, Sparta, 1881–83.

Zachary Daniels House, Augusta. The house was built in 1891, a decade later than the style would indicate.

Samuel P. Hamilton House, Savannah, 1873.

The Queen Anne Style

"Queen Anne" is a misnomer for the style that goes by that name. Architects of the 1870s and 1880s might have been inspired by certain aspects of bygone styles, but they used these more as points of departure on which to build new designs than as models to copy. They boasted of the originality of their work, though they as well as most critics of the time felt that all good architecture should bear the imprimatur of an accepted style. English farmhouses of the original Queen Anne period had features which, along with features from other periods, were adapted in the new style. Although it was called "Queen Anne," some of the contemporaneous critics felt that "Elizabethan" was a more appropriate term. At any rate, the style began in England, where it was distinguishable by its picturesque irregularity, its restless roof lines and superfluous gables, prominent chimneys, and numerous windows randomly placed. It usually employed two or more wall materials. Since the wall and roof materials—principally brick, tile, slate, and

Springer Opera House, Columbus, 1871.

sometimes half-timber—were subdued in color and harmonious with each other, and since much less painted ornamentation was used, the English version was less bizarre than the typical American version of the style.

The Queen Anne style was introduced to this country through illustrations in English architectural magazines, but its popular success dates from the Philadelphia Centennial Exposition of 1876. In Georgia, the style remained popular into the early years of the twentieth century. In some respects it is similar to the ante-bellum Gothic Revival style. Like that style, it was irregular in plan, and picturesque. The informal planning permitted rooms to emerge from the principal mass of the building without the restrictions of symmetry; it also permitted the space of one room to merge with the space of another, frequently separated only by open arches and dividers with weblike spindle decorations. The upper and lower floors were interrelated by spacious open-well stairways that accentuated the unity of the different levels. Bay windows, oriel windows, and the practice of breaking the corners of some rooms by opening them into round or octagonal "nooks" gave the illusion of ever-expanding space and helped integrate the interior with the exterior. Instead of the separate boxlike rooms of classical architecture, the rooms opened out and the emphasis was on space, space that flowed from room to room, from floor to floor, and from inside to outside. The advent of central heating was a factor in the development of such open planning. In Georgia, central heating was a rare luxury, and in winter the spacious interiors were apt to be bitterly cold except near the fireplaces, usually coal-burning fireplaces that seemed pitifully small for the spaces to be heated.

On the exterior, steep roofs (sometimes with patterned slates or shingles), turrets and towers, tall and ornate chimneys, and porches and balconies of various shapes, all decorated with brackets, scroll-saw work and spindle work reflected the vitality of the interiors.

There were innumerable variations including the Stick style and the Eastlake style. Decoration of the Stick style tended toward straight sticklike lines, frequently inspired by medieval half-timber work. It originated before the Queen Anne style, and its basic similarities suggest that the name Queen Anne and various details were applied to a style already partially developed. The Eastlake style derived from the writings and illustrations of the English architect Charles Lock Eastlake, whose book *Hints on Household Taste* was extremely popular in this country. The book dealt primarily with interiors and furniture, the latter being widely copied from the illustrations and sold under the name "Eastlake furniture." Peculiarities of the furniture—its flat carving, gougework, knobs, the shape of the turned work—were reflected in the decorations of buildings in that style.

Queen Anne interiors, including those of the stick style and the Eastlake style, featured wainscoting, intricate stair railings, dropped picture moldings with patterned borders above, and mantels with mirrors and shelves of various sizes for the display of *objets d'art*. Woodwork was generally stained or natural, and the colors of walls muted; wallpaper patterns might be intricate, but the design was deliberately flat. Numerous windows, sometimes edged with stained glass squares, counteracted the somber interior colors and produced interesting light effects, some of them not unlike those in paintings by Vermeer or other seventeenth-century Dutch artists.[4]

As built in Georgia, houses of the style seem well adapted to the climate, and are less overburdened with decoration than those in more fashionable areas. Numerous and generous porches gave protection from the sun and provided pleasant outdoor living areas. The spacious interiors, interrelated with the porches as well as with the outdoors, were especially suited to the hot Georgia summers, although the houses were apt to be fearfully cold in winter.

One-story cottages with projecting rooms and wide porches, frequently wrapped around two or three sides, were particularly popular. The Parr House★ and the Merk House★ in Athens are not

Parr House, Athens, ca. 1890.

Merk House, Athens, ca. 1890.

untypical. Most of the houses today are painted white; probably some of them were painted white when they were built, though that was not a fashionable color at the time. A popular combination was a very deep cream, almost yellow, with white trim and bright green blinds. Shingles laid in a pattern of contrasting colors often decorated gables or special areas of the outside walls. For the really fashionable there was a variety of popular colors to choose from—generally muted colors such as various shades of gray, tan, brown, terra-cotta, and dull green, though bright cream trimmed with white was a common exception. Two or more colors were usually used in combination. The profusion of color and ornament and the freedom with which they were handled produced a kind of blithe fantasy that at times was incongruous, but at its best, sheer delight.

New Haywood★ in Washington is a delicately flamboyant version of the style with a two-story bay window crowned with an open gazebolike cupola. A simpler example is the Martin Luther King, Jr., Birth Home★ in Atlanta. Likewise two stories high and built of wood, it has a porch on two sides which has turned columns, fanciful brackets, and a stick style balustrade; it also has a small second-story porch. Both Atlanta's Sweet Auburn Historic District★ and Savannah's Victorian Historic District★ are rich in Queen Anne type architecture, Savannah's even including some fences and landscape features.

The Queen Anne style and its substyles seem to have been particularly appropriate for smaller churches, and there are examples throughout Georgia: the Seney-Stovall Chapel (1885) at the Lucy Cobb Institute★ in Athens, Christ Episcopal Church (1884) on St. Simons Island, Emmanuel Episcopal Church (1894) in Waynesboro, and the Watkinsville Methodist Church (1893) in Watkinsville.

Richardsonian Romanesque

As the Queen Anne style dominated the design of residences, so the Richardsonian style dominated the design of public buildings in Georgia in the period between the Second Empire style and the return to classicism. Henry Hobson Richardson, originator of the style, was the most influential architect of his time. He was the mentor of Louis Sullivan, who in turn was the mentor of Frank Lloyd Wright, and his influence on the work of both men was significant.

Architects of the earlier Romanesque Revival period tried to adhere to the prototypes as closely as the different requirements and structural methods would permit. Richardson, however, used the ancient models as inspiration for his own imaginative work, adapting elements of original Romanesque architecture, but altering and using them to emphasize the character and unity of his own design. His architecture was characterized by massive arches, broad expanses of unbroken masonry, and the elimination of distracting detail. Richardsonian architecture appears substantial, as if built for the ages.

New Haywood, Washington, ca. 1890.

Arched openings were frequently wider than they were high, with exaggerated, rusticated voussoirs. Columns, when used, were short and heavy, with deliberately crude capitals. Roofs were generally steeply pitched and made of slate or tile. Small windows were grouped so that the effect was horizontal, and the window sash usually contained one large pane of glass, unbroken by muntins. In Georgia, Richardsonian Romanesque buildings were usually of brick, with a granite base and granite trim, though Richardson's own buildings were more often of stone.

Houses built in the style were irregular in outline, with open plans like those of the Queen Anne style, where space seemed to flow from room to room and floor to floor; they were also expensive. Fine woodwork with a natural finish, simpler and heavier than the Queen Anne type, wide open-well stairways with large landings, and massive masonry fireplaces were characteristic of the interiors. The

Martin Luther King, Jr., Birth Home, Atlanta, late nineteenth century.

House at 16 West Duffy Street, Savannah Victorian Historic District, ca. 1890.

Interior of house at 803 Whitaker Street, Savannah Victorian Historic District, ca. 1890.

Edward C. Peters House★ in Atlanta is primarily Queen Anne, but reflects Richardsonian influence as well as a medley of interior styles, including Adam and Louis XV.

A provocative example of the Richardsonian style is the Oglethorpe County Courthouse★ in Lexington. Built of brick and trimmed with granite, it has the typical massive arches (also some untypical small ones with skinny piers) and a square tower that was apparently modeled on the one designed by Richardson for Trinity Church in Boston. The tower has round brick turrets on the four corners, those in front extending from two heavy stone columns at the base, and all terminating with conical pinnacles at the top. The building has the boldness and power of Richardson's own work, but neither the unity nor the restraint. Yet its awkward qualities are expressed with such defiant vigor that they seem assets, intensifying the vitality of the design.

Other architects besides Richardson used the Romanesque as a point of departure for highly imaginative architecture, sometimes freely combined with other styles. The Sacred Heart Church★ in Augusta, with its arched portals and other arches soaring above, its gables, towers, and turrets, its incredibly intricate ma-

Seney-Stovall Chapel (1885), Lucy Cobb Institute, Athens.

sonry and exquisite craftsmanship in woodwork, mosaic, sculpture, painting, and stained glass, is an example of a fantastic architecture that is primarily Victorian but contains Romanesque and Byzantine elements.

Similarly eclectic was Dungeness★on Cumberland Island, a mansion of more than twenty rooms begun by Thomas Carnegie about 1884 and not completed until after his death in 1886. Rambling and nonsymmetrical, it was built of stone

Oglethorpe County Courthouse, Lexington, 1886–87.

Savannah Cotton Exchange, 1886.

and featured an off-center tower, a prominent three- or four-story bay window, an arcaded loggia, gracefully sloping roofs with flared eaves, and innumerable dormers, arched windows, and chimneys. Judging from photographs, the exuberant Victorian architecture presented an amazingly unified composition. Ravaged by fire in 1953, parts of the towering brick walls and chimneys remain, forming a desolate but picturesque ruin.

Nineteenth-Century Skyscrapers

The first skyscraper built in Georgia was the Equitable Building★ (1891), later called the Trust Company of Georgia Building in Atlanta. Locally, along with Stone Mountain, it was considered the greatest wonder of Atlanta when it was finished. Higher buildings were common in Chicago, and the firm of Burnham and Root had designed a number of them. John Wellborn Root, who was a native of Lumpkin, Georgia, and who had grown

Sacred Heart Church, Augusta, 1898–1900.

Equitable Building, Atlanta, 1891–92.

up in Atlanta, was chief designer of the Equitable Building. He had just finished designing the Monadnock Building in Chicago, possibly the greatest of the nineteenth-century skyscrapers. Its design was a synthesis of sculpture and a logic that held that form should follow function and structure without extraneous details. Yet the architect who eschewed all ornament for the earlier building, producing a masterpiece still considered to be a milestone in the development of architecture, seems to have regressed when designing a building to be constructed in his native state. Perhaps he did not wish to risk two buildings so radically different from accepted styles, or possibly the client would not accept the radical simplicity of the Monadnock Building, which was unfinished when the Equitable Building was being designed. Whatever the reason, the Equitable Building, with its arches, belt courses, and ornamented columns, was a good building representative of its time, but missed the quality of greatness that Root was capable of producing.

In other ways it was decades ahead of its time. The developer, Joel Hurt, did not conceive of the building as an isolated unit, but as an integral part of the whole of Atlanta and its environs. At the same time that he was designing the downtown skyscraper, he was developing the subdivision Inman Park as a picturesque garden suburb, with winding streets and irregular building lots, and was connecting the new subdivision with his skyscraper via the rapid-transit system of the day, electric street cars. He was also one of the chief promoters of the Cotton States and International Exposition of 1895, which was to advertise Atlanta to the world.

The Return of Classicism

Throughout the postwar period, buildings were occasionally erected in the classical style. Several of the buildings at the Centennial Exposition in Philadelphia were classical, including the Palace of Fine Arts. Such buildings were usually based on Roman or Renaissance precedent.

Many of the architects of the last half of the nineteenth century had received at least part of their training at the Ecole des Beaux Arts in Paris, where classical design was emphasized. Upon their return, some, like Richardson and Louis Sullivan, eagerly seized upon the freer method of designing that was common in America; others, inspired by the sheer beauty of classical architecture, kept returning to those concepts.

To oversimplify, the new American method was to design from the inside out, the exterior being an expression of the plan and function of the building, modified by demands (likewise frankly expressed) of the structure and of the site; the classical architecture was designed from the outside in, the symmetrical exterior to a large extent dictating the interior arrangement.

Architects of the first group felt that theirs was a distinctive American architecture, representing a new and viable approach that was adaptable to ever-changing conditions. Architects of the second group felt that their approach also represented America, as most of the early buildings in this country were based on classical architecture. They also felt that with their European training they could produce a grander architecture in that same tradition.

The second group decided the style of the buildings at the 1892 Columbian Exposition in Chicago. With a few exceptions, buildings at the exposition were classical. They presented a panorama of fantastic beauty, and visitors from all parts of the country returned home filled with enthusiasm for classical architecture. For several decades thereafter, most buildings in America would be based on classical precedent. The late nineteenth-century classical buildings were, almost without exception, more ornate than those of the Greek Revival period. The Ionic or Corinthian orders were generally preferred to the simpler Doric, though the ornate capitals were often made of a composition that would deteriorate if not kept painted. Arches were frequently used and porches were sometimes curved.

Marble was the favorite exterior material, but most public buildings were of less expensive stone, stucco, or cream-colored brick. Ornamental exterior work might be of marble, terra-cotta, the previously mentioned composition, or pressed metal. Pressed metal ceilings were widely used. In Georgia most of the houses were of wood or brick with wood and composition trim.

The classical buildings were symmetri-cal, and in houses the central hall returned to favor. It was not, however, the corridor type which opened to the rear as well as to the front, but a large reception hall whose major feature was usually an elaborate stairway with prominent turns and landings.

There were variations or substyles, one of which is known as Beaux Arts classicism. Very ornate, the design was usually a composition of carefully balanced masses with advancing and retreating planes, so that in addition to the use of sculpture as part of the design, the buildings themselves became sculptural. Columns were frequently coupled, and classical ornament in the form of swags, wreaths, and naturalistic motifs was widely used in addition to the traditional classic elements.

The Thomas-Carithers House* in Athens is an outstanding example of a residential building designed in the Beaux Arts tradition. Masterfully unified, it also projects a sense of the movement of advancing and receding planes in the form of broken wall surfaces and of the major and minor rows of Ionic columns on its widespreading porches. Pedimented windows and lavish friezes add to the decorative effect.

Interiors are classically inspired with doorways framed by pilasters, and mantels with built-in mirrors, engaged columns, and applied ornament. Most of the woodwork is stained and varnished. High paneled wainscoting is a feature of some of the rooms, possibly a carryover from the Queen Anne period.

The neoclassical revival was less or-

Thomas-Carithers House, Athens, 1895.

nate than Beaux Arts classicism, but was rarely as restrained as the Greek Revival. The Georgia State Capitol★ in Atlanta, a fine example of the style, was finished in 1889, three years before the opening of the Columbian Exposition. Obviously inspired by the United States Capitol, it has a raised central portico with giant Corinthian order columns, intermediate wings with pedimented windows, and end wings with pilasters and pedimented roofs. It is built of Indiana limestone. The architecture is restrained, with few of the clichés of the period.

So-called Southern Colonial houses became popular. They featured two-story classical porticoes, rarely if ever used on houses during the colonial period, but somewhat reminiscent of the Greek Revival style. Since most of the ones in Georgia were built during the early years of the twentieth century, they will be discussed in the next chapter.

The years 1861 to 1900 appear to have been years of confusion and clutter. Actually, it was during these years that major concepts of modern architecture developed. The functional expression and open planning of Queen Anne architecture, the relationship of architecture to

Georgia State Capitol, Atlanta, 1884–89.

site, the unifying quality and the forth-right vigor of Richardsonian architecture, and the frank structural expression of the better-designed skyscrapers were qualities that architects like Frank Lloyd Wright would expand and carry over into the new architecture of the twentieth century. To Wright, Sullivan, and other architects of their persuasion, the return to classicism seemed a disaster, threatening the development of the new and viable architecture they envisioned.

The Landscape

Grounds of the houses built in the style of the Second Empire were generally urban in feeling, even when developed in a rural setting. They were usually enclosed by ornamental iron fences, and had clipped lawns, with one or more geometrical flower beds featuring such exotic plants as coleas and cannas. Carefully placed cast-iron deer and a spurting fountain might indicate the owner's appreciation of the beauties of nature.

Except for that brief phase, landscape principles of the naturalistic school, as espoused by Downing in the 1850s and expanded by his successors Calvert Vaux and Frederick Law Olmsted, were the authoritative guide to the design of gardens, grounds, parks, and subdivisions until the revival of classicism, when more formal designs prevailed.

Ideally, buildings of the time were designed to fit into the topography, so that little had to be done to alter the existing landscape. An admirable quality of the Queen Anne and Richardsonian styles was their interrelation with the surroundings. This was particularly noticeable when the buildings were nonsymmetrical and located in irregular and picturesque sites.

Fences were generally regarded as necessary evils by most landscape gardeners. Walls and hedges were preferred, but walls were expensive, and hedges not always reliable. In some areas there was a move to do away with all such barriers, so that adjoining grounds could merge, presenting a continuous parklike effect. This idea was not generally accepted in Georgia until the twentieth century. In the country, however, hedgerows and rail fences gave way to barbed wire, radically changing the appearance of the countryside.

Foundation planting, avoided altogether in antebellum days, began to make its appearance at the corners or along the sides of some of the houses, though rarely as a solid planting in front. Photographs of Georgia houses of the period generally show fenced lawns with large trees, and little or no foundation planting.

Cities and Towns

Antebellum towns and cities in Georgia were integrated, at least so far as proximity was concerned, since house servants generally lived in or near their masters' houses. After they were freed, blacks began moving out of white-dominated residential areas into sections that were predominately black, augmenting a pattern of segregation that would become increasingly rigid for the next hundred years.

Industrial growth after the Civil War was erratic but continuous. As in antebellum times, mill-owned villages were built in the vicinity of the larger plants. The mill towns were usually drab affairs, with the plainest of houses, but each house had room for a vegetable garden and for stabling a cow; nearby would be a large common that doubled as a pasture and playground.

Coupled with industrial growth was the continuous movement of discouraged farmers into the towns and cities, most of which continuously increased in size after the war. An exception was the former capital of the state, Milledgeville, which preserved its antebellum air of tranquility well into the twentieth century.

Atlanta, almost destroyed during the Civil War, recovered and expanded to become the state's largest and most dynamic city. In 1867 the seat of state government was informally removed from Milledgeville to Atlanta, and in 1877 Atlanta officially became the capital city. Before the century was out, suburbs with transit systems were being developed, skyscrapers were built, and parks were created. In 1895 Atlanta sponsored the Cotton States and International Exposition, which, though not particularly significant architecturally, gave Atlanta worldwide publicity.

With growth and prosperity, there were the usual problems of urban sprawl and poverty. The tenor of the city in the 1890s is probably summed up in Elizabeth Stevenson's account of Frederick Law Olmsted's impression: "He returned to the city to drive down Peachtree Street and to take a sympathetic look at the bustling business center of Atlanta, a place full of naive hope and unsolved problems, thriving in spite of poverty on all its edges."[5]

Having developed the last of her municipally owned land, Savannah's postwar growth consisted mostly of urban sprawl, without the parks and open spaces that make the older part of the city so appealing. But there were areas like the Victorian District* which have a charm of their own, and more open space than is generally found where there is urban housing.

The Augusta canal was greatly enlarged in 1875 by Chinese laborers who were imported to do the work and provided the first major settlement of Orientals in Georgia. In Augusta, Columbus, and Macon, industry continued to grow, as did the port facilities in Savannah. In most cases, this growth was precarious, dependent on low wages and the fluctuations of the market.

Antebellum travelers commented on the tree-lined streets and the shiny white houses of such cities as Savannah, Augusta, and Macon. Postwar towns and cities were, in general, drab by comparison. Most of the buildings remained unpainted for years at a time; there was not much concern and little time for street beautification. Streets that had been lined with trees showed signs of attrition; photographs of Augusta's Broad Street*, which was described in 1801 as "a handsome, well-built street . . . [with] a row of trees for nearly a mile on each side,"[6] indicate that by 1884 the street boasted more power lines and garish signs than it did trees.

Civic pride revived about the turn of the century, and there were widespread but often ineffectual attempts at improvement. Most towns of any size had baseball teams, and municipal baseball fields with adjoining parks became common. Bands were organized, and even small towns had bandstands, either on the public square or in a special park. Public squares were "beautified" and memorials were erected. At the turn of the century, most of Georgia, like Atlanta, was "full of naive hope and unsolved problems."

Chapter Six   The Twentieth Century

By the turn of the century, the conventional house plan with a central hall had been largely superseded by plans in which the principal rooms could be more freely interrelated, and which reflected increasing concern for convenience and practicality. Kitchens, which had once been relegated to outbuildings, were now generally incorporated into the house, closets were replacing wardrobes, bathrooms superseding privies, and electric lights replacing gas lights or oil lamps.[1] Books and magazines relating to architecture proliferated, and Georgians planning to build were confronted with an unprecedented array of styles.

The diversity of architecture in the twentieth century, even when limited to the state of Georgia, is overwhelming, and the styles are too profuse to be surveyed here. For this reason, the architecture included herein will be limited to the classical styles (which were, in a sense, a continuation of older architecture), to a ubiquitous, nameless type of architecture called "anonymous," to a few other styles that seem to have been particularly significant, and to Georgia buildings that pioneered new approaches to design.

Twentieth-Century Classicism

Beaux Arts classicism and neoclassicism continued to be favored into the second decade of the twentieth century. Concurrent with these styles, though less common in Georgia, was the Second Renaissance Revival. Both were based on secular buildings (particularly the palaces) of the Italian Renaissance. In general, the plans were rectangular, the masses simple, the roofs comparatively flat (frequently with balustrades), and the façades dominated by the repetition of arches or pedimented windows rather than porticoes. Numerous post offices of the early twentieth century were built in the style; many are still standing, usually remodeled on the interior for other uses.

In Georgia the most popular of the early twentieth-century classical styles was the so-called Southern Colonial house. As previously mentioned, this was a misnomer, since there were few, if any, houses in colonial America with the large columns typical of the style. The misnomer apparently grew out of confusion with the numerous old southern homes of the Greek Revival period. Like the Greek Revival homes, the main feature of the twentieth-century version was usually a large porch with two-story columns. Columns and houses tended to be more ornate than those of the Greek Revival period, the Ionic or Corinthian being the preferred orders, and the columns were frequently coupled. Pediments were often more steeply pitched than those of the classical prototypes and the porches were sometimes semicircular or partly curved. Windows were large, usually with one pane per sash; elaborate entrances with sparkling beveled glass were typical of the more expensive houses. Modillions and dentils were usually oversized in comparison to the classic prototypes. Inside, the large scale and heavy ornamentation were repeated; stairways, mantels, moldings, and details were usually heavy and ornate. Twentieth-century requirements complicated the floor plans, few of which maintained the grand simplicity of the older examples, though a wide entrance hall with an impressive stairway and with large chambers symmetrically placed on each side were common to most. Open stairwells and oversize openings frequently gave the effect of one huge space that included part of the upstairs hall as well as the flanking rooms. As they had in the Greek Revival period, designers often disregarded classical precedent, generally with less success. During the Greek Revival period the aim was to simplify or lighten the classical effect; during the early years of the twentieth century, designers tended toward complexity, heaviness, and added ornamentation. The style was at the height of its popularity during an era of unusual prosperity. It was found through-

out the state, and numerous examples are still extant in both rural and urban areas. Many of them have been adapted for other uses—prestigious office buildings, fraternity houses, and funeral parlors—and many are still used as residences. Good examples are the H. C. White House★ in Athens and the Holt House in Sandersville.

The heavy ornamentation of the architecture of the Southern Colonial style gradually gave way to simpler designs based on Federal or Greek Revival styles. Adherence to these varied from extremely free interpretations to literal copies of antebellum façades. The adherence to and deviation from precedent manifested in the design of the Roosevelt's Little White House,★ built in Warm Springs in 1932, is probably representative. With its simple lines, exterior symmetry, and Doric porch, the façade could pass as an antebellum Greek Revival cottage. The interior, like most twentieth-century examples, bears little relation to the prototype. Though carefully worked out to conform to its formal exteriors, the interior is informal, nonsymmetrical, and planned for casual twentieth-century living. Despite the lack of unity between the interior and exterior, its charm and appeal cannot be denied. "Ike's Cottage,"★ President Eisenhower's vacation house on the grounds of the Augusta National Golf Course, is not dissimilar.

Variations of classical designs are still being built. Throughout the centuries, classical architecture has repeatedly been superseded and pronounced obsolete, only to revive with new vigor. Before dis-

H. C. White House, Athens. The house was built ca. 1870 and remodeled with the porch added in 1901.

missing it completely, or relegating it to whimsical usage as do some of the post-modernists, a deeper study of the underlying reasons for its viability is in order.

Twentieth-Century Eclecticism

Eclecticism is an ambiguous term. At one time it referred to the combination of two or more styles in one building, such as the use of classical columns with

Putnam County Courthouse, Eatonton, 1905.

Gothic arches. Today it generally refers to architecture designed in the style of a past era. In either case, the term is usually a disparaging one. Classicist architecture, though undeniably eclectic in the modern sense, could be considered a continuation of the traditional architecture of the South, and has therefore been treated separately. Colonial styles that were concurrently popular were the Dutch Colonial, New England Colonial, Cape Cod, and Williamsburg styles, all of

Roosevelt's Little White House, Warm Springs, 1932.

Ike's Cottage, Augusta, 1953.

Charles Hayes House, Athens, ca. 1920.

which were built throughout Georgia without regard to climate or suitability. An unhappy result of their popularity was the conversion of many well-designed old houses with comfortable porches to more stylish New England types. Porches were often replaced by pedimented doorways, and blinds were frequently removed in the hope that the remodeled house would resemble a New England Colonial one, which it rarely did. The house thereafter was not only less suitable for the Georgia climate, it was also apt to be badly proportioned without the horizontal lines of the porch and the open blinds.

Though less common than the colonial styles, Gothic style houses were not uncommon. They were usually modified versions of English village or farm houses of the Tudor period and built of masonry or imitation half-timber. At Avondale Estates, a planned suburban community of the 1920s near Decatur, all buildings were in that style, and the commercial center was designed to resemble an English village. There were few examples in Georgia of the collegiate Gothic architecture that was popular in many areas before the stock-market crash and ensuing depression. Gothic styles continued to be used for churches, becoming increasingly modified as the century progressed, and finally merging into forms that are more expressive of the present than the Gothic era.

There were numerous other styles, particularly for houses. The most popular was the bungalow style, usually one story high, with exceedingly wide eaves, generous porches, and horizontal lines. Very

Swan House, Atlanta, 1920s.

short columns set on high piers or on a low wall often emphasized the horizontality. The porches and wide eaves were particularly well suited to the Georgia climate, but this advantage was frequently offset by small rooms, low ceilings, and lack of cross-ventilation. Elimination of entrance halls was apparently a characteristic practice followed thereafter in all but the more traditional or formal houses. The style has been traced to a seasonal type of shelter used in India,[2] but the American version was developed primarily in California; in fact, such houses were at first called California bungalows.

Some of the eclectic architecture was truly outstanding. The Andrew Calhoun House and the Swan House★, both built in Atlanta in the 1920s, have a unity with the landscape and a commanding presence that sets them apart from ordinary architecture. Both houses combine baroque elements from several small Italian villas, both are approached by magnificent steps and terraces. Philip Shutze designed the Swan House★; he and Neel Reid, the Calhoun House. Both architects practiced extensively in Georgia and both were masters of the styles in which they practiced. The undeniably high

The Fox Theater, Atlanta, 1927–29.

quality of their work indicates that all eclectic architecture is not to be disparaged, and that, as with classical architecture, a reassessment of its valid qualities is overdue.

The architecture of the Fox Theater★ in Atlanta displays eclecticism at its most flamboyant. Built in the days of silent movies, it is a Hollywood version of Moorish architecture, complete with Moorish arches, onion domes, battlements, and minarets. Inside, the audito-

Interior of the Fox Theater.

rium is like an open court, surrounded on three sides with battlemented walls, while overhead, clouds float across a realistic sky with twinkling stars.

The popularity of the eclectic styles peaked at various times. Dutch Colonial and bungalow styles were most popular during the decades immediately before and after World War I; the New England, Cape Cod, and Williamsburg styles seem to have been most popular during the late twenties and thirties. Popularity of Gothic styles was spasmodic throughout the first half century. As might be expected, lavish architecture such as that of the Swan House★, the Calhoun House, and the Fox Theater★ was primarily a product of the boom years of the 1920s.

"Anonymous" Architecture

The most pervasive domestic architecture in twentieth-century Georgia was a hybrid type that can best be designated "anonymous." Plans for most of the residences were adapted from plan books that circulated throughout the nation, and were selected primarily for convenience, comfort, and economy. Though not designed in a specific style, features of current styles were assimilated, so that characteristics varied from decade to decade; unlike indigenous architecture, anonymous architecture tended to represent the era during which it was built more often than it did the region.

Houses of the first two decades were probably the most suitable for the Georgia climate. They were usually simple, substantial, and comfortable, with wide eaves and generous porches, frequently including sleeping porches and sun porches. Porches were generally one story high, and columns were often built of brick. Rooms, though generally not as large as those of preceding eras, were ample, with fairly high ceilings. Ceiling cornices and crown moldings were rare, but picture moldings placed about a foot below the ceiling were nearly always used. One or more rooms might have a high wainscot, usually of pine and stained very dark, and occasionally there would be a beamed ceiling, the beams constructed of boards and obviously nonstructural. Mantels and fireplaces were of various types, but principal fireplaces were usually bold, often of brick and surmounted by a wooden shelf.

Mission furniture was popular at the time, and the contemporaneous proclivity toward its sturdy simplicity and exaggerated structure is also exemplified in architecture of the period. In the first decade, floors of the better houses were most often of rift pine, the boards narrower than in the nineteenth century. Oak floors, however, became increasingly popular, and by the end of the second decade were nearly always used in the more important rooms. Windows usually had one large pane in the lower sash, several smaller ones in the upper. Most interior doors had five or six horizontal panels, but two-panel and occasionally one-panel doors were also used, especially toward the end of the second decade. French doors were often employed where privacy was not a factor.

Jimmy Carter's Boyhood Home, near Plains. The house was built ca. 1910; the metal awning added sometime thereafter.

Roofs were in general simple, though unnecessary gables were frequently added for visual effect, and there were occasional variations such as gambrel and jerkinhead roofs. Clapboarding, with wider boards than in previous years and frequently with mitered corners, was the most common exterior wall material; wood shingles, brick, and occasionally stone or stucco were also used. Clapboarding and shingles were often stained dark brown; cream, ivory, and gray were other popular colors. Very expensive houses might have slate or tile roofs, but most of the roofs were of cedar shingles. Heavy, sturdy-looking brackets that were usually nonstructural appeared to support the wide eaves of many of the houses. Features from other eras were often adapted, the adaptations being so free that today they appear more repre-

sentative of early twentieth-century architecture than of their original source.

Jimmy Carter's Boyhood Home★ (ca. 1910) in Plains has some features, such as its half-columns, that were adapted from the bungalow style, but it is fairly representative of the anonymous architecture of the period, with its generous porch and forthright expression of structure. So is the Rockefeller Cottage★ on Jekyll Island, which, with its twenty-odd rooms, was probably as lavish as could be built in so plain a style. The original part was built in 1892, but the sprawling porch and other parts that were added by William Rockefeller in the early 1900s dominate the design. Despite its size, the house appears comfortable and unpretentious.

Anonymous houses built during the twenties and thirties tended to be more compact, with smaller rooms, few if any

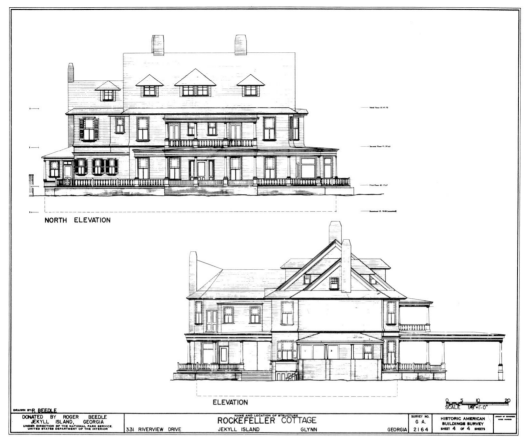

NORTH ELEVATION

ELEVATION

DRAWN BY R. BEEDLE
DONATED BY ROGER BEEDLE
JEKYLL ISLAND, GEORGIA
UNDER DIRECTION OF THE NATIONAL PARK SERVICE.
UNITED STATES DEPARTMENT OF THE INTERIOR

331 RIVERVIEW DRIVE

NAME AND LOCATION OF STRUCTURE
ROCKEFELLER COTTAGE
JEKYLL ISLAND   GLYNN

GEORGIA

SURVEY NO.
G A.
2164

HISTORIC AMERICAN
BUILDINGS SURVEY
SHEET 4 OF 4 SHEETS

Rockefeller Cottage, Jekyll Island. The "cottage" was built in 1892 and enlarged and remodeled to its present form between 1910 and 1920.

entrance halls, and fewer and smaller porches. During the thirties, eaves became narrower and were often omitted on gable ends. Most of the houses were painted white, occasionally even those that were made of brick. Asbestos shingles were often used for siding, and asphalt composition shingles superseded wooden shingles as the favorite roofing material. Central heating was still a luxury to most Georgians. Design of the houses rarely bore much relation to climate, and those built in Georgia differed little from houses designed for cooler areas. Stock millwork was often based on colonial designs, and six-panel doors, windows with a divided sash, and mantels based on colonial designs were popular, especially during the late thirties and early forties. A modish feature consisted of a large sheet of plate glass flanked by operable windows. The ensemble was called a picture window and was usually placed facing the street, evidently for the display of an ornate lamp, which seems to have been a standard accessory.

Anonymous type houses built after World War II were in general more expansive, tending to be spread out and having low ceilings, like ranch houses. The one-story or split-level houses with low pitched roofs and fairly wide eaves were the most representative of the type. Carports became standard; but high foundations, high ceilings, cross ventilation, and porches were apt to be eliminated, being compensated for by air conditioning, sliding glass doors, and freer use of windows and patios. Leisure time for front-porch sitting seemed to have disappeared, along with regional differences which, though not nearly so pronounced as in the previous century, had not completely disappeared in recent architecture. The nationwide trend toward simplicity and informality, inside and out, was generally manifested. Wall-to-wall floor coverings, flush doors, and minimal moldings were characteristic, as was the practice of eliminating formal rooms in favor of multipurpose rooms. An "all-purpose" or "family" room for cooking, eating, and recreation became a favorite. Bricklaying remained a viable craft, and in Georgia brick all but replaced other materials for exterior walls. Low, wide-spreading, brick veneer houses have remained the choice of the greater number of Georgians for almost four decades, although prefinished plywood siding has to some extent supplanted brick for exterior walls. Despite their susceptibility to the vagaries of fashion and despite the fact that sun control is too often ignored, the best of these houses have many of the admirable qualities of indigenous architecture, including a frank expression of contemporary construction practices and an almost classic simplicity. Though more elegant than most, the Jimmy Carter House* in Plains is an outstanding example of the type.

In the early sixties, modified forms of the mansard roof began to reappear, the earliest example apparently being the Benton House (1963) in Atlanta, where it was masterfully used with logic and vigor by architect Fred Bainbridge of the firm of Martin and Bainbridge. The success of the early adaptations led to a host of copies, many of them fake, and nearly all trivialized. Like a "one size fits all," similar roofs appeared on filling stations, apartment houses, hamburger stands, and government buildings.

Current fads in Georgia that reflect a reaction against disciplined "modern" architecture and that may become a phase of tomorrow's historic architecture include prefabricated log cabins and adaptations of Victorian styles, also erratic roof lines, floor plans slashed diagonally, redwood siding applied diagonally, wood constructed arches, circular windows, and various whimsies, these sometimes occurring in buildings that display a masterful handling of space and light.

Jimmy Carter House, Plains. The house was built in 1971–72 and enlarged in 1974.

Wrightian Architecture

During the first decades of the century, when eclectic architecture dominated the field, Frank Lloyd Wright continued developing his own style, partly inspired by the architecture and philosophy of Louis Sullivan and H. H. Richardson. Its form was not predetermined, but evolved from requirements of function, circulation, structure, topography, and climate, in a sense as does the form of a living organism. For this reason Wright liked to call his architecture organic. It was also an architecture of space, with space that seemed almost tangible pervading his work. As with Queen Anne and Richardsonian architecture, this space was continuous, interrelating room with room, floor with floor, and interior with exterior. Materials were always frankly expressed; and local materials such as native wood and stone from the site gave a kind of mystical relation between the re-

Benton House, Atlanta, 1963.

gion and the building. New materials were also used, always in a forthright manner that expressed their basic characteristics. Smooth finish concrete, concrete blocks, metal, plastic skylights, glass tubing—all inspired new forms that exploited their peculiar qualities.

Wright's most obvious talent was that of relating a building to its site, particularly if the site were a natural one. In such cases the building and site frequently became so interrelated that it would be difficult to visualize the one without the other.

Although the Union Station (1910) in Albany is an outstanding example of ar-

chitecture inspired by his early work, and although there are occasional examples that successfully assimilated aspects of his later, more sophisticated work, it is difficult to say how much Wright has influenced contemporary Georgia architecture. Combining rooms and eliminating unnecessary partitions, planning for informal living, the use of natural materials, corner windows, slab floors, and many other features he introduced or advocated have since become standard. He was, however, a genius and his work is probably inimitable. Attempts to emulate his work have too often been superficial, retaining the stylistic features but not the logic. Probably the best work done in that vein has followed the logic, but not attempted to copy details.

The International and Miesian Styles

The International style, an outgrowth of the German Bauhaus, has elements in common with Wrightian architecture, but there are also major differences. Both types eschewed borrowed ornamentation and relied largely on the frank expression of function, structure, and materials for effect. With both types, space was the essence of the architecture, interrelating the parts. With both, the plans were free, unrestricted by symmetry or formalism; with both the plans were usually modular.

A major difference was in the relation of building to site. Wright's buildings were usually integral with the site, while architects of the International school assumed that the building was one thing and the site another. They tended to emphasize the contrast between building and site, frequently raising the buildings so that they seemed to float above the ground.

Wright liked to feel that he was designing in collaboration with nature. Architects of the International school stressed the affinity of their architecture with machines, and with the mass-production techniques of the twentieth century. They tended to ignore the relation of climate to architecture, and disdained regional preferences. Where Wright's architecture was usually constructed of materials that would acquire a patina and grow more beautiful with age, most of the buildings of the International school were at their best when new; many, like automobiles and other products of the twentieth century, were deliberately designed to last for a limited period of time. In general, buildings of the International style were of steel, framed with flat roofs. Interior columns were frequently exposed. Exterior walls were usually stucco or concrete; when brick was used, it was often a glazed type. Glass brick was extensively, sometimes badly used. Arches were avoided, but the corners of buildings were sometimes curved as if in imitation of the "streamlined" automobiles of the day. Except for the metal portions, walls were nearly always white or off-white, color being used primarily for accent. Purists—and most of the architects regarded themselves as purists—used only the primary colors: red, blue, and yellow. The Briarcliff Apartments, designed by David S. Cuttino of the firm Cuttino, Howard, and Ellis, Architects, and built circa 1947 at 1136–42 Briarcliff Road in Atlanta, are fairly typical of the style as transplanted to Georgia.

The potential elegance of the International style is evinced by the Kemp Mooney House at 68 N. Muscogee Street in Atlanta and the Jerry Lominack House at 400 E. Jones Street in Savannah. The Mooney House was enlarged and redesigned to its present form in 1970; the Lominack House was built in 1973. Both houses were designed (or redesigned) by architects for themselves, and both are elo-

Kemp Mooney House, Atlanta. Built in the 1920s, the house was enlarged and completely remodeled in 1970.

Jerry Lominack House, Savannah, 1973.

quently sculptural. The Mooney House is based on rectilinear forms and is, in a sense, a space sculpture with spatial forms emphasized. The Lominack House accentuates mass as well as space, and exploits plastic as well as rectilinear forms. It blends and contrasts pleasantly with the architecture of old Savannah. Both houses are designed with a freedom and exuberance not always associated with the style, but their dramatic silhouettes, the interplay of space and mass, the plain wall surfaces, and the avoidance of applied ornament affirm its influence.

In the medley of stylistic decoration which typified architecture of the first half of the century, the clean simple lines and smooth surfaces of the International style provided a welcome relief, as does an ornate Victorian building when surrounded by today's simplistic architecture. The International style has strongly influenced commercial and industrial buildings in Georgia, but its influence on residential design has been limited, though the mass-produced housing advocated by proponents of the style has in a sense been accomplished. Prefabricated houses in the form of "mobile homes" litter the countryside. Unfortunately, instead of following the theories of the architects of the International style and exploiting the characteristics of prefabricated construction, most of the designs are imitative, with fake wood siding, fake blinds, and fake underpinning. Even the names given the various models are misleading: Stratford, Oxford, Cambridge, and the like, all suggestive of centuries of tradition. Flimsy construction and disregard of climatic and regional factors are further disadvantages. Yet the future of housing probably lies in the potential savings inherent in mass production. The application of the design principles of the International style, combined with proper climate control, could go a long way toward making the architecture of the ubiquitous "mobile home" acceptable.

Most of the architects who practiced in the International style modified their designs in later years, accepting native materials, climate control, and some regional differences. One architect, Mies van der Rohe, steadfastly followed the original ideal, continually seeking greater simplicity and machinelike precision in his designs, obtaining elegance by following his axiom, "less is more."

His major contribution to Georgia architecture was his part in the development and popularization of the modular curtain wall, particularly for exterior wall facings. In his own buildings (the Seagram Building in New York is an example) the rhythmic repetition of carefully proportioned wall units, most of them glass, set a fashion that became standard for commercial buildings throughout the world. Part of its popularity was due to the economy and speed with which such walls could be erected. Few of the copies were as successful as the Miesian prototypes, but they had the virtue of simplicity and a pleasant rhythmic effect, and their use raised the quality of urban design.

The most spectacular Miesian architecture in Georgia can be seen in the metal and glass towers that dominate the Atlanta skyline. Though blatantly ignoring climate and energy conservation, they are still a thrilling sight.

Industrial Architecture

Georgia's twentieth-century industrial architecture is too complicated a subject to cover here, but an outline of the major changes in its multitudinous forms is in order. Except in size, buildings for textile mills at the beginning of the twentieth century differed little from those of the pre–Civil War period; many of the nineteenth-century textile buildings are still in use. Space requirements for most of the mills, however, increased, and early in the century some plants were so large that windows were insufficient to light the complete interior. Resourceful architects made use of the sawtooth roof, which admitted north light to all parts of one-story buildings. With the advent of continuous operations, natural light became a minor factor, and large industries switched to twenty-four-hour artificial lighting, often bricking up windows in existing buildings to avoid fluctuating

Southworth Division of the Morris-Bryan Plant, Jefferson, 1966.

conditions. Buildings for the manufacture of textiles and similar industries became blank shelters, with no distinguishing expression of function except as an envelope for increasingly complicated machinery. After World War II prefabricated metal or concrete panels superseded brick as the standard wall material, and a sign bearing the name of the company became the principal clue to the operations inside.

Buildings for such plants are usually laid out in rectangular bays large enough to accommodate one or more machines and the surrounding work space, but small enough to be practical structurally. Because machines are constantly being improved and their sizes changing, build-

ings designed on a bay system are not as flexible as could be desired; uninterrupted floor space would be preferable. An ingenious solution was reached in the design of the Southworth Division Building (1966) of the Morris Bryan Plant in Jefferson, where exposed suspension trusses, similar to those of a suspension bridge, support the roof. The steel towers and catenary curves of the cables express the vitality of the structure, if not of the manufacturing process the building conceals.

The Procter and Gamble Company (1962) at 3464 Savannah Road, Augusta, instead of screening the operations inside its plant, uses a design in which the manufacturing process is visually expressed

Procter and Gamble Plant, Augusta, 1962.

and form follows function, with spectacular results. The building was designed by the Procter and Gamble Engineering Department.

A major benefit of the automobile age was that employers no longer had to provide housing to be assured of an adequate work force. By the mid-twenties, the practice of constructing industrial housing was just about at its end, and by the fifties, nearly all such existing housing had been sold to the tenants. Most of those houses have since been renovated and the grounds improved. The drab, occupationally segregated mill villages of the past are, in many cases, now attractive if modest suburbs.

Twentieth-Century Vernacular and Strip Architecture

Early in the century a new kind of vernacular architecture began to emerge. Earlier vernacular architecture was built of logs and native materials. The economical and easily available materials of the twentieth century were at first light wood members and galvanized metal, and a little later concrete blocks. Still later, porcelain-faced metal and plastics could be added to the list. Silos, barns, and cheap commercial buildings were constructed of the newer materials and had a picturesque though obtrusive quality of their own. It was a new form of folk architecture, as ubiquitous in twentieth-century America as the log cabin was in the nineteenth century. The Billy Carter Service Station* in Plains is a good example of the rural or small-town commercial type.

On major highways, particularly near the larger cities, where filling stations, restaurants, night clubs, and similar enterprises compete for patronage, advertising became a major function of architecture; presumably the more obtrusive and easily recognizable the building and the signs, the better the business. The resultant conglomeration of signs, lights, buildings, and highway has become known as "the strip," and the design of such buildings as "strip architecture." Strident, discordant, colorful, and raucous, it is incompatible with architecture not designed to accord with it. In its own milieu, it has possibilities of being a new art form, fantastic and exciting, the acid rock[3] of modern architecture.

An unplanned and unexploited feature of modern architecture is the lyric beauty of city lights as seen from an airplane; the possibility of transforming the garish effect of neon lights to the serenity of such a view seems not to have been explored.

Georgia in the Vanguard

Georgia has rarely been in the forefront of architectural progress. In the last decade, however, some of the state's architecture has led the way to new approaches in design.

The Hyatt-Regency Hotel, designed by John C. Portman and Associates and completed in 1967 in Atlanta, reintroduced fun, excitement, and drama to hotel ar-

Billy Carter's Service Station, Plains. The structure, built in 1935, was moved and converted to a service station in 1956. There have been other changes and additions since.

chitecture. Entered by way of a comparatively low foyer, the twenty-three-story-high skylighted lobby seems by contrast overwhelmingly lofty. For the first time, the drama of a truly high-rise building was repeated on the interior. The excitement of the interior was emphasized by swiftly ascending and descending elevators with baroque glass-enclosed cabs decorated with jewellike rows of lightbulbs. The open lobby, exposed elevators, and decorative lightbulbs had been used decades earlier, notably in the Brown Palace Hotel in Denver, Colorado. Through the years, hotel design had grown more discreet—the elevators enclosed, the lighting indirect, the lobbies

minimal. In the Hyatt-Regency, the wonder, the joy, and the exhilaration of modern architecture were brought back on a grander scale than was possible when the architects of the early high-rise buildings dramatized their achievements. Hotel design has not been the same since the Hyatt-Regency was opened.

As deliberately unobtrusive as the Hyatt-Regency is conspicuous, the Jones Bridge Headquarters of the Simmons Company, which was designed by Thompson, Hancock, Witte and Associates and which was completed in 1975, blends into its natural surroundings in Gwinnett County about fourteen miles north of Atlanta.

Lobby of the Hyatt-Regency Hotel, Atlanta, 1972.

Jones Bridge Headquarters of the Simmons Company, Atlanta vicinity, 1975.

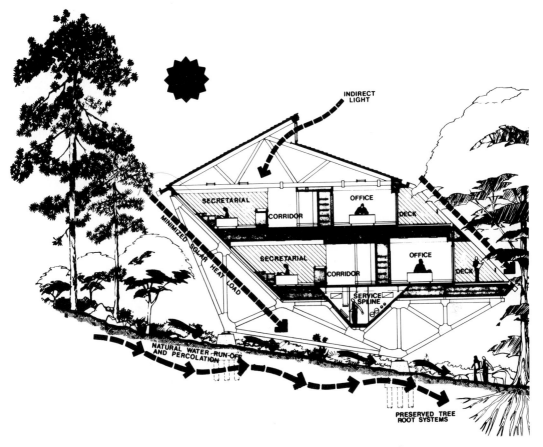

Diagrammatic drawing of the Jones Bridge Headquarters of the Simmons Company, showing the relation of building form to solar angles and other ecological factors.

The building, supported by giant inverted steel trusses, is raised above its site on a wooded hillside overlooking the Chattahoochee River. A V-shaped spine under the floor extends the length of the building and contains wires, pipes, ducts, and mechanical equipment. It repeats the shape of the inverted trusses, permitting sunlight to penetrate under the building so that plants grow there, leaving the natural watershed undisturbed. On the

south side of the building, the outward slope is continued upward, excluding direct summer sun from the glass walls of that side of the building but providing ideal lighting as well as views.

The long building is divided into bays that are staggered to fit the contours and to preserve important trees. Except for the steel trusses beneath, all framing is natural wood, as are the wall finishes, interior and exterior. Walls on the north and south sides are mostly glass; from within the view is through the tree tops, and the effect not unlike that of a tree house.

The affinity with the site was carried into the design of the drives and parking areas. While the building was under construction, workers parked erratically among the trees; later the worn places where the cars had parked were paved, thus providing parking space that is unobtrusive and that did not destroy the existing trees. Thereafter landscape design consisted primarily of restoring native flora.

The building, designed for the climate and for the conservation of energy, is in empathy with the topography and natural surroundings. It is the type of architecture anticipated for an increasingly energy-conscious, earth-respecting age. In a sense, the building and grounds could also be considered the extreme limit to which the theories of the naturalistic school of landscape gardening, begun in England two centuries earlier and promulgated in this country by Downing, Vaux, and Olmsted, could be carried. As with nearly all buildings that signify radically new directions, unforeseen complications have arisen. A major complaint is that many of the employees dislike the idyllic surroundings eight hours a day; as Jane Jacobs (proponent of city living and author of *The Death and Life of Great American Cities*) might have predicted, some prefer pavement, action, and people to sylvan views and trees. Eventually, perhaps, architecture can provide both rural serenity and urban excitement.

Probably this ideal is now as nearly attained in buildings favorably located in the older sections of Savannah as in any place.

As the Hyatt-Regency led the way with new hotel design and the Simmons Building led the way in design with climate and environment, so the city of Savannah is now in the forefront of a third major trend in architecture, that of conserving, using, and restoring existing buildings. Beginning in earnest in 1955 with the formation of the Historic Savannah Foundation, the conservation movement has been so effective that most of the rundown areas within the two square miles of the old city have been restored, bringing life back to the once-decaying downtown, reviving business, and making Savannah one of the most beautiful cities in America.

The Landscape

At the beginning of the eighteenth century, Georgia was populated by Indians and primeval forest covered most of the state. At the beginning of the nineteenth century, most of the state was still forested, and much of it inhabited by Indians. By the beginning of the twentieth century, the mountain and coastal areas remained largely forested, and there were some large tracts of forest in other sections, but most of the land was cultivated, and most of the forests cut over. Hedgerows and rail fences, ubiquitous in antebellum Georgia, had been largely replaced with barbed wire by the end of the century. Wild game, formerly abundant, became increasingly scarce. The destruction of the forests continued throughout the first two decades of the century. During the 1930s a reversal set in, in part because the worn-out land could no longer support the numbers who were trying to wrest a living from it. Though most have disappeared, dilapidated ruins of deserted tenant houses are still spotted throughout the Georgia countryside. Machinery, new types of crops, and new methods of farming have in various ways changed the appearance of cultivated fields. The patterns of concentric curves which are such a striking feature of the piedmont landscape when seen from the air are the result of contour plowing and terracing, practices advocated by a few progressive planters before the Civil War, but not characteristic of the region until after World War I.

Of utmost importance for timber, for recreational and inspirational areas, and for maintaining the precarious ecological balance of natural systems threatened by overpopulation and pollution are the national forests and the national and state parks. Much of the land for these areas was acquired when the government bought up abandoned farmland in the aftermath of the depression, but state control of many of the barrier islands was accomplished by propitious cooperation among conservationists, legislators, and concerned landowners. Properly administered, these islands should continue their role as guardians of the Georgia coast, maintaining the intricate balance of land, marsh, and sea which is essential for their own preservation, for the flora and fauna of the coastal area, and for Georgia's related fishing industry. It is hoped that future generations will enjoy their many benefits and the incredible beauty of Georgia's "golden islands."

Features of similarly protected areas vary from mountains to beaches, from granite cliffs and wild icy rivers to the trembling earth and the quiet dark waters of the Okefenokee Swamp. There are also privately endowed parks such as the famed Callaway Gardens with its hundreds of acres of native and exotic flora.

Both the government and the power companies have altered the landscape by the creation of vast lakes. In central Georgia, large-scale strip mining for kaolin has formed a new and rugged landscape of hills, mounds, valleys, gulleys, and small lakes; it is a surrealistic landscape, without plants, but with marvelously colored earth and occasional lakes of sometimes turbid and sometimes clear blue water. Though none has been developed as such, some of the areas have been arbitrarily usurped for recreation, the lakes and fantastic scenery unintentionally forming an extraordinary park. In recent years, much of this wasteland has been planted in pines, and efforts are underway to restore its productivity.

The greatest change has been caused by the automobile and the network of roads that crisscross the state. From the grand beauty of the highways, bridges, and cloverleaf intersections to the ugliness of most of the strip architecture, the automobile has affected nearly all aspects of the landscape, including the growth of the suburbs and even the disappearance of the suburban barnyard, with its provisions for cows and chickens as well as horses.

The landscape of the better suburbs is surprisingly close to that advocated by nineteenth-century landscape gardeners of the naturalistic school. Fences have been dispensed with, lawns merged with one another, and the desired parklike effect is often achieved, nowhere better exemplified than in the suburbs of Atlanta, which were developed in rolling woodlands whose natural beauty was preserved.

Less successful are the suburbs with small lots, where the houses are so close together that they dominate the landscape and need some barrier to separate them. Questionable also is the twentieth-century custom of surrounding every house with a mass of shrubbery known as foundation planting.

The landscaping of the Swan House★ and the Andrew Calhoun House, both in Atlanta, is masterful. Both houses are located on the crests of hills, overlooking a broad expanse of lawn and valley. In both cases the entrance to the house is from the rear, and the view to the front. In both cases the transition from house to lawn is effected by a series of steps and landings; each has a large intermediate terrace with a traditional parterre garden. Rarely have the geometric forms of such gardens been more valid, repeating as they do the geometry of the architecture while the flora relates to the more naturalistic vista beyond.

Unfortunately, flower gardens as a part of the home grounds have become increasingly rare during the twentieth century because they are costly to maintain. The loss has to some extent been compensated for by very small gardens requiring minimal upkeep, by areas for outdoor cooking and entertaining, and by public parks and gardens.

Cities and Towns

The movement from rural to urban areas continued throughout the first half of the twentieth century. During the first and part of the second decade, villages as well as towns and cities grew and prospered; they also had a strong sense of pride and community feeling. Most towns and cities had baseball teams, bands, and civic groups, the latter primarily dedicated to beautifying public areas. The practice of planting street trees was revived, squares were landscaped, bandstands built, and innumerable monuments erected. Parks, ballfields, and playgrounds were developed and old parks improved. A tract of nearly two hundred acres which had been the site of the Cotton States and International Exposition was purchased by the city of Atlanta in 1904 and redesigned into Piedmont Park by the Olmsted firm, successors to Frederick Law Olmsted.

In the second decade, as the automobile came into general use, the smaller towns and villages declined in population. Throughout Georgia, the boarded-up fronts of village stores, banks, and other commercial buildings stand as relics of the time when villages were important centers of rural communities.

The resultant growth of the larger towns and cities produced dramatic changes in their composition. Rapid growth of commercial institutions created an unprecedented demand for urban space; stores and office buildings were expanded and urban land values and rents rose to new and inflated heights. Almost unnoticed in the excitement of mushrooming values and new construction was the destruction of fine old town houses and the fact that renters were abandoning the apartments they formerly occupied over most of the commercial establishments. At the same time, streets were being widened at the expense of trees, sidewalks, medians, and parks to accommodate ever-increasing traffic and ever-increasing demand for parking spaces. Eventually, the limit was reached, and the commercial enterprises that had displaced the amenities and the residents began moving to suburban areas, away from the downtown areas they themselves had made uninhabitable.

After World War II, the shopping centers increased dramatically in number and size, the larger ones drawing shoppers from entire regions and from the cities themselves. Georgia cities were faced with problems common to most American cities since the middle of the century: increasing congestion in the poorer neighborhoods, the flight of the well-to-do to the suburbs, loss of business to the shopping centers, decay and crime in the central city. The problems were and remain most acute in Atlanta, the largest city. Efforts to keep the city viable have been Herculean, though some of them are questionable in view of the impending energy crisis.

A major move to revitalize the city was marked by the completion of the Atlanta Stadium in 1965, the Memorial Arts Center in 1967, the Atlanta Civic Center in 1968, the Omni in 1972, and the Georgia World Congress Center in 1976.

Partly completed is MARTA, a rapid-transit system interconnecting the various parts of the city. A welcome retreat has been created in the heart of the city by clearing nearly two acres of old buildings and converting that area into Central City Park, a rolling, grassy area much used for sunning, lolling, lunching, and people-watching.

Since 1970 spectacular, self-contained urban complexes have been erected, some concentrated in the center of the city, others farther out. Their glass and part-glass towers have radically changed the appearance of the city. Bridges at dizzying heights connect the upper stories. Within the complexes, hotel, office, commercial, and recreational facilities are combined with pleasant open spaces, trees, large-scale and often dynamic abstract sculpture, fountains, and sunken plazas.

These and similar enterprises are bright spots in a city plagued with problems. It is hoped that the vigor and enthusiasm which have revitalized disparate parts of

Atlanta skyline (ca. 1967) with the Atlanta Stadium in the foreground.

Atlanta will spread to the more blighted areas, eventually effecting the renewal of the whole city.

Sweet Auburn★ is a part of Atlanta that is experiencing renewal and revitalization partly because of the life and tragic death of Martin Luther King, Jr., whose birthplace is nearby and whose burial place is within the area. The neighborhood is predominately black, and is a mixed residential, institutional, and commercial area. Of special interest is the restored late Victorian home in which Dr. King was born; Ebenezer Church, where his father has long been pastor; and the site containing the memorial to Dr. King, Jr., and his mausoleum. The memorial and mausoleum have become shrines, drawing people from around the world. Because of its associations with Dr. King and with Atlanta's black history, Sweet Auburn is the center of much interest in preservation.

A number of blighted areas throughout old Atlanta are being rejuvenated. Victorian houses in Inman Park and other areas that were formerly elegant suburbs but that had long since deteriorated are being brought up and zestfully restored by enthusiastic purchasers, most of them youthful. Valiant efforts are being made to save the Fox Theater★, the fantastic

Herndon Building, Sweet Auburn Historic District, Atlanta, 1924.

building of Moorish inspiration built in the 1920s for silent movies.

By a unique set of circumstances, streets in one section of downtown Atlanta were elevated during the early part of the twentieth century, thus leaving an underground area of deserted shops, saloons, and commercial establishments. These have been restored, and the area extended with some new buildings. Most of them, old and new, have been embellished with generous additions of gingerbread salvaged from demolished buildings. The area now constitutes a nighttime entertainment center with a colorful turn-of-the-century atmosphere. Atlanta's

basic, ingrained tradition, however, will probably continue to be that of building anew, ever grander than before, on the ashes of the old.

Unlike Atlanta, Savannah has concentrated on enhancing those timeless qualities which have long made the old city such a desirable place in which to live. Though other cities had started similar moves earlier, Savannah assumed the forefront in the move to revitalize blighted areas by restoration, and most of the remaining old buildings within the original city have been restored. Long-neglected parks have been landscaped, needed features and plantings added, and their up-

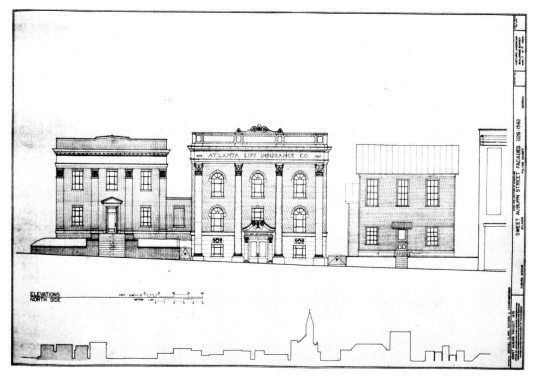

Atlanta Life Insurance and Sweet Auburn Street façades.

keep assured. So successful was the move to restore the city that Victorian houses in areas adjoining the original city are now being eagerly sought by prospective buyers.

The rehabilitation created a problem unusual in large cities; whites buying up the town houses and moving into areas that had been predominately black were displacing vast numbers of blacks. The plan at present is that further restoration of blighted areas will provide sufficient housing for the current residents, much of it in restored homes, so that they will not be forced to leave. It is hoped that this will result in restored areas of economic and ethnic diversity. This unusual approach has been sponsored by a group of citizens incorporated as the nonprofit Savannah Landmark Rehabilitation Project. Their pilot project is known as the Savannah Victorian Historic District★, and restoration of the area is well under way.

The project has additional interest in that it probably represents the extreme of a strong reaction against the dreary public-housing projects of the past, projects for which countless houses, many of which could have been rehabilitated

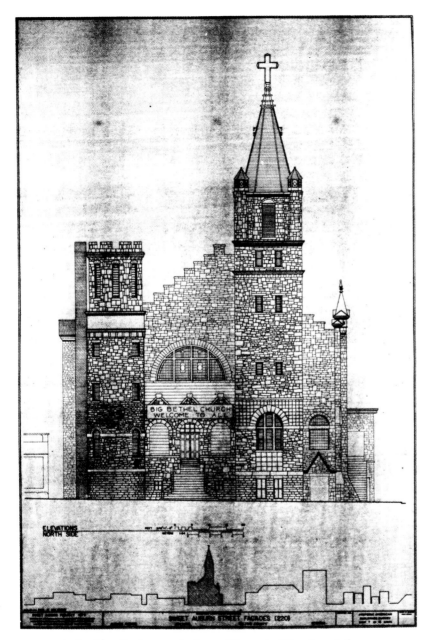

Big Bethel Church, Sweet Auburn Historic District, Atlanta, 1922.

economically and which would have lent interest and character to renewal areas, were destroyed.

Savannah's ancient city plan has proven amazingly adaptable to modern city life. In an increasingly mechanized world, the parks, pleasant with trees and plants, are probably more important than ever before. The streets bounding the old wards have been converted to one-way expressways permitting rapid movement of traffic throughout the city, while the series of squares forces a leisurely pace where it is desirable. Much of old Savannah is now a pleasant mixture of municipal buildings, offices, shops, stores, restaurants, and nightclubs—all the urban amenities conveniently and unobtrusively intermingled with houses and apartments. Though aspects of the recent development of the river front have been questioned, so far Savannah seems to have avoided the over-exploitation of past glories which threatens to change the lower part of Charleston from the most genuine and livable of urban areas to a traffic-congested tourist mecca, teeming with affluent visitors and spawning such architectural anomalies as a proposed twelve-story convention center with a façade of preserved storefronts decorating its base. From the harbor, the massive building will dominate a skyline previously noted for its graceful church spires.

Cities and larger towns throughout Georgia are faced with problems similar to those of Atlanta and Savannah. Means of combating urban decay vary, but most cities are following Savannah's lead in attempting to make the downtown areas

217 West Duffy Street, Savannah Victorian Historic District, 1890.

pleasant places in which to live, shop, relax, and play; there is also an attempt to restore a favorable balance of people, automobiles, and commercial enterprises. To date, however, none has followed the example of progressive European cities in providing adequate and safe bicycle lanes.

Parts of Broad Street in Augusta, which for decades had been a dreary expanse of pavement, automobiles, overhead wires, and garish signs, have been transformed with medians which include trees and semiconcealed parking, fountains, miniparks, and an ingenious if dubious small civic building raised on pilotis. Plans are to improve and extend the rejuvenated

217–225 East Bolton Street, Savannah Victorian Historic District, 1885.

area, and eventually to integrate the Augusta Canal and the Savannah River into a system of related urban parks. Few cities have the potential for as exciting a system of parks. Publicly owned land, a legacy from the time when the canal and its branches were vital shipping arteries, interpenetrates the city and merges into an extensive area which contains the main body of the canal and related lakes, locks, and dams. It also contains historic structures, archaeological sites, beautiful bogs and woodlands, and scenic sections of the Savannah River. The nine-mile boat ride from the business district of Augusta, through an industrial district, past the great chimney of the Confederate States Powder Works★, and on to the wilds of the lower part of the canal is an unforgettable experience.

Many of the apartments over the Broad Street Stores★ originally were stylish dwellings with graceful stairways, fine woodwork and plaster work, and floor-length windows opening onto balconies. HABS photographs of the Broad Street Stores show these as they appeared in 1884, when they were somewhat run down but still in use. A few are occupied to this day, and at least one is in the process of being restored. Restoration and reuse of apartments over places of business may prove to be the greatest single factor in reviving downtown areas.

Probably the most resplendent ante-bellum apartment in Georgia was located over a dentist's office in the Emerson-Holmes Building★ in Macon. With ex-ceedingly high ceilings, ornate plaster work, silver-plated door knobs, crystal chandeliers, marble mantels, and full-length arched windows opening onto a balcony overlooking Mulberry Street, its lavish interiors rivaled those of the finest homes. Long-deserted apartments such as this indicate that the death of the city, as a place to live, occurred years before the advent of the shopping center.

Though little as yet has been done to attract residents back to the city, Macon is planning a novel method of enticing shoppers. Blocks of the downtown area are bisected in both directions by alleys. Tentative plans are to convert the alleys into pedestrian malls, thus in a sense turning the blocks inside out with park-ing and services on the periphery.

Columbus has restored and revitalized blocks of derelict buildings as well as the old promenade along the Chattahoochee River and down the median of First Street. Similar rejuvenation projects have been implemented in Macon, Albany, and other cities and towns in Georgia.

Most of the older commercial build-ings originally had balconies, awnings, or some type of canopy to protect window displays from sun and to provide shelter for window shoppers and for the side-walk displays that were then an impor-tant mode of advertising. Restorationists have too often neglected the need for such protection, a mistake never made by designers of successful new shopping centers.

Another aspect of nineteenth-century city life that is too often ignored by mod-ern planners and by historic preserva-tionists was the lively, sometimes rau-cous, street life that made cities exciting places in which to live. Mid-nineteenth-century accounts of Augusta mention firemen's parades with displays of water pumped some ninety feet high, bands, public balls, an open market, and canvas booths set up on Broad Street, including one where "Professor Donnell swallows a sword twenty-three inches long, and no deception"; there were also cockfights, "gamblers of high and low degree," and "drinks for the crowd."[4] Sword swal-lowers and cockfights probably have no place in the twentieth century, but twen-tieth-century cities still need a place for carnival, a place where music can blare, garish signs shriek, and neon lights daz-zle; an updated Times Square.

In general, the accomplishments of Georgia cities and towns are encourag-ing, and, given time, should be success-ful in restoring the favorable balance of people, commercial enterprises, and transportation that they enjoyed before being overwhelmed by the automobiles. It has, however, been more than half a century since urban living was generally fashionable in Georgia. The advantages are becoming increasingly obvious, but the town houses and the apartments over stores will have to be equipped with the conveniences expected in modern houses combined with some of their former elegance before they can be rented successfully or before any but the most enlightened of the suburbanites will risk purchasing them.

Efforts to keep the larger department stores and similar establishments in downtown areas have usually proven futile, and will likely continue to be so. In most cases, the combined parking areas of the great commercial enterprises that are located on the outskirts of cities is larger than the whole of the old downtown area. No traditional city contains space enough for the parking required; if sufficient parking could be provided the units would become too dispersed to be practical. Malls cannot provide the concentration of diverse types of stores, shops, offices, dwellings, and municipal amenities that are found in cities; malls and cities are radically different yet interdependent. So far there has been little attempt in Georgia to interrelate the city with its malls, or even to relate the various malls with each other so that they could form a convenient unified entity, thus saving customers miles of driving. A beginning may have been made in Atlanta, where a rapid transit system is being constructed. Planning within the cities of Georgia has come a long way in a few years; overall planning of cities, including their surrounding malls and shopping centers, has a long way to go.

The villages and smaller towns have reacted in diverse ways to keep business viable and to attract those who are leaving the cities in search of a more tranquil way of life. Some, including Dahlonega, Madison, Eatonton, Sparta, and Washington, have capitalized on the beauty of their shady squares, tree-lined streets, and heritage of old buildings. Like Savannah, they have rejuvenated their squares, promoted further planting, and restored deteriorating buildings. A few have even managed to get rid of unsightly signs.

Other towns and villages have made use of other methods to regain their vitality. One small mountain town was remodeled into an imitation Alpine village and attracted so many tourists that it became a combination Disneyland and traffic jam, traffic predominating. A county seat that was formerly an attractive town with a large square that was pleasant with trees and grass, converted the square to a parking area, thus giving the town ample parking and the dismal appearance of one large used-car lot. A widely copied and ingenious method of introducing trees into the downtown area was developed in Athens in 1975, when dead spaces between sidewalks and traffic lanes at intersections of streets with angled parking were converted into mini-parks with clumps of trees. Concomitant advantages were the shortened crosswalks and the protection that the parks gave to the cars parked nearest the corners.

Several new preplanned cities complete with industries, civic amenities, and residential, commercial, and recreational facilities are in the planning stage or are being developed within the state. Among these is Peachtree City, about thirty miles from Atlanta in Fayette County. Consisting of some fifteen thousand acres, it is planned for an ultimate population of about eight thousand residents before the turn of the century.

The plan, which is subject to some change as it evolves, calls for the development of a number of neighborhood centers that will be grouped into villages, where schools and shopping facilities will be within walking distance of the residences. Pedestrian and bicycle paths interconnect the residences with those facilities as well as with larger shopping centers and other neighborhoods, so that it will be possible to live there without being dependent on the automobile. A natural and permanent green belt surrounds the area, and open green spaces interpenetrate all parts of the city.

About the same distance from Atlanta and near Newnan in Coweta County is Shenandoah, another new town. Although it is smaller than Peachtree City, it is similar in that it is planned with pedestrian and bicycle paths, and with open green spaces interpenetrating all areas. It will have commercial and industrial areas, as well. Of particular interest is its community center, which is heated and cooled by solar energy.

The most provocative new town, and possibly the one that will exert the most influence on future cities, is still in the preplanning stages. It is to be developed by a nonprofit corporation called the Club of 1000, most of whose members are also members of the Passive Solar Energy Society of Georgia, founded by Professor George Ramsey of the College of Architecture of the Georgia Institute of Technology. Many of the unusual features proposed doubtless emanated from his research and from the research at that institution. The intent of the club is to develop a combination urban-agrarian community which will be as self-sustaining, as energy efficient, and as ecologically sound as a diverse set of technologies will permit, and to encourage by example future growth patterns throughout the United States.[5]

The community will occupy approximately two thousand acres, of which about sixty will be divided among members for their private homes, gardens, and places of business. The remainder of the land will be owned jointly. About one thousand acres of this will be devoted to organic agriculture, and it is estimated that this will produce more food than is needed for the community. The rest of the acreage will be used for other community needs such as water, energy, and food processing; also for open space, recreational areas, a forest, and a wildlife habitat.

Buildings will be designed and oriented for sun and wind control, and to take advantage of systems consuming little energy. Wherever possible, local materials will be used in their construction and it is anticipated the architecture will be of an indigenous type. Units will be grouped so that they can share interior walls for energy conservation. Their height will be limited to comfortable access by stairs, usually two or three stories. Living quarters will be adjacent to or over the owner's place of work. The community, which is being planned for one thousand families, will be small enough so that only pedestrian or bicycle paths will be needed for circulation. Energy-producing systems,

*South side of the 200 block of East Henry Street, Savannah Victorian
Historic District, ca. 1890.*

recycling of waste materials, agricultural
methods, and forest management will be
conducted according to sound ecological
principles.

Members cite among the advantages of
such a community a higher quality of
life, health, longevity, personal liberty,
private familial enterprise, security, and
self-reliance. Also, assuming that the
plan is widely adopted, it will encourage
preservation of natural resources, national energy independence, and a more
pleasurable and enduring nation. In
studying plans for this community, one
cannot but be impressed by their similarity to the idealistic plans of many of

this country's founders, especially those
of Oglethorpe and the trustees for Georgia, which in turn hark back to the Utopian plans of Sir Thomas More. The indigenous architecture proposed for the
buildings, prototypes for the future, will
likewise have features in common with
much of Georgia's earlier architecture.
In its complexities, the amalgam that is
architecture is simultaneously pioneer-
ing new paths, returning to basics, being
born again, revived, rerevived. . . .

Notes

Chapter 1. Out of the Clouded Past

1. Erich Von Däniken, *Chariots of the Gods? Unsolved Mysteries of the Past*, pp. 32–34; and *Gods from Outer Space: Return to the Stars, or Evidence for the Impossible*, pp. 117–19.

2. Charles Hudson, *The Southeastern Indians*, p. 78.

3. Warren King Moorehead, *Exploration of the Etowah Mounds Site in Georgia*, p. 15.

4. Charles Colcock Jones, Jr., *Antiquities of the Southern Indians*, p. 213.

5. Garcilaso de la Vega, *The Florida of the Inca*, translated and edited by John Grier Varner and Jeanette Johnson Varner, pp. 314–15. Talomico may have been on the South Carolina side of the Savannah River. The editors note that another account, Ranjel's, describes the temple in "less gaudy form." Garcilaso de la Vega's mother was an Incan princess and he may have exaggerated the splendors of a related civilization. Nearly all the accounts mention the vast quantities of pearls. These were primarily freshwater pearls, not as highly valued as saltwater ones. Apparently mussels are no longer gathered in the area for food or for pearls.

6. Hudson, *The Southeastern Indians*, p. 213.

7. Ibid., p. 216.

8. Jones, *Antiquities of the Southern Indians*, p. 176.

9. Gustavus James Nash, *The Early History of Jackson County*, p. 27.

10. Michael D. Roethler, "Negro Slavery among the Cherokee Indians, 1540–1866," Ph.D. dissertation, Fordham University, 1964, p. 148.

Chapter 2. The Colonial Period

1. E. Merton Coulter, *A Short History of Georgia*, p. 20; Kenneth Coleman, ed., *A History of Georgia*, p. 18.

2. Frederick Doveton Nichols, *The Architecture of Georgia*, p. 22.

3. Ibid.

4. Frances B. Johnston and Thomas T. Waterman, *The Early Architecture of North Carolina*, p. 173.

5. Frances Anne Kemble, *Journal of a Residence on a Georgian Plantation in 1838–1839*, p. 67; Sir Charles Lyell, *A Second Visit to the United States of North America*, 1:249; Frederick Law Olmsted, *A Journey in the Seaboard Slave States in the Years 1853–1854*, 2:49–50.

6. E. Merton Coulter, ed., *Georgia's Disputed Ruins*, p. 16.

7. Charles H. Fairbanks, "The Excavations of the Hawkins-Davison Houses," *Georgia Historical Quarterly*, vol. 40, no. 3 (September 1956): 214.

8. Ibid., p. 204.

9. Coulter, ed., *Georgia's Disputed Ruins*, p. 63.

10. Coulter, *A Short History of Georgia*, p. 32.

11. William Harden, *A History of Savannah and South Georgia*, 1:17.

12. Coulter, ed., *Georgia's Disputed Ruins*, p. 189.

13. William M. Kelso, *Captain Jones's Wormslow: A Historical, Archaeological, and Architectural Study of an Eighteenth-Century Plantation Site near Savannah, Georgia*.

14. Frederick Doveton Nichols, *The Early Architecture of Georgia*, p. 2.

15. Kenneth Coleman, *Georgia History in Outline*, pp. 10–11.

16. Historic-Savannah Foundation, *Historic Savannah*, p. 5.

17. Nichols, *The Early Architecture of Georgia*, p. 45.

18. The first building for St. Paul's Church in Augusta (1749) was similar, but both entrances were on the long side. Ibid., p. 280.

19. Ibid., pp. 26–27.

20. Augustus B. Longstreet, *Georgia Scenes, Characters, and Incidents*, p. 7.

21. Nichols, *The Early Architecture of Georgia*, p. 126.

22. Ibid., p. 2.

23. Samuel Gaillard Stoney, *Plantations of the Carolina Low Country*, p. 47.

24. John W. Reps, *Town Planning in Frontier America*, p. 141.

25. Oglethorpe noted that the fiercest winter winds are from the southwest, but prevailing winter winds are northwest.

26. Edward Surtz and J. H. Hexton, eds., *The Complete Works of St. Thomas More* (New Haven: Yale University Press, 1965), vol. 4, *Utopia*, p. 121.

27. Nichols, *The Early Architecture of Georgia*, p. 13.

28. Charles Colcock Jones, Jr., and Salem Dutcher, *Memorial History of Augusta, Georgia*, p. 149.

Chapter 3. The Federal Period

1. William H. Pierson, Jr., *American Buildings and Their Architects*, p. 216.

2. Ibid., p. 218.

3. George G. Smith, *The Story of Georgia and the Georgia People 1732 to 1860*, p. 234.

4. Identified by Ed Polk Douglas, specialist in the field of French panoramic wallpapers.

5. Samuel Carter III, *Cherokee Sunset: A Nation Betrayed*, pp. 24, 30.

6. Nichols, *The Architecture of Georgia*, p. 57.

7. H. M. Pierce Gallagher, *Robert Mills, Architect of the Washington Monument, 1781–1855*, p. 170.

8. Ibid., pp. 175–76.

9. Nichols, *The Architecture of Georgia*, p. 47.

10. A series of ceramic works called "Beauties of America" was produced in England before 1830 by John and William Ridgeway. An example with a view of the bank is on display at the Scarbrough House, a loan from Mrs. C. M. Theus. See also, James Vernon McDonough, "William Jay, Regency Architect in Georgia and South Carolina," Ph.D. dissertation, Princeton University, 1950; *Commercial Directory of the United States* (Philadelphia: J. C. Kyser and Co., 1823), p. 34; and J. H. Hinton, *History and Topography of the United States of America* (London: Hinton, Simphius and Marshall, 1831), vol. 2, pl. 71.

11. McDonough, "William Jay," p. 42.

12. Mills Lane IV, *Savannah Revisited: A Pictorial History*, p. 112.

13. Ibid., p. 48.

14. Florence Marye, *Garden History of Georgia 1733–1933*, p. 23.

15. Ibid.

16. Nichols, *The Early Architecture of Georgia*, p. 36.

17. Reps, *Town Planning in Frontier America*, p. 258.

18. Nichols, *The Early Architecture of Georgia*, p. 16.

19. Ibid., p. 16.

20. Jones and Dutcher, *Memorial History of Augusta, Georgia*, pp. 151–52.

21. Ibid., p. 148.

22. Lane, *Savannah Revisited*, p. 48.

Chapter 4. The Antebellum Period

1. Talbot F. Hamlin, *Greek Revival Architecture in America*, p. 319.

2. John Summerson, *The Classical Language of Architecture*, pp. 19–20.

3. *Southern Cultivator*, vol. 15, no. 8 (August 1857): 242–45.

4. Robert Manson Myers, ed., *The Children of Pride: A True Story of Georgia and the Civil War*, p. 1336.

5. Leola Selman Beeson, *The One Hundred Years of the Old Governor's Mansion, Milledgeville, Georgia, 1838–1938*, p. 67.

6. James C. Bonner, *Milledgeville: Georgia's Antebellum Capital*, p. 21.

7. Andrew Jackson Downing, *Cottage Residences*, p. 25.

8. "Sanded" by applying sand to the paint before the paint has dried, thus giving it a grainy, stonelike finish.

9. Andrew Jackson Downing, *The Architecture of Country Houses*, pp. 202–4, 403–4, 367.

10. William Howard Russell, *My Diary North and South*, p. 80.

11. Downing, *The Architecture of Country Houses*, pp. 338–42.

12. Thaddeus B. Rice and Carolyn W. Williams, *History of Greene County, Georgia, 1786–1886*, pp. 347–48; but see Nichols, *The Early Architecture of Georgia*, p. 261.

13. *Journal of the Society of Architectural Historians*, vol. 28, no. 3 (October 1969): 173–83.

14. Downing, *The Architecture of Country Houses*, p. 173.

15. Kemble, *Journal*, p. 67.

16. Lyell, *A Second Visit to the United States*, 1:249.

17. Olmsted, *A Journey in the Seaboard Slave States*, 2:49–50.

18. John Solomon Otto, "Status Differences and the Archaeological Record," p. 372.

19. Russell, *My Diary North and South*, p. 80.

20. Marye, *Garden History of Georgia 1733–1933*, p. 113.

21. *Southern Cultivator*, vol. 14, no. 6 (June 1856): 185.

22. Myers, ed., *The Children of Pride*, p. 35.

23. Kemble, *Journal*, p. 63.

24. *Southern Cultivator*, vol. 14, no. 6 (June 1856): 184–85.

Chapter 5. The Civil War to the End of the Century

1. Coulter, *A Short History of Georgia*, p. 348.

2. The quotation is from Margaret Armstrong, *Fanny Kemble: A Passionate Victorian*, p. 353. The diary is Frances Butler Leigh's *Ten Years on a Georgia Plantation since the War*.

3. Florence Fleming Corley, *Confederate City: Augusta, Georgia, 1860–1865*, p. 60.

4. Copies of Flemish woodcuts and etchings were rich sources for architectural precedent; they were also sources for chiaroscuro technique and their influence may be more apparent in nineteenth-century illustrations of interiors than in the interiors themselves.

5. Elizabeth Stevenson, *Park Maker: A Life of Frederick Law Olmsted*, p. 407.

6. Jones and Dutcher, *Memorial History of Augusta, Georgia*, pp. 151–52.

Chapter 6. The Twentieth Century

1. Before the twentieth century, bathrooms in Georgia generally were found only in the more expensive houses or in houses located in the few cities that had public waterworks.

2. Marcus Whiffen, *American Architecture since 1780: A Guide to the Styles*, p. 218.

3. A type of music—loud, syncopated and hypnotic—popular when this was written.

4. Corley, *Confederate City*, pp. 22–23.

5. Kibbutzes, operating successfully in Israel, attest the validity of the basic ideas.

Bibliography

Allen, Ivan Earnest. *The Cherokee Nation, Fort Mountain, Vann House, Chester Inns, New Echota.* Atlanta: Ivan Allen Co., 1959.

Anderson, Mary Savage; Elfrida de Renne Barrow; Elizabeth Mackay Screven; and Martha Gallaudet Waring. *Georgia: A Pageant of Years.* Richmond: Garrett and Massie, 1933.

Andrews, Wayne. *American Gothic: Its Origins, Its Trials, Its Triumphs.* New York: Random House, 1975.

Armstrong, Margaret. *Fanny Kemble: A Passionate Victorian.* New York: Macmillan Co., 1938.

Art Work of Augusta and Savannah, Georgia. Chicago: Gravure Illustration Co., 1902.

Art Work of Northern Central Georgia. Chicago: Gravure Illustration Co., 1919.

Bartram, John. *Diary of a Journey through the Carolinas, Georgia and Florida from July 1, 1765 to April 10, 1766.* Annotated by Francis Harper. 1943. Reprinted from *Transactions of the American Philosophical Society,* n.s. vol. 33, pt. 1 (December 1942).

Bartram, William. *The Travels of William Bartram.* Edited by Francis Harper. New Haven: Yale University Press, 1958.

Beeson, Leola Selman. *The One Hundred Years of the Old Governors' Mansion, Milledgeville, Georgia, 1838–1938.* Macon, Ga.: J. W. Burke Co., 1938.

Benjamin, Asher. *The American Builder's Companion.* New York: Dover Publications, 1969. Reprint of the 6th (1827) edition.

———. *The Practical House Carpenter.* New York: Da Capo Press, 1972. Reprint of the 1835 edition.

Bonner, James C. *A History of Georgia Architecture, 1732–1860.* Athens: University of Georgia Press, 1964.

———. *Milledgeville: Georgia's Antebellum Capital.* Athens: University of Georgia Press, 1978.

Bremer, Fredrika. *The Homes of the New World: Impressions of America.* Translated by Mary Howitt. London: Arthur Hall, Virtue and Co., 1853.

Brown, Ira L. *The Georgia Colony.* New York: Crowell-Collier Press, 1970.

Carter, Hugh Alton. *Cousin Beedie and Cousin Hot: My Life with the Carter Family of Plains.* Englewood Cliffs, N.J.: Prentice-Hall, 1978.

Carter, Samuel, III. *Cherokee Sunset: A Nation Betrayed.* New York: Doubleday, 1976.

Chase, Judith Wragg. *Afro-American Art and Craft.* New York: Van Nostrand-Reinhold Co., 1971.

Coastal Georgia Historical Society. *Historic Glimpses of St. Simons Island, Georgia, 1736–1924.* St. Simons Island, Ga., 1973.

Coleman, Kenneth. *Colonial Georgia: A History.* New York: Charles Scribner's Sons, 1976.

———. *Georgia History in Outline.* Athens: University of Georgia Press, 1960.

———., ed. *A History of Georgia.* Athens: University of Georgia Press, 1977.

Conger, Ledlie William, and Ruth Dunlap Conger. *Sketching and Etching in Georgia.* Atlanta: Conger Printing Co., 1971.

Corley, Florence Fleming. *Confederate City: Augusta, Georgia, 1860–1865.* Columbia: University of South Carolina Press, 1960.

Coulter, E. Merton. *A Short History of Georgia.* Chapel Hill: University of North Carolina Press, 1933.

———. *Wormsloe: Two Centuries of a Georgia Family.* Athens: University of Georgia Press, 1955.

———., ed. *Georgia's Disputed Ruins.* Chapel Hill: University of North Carolina Press, 1937.

Cumming, Mary Gairdner Smith. *Two Centuries of Augusta: A Sketch.* Augusta, Ga.: Ridgely-Tidwell-Ashe Co., 1926.

Davidson, William H. *Brooks of Honey and Butter: Plantations and People of Meriwether County, Georgia*. Alexander City, Ala.: Outlook Publishing Co., 1971.

———. *Pine Log and Greek Revival: House and People of Three Counties in Georgia and Alabama*. Alexander City, Ala.: Outlook Publishing Co., 1964.

Denmark, Ernest Ray. *Architecture of the Old South*. Atlanta: Southern Architect and Building News, 1926.

Downing, Andrew Jackson. *The Architecture of Country Houses*. New York: D. Appleton Co., 1853.

———. *Cottage Residences*. 4th ed. New York: Wiley and Halsted, 1856.

Ellis, John O. *The Log Cabin: Homes of the North American Wilderness*. Barre, Mass.: Barre Publishing Co., 1978.

Fine, Elsa Honig. *The Afro-American Artist: A Search for Identity*. New York: Holt, Rinehart, and Winston, 1973.

Fletcher, Sir Banister. *A History of Architecture on the Comparative Method*. 17th ed. New York: Charles Scribner's Sons, 1961.

Forman, Henry Chandlee. *The Architecture of the Old South: The Medieval Style, 1585–1850*. Cambridge: Harvard University Press, 1948.

Gallagher, H. M. Pierce. *Robert Mills, Architect of the Washington Monument, 1781–1855*. New York: Columbia University Press, 1935.

Garcilaso de la Vega. *The Florida of the Inca*. Translated and edited by John Grier Varner and Jeanette Johnson Varner. Austin: University of Texas Press, 1951.

Gould, Mrs. James, and the St. Simons Library Commission. *Old Mill Days 1874–1908*. St. Simons Island: St. Simons Library, n.d.

Goulding, Rev. Francis R. *Nacoochee; or, Boy-Life from Home*. New York: Dodd, Mead and Co., 1888.

Guthrie, Jim. *Athens Sketchbook*. Athens: William Murray, 1975.

Hajos, Albin. *Hajos' Athens, Georgia*. Brooklyn, N.Y.: Albertype Co., 1900.

Hamlin, Talbot F. *Greek Revival Architecture in America*. New York: Oxford University Press, 1944.

Hanie, Robert. *Guale, the Golden Coast of Georgia*. Edited by Kenneth Brower with photographs by James Valentine. San Francisco: Friends of the Earth, 1974.

Harden, William. *A History of Savannah and South Georgia*. Atlanta: Cherokee Publishing Co., 1969. Reprint of 1913 edition.

Heye, George G.; F. W. Hodge; and George H. Pepper. *The Nacoochee Mound in Georgia*. New York: Museum of the American Indian, Heye Foundation, 1918.

Historic-Savannah Foundation. *Historic Savannah*. Savannah: Historic-Savannah Foundation, 1968.

Hoffman, Donald. *The Architecture of John Wellborn Root*. Baltimore: Johns Hopkins University Press, 1973.

Holly, Henry Hudson. *Holly's County Seats* (1863) and *Modern Dwellings* (1878). Watkins Glen, N.Y.: American Life Foundation, 1977. Reprinted in one volume.

Hudson, Charles. *The Southeastern Indians*. Knoxville: University of Tennessee Press, 1976.

Jacobs, Jane. *The Death and Life of Great American Cities*. New York: Random House, 1961.

Jacques, Daniel Harrison. *The House: A Pocket Manual of Rural Architecture*. New York: Fowler and Wells, 1859.

Jarrell, Charles C. *Oxford Echoes*. Oxford, Ga.: no imprint, 1967.

Jeane, D. Gregory, ed. *The Architectural Legacy of the Lower Chattahoochee Valley in Alabama and Georgia*. Tuscaloosa: University of Alabama Press, 1978.

Johnston, Frances B., and Thomas T. Waterman. *The Early Architecture of North Carolina*. Chapel Hill: University of North Carolina Press, 1958.

Jones, Charles Colcock, Jr. *Aboriginal Structures in Georgia*. Washington, D.C.: Government Printing Office, 1878.

———. *Antiquities of the Southern Indians, Particularly of the Georgia Tribes*. New York: D. Appleton and Co., 1873.

———. *The History of Georgia*. Boston, New York: Houghton Mifflin and Co., 1883.

———. "Some of the Early Memories Connected with Augusta, Georgia." Augusta, Ga., 1883.

———, and Salem Dutcher. *Memorial History of Augusta, Georgia*. Syracuse, N.Y.: D. Mason and Co., 1890.

Kahn, E. J., Jr. *Georgia from Rabun Gap to Tybee Light*. Atlanta: Cherokee Publishing Co., 1978.

Kelso, William M. *Captain Jones's Wormslow: A Historical, Archaeological, and Architectural Study of an Eighteenth-Century Plantation Site near Savannah, Georgia*. Athens: University of Georgia Press, 1979.

Kemble, Frances Anne. *Journal of a Residence on a Georgian Plantation in 1838–1839*. Edited by John A. Scott. New York: Alfred A. Knopf, 1961.

Knight, Lucian Lamar. *Georgia's Landmarks, Memorials, and Legends*. Atlanta: Byrd Printing Co., 1913–1914.

———. *A Standard History of Georgia and Georgians*. Chicago and New York: Lewis Publishing Co., 1917.

Lafever, Minard. *The Beauties of Modern Architecture*. New York: Da Capo Press, 1968. Reprint of 1835 edition.

———. *The Modern Builder's Guide*. New York: Dover Publications, 1969. Reprint of 1833 edition.

Lane, Mills B., IV. *The People of Georgia: An Illustrated Social History*. Savannah: Beehive Press, 1975.

———. *Savannah Revisited: A Pictorial History*. Athens: University of Georgia Press, 1969.

LeConte, Emma. *When the World Ended*. Edited by Earl Schenck Miers. New York: Oxford University Press, 1957.

Leigh, Frances Butler. *Ten Years on a Georgia Plantation since the War*. New York: Negro Universities Press, 1969. Reprint of 1883 edition.

Linley, John. *Architecture of Middle Georgia: The Oconee Area*. Athens: University of Georgia Press, 1972.

Longstreet, Augustus B. *Georgia Scenes, Characters, and Incidents*. Savannah: Beehive Press, 1975. Reprint of 1835 edition.

Loth, Calder, and Julius Trousdale Sadler, Jr. *The Only Proper Style: Gothic Architecture in America*. Boston: New York Graphic Society, 1975.

Lyell, Sir Charles. *A Second Visit to the United States of North America*. New York: Harper and Brothers, 1849.

Lyon, Elizabeth Ann Mack. *Atlanta Architecture: The Victorian Heritage*. Atlanta: Atlanta Historical Society, 1976.

———. "Business Buildings in Atlanta: A Study in Urban Growth and Forms." Thesis, Emory University, 1971.

Manucy, Albert C. *The Fort at Frederica*. Tallahassee: Department of Anthropology, Florida State University, 1962.

Marsh, Kenneth, and Blanche Marsh. *Athens: Georgia's Columned City*. Asheville, N.C.: Biltmore Press, 1964.

Marye, Florence. *Garden History of Georgia, 1733–1933*. Edited by Hattie C. Rainwater. Atlanta: Peachtree Garden Club, 1933.

McDonough, James Vernon. "William Jay: Regency Architect in Georgia and South Carolina." Ph.D. dissertation, Princeton University, 1950.

McKay, John J., Jr., and Nelle Edwards Smith. *A Guide to Macon's Architectural and Historical Heritage*. Macon, Ga.: Middle Georgia Historical Society, 1972.

Middle Georgia Planning and Development Commission. *Architectural Heritage of Middle Georgia*. Macon, Ga., 1976.

Mitchell, William R. *Handbook for Historical Preservation in Georgia*. Atlanta, Ga.: Georgia Historical Commission, 1971.

Moorehead, Warren King. *Exploration of the Etowah Mounds Site in Georgia*. New Haven: Yale University Press, 1932.

Morrison, Mary L., ed. *Historic Savannah: Survey of Significant Buildings in the Historic and Victorian Districts of Savannah, Georgia*. 2d ed. Savannah: Historic Savannah Foundation and the Junior League of Savannah, 1979.

Nichols, Frederick Doveton. *The Architecture of Georgia*. Savannah: Beehive Press, 1976.

———. *The Early Architecture of Georgia*. Chapel Hill: University of North Carolina Press, 1957.

Norwood, Martha F. *A History of the White House Tract, Richmond County, Georgia, 1756–1975*. Atlanta: Georgia Department of Natural Resources, Historic Preservation Section, 1975.

Olmsted, Frederick Law. *A Journey in the Seaboard Slave States in the Years 1853–1854*. New York and London: G. P. Putnam's Sons, 1904. Reprint of 1856 edition.

Otto, John Solomon. "Status Differences and the Archeological Record: A Comparison of Planter, Overseer, and Slave Sites from Cannons Point Plantation (1794–1861)." Thesis, University of Florida, 1975–1976.

Perkerson, Medora Field. *White Columns in Georgia*. New York: Rinehart and Co., 1952.

Peterson, Merrill D. *Thomas Jefferson and the New Nation: A Biography*. New York: Oxford University Press, 1970.

Pevsner, Nikolaus. *Ruskin and Viollet-le-Duc: Englishness and Frenchness in the Appreciation of Gothic Architecture*. London: Thames and Hudson, 1969.

Pierson, William H., Jr. *American Buildings and Their Architects.* Garden City, N.Y.: Doubleday, 1970.

Powell, Helen Cline. *The Building Materials of the Piedmont and Coastal Plain of Georgia.* M.L.A. thesis, University of Georgia, 1977.

Rains, George Washington. *History of the Confederate Powder Works.* Augusta, Ga.: Chronicle and Constitutionalist Printers, 1882.

Reps, John W. *Town Planning in Frontier America.* Princeton, N.J.: Princeton University Press, 1969.

Rice, Thaddeus B., and Carolyn W. Williams. *History of Greene County, Georgia, 1786–1886.* Macon, Ga.: J. W. Burke Co., 1961.

Rodgers, Ava D. *The Housing of Oglethorpe County, 1790–1860.* Tallahassee: Florida State University Press, 1971.

Roethler, Michael D. *Negro Slavery among the Cherokee Indians, 1540–1866.* Ph.D. dissertation, Fordham University, 1964.

Rowland, Arthur Ray. *A Guide to the Study of Augusta and Richmond County, Georgia.* Augusta, Ga.: Richmond County Historical Society, 1967.

Russell, William Howard. *My Diary North and South.* Edited by Fletcher Pratt. New York: Harper and Brothers, 1954.

Sams, Anita B. *Wayfarers in Walton: A History of Walton County, Georgia, 1818–1967.* Monroe, Ga.: General Charitable Foundation of Monroe, Ga., 1967.

Schwarze, The Reverend Edmund. *History of the Moravian Missions among the Southern Indian Tribes of the United States.* Bethlehem, Pa.: Times Publishing Co., 1923.

Sears, Joan Niles. *The First Hundred Years of Town Planning in Georgia.* Atlanta: Cherokee Publishing Co., 1979.

Shaw, Edward. *Civil Architecture; or, A Complete Theoretical and Practical System of Building.* 4th ed. Boston: Marsh, Capen, and Lyon, 1836.

Smith, George G. *The Story of Georgia and the Georgia People 1732 to 1860.* Macon, Ga.: George G. Smith, 1900.

Spalding, Phinizy. *Oglethorpe in America.* Chicago: University of Chicago Press, 1977.

Stanton, Phoebe B. *The Gothic Revival and American Church Architecture: An Episode in Taste, 1840–1856.* Baltimore: Johns Hopkins University Press, 1968.

Stevenson, Elizabeth. *Park Maker: A Life of Frederick Law Olmsted.* New York: Macmillan Co., 1977.

Stoney, Samuel Gaillard. *Plantations of the Carolina Low Country.* Edited by Albert Simmons and Samuel Lapham, Jr. Charleston, S.C.: Carolina Art Association, 1939.

Summerson, John. *The Classical Language of Architecture.* Cambridge, Mass.: MIT Press, 1963.

Thomas, Kenneth H. *The Rock House, McDuffie County, Georgia: An Analysis of an Historic Site.* Atlanta: Georgia Department of Natural Resources, Historic Preservation Section, 1974.

Thomas, Mrs. Z. V. *History of Jefferson County.* Macon, Ga.: J. W. Burke Co., 1927.

Von Däniken, Erich. *Chariots of the Gods? Unsolved Mysteries of the Past.* Translated by Michael Heron. New York: Putnam, 1970.

———. *Gods from Outer Space: Return to the Stars or Evidence for the Impossible.* Translated by Michael Heron. New York: Putnam, 1971.

Waring, John Frederick. *Cerveaux's Savannah.* Savannah: Georgia Historical Society, 1973.

Whiffin, Marcus. *American Architecture since 1780: A Guide to the Styles.* Cambridge, Mass.: MIT Press, 1969.

White, The Reverend George. *Historical Collections of Georgia.* New York: Pudney and Russell, 1854.

Williams, George Walton. *Nacoochee and Its Surroundings.* Charleston, S.C.: George W. Williams Co., 1874.

Williford, William Bailey. *The Glory of Covington.* Atlanta, Ga.: Cherokee Publishing Co., 1973.

Willingham, Robert M., Jr. *We Have This Heritage: The History of Wilkes County, Georgia, Beginnings to 1860.* Washington, Ga.: Wilkes County Publishing Co., 1969.

Wilson, Gustavus James Nash. *The Early History of Jackson County, Georgia.* Atlanta: Foote and Davis Co., 1914.

Woodward, Emily, ed. *Empire: Georgia Today in Photographs and Paragraphs.* Atlanta: Ruralist Press, 1936.

Woodward, George E. *Woodward's Architecture and Rural Art.* Vol 2. New York: George E. Woodward, 1868.

———, and Edward G. Thompson. *Woodward's National Architect.* New York: George E. Woodward, 1869.

Writer's Program of the Work Projects Administration in Georgia. *Georgia: A Guide to Its Towns and Countryside*. Athens: University of Georgia Press, 1940.

Periodicals

Brown's Guide to Georgia. Alfred Brown Publishing Co., College Park, Ga. Winter 1972/73–.
Georgia Historical Quarterly. Georgia Historical Society, Savannah, Ga. March 1917–.
Georgia Life. Decatur, Ga. Summer 1974–Spring 1980.
Southern Accents. WRC Smith Publishing Co., Atlanta, Ga. Fall 1977–.
Southern Cultivator, Southern Cultivator and Farmer. Augusta, Ga., 1843–1935.
Southern Living. Progressive Farmer Publishing Co., Birmingham, Ala. February 1976–.

Part II

A Catalog of Buildings Included in the Historic American Buildings Survey

In accordance with HABS policy, buildings included herein are cataloged according to the name of the building itself or according to the name of the first owner. Exceptions occur when a building was connected with a nationally prominent figure. In cases where, because of the previous HABS listing or because of long association, a building is known by the name of a later owner, the names of both owners are listed. If, however, the building is a public structure and the official designation includes more than one name, the official designation is used. In the case of buildings that were greatly enlarged or changed, the name of the original owner (if known) and the name of the later owner who made the changes are both used. Buildings are listed by town or city, or by their vicinity to the nearest town or city in the county within which they are located. Following the name of the building is the HABS number (e.g., GA-105). These numbers should be used when inquiring about a structure or when ordering reproductions from the Library of Congress.

Descriptions follow the standard HABS format, listing the material of which the building was constructed, the dimensions or shape of the building, the number of bays in front, the number of stories, the type of roof, the position

and number of chimneys, notable exterior details, notable interior details, outbuildings and dependencies, the chronology, the architect if known, changes, the present condition if different from the original, and, if applicable, a statement regarding special architectural or historic significance. Because of the number of Georgia buildings included in the survey, the descriptions are of necessity brief, and in the interest of brevity abbreviations and technical terms are used freely. A glossary of technical terms follows the catalog. Following the architectural and historical descriptions of the individual entries is a listing of the records in the Georgia HABS collection at the Library of Congress in Washington. The term *sheets* refers to architectural measured drawings, *ext. photo* and *int. photo* to exterior and interior photographs, and *data pages* to written historical and architectural data. These records may be consulted at the Library of Congress, Prints and Photographs Reading Room. Copies of the material may be purchased by writing the Library of Congress, Prints and Photographs Division, Washington, D.C. 20540.

Arnoldsville Vicinity

Oglethorpe County (111)

Langston House (Old Daniels Place) GA-1109. N side of U.S. Hwy. 78, ⅔ mi. w of intersection with County Rd. 915 in Arnoldsville. House faces S. Brick, Flemish bond (façade only), rectangular, five-bay front (50'2''), three-bay sides, two stories, gable roof with end parapets. Four ext. chimneys flush with end wall. Two-tiered one-bay entrance porch with attenuated pilasters and heavy square columns. Cornice of porch and house has odd triangular "dentils" (a sawtooth board) on face of corona. One-story shed porch on E side. Second-floor front and side windows nine panes over six, first floor nine over nine, rear windows twelve over twelve. Six-panel entrance door with sliding sash type sidelights, upper sash two panes wide, three high, lower sash two panes wide, two panes high. Central hall plan. Mantels with fluted pilasters, one with sunbursts. Windows with paneled reveals.

Smokehouse, frame with clapboarding, gable roof. Log carriage house built in the form of a dog trot cabin, open space presumably for carriage.

Built ca. 1816–29. Front porch columns replacements. One-story porch and kitchen ell replaces original two-story rear porch. E side above porch later stuccoed. Pinkish cast of brickwork suggests whitewash, though meticulous jointing, once painted, indicates coating was not original. 5 ext. photos (1936); 1 data page (1936).

Old Daniels Place. See *Langston House.*

Athens

Clarke County (30)

Alpha Gamma Delta Chapter House. See *Thomas-Carithers House.*

Anderson House (Lyle House; Lyle-Hunnicutt House) GA-1129. 320 Lumpkin St. facing E. Frame with clapboarding, flush siding under portico. Three-bay front, rectangular with rear additions. Two stories, hipped roof, apparently two int. chimneys. Corner pilasters and deep entablature around original structure. One-story portico with four fluted Greek Doric columns. Double entrance door with transom and sidelights. One room deep with additions at rear. Greek Revival, mid 19th C. Demolished ca. 1950. 1 ext. photo (1936); 1 data page (1936).

Athens Hardware Company (Old Hotel). See *Franklin House.*

Camak House GA-14-67. 297 Meigs St., facing N. Brick (painted) 59'2" (five-bay front) × 46'2" (four-bay sides). Two stories, raised basement, hipped roof, four chimneys flush with ext. walls. Pilasters at corners and on each side of center bay, front and back. Three-

bay entrance porch with cast-iron columns, railing, frieze, brackets, and acroteria. Heavy blinds with stationary louvers and hand-wrought hardware originally at all windows including basement. Intricately paneled entrance door with fan and sidelights. Central hall plan. Transitional, Federal and Greek Revival elements. Built 1834–35. Combination well and bathhouse which stood behind the house demolished after 1934. House used by fraternal orders since 1947 with many int. changes. Purchased by Coca-Cola Bottling Company 1979. Plans to restore for office use. 4 sheets (1934); 2 ext. photos (1934); 2 data pages (1936). Illustrated on p. 149.

Chapel GA-1164. N campus, University of Georgia, facing E. Brick with stucco, retangular three-bay front, five-bay sides, apsidal type projection on rear. Corner pilasters. Temple form with modified Greek hexastyle portico. Columns fluted and tapered, but without entasis. Very tall paired double windows extending past balcony. Main entrance with double doors and transom, smaller single doors each side. Meetinghouse plan. Balcony on three sides, supported by slender cast-iron columns with unorthodox acanthus leaf capitals. Cove ceiling. Greek Revival, 1832.

Square tower with louvers and free-standing columns at each corner, originally located over vestibule, was removed and a scaffold type bell tower erected at rear before 1935. Cymatium of raking cornice of pediment was replaced by a flat board ca. 1975. Doors and transom of main entrance appear to be replacements; sloping floor of chapel and steps in ves-

tibule are apparently not original. Old photographs indicate apse at the rear of the platform instead of present straight top recess with pilasters and entablature. Large painting by George Cook on rear wall of the recess was donated by Daniel Pratt in 1867. 1 ext. photo (1935).

Chase House (Reed House) GA-1112. 185 N. Hull St., facing E. Brick with stucco scored, rectangular, three-bay front, two-bay sides. Two stories, low hipped roof, four chimneys flush with ext. walls. One-story, three-bay Greek Doric entrance porch, the proportions lightened, but with full entablature except that triglyphs appear only at corners and over center columns. Entrance door with transom and sidelights, muntins arranged in rectangular lattice pattern. Central hall plan. One-story brick house at rear was probably a combination kitchen and servants' house. Greek Revival style, 1840–41. Plinths at bottom of porch columns may have been added as shaft deteriorated. Some triglyphs may have been removed. House now converted into apartments; deteriorated but basically sound. 1 ext. photo (1936); 1 data page (1936).

Cobb House. See *T. R. R. Cobb House.*

Cobb Institute. See *Lucy Cobb Institute.*

John A. Cobb House GA-1166. 1234 S. Lumpkin St., facing SE. Frame with clapboarding, flush siding under porch. Rectangular, three-bay front, four-bay sides. Two stories, hipped roof, four end chimneys. Two-story-high porch across front with eight slender columns of a type apparently unique to the Athens-Lexington area. Cross section of columns similar to Greek cross with rounded arms. Center and side bays of porch wider than others. Brackets form pseudo arches in wide bays, elliptical arches in others. Balcony with scroll-saw banisters over entrance. Main entrance and entrance to balcony with transoms and sidelights. Central hall plan, two rooms each side. Mid 19th C. Additions to rear. 1 ext. photo (1935). Illustrated on p. 156.

Lucy Cobb Institute (Cobb Institute) GA-1120. 220 N. Milledge Ave., facing E. Brick with stucco, U-shape, eleven-bay front (second story twelve bays), two stories over raised basement. Hipped roof with parapet in front, parapet flat in center, pediments on each side. One-story, thirteen-bay, cast-iron veranda with concave roof across front. E (front) windows have cast-iron cornices, windows on porch full length. Entrance door with arched panels, sidelights, and transom, framed by pilasters with entablature. One-story porch between rear ells. Separate brick kitchen and brick servants' house, the latter with a second story of wood which appears to be of later date. Built 1858–59.

Old photos (1936) show the stucco scored, also a six-bay third floor with pediment type parapet (similar to pediments on each end). Adjacent Seney-Stovall octagonal brick chapel with stick style woodwork erected 1885. Several undistinguished wood frame with clapboard buildings added early 20th C.

Lucy Cobb Institute served as a finishing school for young ladies from 1859 to 1931. Building used for various purposes several decades thereafter. Now deserted and deteriorating. 1 ext. photo (1936); 1 int. photo (1936); 2 ext. photos (1940); 1 ext. photo chapel (1980); 1 data page (1936). Illustrated on pp. 150, 203.

T. R. R. Cobb House (Cobb House) GA-1116. 194 Prince Ave., facing S. Frame with clapboarding, flush siding under porch. Rectangular, octagonal wings projecting toward the front on each side; central portion three bays; three sides of each wing toward front, the central one with one window per floor, the diagonal one with none. Central portion and wings two story; sides and back irregular, part one-story, part two-story. Roof flat, gable, and shed types; front and part of wings with entablature type parapet. Two end chimneys, five int. chimneys. Front corner pilasters. Two-story-high modified Greek Doric porch in antis; balcony with concave center portion, cast-iron railing. Front entrance and front windows framed by pilasters with entablatures. Entrance with sidelights and transom; front first-floor windows full length. No records of earliest portion. Greek Revival porch and wings added 1852. Marble floor of porch probably later. Sidelights, transom, and some window sashes later changed to single-pane type. Int. greatly changed early to mid 20th C. Adaptive restoration for parish house and rectory for Saint Joseph's Catholic Church in 1976. Residence from 1852 to 1862 of T. R. R. Cobb, author of the Constitution of the Confederate States of America. 2 ext. photos (1936); 2 ext. photos (1940); 1 ext. photo (1980); 1 data page (1937). Illustrated on p. 102.

Crane House (Sigma Alpha Epsilon Chapter House) GA-1111 G. 247 Pulaski St., facing E. Brick (painted), stone foundation. Main body five bays wide, rectangular, with wings, hipped roof, four end chimneys flush with ext. walls. Two-story-high modified Doric porch with square (brick with stucco) tapered columns across front. Entrance with transom, corner lights, and sidelights framed by pilasters with entablature. Central hall plan (walls between hall and other rooms brick with plaster), two rooms each side, open-well stairway with simple rectangular balusters and end volute. Remnants of extensive parterre gardens remain near the house. Greek Revival, 1845. Ross Crane, builder and first owner. A former ell was demolished, a rear entrance porch and wings added ca. 1935 when converted to a fraternity house. Two brick servants' houses demolished after 1936. 3 ext. photos (1936); 2 int. photos (1936); 1 data page (1936).

Albin P. Dearing House (Dearing House; Kappa Alpha Theta Chapter House) GA-1133. 338 S. Milledge Ave., facing E. Brick, rectangular except one-story ell across back projects both sides. Four end chimneys flush with ext. walls. Heroic Greek Doric porch (modified) three sides; six columns (brick with stucco) in front, four each side. Center and end columns spaced closer than intermediate ones. Full-length windows open onto porch. Entrance with sidelights and transom framed by pilasters with entablature. Central hall plan, two rooms each side. Walls between hall and adjoining rooms brick with plaster. Interior woodwork curly maple. Greek Revival, 1856. Converted to sorority house in 1936–37. Three-story wing added to rear in 1957. 2 ext. photos (1936); 1 ext. photo (1940); 1 data page (1936).

Mrs. William Dearing House (House, 225 S. Milledge Ave.) GA-1163. 225 S. Milledge Ave., facing w. Frame with clapboarding, apparently rectangular. Three-bay front, two stories high. Roof probably hipped, with entablature type parapet three sides. Heroic Greek Doric (modified) porch three sides. Six fluted columns across front; several each side. First-story windows on porch full length. Entrance door with sidelights and transom framed by pilasters with entablature. Reputedly a smaller version in wood of the Albin P. Dearing House. Greek Revival, 1858. Demolished ca. 1965. 1 ext. photo (1940).

Delta Tau Delta House. See *Joseph Henry Lumpkin House.*

Demosthenian Hall GA-14-87 G. N campus, University of Georgia, facing E. Brick with stucco, rectangular, three-bay front and three-bay sides, hipped roof with flared eaves, two end chimneys. Stone stoop, entrance with fan and sidelights, Palladian window with intricately carved casing over entrance. Apparently first floor was originally central hall type with two rooms each side and a transverse stair hall at rear; second floor one large assembly room plus stair hall. Plaster ceiling of assembly hall coved and elaborately decorated in the Adam manner. Traditional Federal style. Built 1824. Entrance door since removed, front part of hall converted to a semienclosed porch with the former doorway (without door) as entrance. First-floor plan greatly changed; stairway ap-

parently not original. Old photos (pre-HABS) show ext. trim, lintels, and archivolts (the latter apparently projecting slightly) painted in a darker color than the body of the building. 5 sheets (1934); 2 ext. photos (1934); 5 int. photos (1936). Illustrated on p. 54.

First Presbyterian Church GA-1165. 185 E. Hancock St., facing s. Rectangular, three-bay front, six-bay sides with wings at rear. Two stories over raised basement, temple form with Greek Doric hexastyle portico. Entablature complete with triglyphs and mutules carries around the original part of the church. Windows with three sashes, each sash seven lights wide, six lights high; louvered blinds. Pilasters at corners and between windows. Meetinghouse plan with balcony over vestibule. Greek Revival, 1855. Original structure had recessed Greek Doric porch with columns in antis and octagonal steeple with cupola over. At one time, the cupola was surmounted with a hand pointing heavenward. The present portico was added to the original building, and the recessed porch converted to a vestibule in 1902. Rear wings (educational annex) added in 1964–66. Entrance door enlarged by addition of flanking doors ca. 1970. 1 ext. photo (1935).

Franklin House (Athens Hardware Company; Old Hotel) GA-1122. 480 E. Broad St., facing N. Approximately 75' (eight-bay) front × 50' with rear ell and other additions. Three stories; gable roof with stepped parapet. Four int. chimneys, four ext. chimneys flush with end walls in original part. Heavily paneled door, fan and sidelights framed by pilasters with entablature at second-floor level of front façade and on E side;

windows with similar treatment on third floor over doors; also in attic on E side. Simulated lintels in stucco over other windows. Hinges for blinds; a few blinds with very heavy stationary louvers stored in attic. First floor has cast-iron front. Neoclassic, traditional phase, simplistic Federal. Built 1845–47. Additions to the rear (blocking windows, light, and ventilation) before 1860. Second-floor balconies probably removed when cast-iron front was installed in 1886. Building used exclusively as hotel until end of Civil War, when Athens Hardware Company was housed in it. By 1885 the whole building was used by the hardware company, which operated continuously in that location until 1972. 1 ext. photo (1936).

Dr. Marcus A. Franklin House (Upson House) GA-14-66. 1022 Prince Ave., facing s. Brick with stucco scored, rectangular (five-bay front), two stories, hipped roof with entablature type parapet three sides. Four end chimneys flush with ext. walls. Two-story-high hexastyle modified Greek Doric porch across front, columns stucco on brick, fluted. Raised stucco belt course at second floor, raised stucco lintels over openings. First-floor windows full length. Entrance door with two vertical panels and with sidelights and transom. Central hall plan, two rooms each side, rooms w side connected by sliding doors. Open-well stairway curved at turns. Greek Revival, 1847. Porches at rear changed and partially enclosed after 1885; removed 1979. Adaptive restoration by Group Five Architects, Atlanta, for offices for First National Bank of Athens, 1979–80. 4 sheets (1934); 4 ext. photos (1934); 2 data pages (1934). Illustrated on p. 103.

Gerdine House. See *Tinsley House.*

Grant-Hill-White-Bradshaw House. See *President's House, University of Georgia.*

Hamilton House. See *Phinizy House.*

Charles Hayes House GA-2101. 1720 S. Lumpkin St., facing ESE. Wood frame with shingle siding, irregular shape, three-bay front, one story, roof gabled at front and sides, hipped at rear. Three int. chimneys. Wide eaves with braced roof brackets. Two-bay front porch with shingled piers and shingled railing with an inset lattice panel. Shingle courses alternately wide and narrow. Irregular plan, entrance from porch directly into living room. Bungalow style, ca. 1920. 1 ext. photo (1980). Illustrated on p. 219.

Ben Hill House. See *President's House, University of Georgia.*

Hodgson House. See *Lane House.*

House, 1234 Lumpkin Street. See *John A. Cobb House.*

House, 225 Milledge Avenue. See *Mrs. William Dearing House.*

House, 897 Milledge Avenue. See *Lampkin-Mell House.*

Hunnicutt House. See *Phinizy House.*

Kappa Alpha Theta Chapter House. See *Albin P. Dearing House.*

Lampkin-Mell House (House, 897 Milledge Ave.) GA-1167. 897 S. Milledge Ave., facing w. Frame with clapboarding, flush siding under porch. Rectangular (three-bay front) with rear ell. Two stories, roof not visible from eye level. Seven-bay two-story-high porch across front with slender columns supporting heavy bracketed entablature. Cross section of columns similar to Greek cross with rounded arms; double cyma recta brackets at top of columns, the outer one meeting its counterpart of the adjacent column, a flat pendant marking the juncture. Cast-iron railing. First-floor windows on porch full length; entrance door with transom and side- and corner-lights. Flamboyant combination of Greek, Gothic, Italianate, and vernacular elements. The shape of the columns is structurally logical, and of a type apparently unique to the Athens-Lexington area. Built on Jackson St. ca. 1840. Moved to Milledge Ave. ca. 1910 by John D. Mell. Demolished ca. 1965. 1 ext. photo (1935). Illustrated on p. 156.

Lane House (Hodgson House) GA-1160. 287 Oconee St., facing sw. Wood frame with clapboarding, rectangular (five-bay front), two stories, with attached annex on the southeast side. Gable roof, two end chimneys. Two-tier, three-bay porch; also one-story porch connecting main porch with annex. Porch columns chamfered, with scroll-saw brackets and banisters. Palladian type entrances first and second floors. Early 19th C. Scroll-saw work and annex obviously later. Demolished ca. 1942. 1 ext. photo (1933); 1 ext. photo (1940). Recorded in 1933 and 1940 under several names and addresses.

Joseph Henry Lumpkin House (Judge Lumpkin House) GA-1115. 248 Prince Ave., facing s. Frame with clapboarding, flush siding under porch. Rectangular with wings and with T-shaped ell on back. Five-bay front, two stories, principal roof hipped with entablature as a parapet on three sides; other roofs hipped, gable, and shed types. Two int. chimneys, four end chimneys. Two-story porch three sides terminating at wings. Greek Doric columns with modified entablature carried over ends of wings. First-floor windows full length framed by pilasters with entablatures, as is the entrance door with its transom and sidelights. Balcony (wood lattice railing) over. Front portion central hall plan; cross hall with more rooms behind. Greek Revival. Original part (facing w) built before 1837 by Charles McKinley (not documented). Greatly enlarged, front portion and porches probably added by Joseph H. Lumpkin ca. 1850. Moved much closer to street ca. 1906. Now used as alumni house by University of Georgia School of Law. Joseph Henry Lumpkin, first chief justice of the Georgia Supreme Court, lived here from 1843 to 1867. 1 ext. photo (1936); 1 ext. photo (1940).

1234 Lumpkin Street. See *John A. Cobb House.*

Lumpkin-Barrow-Childs House. See *Joseph Henry Lumpkin House.*

Lyle House. See *Anderson House.*

Lyle-Hunnicutt House. See *Anderson House.*

McKinley-Lumpkin-Cobb House. See *T. R. R. Cobb House.*

Mell House. See *Lampkin-Mell House.*

Merk House GA-2102. 735 Prince Ave., facing N. Frame with clapboarding, brick piers with wood lattice underpinning, irregular shape, three-bay front, one-story gable roof, three int. chimneys. Projecting room (right of entrance) with floor-length window opening onto balcony with concave hood (on console brackets) over. Wraparound porch on part of N and E sides, breaking out into an octagonal gazebolike form at the corner. Slender square porch columns with scrollwork brackets; scrollwork porch railing. Entrance door with glass panel, sidelights, and transom. Irregular plan with central hall. Attached rear wing with kitchen and servant's room. Queen Anne style, ca. 1890. Minor int. changes. 1 ext. photo (1980). Illustrated on p. 198.

225 Milledge Avenue. See *Mrs. William Dearing House.*

897 Milledge Avenue. See *Lampkin-Mell House.*

Nicholson House. See *Wray-Nicholson House.*

Old Hotel. See *Franklin House.*

Parr House GA-2103. 227 Bloomfield St., facing W. Frame with clapboarding, irregular shape, three-bay (counting bay window as one bay) front, one story, gable roof, three int. chimneys. Gables with fans of overlapping tapered clapboarding. Projecting room with bay window right side of entrance, wraparound porch part of front and N side. Slender chamfered porch columns, scrollwork banisters. Entrance door with arched etched glass panel. Irregular plan with central hall. Attached kitchen at rear. Interior walls and ceilings decorated with stenciled and painted designs. Vernacular Queen Anne style, 1889. Scrollwork porch brackets since removed. The gable fans are of a type not uncommon in NE Georgia, but may be unique to the area. 1 ext. photo (1980). Illustrated on p. 198.

Phi Kappa Hall GA-1117. N campus, University of Georgia, facing W. Brick, rectangular (one-bay front), two stories, gable roof. Vernacular version of a prostyle tetrastyle Doric temple. Two-story-high columns brick with stucco. Double entrance door with lintel simulated in stucco; simulated stucco lintels over windows. Vestibule with dog-leg stairs either side. Several rooms first floor; second-floor vestibule and meeting room. Vernacular Greek Revival, 1836. Original chimney removed; later one built against side of building. Minor changes first floor. 2 ext. photos (1936); 1 data page (1936).

Phinizy House (Hunnicutt House) GA-1128 I. 325 N. Milledge Ave., facing E. Wood frame with clapboarding, kitchen ell brick. Rectangular, rear ells, five-bay front, two stories, hipped roof, four end chimneys. Bracketed cornice with paneled frieze. Five-bay cast-iron veranda with concave roof across front and returning down S side. Wood lattice between porch piers. Window and door openings with simple shouldered pediments; full-length windows on porch, entrance with sidelights and transom. Central hall plan, two rooms each side. Brick smokehouse and wood frame servants' house. Built ca. 1858. Minor changes and additions. 1 ext. photo (1936); 1 data page (1936).

President's House, University of Georgia (Grant-Hill-White-Bradshaw House) GA-1-20. 570 Prince Ave., facing S. Frame with clapboarding, flush siding under porch. Rectangular, wings projecting front and rear. Porches flush with wings on sides and between wings at rear, so that overall shape is rectangular. Five-bay front, two stories over raised basement. Hipped roof, four end chimneys. Two-story-high Corinthian porch front and sides; two-story Doric porch in antis at back. Pilasters at corners of house, entablature continuous. Of surviving Greek Revival houses with heroic porches, this is one of the few with an entablature wholly below the roof line and wholly above the windows. Pilasters with entablatures frame door and window openings. First-floor windows on porch full length; entrance recessed and with sidelights and transom of etched glass. Balcony with turned banisters over. Central hall plan with double room (two fireplaces) on E side, two rooms on W side. Ornate plaster cornices and ceiling medallions; original chandeliers in E room. Intricately carved marble mantels with arched openings for coal grates.

At rear a plantation type cottage showing Greek Revival influence; may once have occupied site of house. Front yard with boxwood parterre garden enclosed by a picket fence.

Greek Revival, built 1857–58. A list of "Expenses of building in Athens" by John T. Grant, the first owner, itemizes materials and expenses, total cost $25,355.25. Copy of list is included in account of the house written by Patricia I. Cooper (vertical files, Georgia Room, University of Georgia Library).

Wings and two-story porch at the rear replace one-story porch; original straight flight of steps leading to entrance has been replaced by a more complicated double type; and the wide flat arches which originally had visually divided the central hall and the E drawing room have been removed. These changes were made in 1949; architects for the remodeling were Cooper, Bond, and Cooper. The rear gardens, planted about the same time, were designed by Hubert B. Owens, A.S.L.A. American boxwood was substituted for the original dwarf English boxwood of the front gardens, and brick walks replaced sand walks ca. 1965. Possibly the most elegant Greek Revival house left in Georgia. 1 ext. photo (1934); 1 ext. photo (1940); 1 ext. photo outbuilding (1980); 2 data pages (1936). Illustrated on pp. 100, 110.

Reed House. See *Chase House.*

Seney-Stovall Chapel. See *Lucy Cobb Institute.*

Sigma Alpha Epsilon Chapter House. See *Crane House.*

Sigma Phi Epsilon Chapter House. See *H. C. White House.*

James Sledge House GA-2104. 749 Cobb St., facing NE. Brick with stucco, ells frame with clapboarding. Rectangular, rear ells, three-bay front, one-and-a-half stories, gable roof, dormers with scroll-saw barge boards, four int. end chimneys, five-bay front veranda with concave hipped roof and filigree cast-iron columns, frieze, brackets, railing, and acroteriae. Windows under veranda floor length. Double entrance doors with etched-glass sidelights,

transom, and modified pediment. Divided central hall, two rooms each side. Ogee arch with double doors between halls. Principal rooms downstairs have plaster cornices, walnut woodwork trimmed with oak, marble mantels, silver hinge bolts; downstairs hall with walnut and oak (alternating) flooring. Mid-Victorian, Gothic Revival influence, 1860. Ells at rear probably early additions. 3 ext. photos (1980). Illustrated on pp. 151, 155.

Taylor-Grady House GA-1114. 634 Prince Ave., facing S. Frame with clapboarding, flush siding under porch. Reverse t-shape (rectangular if porches included), three-bay front, two stories over semi-raised basement. Hipped roof with entablature type parapet three sides, one int. chimney, two end chimneys. Pilasters at corners and between bays, belt course between floors. Two-story-high porch three sides, flush with and dying against wings. Fluted Greek Doric columns, brick with stucco, simplified entablature. Six columns in front, three (including corner column) on E side, four on W side, total said to represent the thirteen original colonies. Retaining wall between piers that support columns, the portion above grade with segmental arched openings with very delicate wood lattice. Twisted wire railing on porch. Entrance with side- and corner-lights and transom; first-story windows full length. Windows and entrance framed by pilasters with entablature. Central hall plan, two rooms each side. Ext. corners of E rooms rounded, rooms connected by sliding doors.

Unique outbuildings include kitchen (?), storage house, and wellhouse. Kitchen brick with

stucco, square, with a pyramidal roof. Heavy unorthodox pilasters with bold cyma reversa capitals in stucco at corners. Bottom of entablature curiously scalloped with square indentations. Holes under entablature and over dropped ceiling within. Holes and scallops about the size and shape of large brick headers. Storage or ice-house is brick with stucco, with gable roof which appears to be concrete; the building similar to mausoleums in old New Orleans cemeteries. Classic well-house with pyramidal roof supported by Doric columns of wood; design thought to be original, but most parts replaced over the years.

Greek Revival, 1845; restored by Athens Junior Assembly and the city of Athens 1977. Home of Henry Grady, 19th C. orator and journalist, 1865–68. House museum. 3 ext. photos (1936); 1 ext. photo kitchen (1980); 1 int. photo (1936); 1 data page (1936). Illustrated on p. 161.

Taylor Monument GA-2105. Oconee Hills Cemetery. Marble, square base (7' × 7') plus rectangular mausoleum with gable roof. Monument approximately 28 ft. high overall, consisting of base, pedestal, and pinnacle-type canopy supported by a framework of pointed arches resting on four colonnettes. Classical figure of winged angel under canopy, statue enframed by colonnettes and Gothic arches. Marble door in pedestal and inscription on one side to the memory of Mrs. Sarah Jane Taylor, who was born in 1832 and died in 1860; inscription on the other side in memory of two of her children, who were interred there later. Gothic Revival style ca. 1860. Wings, one arm, and nose of the figure broken before

1980. Figure destroyed by vandals, 1981. 2 ext. photos (1980). Illustrated on p. 134.

Thomas House GA-1113. 347 W. Hancock St., facing N. Wood frame with clapboarding, flush siding under porch. First floor T-shaped, second floor rectangular. Five-bay front, two stories with one-story ell across back and extending each side, thus the T-shape. Pyramidal roof with entablature as parapet around porch and down W side, four end chimneys. Two-story-high hexastyle modified Greek Doric porch across front. Full-length windows opening onto porch. Entrance with sidelights and transom framed by pilasters with entablature; balcony with wooden railing over. Originally faced E (Pulaski St.), was raised high off the ground, and was approached through parterre gardens set behind a picket fence. Transferred to present location on the same site before 1933. 1 ext. photo (1936); 1 data page (1936).

Thomas-Carithers House (Alpha Gamma Delta Chapter House) GA-1131. 530 Milledge Ave., facing E. Wood frame with clapboarding, rectangular, end pavilions, wings each side. Seven-bay front, two stories, principal roof hipped, others flat or gable, some with balustrades. Two int. chimneys, two int. end chimneys. Floriated frieze on pavilions. Twelve-bay Ionic porch across front, three central bays project over steps, wide end bay forms porte-cochère north side. Seven-bay second-story porch between pavilions. Large central entrance hall. Principal rooms have paneled wainscot, dentil cornices, and friezes with plaster swags similar to those on ext. Beaux Arts style, 1895.

W. W. Thomas, architect and first owner. Additions include dormitory at rear. 1 ext. photo (1980). Illustrated on p. 210.

Tinsley House (Gerdine House) GA-1130. 129 Dougherty St., facing S. Wood frame with clapboarding, rectangular, five-bay front, two stories, gable roof, two int. chimneys. Two-tiered, three-bay simplified Doric portico. Plan apparently central hall with two rooms each side. Built ca. 1836. Demolished ca. 1947. 1 ext. photo (1936); 1 data page (1936).

Treanor House. See *John A. Cobb House*.

University of Georgia. See individual buildings: *Chapel, Demosthenian Hall, Phi Kappa Hall, President's House*.

Upson House. See *Dr. Marcus A. Franklin House*.

H. C. White House (Sigma Phi Epsilon Chapter House) GA-2106. 327 S. Milledge Ave., facing W. Frame with clapboarding, rectangular, additions and ells at rear, five-bay front, two stories, truncated pyramidal roof, one int. chimney, two int. end chimneys. Giant order tetrastyle Ionic porch, central bay projecting slightly and with pediment over. Modillion cornice. Two rooms at front, one the equivalent of entrance hall plus chamber, high wainscot and built-in bench one end. Rear hall with mid 19th C. type open-well stairway, curved at corners. House originally Second Empire style, probably built ca. 1870–80. Remodeled by Prof. H. C. White in 1901 in 20th C. Classic Revival ("Southern Colonial") style. Late additions at rear. 1 ext. photo (1980). Illustrated on p. 216.

Wray-Nicholson House (Nicholson House) GA-1134. G. 298 Hull St., facing E. Wood frame with clapboarding, flush siding under porch. Rectangular, with rear ell, five-bay front, two stories over raised basement. Brick kitchen attached to basement. Hipped roof with concealed gutters, except ell and kitchen have gable roofs. Four end chimneys, one int. chimney. Two-story-high hexastyle Greek Doric (modified) porch across front; one-story porch on S and W sides. Full-length windows open onto front porch. Entrance with sidelights and transom, framed by pilasters with entablature. Balcony over. Central hall plan, two rooms each side. Original part (no records), early 19th C., may have been University of Georgia dining room. Remodeled and enlarged to (approximately) its present appearance by Thomas Wray in 1840. Porch changed to two-tier type late 19th C. Restored by M. G. Nicholson in 1916, with new porch foundation and with old columns from the Whaley Place (originally at 771 Prince Ave.). Several minor additions N and W sides. Minor int. changes since 1970. 1 ext. photo (1936); 1 data page (1936).

Atlanta

Fulton County (61)

Equitable Building (Trust Company of Georgia) GA-2107. 25 Pryor St., N.E. Brick, stone columns and trim, modified triangular shape with interior open court, three entrance fronts, one at apex, one each side. Three-bay front at apex, eleven-bay sides, except eight bays at first floor, since entrance takes up three bays. Windows over entrance at apex combined into multistory bay window; three windows over entrances at sides combined into multistory bow windows. Building rises in five stages; the bottom stage being the first floor, in which the bays (except at side entrances) are separated by heavy columns with Romanesque-type Corinthian capitals; second stage is the second floor, with bands of light and dark brick and an entablature over; the third stage is floors three and four, with windows unified vertically and with entablature over; the fourth stage is floors five, six, and seven, whose windows are likewise unified, the top ones arched; the fifth stage is the eighth floor, and has an elaborate entablature.

Entrance at apex set behind columns. Entrances at sides within elliptical arch flanked by column-like projections that rest on stone brackets and support an entablature over the second-story windows. Floriated reliefs around arch, across architrave, on each side of bow windows, and on each side of and below top-floor windows at apex. Courtyard windows almost wall-to-wall glass, the structure there simply and frankly expressed with minimal ornament. Interior rich with curving stairway, marble, hardwood, and ornamental metal work. Early skyscraper with Richardsonian Romanesque decorative details; Burnham and Root, architects. Built 1891; demolished 1971. 12 ext. photos (1970); 2 int. photos (1970). Recorded in 1934 as in De Kalb County. Illustrated on p. 207.

The Fox Theater GA-2108. NW corner Ponce de Leon Ave. and E. Peachtree St. Cream and buff brick with cast stone and terra cotta trim. Basically rectangular but with many projections and recesses; appears to be a group of buildings. Peachtree side eight structural bays, one being the main entrance, deeply recessed and with six double doors; the other major bays contain a central entrance door flanked by display windows, all one story high. Ponce de Leon side has five similar structural bays, then a higher irregular portion with projections and recesses, with seventeen minor bays. Building varies from one to seven stories above street level and one to four stories below. Roofs primarily flat, with crenellated parapets. Main entrance Peachtree side with marquee flanked by minarets. Irregular roof line on Ponce de Leon side, the varying levels accentuated by crenellations, minarets, and onion domes; the façade accentuated by horizontal bands of brickwork alternately cream and buff, by the silhouette of an ext. stairway, by arched recesses and loggias, and by windows with lancet and horseshoe arches.

The auditorium (roughly 6500 sq. ft.) is surrounded on three sides by oriental castellated walls with turrets, balconies, and barred windows; the proscenium, with its arch built to resemble a bridge with lanterns, forms the fourth side. Ceiling designed to give the effect of the sky—day, night, sunrise, or sunset—with billowing clouds, twinkling stars, changing colors, as needed. Auditorium designed for 5,000 but later reduced to 3,934 to provide more modern seats. Exotic decor throughout, principally based on Arabian or Egyptian motifs. The famous Moller pipe organ has a system of more than 3,500 pipes, and can be raised or lowered on its own elevator. When installed, the electric power serving the Fox was equal to that serving all of Greenville, S.C., in 1929.

Rental storerooms, offices, and a Shriners' mosque for the use of the first owners, the Yaarab Temple of the Mystic Shriners, were also included in the building. Eclectic design of Moorish influence, built 1927–29. Marye, Alger and Vinour, architects. 1 ext. photo (1980); 1 int. photo (1980). Illustrated on pp. 221, 222.

Georgia State Capitol GA-2109. Capitol Square, facing w. Indiana limestone, basement story vermiculated rusticated, first story smooth rusticated, second and third stories smooth cut stone. Rectangular, projecting center pavilion (seven bays) and wings with projecting end pavilions. Nineteen-bay front, three stories over raised basement. Flat roof with parapet and center dome. Six square stone columnar pedestals at entrance support a giant order hexastyle Corinthian portico at second-floor level of central pavilion. End pavilions have matching pilasters with pediments. E front similar but instead of portico there is an enclosed pavilion with pilasters. Drum of dome has pedimented windows with bull's-eye windows over and with engaged Corinthian columns between. Lantern of dome surmounted by statue of Liberty, her torch 258 ft. above ground.

Central rotunda with flanking rectangular lobbies, lobbies with balconies supported by Corinthian columns and lighted by clerestory arched windows. Floors, wainscot, and stairways of principal rooms of Georgia marble. Neoclassical Revival style, 1884–89; Edbrooke and Burnham of Chicago, architects. Gold leaf from Dahlonega, Ga., applied to dome in 1958. 1 ext. photo (1980). Illustrated on p. 211.

Martin Luther King, Jr., Birth Home GA-1171. 501 Auburn Ave. N.E., facing N. Frame with clapboarding, shingles in gables, irregular shape, four-bay front first story, three-bay front second story. Hipped roof with secondary gables, one end, two int. chimneys, porch with shed roof, turned posts, scroll-saw brackets front and one side; smaller second-story porch over. Irregular plan. Queen Anne style, late 19th C. Restoration begun 1974. House museum. 6 ext. photos (1979); 2 int. photos (1979); 1 ext. photo (1980). Illustrated on p. 201.

Edward C. Peters House GA-179 Ponce de Leon Ave., facing w. Brick, terra cotta, half-timbered, wood frame with shingle siding, stone foundation and trim; slate roof with metal ridges. Irregular, two-bay front, side porch, wings, hipped roof with projecting gables, two ext. chimneys with carved stone weatherings, three int. chimneys. Porte-cochère at entrance with one large arch on each of three sides. Side porch on w side with semicircular end, fanciful turned columns with Romanesque type Corinthian columns, Victorian brackets and railing. Sunporch adjoining on NW side. Belt course at second-floor level with splayed band of decorative terra-cotta shingles over. Window and door opening with segmental arches, sunbursts on tympanum; sashes vary from one-over-one type to complicated patterns. Small entrance foyer opening into large stair hall with fireplace. Heavy open-well oak stairway with turned balusters, carved solid quarter-circle panel at landing, carved newel post. Beveled leaded glass window over landing. High oak wainscot, paneled; top panel of doors carved in low relief; ceiling paneled with oak and plaster. No two rooms shaped alike. Small parlor Victorian version of Adam style; large parlor Victorian version of Louis XV style. Upstairs hall with Queen Anne spiderweb arch with spindles. All mantels unusual; one bedroom mantel with asymmetrical arrangement of shelves and mirrors in overmantel.

Carriage house frame with clapboarding, one-and-a-half stories, steep picturesque roof with dormers. Queen Anne style, 1885. 1 ref. photo. Recorded in 1934 as in De Kalb County.

Swan House GA-2111. 3099 Andrews Dr., facing NW. Brick with stucco, rectangular, center and end pavilions, nine-bay front, two stories, hipped roof, the parapet over the center pavilion pedimented and supporting sculpture. Two int. chimneys. Street (NW) front approached via a series of terraces and fountains that culminate with horseshoe steps leading to entrance which has stone trim and pediment surmounted by an urn. Two-story-high tetrastyle Doric porte-cochère on sw side leads to circular entrance hall interrelated with a rectangular stair hall with freestanding circular stairway with bronze balustrade. Principal rooms have ornamental plaster cornices and medallions, richly carved door headers and mantels. Elements of early 18th C. English architecture and earlier prototypal Italian villas adapted to create a classical design, masterful in the unity of its parts and in the unity of house and grounds. Built by Edward H. Inman in 1920s, Philip T. Shutze, architect. Woodcarving primarily by H. J. Millard. 3 ext. photos (1980). Illustrated on p. 220.

Sweet Auburn Historic District GA-1170-1172. That area bounded by Courtland and Houston Sts., Auburn and Piedmont Aves., also both sides of Auburn Ave. between Piedmont and Bell Sts., and extending to Edgewood Ave.; E side of Bell St. between Auburn and Edgewood Aves.; and triangular area bounded by Butler St., Edgewood Ave., Bell St., and the first diagonal street sw of Bell St. and Butler St. Predominantly black commercial-residential area which has been called "the richest Negro street in the world." Within or near the area are the birthplace of Martin Luther King, Jr., (GA-1171), his grave, the memorial buildings and park dedicated to his memory, and Ebenezer Baptist Church, where both he and his father preached and where his mother was fatally shot.

Buildings there are put to religious, social, civic, and commercial uses; there are detached and row houses; styles range from modest to elegant, from late 19th C. to the present. 32 sheets (1979); 76 ext. photos (1979); 5 int. photos (1979); incomplete data (1979). Illustrated on pp. 245, 246, 247.

Trust Company of Georgia. See *Equitable Building.*

Atlanta Vicinity
Cobb County (34)

Covered Bridge over Soap Creek. See *Covered Bridge over Sope Creek*, Marietta Vicinity.

Atlanta Vicinity

De Kalb County (45)

Latimer-Felton House GA-1106. W side of Hwy. 155, 9 mi. SE of intersection with Memorial Dr. in Atlanta. One-tenth mile s of South River, facing E. Frame with clapboarding, flush siding under porch and as sheathing under clapboards. Foundation large squared granite stones. Rectangular, three-bay front, two stories, hipped roof flattening at eaves, two int. chimneys. One-story porch across front, center portion probably two-tiered. Entrance door with sidelights and transom framed by pilasters with entablature; similar door second story. Central hall plan, two rooms each side. House framed with heavy hand-hewn timbers: 10″ × 10″ sills, approximately 3¼″ × 10″ first floor joists, 5 in. studs. Built mid 19th C. Rebuilt as one-story house after 1937. Destroyed by fire ca. 1978. Childhood home of Rebecca Latimer Felton, first woman U.S. senator. 2 sheets (1936); 1 ext. photo (1936); 2 data pages (1937).

Augusta

Richmond County (123)

Academy of Richmond County (now the Augusta Museum) GA-229. 540 Telfair St. Faces NNE. Brick with stucco scored. 112′ (eleven-bay front) × 93′8″, H-shaped. Central unit 44′ (five-bay front); wings 34′ (three-bay front) × 93′8″. Two stories, central unit higher than wings. Flat or nearly flat roofs with crenellated parapets. Six int. chimneys, stuccoed, with ornamental chimney pots. Central unit with five-bay porches front and back, extending from wing to wing. Porches have compound Gothic type piers with Tudor arches over, the piers cast iron and the arches of wood construction. Crenellations over the porches, presumed to be wood construction like the arches, are covered with sheet metal. Wood, iron, and sheet metal of the porches have sanded paint finish. Terra cotta hood moldings over windows continue at a lower level between windows, thus forming a continuous fret.

Central unit one large room each floor, stairs in wings. A lattice brick wall in front of the building continues on in front of the adjacent Old Medical College★. Gothic Revival Tudor style, opened as an academy in 1802. A contemporary account gives the following description: "an academy, containing a central building 45 feet by 36 feet, and wings 33 feet by 100 feet [93 feet 8 inches, actually] is now building. This building is ornamented with a cupola." Antebellum illustrations show few changes have been made to the ext. since 1860. Int. arrangement changed many times. Major repairs and some renovations executed in 1856–57 under the supervision of William Goodrich, architect-builder; it is assumed that the Gothic elements date from that time. The old stucco is currently being replaced, and in the process filled-in arches over side entrance doors have been revealed. This could indicate that those doors formerly had fanlights and that the building was originally of a different style. The cupola mentioned in early accounts does not appear in extant illustrations. If originally built in its present style, this would be the oldest surviving Gothic Revival public building in the U.S. 1 ext. photo (1936); 2 data pages (1936). Illustrated on p. 133.

Allen Fuqua Center. See *Montrose.*

Appleby-Kilpatrick House (Kilpatrick House) GA-233. 1314 Comfort Rd., facing N. Frame with flush siding, five-bay front, rectangular, two-and-a-half stories (dormer and entablature windows) on raised basement, low pitched roof with parapet. Four int. end chimneys. Pilasters at corners, full entablature around house, small Doric entrance porch with two sets of paired unfluted round wood columns, horseshoe steps granite with iron railing. Eight-panel entrance door with leaded side and fanlight, the latter with an eagle at pivotal center. Rear doorway with sidelights and blind arch over, tympanum of arch carved and with a small fanlight over door proper. Central hall with dividing arch, the part behind the arch larger and containing the open-well three-flight stairway. Older, Adam type mantel with reeded pilasters in E room; marble mantels, sliding doors, floriated ceiling medallions, and windows with hinged panels at bottom (where opening onto porch) in rooms on W side of hall. Built late 18th or early 19th C. Probably remodeled in mid 19th C. House was originally located on sw corner Greene and 7th Sts., facing NNE. Moved to present site in 1929, when a two-story porch and other appurtenances were removed from rear, porch and wing on side were added, and minor int. changes made. Steps and landing at rear, and possibly rear doorway and the dormer windows date from this period. Lafayette was a guest in this house on two occasions. 2 ext. photos (1937); 3 int. photos (1936); 1 photo of sketch of entrance (1936).

Augusta College. See *United States Arsenal.*

Augusta Museum. See *Academy of Richmond County.*

Augusta National Golf Club. See *Fruitlands* and *Ike's Cottage.*

Azalea Cottage GA-272. 2 Indian Creek Rd., facing NNW. Frame with beaded siding, 37' (five-bay front) rectangular, with small projection on E and additions to the rear. One and a half stories, gable roof with dormers, three ext. end chimneys. Three-bay front porch with solid square wooden posts and railing with vertical pickets (⅝'' × 1⅜''). Four-panel entrance door (upper panels arched) with heavy moldings, simple transom and sidelights with rectangular panes. Central hallway, small curving stairway to one side, fanlight door at rear. Adam type mantels, some with carved sunbursts. Sand Hills cottage built 1813, originally located at 2236 Walton Way, facing NNE. Front door mid 19th C., several alterations to rear before 1937. Moved to present site in 1971, when further alterations were made, including changes in rear roof line. Small side porch with combination cast- and wrought-iron work shown in one of the 1936 photos is not part of the present house. 2 ext. photos (1936); 1 data page (1936).

Bennoch House GA-230. 118 Ninth St. (not 119 Eighth St. as originally listed) facing WNW. First story brick, upper stories frame with clapboarding. Six-bay

front, rectangular, 3½ stories. Hipped roof with flared eaves, dormer windows. Two int. chimneys. Doric entablature with triglyphs and mutules, paterae applied to metopes. Balcony (full width of building) with cast-iron railing and brackets.

Four first-floor entrance doors, all with paneled jambs. Door patterns vary, but one with four panels matched the jambs and was evidently original. Dormer windows with louvered fanlights framed by pilasters with open base pediments. Int. divided into two apartments, each with stairways with mahogany handrails and balusters, and each extending from basement to attic. Traditional Federal style, built ca. 1820. Demolished ca. 1954. 1 ext. photo (1936); 2 data pages (1936).

BROAD STREET BUSINESS DISTRICT, 1884

Broad Street Stores, 500 block GA-273. 582–590 Broad St., facing NNE. Brick, standing-seam metal roof. 78 ft. (nine-bay, three-unit front), rectangular, three int. courtyards. Two-and-a-half stories. Gable roof flaring at the eaves, dormer windows, parapets between units and at end walls. Two end chimneys, four int. chimneys (exclusive of those in ells and in rear wing), all integral with parapets. Dormer windows have molded face pilasters and open-base pediments. Brick cornice with brick dentil course, quarter-round masonry units, and molded-edge metal gutter. Second-story windows have carved granite lintels. Balcony with cast-iron railings and brackets across front. Three-unit building (apartments over stores), each unit with courtyard. Connecting rooms in

ell on E side of courtyard, blank wall of adjoining apartment on W side. Balcony, similar to one on street side, full length of ell. Units have side hall plan, delicate and graceful open-well two-flight staircase with continuous rail curved at turns. Bottom floor (except for stair hall, courtyard, and service rooms on E and S sides of courtyard) commercial. Second story contains hallway, two parlors, and other rooms in ell and in rear wing. Principal rooms have traditional Federal style mantels with pilasters, of simple but elegant design. Parlors separated by double sliding doors; walls of rear parlor curved each side of sliding doors to form triangular closets with six-panel doors that curve with wall. Probably built early 19th C. Cast-iron fronts with plate glass installed on first floor in mid or late 19th C. Plate glass since covered with various types of ext. wall coverings. Blinds on upper-floor windows have been removed, as have balconies overlooking street, except at center unit where iron railing has been covered with a sign advertising "EDDIE PEACE—TATTOO ARTIST." Upper floors of center unit still used as residences; upper floors of other units vacant and deteriorating. Living quarters of center unit surprisingly light and airy; courtyard even in its present unkempt state pleasant, with old brick walls, remnants of brick paving, weeds, and vines. Reminiscent of Pieter de Hooch's painting "Courtyard of a Dutch House." 1 ext. photo (1936). Illustrated on p. 92.

Broad Street Stores, 600 block, south side GA-273. 600 block, S side of Broad St., facing NNE. 1884 photo shows buildings of brick, some of brick with stucco, and a few of light-colored masonry which appears to be cut stone. Most had cast-iron fronts on the bottom floor, though a few older ones had not been "modernized." Heights varied from two to three-and-a-half stories; roofs of the older buildings were predominantly gable type with parapet walls between units (the parapets important as fire stops), but there were also flat roofs or roofs concealed behind false fronts, many of the latter with elaborate cornices. One of the two buildings still standing had a mansard roof. Most of the older buildings had louvered blinds at windows and balconies with cast-iron railings overhanging sidewalk. Newer buildings had awnings or canopies which, like the balconies, provided pedestrians with some protection from rain. A foretaste of 20th C. visual pollution in the form of garish signs and of unsightly telegraph lines and poles had already (1884) disfigured buildings and cluttered sidewalks. There is no evidence of trees and parks, which were part of original plan. The most blatant sign was raised on posts, billboard fashion, in front of the second floor of what is now 608–612 Broad St., one of two buildings shown in 1884 photograph that are still standing. Brick, 54 ft. (five-bay front) wide, rectangular, two rear ells with a narrow courtyard between them. Ells are one story, but main rectangular part is two-and-a-half stories, gable roof with front and end parapets, dormer windows. Four end chimneys integral with parapets; there was a cast-iron balcony across the front. Details are similar to those of the Broad Street Stores at 582–590 Broad Street*. Bottom-floor stores have cast-iron fronts. Probably built early 19th C., cast-iron fronts installed during mid or late 19th

C. Since 1936 the chimneys have been lowered, second-story windows and some of first-story plate-glass windows have been boarded up, and balcony has been removed. The other building still standing is the Augusta Hotel (recently closed) on the corner of Broad and Sixth Sts. It is brick with stucco, four bays wide, three-and-a-half stories high, and has a mansard roof with dormer windows. Window frames have segmental pediments supported by console brackets, pediments and brackets formed of sheet metal and sanded to resemble stone. Probably erected shortly before or after the Civil War. Lower slope of mansard roof has been covered with composition shingles; cast-iron balcony that extended across front of building has been removed. False balconies, the railings apparently from the original, have been added to the upper-story windows. Broad St. side of first floor has been projected about 2 ft. toward street and covered with a concave hood roof. Vari-colored brick and a series of picture windows with muntins give this part a pseudo-colonial look that contrasts oddly with the elegant Second Empire style of the original. Other buildings shown in the photographs have been demolished. 2 ext. photos (1884); 1 ext. photo (1936).

Broad Street Stores, 700 block, north side, GA-273. 721–729 Broad St., facing ssw. Buildings brick, of various heights and various types. Two buildings in foreground still retained their complete masonry fronts in 1888. Others had more fashionable cast-iron and plate-glass façades at ground level. Though changes (lower floors painted, single-paned windows substituted for muntined ones,

etc.) had obviously been made, those with masonry fronts retained a unity lacking in the buildings with cast-iron open fronts at ground level and fenestrated masonry above. The older buildings with their gable roofs likewise had a unity with each other that was lost with intrusion of flat-roof and false-front types. Despite garish signs and the aforementioned changes, this section of Broad St., with its trees, its iron balconies, its small paned windows, louvered blinds, and shadow-dappled brick walls, must have been reminiscent of its better days. All buildings shown in the HABS photograph have been demolished or remodeled beyond recognition. 1 ext. photo (1888).

Carnes House (Chafee House) GA-26. 914 Milledge Rd., facing w. Frame, clapboarding beaded except under porch and where replaced. Clapboarding under porch may replace older flush siding or plaster. 38'4" wide (five-bay front), rectangular, irregular wings and additions at rear. One and a half stories plus semi-raised basement (basement fully raised at rear of house). Spraddle roof with dormers, three end chimneys, full-width three-bay front porch, back porch full width except s end enclosed. Porch posts solid, 5½ ins. square, chamfered above railing. Floor-length windows opening onto front porch. Front door Dutch type, with lower part higher than customary, top part with two arched panels (Italianate), lower part with two rectangular panels, all with very heavy moldings. Central hall plan, but generally irregular. Interesting 18th and early 19th C. mantels, brought from other houses and installed here in 20th C.

Separate building housing kitchen and servants' quarters in rear is frame with board-and-batten siding, rectangular, two-story with one-story kitchen ell to front. Gable roof and one int. chimney. Deeply scalloped eaves repeat vertical lines of board-and-batten siding, the total effect being similar to a Downing cottage.

House itself added to and changed many times, its present form that of a Sand Hills cottage. Original part said to have been built before 1784; date not documented. Indigenous Federal, enlarged early 19th C., added to twice during mid 19th C. Servants' house and kitchen mid 19th C. 2 ext. photos (1934); 2 ext. photos (1936); 3 ext. photos, kitchen and garden (1936); 2 int. photos (1934); 4 int. photos (1936); 2 data pages (1936). Illustrated on pp. 88, 162.

Chafee House. See *Carnes House.*

Chew House (Chew-Dearing-Battey House) GA-260. 428 Sixth St., facing wsw. Frame with clapboarding. Five-bay front, probably rectangular, three stories. Two-story tetrastyle porch with full-length round fluted wooden columns. Main door one panel with flat face moldings, the widest of which was decorated with paterae. Lattice design sidelights and transom. Outside moldings of doorframe mitered at corners, but casing between door and sidelights fluted and with corner blocks. Balcony (simple wooden railing with rectangular pickets) extending to and partly supported by columns. Doorway to balcony similar to main entrance, but with blinds and plain rectangular lights in transom and sidelights. Doorframe differs in that, like

door, it is decorated with paterae. Apparently central hall plan.

Greek Revival; mid 19th C. Awkward stucco piers under columns were probably replacements of deteriorated column bases; one-story circular porches added to each side of main porch, these changes before 1937. House demolished ca. 1955. 2 ext. photos (1936); 1 data page (1936). Illustrated on p. 117.

Chew-Dearing-Battey House. See *Chew House.*

Clanton House GA-224. 503 Greene St., facing ssw. Brick; foundation for front porch brick with stucco, T-shaped, stem of T (toward front) five bays wide. Two and a half stories (half-story windows in frieze) over raised basement, gable roof. Two-story-high tetrastyle portico with fluted Greek Doric columns and modified Corinthian entablature. Frieze and architrave repeated in raking cornice of portico. Four unfluted pilasters under portico (int. ones narrower than ext.) flank a two-story recess for first-story and balcony doorways. Wrought-iron railing for front steps and porch with a pattern of pickets, scrolls, and rosettes; porch railing curved outward between columns. Entrance door one panel type with paterae ornamenting wide flat molding which enframed panel. Doorframe with pilaster-type mullions between door and sidelights, the pilasters carrying to the top of and dividing transom. Frame for sidelights and transom ornamented with paterae. Similar doorway at balcony over entrance. Balcony had cast-iron railing and was supported by cast-iron brackets.

Five-bay, two-story rear porch with full-length square wooden

columns, unusual in that it was recessed into NE corner of house. Central hall plan. Four-panel int. doors with molded face trim and corner blocks with carved anthemion motif. Mid 19th C. Demolished ca. 1965. 8 ext. photos (1936); 1 int. photo (1936); 1 data page (1936). Illustrated on p. 115.

College Hill (Harper House) GA-14-69. 2116 Wrightsboro Rd., facing NE. Wood frame with clapboarding, flush siding under porches. Rectangular (seven-bay front), two stories with gable roof and two end chimneys. Across the front is a seven-bay, two-tiered porch with elliptical arches between columns; pickets in railing of second floor arranged in sheaf-of-wheat design, of first floor in diamond design with vertical picket in center of each diamond. One-story porch with shed roof and additions on rear. Double entrance doors with sidelights and transom, muntins of transom arranged in fan pattern. Entrance framed by pilasters with entablature.

Divided central hall, two rooms each side, front and back stairways, front stairway circular. Mantels with reeded pilasters, fluted frieze, and sunbursts. Indigenous Federal, apparently early 19th C. George Walton, signer of the Declaration of Independence, is thought to have had a summer home on this site. Whether he built this house, or whether his house was incorporated into it, or whether this is a different house has not been documented. 11 sheets (1934); 2 ext. photos (1934); 2 int. photos (1934); 2 data pages (1934). Illustrated on p. 55.

Confederate States Powder Works Chimney GA-1101. NE side

of Goodrich St., .3 mi. NW of intersection with W. Broad St. Brick with granite base. Twenty ft. square at bottom, 150 ft. high. Int. dimensions of flue 5 ft. square. Chimney originally rose from within central building of Confederate States Powder Works at Augusta. Lower portion, which was within building, vertical with stucco panels; upper part (115 ft.) tapered except for flare at top. Cornerstone containing documents placed in one of the corners of top coping. Buildings were Industrial Gothic style. Upper, tapered part of chimney is a soaring shaft, rising above its surroundings with powerful simplicity, so inspiring that Gen. George Washington Rains requested that he be buried by it. Request was not carried out, but one of two tablets on chimney bears the following inscription: "George Washington Rains, U.S.M.A., Brigadier General C.S.A., Brevet Major U.S.A., Captain Fourth Artillery, who, under almost insuperable difficulties, erected and successfully operated these powder works, a bulwark of the beleaguered Confederacy." Built 1861–62; designed by C. Shaler Smith, architect, from sketches prepared by C.S.A. Gen. George Washington Rains. Denning and Bowe, Augusta, builders. Demolished (except chimney) ca. 1880. Illustrated on pp. 184, 185.

Courthouse. See *Richmond County Courthouse.*

Zachary Daniels House GA-2112. 448 Greene St., facing N. Brick with wood, marble, and pressed-metal trim. Irregular, except front symmetrical with projecting center pavilion and square cupola over. Five-bay front, two-and-

a-half stories, mansard roof with dormers, five end chimneys. Bracketed cornices, marble quoins, fanciful arches, open-arms steps. Center pavilion flanked by triangular bay windows at first floor. Double entrance door with transom, central hall plan. Very fine period woodwork, hardwood mantels with diverse patterns, some with mirrored and shelved overmantels. Ornamental iron fence at front. Second Empire style, ca. 1891 (a very late date for this style). 1 ext. photo (1980). Illustrated on p. 194.

First Presbyterian Church GA-2113. 642 Telfair St., facing NNE. Brick with stucco scored. Rectangular, 67'6" (three-bay front) × 105'8" (six-bay sides) with additions at rear. Gable roof with crenellated parapet. Square, central projecting buttressed tower with octagonal drum, belfry, and spire. Wheel windows with wooden tracery over entrance. Main entrance arched, flanked by entrances with windows over; windows arched and with Y-tracery, clear glass in lattice-type muntins, int. blinds. Vestibule with rounded stairs and balcony over. Auditorium with vaulted plaster ceiling; main vault elliptical, cross vaults appear to be catenary. Original box pews.

Wooden picket fence mounted on low (approx. 9 in. high) brick wall. Granite posts at 20'6" on center. Rails 3½" × 7¾", top tapered to shed water; pickets 1¾ in. diameter, 4'6" high.

Built 1809–12; Robert Mills, architect. Church originally traditional Federal style. Remodeled to Romanesque style 1892, at which time the buttresses, crenellations, and Romanesque details were added. Windows formerly typical

six-over-six type with separate lunettes over, set in blind arches. Openings for lunettes and windows were combined to permit installation of Romanesque arched windows with Y-tracery. Tower was extended upward, and base of spire simplified to adapt to the newer style. Int. likewise changed to conform with Romanesque Revival style, the installation of suspended vaulted ceiling and arched windows being the major changes. Ironically, the ceiling, with its powerful catenarylike curves is more suggestive (in appearance, if not in structure) of Mills's work at its best than are his own drawings (still kept by the church) for the building.

The Presbyterian Church in the U.S. (Southern Presbyterian) was organized here in 1861 during the pastorate of the Reverend R. W. Wilson, father of President Woodrow Wilson. 1 ext. photo (1980). Illustrated on p. 76.

Fruitlands GA-252. 2604 Washington Rd., facing NNE. Concrete (lime-sand-gravel mix), 50' (three-bay front) × 55', two stories. Pyramidal roof sloping to cupola. Two int. chimneys. Two-story porch completely around house, its roof integral with but flatter than the main roof. Full-height square wooden columns. First-floor windows with heavy shutters, second-floor windows with louvered blinds. Four-panel entrance door with sidelights; door to second story with sidelights and transom. Central hall plan with circular stair in alcove to side. Indigenous Greek Revival, begun 1854, finished before 1857; D. Redmond, original owner, designer, and builder. Drawings of house and descriptions of its design and construction in *The Southern*

Cultivator, vol. 15, no. 8 (August 1857), pp. 242–45; also in several contemporary plan books, including *The House: A Pocket Manual of Rural Architecture* (New York: Fowler and Wells, 1859), pp. 78–83. According to those descriptions and drawings, main entrance was originally by way of a broad flight of steps to second-story porch. Columns were "of solid pine, one foot in diameter, turned tapering, and bored entirely through lengthwise to prevent shrinkage." Main rooms were on second floor, and "two large halls, fifty-three by ten feet, run directly through the building, securing perfect ventilation. . . . The stairs are removed to one side of their usual position in the halls, leaving the latter entirely free and unobstructed." Downstairs were dining room, pantry, fruit room, icehouse, office, bathing room—"in short, all the working rooms." From the description of the planning process, it is apparent that the house was designed primarily for comfort and convenience, and that the Greek Revival character resulted from the frank expression of climate, function, and structure.

Fruitland Nurseries originated here at about the time the house was built, and exotic shrubs and trees, particularly the avenue of magnolia trees planted in 1858, still enhance the grounds, now the Augusta National Golf Course, where the Masters' Tournament is held each spring. The old house is used as the clubhouse, minor changes having been made over the years. 2 ext. photos (1937). Illustrated on p. 113.

457 Greene Street. See *House, 457 Greene Street.*

Greene Street Historic District GA-269. Greene St. from Gordon Hwy. to Augusta Canal Bridge. Ten-block landscaped boulevard containing fine examples of 19th C. architecture. 83 ext. photos (1979); 6 data pages (1980).

Harper House. See *College Hill.*

Harper-Cohen House GA-221. 2150 Battle Rd., facing NE. Frame with clapboarding, flush siding under porch and on sides of dormer windows. T-shaped, the stem of the T being one and one-half stories parallel to the street, and abutting a two-story part (the top of the T). Eight-bay front. Gable roofs, the one and one-half story part being spraddle gable type with dormer windows, and with porches front and back. One int., two ext. chimneys. Front porch seven bays with slender Doric-type columns, unusual in that the moldings representing the capitals are several inches below the top of the columns. Irregular plan. Exceptionally graceful picket fence, copied from one at Mt. Vernon, surrounds the grounds. Indigenous, unusual combination of plantation plain style and plantation cottage types. Probably early 19th C., the two parts apparently built at different times. 2 ext. photos (1936); 1 data page (1936).

Harris-Pearson-Walker House (White House) GA-14-7. 1822 W. Broad St., facing NNE. Frame with beaded siding. 41'10" (five-bay front), rectangular. Two stories, gambrel roof, two end chimneys, one of which is laid in Flemish bond. Two-tiered, five- (unequal) bay porch in front; two-tiered, three- (unequal) bay porch with a room at each end on back; both

porches covered by main roof. Staircase to second floor on back porch. Cornice with modillions front and back. Eighteen-light windows with raised panel shutters. Double entrance doors, each with eight raised panels and with three lights at the top, framed by fluted pilasters and entablature with pulvinated frieze and modillion cornice. Central hall plan, ceiling of hall arched, no int. stairway. Plaster walls with paneled wainscot. Mantels 18th C. types, the one in the principal room having shouldered architrave and pulvinated frieze, a dentil band and a Greek fret. Attic plastered and finished.

Post-colonial, precise date of construction in doubt. When house was restored, it was thought to have been built between 1760 and 1780, and restoration and furnishings were for a house of that period. Further research has revealed that ca. 1797 is the probable date of construction.

Restoration plans were begun in 1956, and the official opening held in 1964. Changes made before restoration included enclosing back porch, enclosing second story of front porch, enlarging remaining porch columns (original columns were left inside the later ones), adding a rear ell, and presumably installing a circular stairway in enclosed back porch. The additions were removed, and the house changed back to its original form during the course of restoration, though the modillion cornice and the corner stiles, which may have been the result of mid 19th C. remodeling, were left.

A Revolutionary War battle took place here in which American forces under Col. (later Gen.) Elijah Clarke attacked the English on September 14, 1780. The battle was fought intermittently until the morning of September 18, when the American forces were forced to retreat, leaving twenty-nine wounded patriots. Of these, the English under Col. Thomas Brown hanged thirteen as spies and turned the remainder over to the Indians for torture. According to local legend, the staircase of this house was used as a gallows from which the thirteen were hanged. House museum. 8 sheets (1934); 3 ext. photos (1934); 2 int. photos (1936); 2 data pages. Illustrated on pp. 42, 43.

High Gate GA-266. 820 Milledge Rd., facing wsw. Frame with clapboarding, H-shaped, eight bays wide. Central unit one and one-half stories with dormer windows, wings two stories. Roofs gable, hipped, shed, and flat, the latter type with balustrades. Three int. chimneys, one end chimney. Front and side porches have heavy square, Doric-type columns; back porch has slender wooden columns with wide cove molding capitals, a unique stairway with curved silhouette and arched ceiling over, and large-scale adjustable louvers. Windows and eaves of two-story wings have Italianate paired brackets. Irregular plan; varying floor levels. Old Adam-type mantels with sunbursts, also marble mantels of later date. Handsome iron fence in front with high gates. Oldest part (north wing with the back porch) ca. 1810, indigenous except for later alterations. South wing built in 1850s; Goodrich, architect and builder. Other additions and changes at various times, mostly between 1850 and 1880. Fascinating combination of indig-

enous, Greek Revival, and Italianate styles. 1 ext. photo (1936); 2 data pages (1937). Illustrated on p. 45.

House, 467 Greene Street (Ironwork) GA-263. Facing ssw. Frame with clapboarding, apparently rectangular, three-bay front, two stories. One-story, three-bay veranda across the front, the veranda having ornamental cast-iron columns, frieze, brackets, fringe, and railings. Two entrance doors, each with sidelights and transom, flank a central window. Mid 19th C. Demolished 1965. 2 ext. photos (1934); 1 data page (1934).

House, 261 Watkins Street GA-265. Facing ssw. Frame with clapboarding, brick basement, standing seam metal roof. Rectangular, three-bay front, one story over raised basement, gable roof with flared eaves, one end chimney with corbel top. Fanciful frieze of scroll-saw cutouts applied flat against building, scroll-saw work with curvilinear motifs applied over heads of windows. Corner stiles with raised panels, one panel wide, eighteen high. Steps, small entrance porch, and picket fence evidently replacements, not up to quality of rest of house. Curious details, seemingly without precedent. Probably mid 19th C. Destroyed ca. 1939. 1 ext. photo (1936); 1 data page (1936). Illustrated on p. 166.

Ike's Cottage GA-2114. Grounds of Augusta National Golf Course, 2604 Washington Rd., facing s. Brick, rectangular with wings, five-bay front (nine including wings), one-and-a-half stories, gable roof with dormers, 1 int. chim-

ney. Recessed front porch with three-bay projecting portico with square columns and figure of American eagle in pediment. Cottage type simplified 20th C. Classical Revival style, 1953. Vacation home of President Dwight D. Eisenhower. 1 ext. photo (1980). Illustrated on p. 218.

Institute of Art. See *Ware-Sibley-Clark House.*

Ironwork. See *House, 467 Greene Street.*

Jail GA-264. sw corner Watkins and Elbert Sts. Brick with slate roof, rectangular, three-bay front, four stories, hipped roof, two end chimneys. High brick wall with piers, both with corbel tops. Built 1819. Demolished ca. 1938. 1 ext. photo (1936). See also *Old Jail.*

Kilpatrick House. See *Appleby-Kilpatrick House.*

Mackay House. See *Harris-Pearson-Walker House.*

Mayor White House GA-226. 2260 Walton Way, facing N. Frame with clapboarding. 52'6'' (five-bay front), rectangular with irregular additions at rear, two and one-half stories, gable roof with large dormer at rear, flat roofs over porches, three end chimneys within ext. walls. Hexastyle Greek Doric porch, giant order, with simplified entablature and roof balustrade with combination X and Greek cross motif across front. Similar porch, except that it projects two bays, across back. Full-length windows and railing with X-cross design on front porch. Entrance doorway with sidelights and transom. Balcony with Chinese lattice design railing, balcony supported by console brackets. Central hall plan. Plaster ceiling cornice with Greek fret in soffit.

Quaint two-story brick outbuilding with one-story wing. Two-story part has gable roof with parapet; one-story wing has flat roof and parapet. No chimney. Probably former kitchen and servants' house.

Greek Revival, ca. 1840. Many changes and additions, including porch at rear. Now used as branch library for the Augusta Libraries System. 1 ext. photo (1936); 1 data page (1936).

Meadow Garden GA-2100. Site occupies block between Nelson and Fenwick Sts., behind stores on NW side of Thirteenth St. House faces SE, or the rear of those stores. Frame with clapboarding, wood-shingle roof. Rectangular six-bay front, built in two stages; older part to SW, adjoining newer part at a higher (two steps) floor level. Older part 18' (three-bay front), newer part 25'2" (three-bay front), total width 43'2". Older part spraddle roof with dormers, one int. chimney, porches front and back. Newer part similar except no back porch. Roof continuous over both sections. Four-bay, full-width front porch; SW part two steps lower than the rest. Turned wooden columns with square bases (8" × 8") to balustrade height, round and tapered above with Doric-type capitals. Two ext. doors, the one to the older part with ten raised panels: three vertical bottom panels, two horizontal panels below lock rail, three vertical panels above lock rail, and two horizontal panels at top. Central hall plan. Chamber on SW side has Colonial-type mantel with pulvinated frieze,

overmantel with raised panels, and ceiling cornice with fret molding. Restored kitchen with fireplace in basement. Indigenous, original part late 18th C., newer part early 19th C. Old photos show broken roof line at front, and dormer windows on the newer part only. George Walton, signer of the Declaration of Independence, died here February 2, 1804. House museum. 4 ext. photos (1934, 1936); 2 int. photos (1936); 2 data pages (1936). Illustrated on pp. 45, 46.

Medical College. See *Old Medical College.*

Montrose (Reid-Jones-Carpenter House) GA-227. 2249 Walton Way, facing SSW. Frame with narrow (3 in. exposed face) clapboarding, basement brick with stucco. Five-bay front, rectangular, wings each side, recessed rear porch. One and one-half stories over raised basement, gable roof with pediments, six int. end chimneys. Two-story tetrastyle Corinthian portico with full-length fluted columns resting on ground floor. Entablature carried completely around house and up pediments; half-story windows in frieze. Doric pilasters at junction of portico and house, and at corners of house. Full-length windows in front. At entrance a one-panel door with enriched moldings, sidelights and transom, all enframed with pilasters and entablature; smaller pilasters between door and sidelights. Divided central hall plan, open-well stair with rounded return, double parlor one side. Symmetrically molded trim with foliated corner blocks, black marble mantels with Ionic pilasters, original chandeliers, fleurated ceiling medallions.

Detached octagonal brick

kitchen has peaked roof with finial. Classical privy, square, frame with clapboarding, pilasters at corners, pyramidal roof. Int. walls plaster.

Greek Revival, 1849. Postbellum home of Charles Colcock Jones, Jr., distinguished lawyer, author, historian; possibly best known for his letters, recorded in *The Children of Pride*, compiled by Robert Manson Myers (New Haven: Yale University Press, 1972). Now the Allen Fuqua Center for young people. 4 ext. photos (1936); 2 int. photos (1936); 1 data page (1936). Illustrated on p. 105.

Murphy House. See *Old Government House.*

Oertel House GA-297. 638 Greene St. (previously incorrectly listed 638 Telfair St.), facing NNE. Brick, five-bay front, rectangular, two stories over raised basement. Flat roof with parapet and corbel brick cornice under; cast-iron insets (anthemion motif) in parapet. Four end chimneys flush with ext. walls. Windows and doorways with marble lintels. Two-tiered five-bay porch with square columns across rear. Front steps and stoop with wrought-iron railing, cast- and wrought-iron insets. At entrance a one-panel door with enriched moldings, transom, and sidelights. Pilasters between door and sidelights, and on each side of sidelights. Central hall divided by three-centered arched opening, open stair with rounded turn. Symmetrically molded trim with foliated corner blocks, black marble mantels. Iron fence, same pattern as stair rails, in front. Simplistic Federal style, early 19th C. Ends of rear porch enclosed and a room added to rear before 1937. Demolished 1963.

3 ext. photos (1934); 4 ext. photos (1936); 2 int. photos (1934); 1 data page (1937).

Old Government House (Murphy House) GA-268. 432 Telfair St., facing NNE. Brick with stucco, 60′5″ (five-bay front), rectangular, wings to rear and side, main body of house has gable roof with parapets, flat roof over veranda, roofs of wings and additions vary. Two stories, six end chimneys flush with ext. walls, two-tiered porch between octagonal wings at rear. Parapet with cast-iron panels, anthemion motif, cornice below. One-story veranda in front, with cast-iron columns, frieze, brackets, roof fringe, and railing at roof and floor. Entrance doorway with sidelights and transom, enframed by pilasters with entablature. Similar but not identical doorway to roof over veranda. Central hall plan with double parlor one side. Rear door with fanlight. Open-well stairway with rounded return. Heavy plaster cornice moldings, parlor cornice with fleurated plaster border. Marble mantels. Gold-leaf pier mirror with matching window cornices, apparently made specifically for parlor.

Iron fence with granite gate posts. Built 1801 as courthouse. Remodeled into residence 1821. Wings added and further remodeling mid 19th C. Picture molding added before 1937. Rear porch enclosed after 1937. 2 ext. photos (1934); 1 ext. photo (1936); 2 int. photos (1934); 2 data pages (1936).

Old Jail GA-264. sw corner Watkins and Elbert Sts. Brick with standing-seam metal roof. Rectangular, two stories, lower story three-bay front, upper story two-bay front. Gable roof with parapet, one int. chimney. Wall buttresses, three in front wall. High, free-standing brick wall with arched gateway, wall integral with wall of building. Pierced brick gable ventilators. Said to have been built about 1740. One of the few remaining Colonial buildings in Georgia at the time the survey was made. Was used as kitchen for the later jail, which was built in 1819. Both jails demolished ca. 1938. 2 ext. photos (1936); 1 data page (1936). Illustrated on p. 18. See also *Jail*.

Old Medical College GA-14-70. SE corner Telfair and Sixth Sts., facing NNE. Brick with stucco. Rectangular with addition to rear. 77′4″ (first story one-bay front, second story seven-bay) × 70′4″. Corner bays project slightly at sides. Low-sloping pyramidal roof with dome and parapet. Heroic hexastyle portico with Greek Doric columns (stucco over brick) and simplified entablature. Belt course under portico sloped to form pediment with bracket light over entrance. Heavy double entrance doors with one raised panel on ext., three panels on int. face. Vestibule with symmetrical divided stairway. Central hall with double doors, sidelights and full semicircular fanlight at each end of hall. Rotunda on second floor lighted by dome with skylight.

Lattice brick wall with wrought-iron gates surrounds property. Greek Revival, 1835; Charles B. Cluskey, architect. Exhibition hall (formerly dissecting room with surrounding observation gallery) added shortly after building was completed. Stucco originally scored. Rotunda, originally open to first floor, has been closed at second-floor level. Original circular stairway has been removed.

Old prints show wooden fence instead of present brick wall. Other changes minor. Building used as medical college until 1915. 14 sheets (1934); 2 ext. photos (1934); 2 int. photos (1934); 2 data pages (1934). Illustrated on p. 123.

Phinizy House GA-223. 519 Greene St., facing SSW. Brick, rectangular, five-bay front, three stories over raised basement, hipped roof. Corbel brick entablature at top of second story. One end chimney. Windows, except at third floor, have granite lintels incised with triple oval relief. Greek Doric tetrastyle entrance porch with simplified entablature, and with entrance to basement beneath. Horseshoe stone steps with bull-nose tread and with wrought-iron railing. Porch railing wrought iron with spiral and anthemion motifs. Entrance with sidelights and full elliptical fanlight; engaged Doric columns between door and sidelights, all set within an elliptical archway with granite jambs, archivolt, and key and spring stones. Similar door to porch roof deck. Central hall plan. Iron fence in front. Transitional house, late Federal with some Greek Revival features, ca. 1835–40.

Tiffany glass installed in front doorways, and mantels and stairway changed about 1900. Third floor and porch on w side added before 1926. Original chimneys removed and replaced by one very large chimney, and wing (replacing porch) added to the w side after 1937. House used as residence until 1926, after which it was used for varied purposes, including a funeral home and a clubhouse. Interiors have been remodeled accordingly. 3 ext. photos (1936); 2 data pages (1936).

Platt House (Platt-Fleming-Walker-d'Antignac House) GA-262. 453 Greene St., facing ssw. Brick, lattice brick foundation under porch. 52'8'' (five-bay front), rectangular with rear ell. Three stories, hipped roof, five end chimneys flush with ext. walls. Corbel brick string course at bottom of third-floor windows, granite lintels over doors and windows, full-width porch with ornamental cast-iron columns, frieze, brackets, and railing. Half windows (six-light) in top story, full-length windows on porch. Entrance door with leaded bevel glass sidelights and transom. Central hall plan, since changed. Mid 19th C. Third floor may be an early addition. Bevel glass and mantels late 19th or early 20th C. replacements; also changes in hall and stairway. Converted to lawyers' offices 1971. 2 ext. photos (1936); 1 data page (1936).

Reid-Jones-Carpenter House. See *Montrose.*

Richmond County Courthouse (Courthouse) GA-239. s side of Greene St., between Fifth and Sixth Sts., facing NNE. Brick with stucco scored. Rectangular central block with nine-bay front and wings. Two stories over raised basement. Hipped roof with balustrade and with center pediment on N side. Tower, progressing from square base to octagonal belfry to domical roof and crowned with statue of Justice rising from center of roof. One-story, three-bay Ionic porch (with end columns paired) at entrances on N and s sides. Windows of principal floor within blind arches with carved stone archivolts; carved stone lintels over windows. Stone belt courses at floor level of main

floor; Ionic entablature at top of wall. Iron fence mounted on granite base and with granite posts surrounded grounds. Traditional Federal style, ca. 1811. Originally brick, stuccoed before 1936. Wings and pediment added before 1936. Demolished 1958. 3 ext. photos (1936); 1 int. photo (1936); 1 data page. Illustrated on p. 34.

Sacred Heart Church GA-2115. NE corner Greene and Thirteenth Sts., entrance on Greene St., facing ssw. Brick with stone trim, basement random ashlar with raised joints. Standing-seam metal roof. Cruciform plan, round towers at front, three-bay 45 ft. porch between towers. Five-bay aisles with chamfered buttresses with stone finials, polygonal apse. One story over raised basement. Gable roof (hipped over apse and with dome at crossing) with gable parapets; brick modillion corbel table under eaves. Two end chimneys, the shafts emerging at the center of the transept gable parapets.

Projecting stone porch with three arched portals, the center portal larger and accentuated by a gabled parapet with flanking tourelles. Three arched widows (the center one stilted) set in deep embrasures in the wall of the front façade over portals. All windows leaded stained glass, large windows with stone tracery. Towers with round belfries and flared conical spires. Round turrets with stone finials at intersection of towers with front of church; also on each side of transept façades. Spires, turrets, and dome surmounted by crosses.

Transepts with three arched windows in façade (center one stilted), set within a blind arch. Wheel windows over. Gauged masonry work: brick moldings, brick

dentils, brick in sawtooth patterns, brick in checker patterns, and brick laid diagonally (sawtooth face) in turrets with resulting pattern of interlaced spirals.

Varicolored marble mosaic (not representational) in tympanum over portals. Portals splayed with a series of Romanesque Corinthian columns separated by nook shafts. Carved archivolts over. Double entrance doors.

Tunnel-vaulted wooden ceiling in nave with cusped cross arches, the arches supported by columns projecting from upper walls and terminating underneath with pendants at ceiling line of side aisles. Clerestory windows, dome at crossing.

Victorian version of Byzantine and Romanesque architecture, some of the features apparently adapted from Ely Cathedral. Begun 1898, dedicated 1900; designed by Brother Otten. Iron fence mounted on low brick wall with molded brick coping.

Probably the most intricate masonry to be found in Georgia; it transcended craft to become an art form. Interesting adaptations of Romanesque stone moldings translated into brickwork. Built as a Roman Catholic church, the building has been deconsecrated and abandoned. 1 ext. photo (1980). Illustrated on p. 206.

St. Paul's Church GA-241. NE corner Reynolds and Sixth Sts., facing ssw. Brick, Flemish bond, with cast-stone trim. Rectangular, projecting entrance tower, annex toward rear on w side. Three-bay front, one story, gable roof. Square brick tower, octagonal wooden belfry with arched openings and Ionic columns at each corner. Octagonal drum over belfry, with dome and lantern surmounted by cross. Tetrastyle portico with Greek Doric columns and Roman Doric entablature, the middle bay of the portico containing the base of the tower. Main entrance in base of tower, side entrances open into narthex behind tower. Entrance doors recessed within brick wall arches with Gibbes surrounds. Arched windows over central door, cartouches over flanking doors. Double doors with half-columns and entablatures. Narthex with stairs to balcony. Nave with elliptical paneled ceiling, paired Corinthian pilasters along wall. Arched stained-glass windows. Apse with elliptical ceiling and Palladian stained-glass windows.

Brick wall (originally with stucco) with corbel brick coping and wrought-iron gates encloses grounds of church and cemetery. Church building traditional Federal, built 1919 to replace a similar building erected in 1820; John Land, original architect-builder; H. T. E. Wendell, architect for the rebuilding. Ext. with the exception of minor changes a replica of the original; int. quite different. 1 ext. photo (1934); 2 data pages (1934).

St. Paul's Parish Cemetery GA-231. NE corner intersection of Reynolds and Sixth Sts. Brick wall (with traces of original stucco) between cemetery and street. Wall three withes thick, five withes at piers, corbel brick coping. Wall height varies from 4 to slightly over 6 ft. at gate. Iron gate with square pickets and cast finials, 9'9'' to top of highest finial. Gate leads directly to entrance to St. Paul's Church (GA-241), which was established at this site in 1750. Interesting markers and epitaphs mark the graves of Geor-

gia citizens and leaders from colonial times to the present. 5 ext. photos (1936); 1 data page (1936).

Sibley Mills GA-2116. NE side of Goodrich St., .25 mi. NW of intersection with Broad St. Brick, roughly T-shaped (530' × 80') with stem of T to rear, thirty-three structural bays, two openings per bay except one at center bay. Four stories, flat roof with crenellated parapet, center pavilion three structural bays wide, five stories high, with twin seven-story towers each side of center (entrance) bay. Towers with crenellated parapets, finials each corner. Main entrance porch brick, one bay, arched. Pavilions (one structural bay wide) each end with similar porches. Intermediate pavilions (two bays wide) with decorative parapets and finials. Flat buttresses between structural bays carried above roof line as higher and heavier merlons. Segmental arched windows. Industrial Gothic Revival style, said to have been modeled on the Confederate States Powder Works buildings which previously occupied site. 1880. Numerous additions to rear and sides. Windows in main parts of building since bricked up. Confederate Powder Works chimney★ remains in front of building. 1 photo (1980). Illustrated on p. 186.

United States Arsenal GA-251. Bound by Arsenal St. (W), Buford St. (N), Fanning St. (E); built around a quadrangle enclosed W by Fanning Hall and high (approximately eighteen ft.) brick walls with embrasures; N by the same wall and by one side of Rains Hall; E by the front of Rains Hall, Payne Hall, and the President's House,

these with a wrought-iron fence (the fence mounted on a brick wall, total height over ten ft.) between buildings; and S by side of the President's House and the old kitchen, mess hall, and stables. All buildings are brick painted, with stone or stucco trim. Kitchen, mess hall, and stables are one story and have gable roofs; other buildings have hipped roofs with parapets.

Fanning Hall rectangular, two stories, the Arsenal St. front eight bays with a three-bay, one-story porch; the quadrangle front five bays with a fanlight entrance door enframed by a blind arch.

Rains Hall facing E, rectangular with additions to rear. Three-bay front, two stories, three-bay, two-tiered porch with unfluted Doric-type columns; first-floor columns brick with stucco, second-story columns wooden. Side hall plan.

Payne Hall rectangular with center pavilions both fronts. Pavilion on Fanning St. front with splayed sides; pavilion facing quadrangle rectangular. Fanning St. pavilion with open arched porch at first floor, two bays each side of pavilion, three bays under porch. Cartouche over center arch, with roundel over that. Pavilion on quadrangle side has triple window set in segmental arched opening, three bays each side.

President's House, facing E, rectangular, additions to sides and rear. Main body of house three-bay front, two stories high. Four-bay, two-tiered porch, S bay being a later addition in the form of a side porch. Columns similar to those on Rains Hall.

Shop building, within quadrangle and facing S, square with additions to rear. Three-bay front, one story. Heavy pilasters at corners, segmental arched windows, entrance door set within blind arch.

Simplistic Federal, built 1827–29, except shop, which was built later in 19th C. Fanning Hall was built as the enlisted men's barracks, Rains Hall as officers' quarters. Payne Hall has been commissary, storehouse, and headquarters building, with a prison in the semiraised basement. President's House was originally the commandant's house.

Fanning Hall had a seven-bay two-tiered porch on the Arsenal St. side, this changed since 1937. Rains Hall and President's House were almost identical when built. The three-bay, two-tiered porches were added about 1840; numerous additions since.

Shop originally had double doors with a semicircular transom over, this changed since 1936. Kitchen, mess hall, and stable have been converted into garages and storage rooms. Complex now part of Augusta College. 6 ext. photos (1936); 3 data pages (1936).

Ware-Sibley-Clark House GA-2128. 506 Telfair St., facing NNE. Frame with clapboarding; front façade flush siding; basement brick, Flemish bond with stone trim. Rectangular except two full-height (three stories) bay windows flanking entrance. 57'2" (seven-bay front) by 44'2". Two and one-half stories over raised basement. Hipped roof with dormers and flared eaves. Four int. end chimneys. Fluted Doric pilasters on stone pedestals (pedestals full height of basement) flanking bay windows; also at ext. corners of bay windows. Doric entablature with medallions on metopes. Ext. window trim molded, with corner blocks. Moldings to simulate panels with concave corners between

first- and second-story windows, front façade only. Heavy raised panel shutters at basement windows, louvered blinds at other windows. Three-bay, three-tiered entrance porch, bowed front. Stone columns, Tuscan order at basement level, fluted Doric columns (wooden) at first and second floors. Dormer with pilasters and broken base pediment, and door with fanlight over porches.

Horseshoe steps of stone with iron pickets and mahogany hand rail lead to first-floor entrance porch. Entrance doorway six-paneled (panels wih concave corners), leaded sidelights and fanlight. Molded face pilasters each side of door and of sidelights, moldings repeated in archivolt, which has carved wooden "keystone." Similar door to second-story porch.

Central hall plan, the hall divided by elliptical arch with reeded pilasters and soffit. Rear door with fan and sidelights similar to but of simpler design than front door. Four-story elliptical flying stairway placed to one side of hallway, leaving axis uninterrupted. Parlors on E side connected by sliding doors with extremely wide and ornate fanlight. Molded door and window trim with ornamental corner blocks. One Adam-type mantel with pilasters, egg-and-dart trim, carved sunbursts; other mantels replacements. Attic story has vaulted ceilings.

High iron fence on stone coping terminating at brick walls on each side. Design of brick walk repeating curves of steps and being of same material as sidewalk produces a strong interrelation of house to street. Traditional Federal style with Adamesque details, built 1818. Architect unknown,

but house has been attributed both to Daniel Pratt and to Gabriel Manigault. Manigault died several years before this house was built, but there are similarities to the Charleston house he built for his brother, Joseph Manigault: the basic concept, the orientation (the Manigault entrance was originally from N), the unusual plan, some of the details, though not the restraint.

Rear porch overlooking garden has been replaced with a deck; a separate octagonal (or hexagonal) kitchen has been removed, and minor int. changes have been made over the years. 8 sheets (1936); 1 ext. photo (1934); 7 ext. photos (1936); 8 int. photos (1936). Illustrated on pp. 33, 34, 35.

261 Watkins Street. See *House, 261 Watkins Street.*

White House. See *Harris-Pearson-Walker House.*

White, Mayor, House. See *Mayor White House.*

Woodrow Wilson Boyhood Home GA-2117. 419 Seventh St., facing E. Brick with stone window and door sills and lintels. Rectangular, rear ell including two-story kitchen and servants' house. Five-bay front, two stories, gable roof, four end chimneys. Three-bay one-story porch with Doric columns and pilasters, and a flat roof with balustrade. First-floor windows in front are floor length. Entrance with sidelights and transom, central hall plan. Two-story brick carriage house and stable. Built ca. 1840. Kitchen and servants' house was originally separate, possibly connected by covered walkway. Picket fence and blinds since removed; minor int. changes.

Typical of substantial conservative architecture of the period. Home of President Woodrow Wilson 1858–70. 1 ext. photo (1980). Illustrated on p. 160.

Woman's Club GA-267. 825 Greene St., facing ssw. Frame with clapboarding, five-bay front, rectangular, one and one-half stories over raised basement gable roof with dormers and with integral lean-to (salt-box type) on back, four end chimneys.

Small entrance porch supported on two brick piers and with two square wooden columns at first floor. Most-used entrance appears to have been at basement level. Central hall plan. Int. with molded wooden cornices and wooden wainscot, the latter consisting of two wide boards.

Brick wall at sides of lot, wrought-iron fence with lattice iron gate in front. Architecture clean and simple, of a type that could have been built from the late 18th C. to the mid 19th C. Probably built early 19th C. House originally set close to the ground; later raised onto a high basement and dormer windows added. Demolished 1957. 2 ext. photos (1937); 2 int. photos (1936); 1 data page (1936).

Augusta Vicinity

Richmond County (123)

Glascock House GA-250. E side old Savannah Rd. (Ga. Hwy. 56) about 100 yds. s of intersection with Lumpkin Rd. House probably faced w. Frame with clapboarding (beaded?), front façade with beaded siding laid flat. Five-bay front, rectangular, two sto-

ries, gable roof, two end chimneys. Five-bay, one-story porch with smaller three-bay second-story porch over. Slender turned columns, Doric type. Double six-panel entrance doors with fanlight, framed by reeded pilasters and archivolt. Similar door to second-story porch. Central hall plan. Built before 1791. Apparently second-story porch originally extended across entire front. An ell projecting slightly to the side was probably an addition. Demolished about 1945. According to a marker on the site, George Washington, on his tour of the South, was met here by local officials, who escorted him into Augusta on the morning of May 18, 1791. 2 ext. photos (1936); 1 data page (1936).

Harper House. See *College Hill,* Augusta.

Barnesville Vicinity

Lamar County (86)

Gachet House GA-14-121. N side of Hwy. 18 at Milners Crossroads, 4 mi. w of Barnesville, 2.75 mi. w of intersection with U.S. Hwy. 341. Frame with clapboarding, flush siding under porch, 41′6″ (five-bay front) × 40′, two stories, plantation plain style with shed rooms on rear, porch between shed rooms on front, semi-detached kitchen, two ext. end chimneys, one ext. chimney at side of shed room, three-bay front porch with square tapered columns, ornamental flat balusters, fascia cut to resemble dentil blocks under cornice crown molding; central hall plan. Wellhouse and kitchen have decorative cornice similar to that on house. In-

digenous, built 1823. Kitchen originally may have been detached and located farther from house. Lafayette visited the owner, a native of France, at this house March 19, 1825. 3 sheets (1934); 2 ext. photos (1934); 2 data pages (1934). Recorded in 1934 as in Pike County. Illustrated on p. 24.

Braselton Vicinity

Jackson County (79)

Cochran House GA-14-23. S side Ga. Hwy. 124, 5.8 mi. E of intersection with Ga. Hwy. 53 in Braselton, orientation unknown. Square, hewn logs with dovetailed corners. Piers and chimney fieldstone, roof hand-split shingles. Rectangular, one side one bay, one side three bays, one opening one end, no openings other end. One and one-half stories, gable roof, two end chimneys. Two rooms each floor, divided by stairway. Built late 18th C., dismantled ca. 1945. Used as headquarters by Gen. Andrew Jackson in 1812 when blazing the Jackson Trail, again in 1814 and 1815 when he was in charge of the Tennessee Volunteers, who protected settlers from Indians. 2 sheets (1934); 2 ext. photos (1936); 1 data page (1936). Illustrated on pp. 18, 19.

Brunswick Vicinity

Glynn County (64)

Elizafield Plantation Sugar Works GA-2118. Grounds of Georgia Youth Estate Incorporated. Entrance to grounds N side of Ga. Hwy. 99, about 12 mi. N of Brunswick, .6 mi. NE of intersection of Hwy. 99 and U.S. Hwy. 95. Ruins of two buildings, both tabby. Northernmost (NNE) building octagonal, sides varying from 15′7″ to 16′3″, 10 in. thick. One window or one door per side, alternating, except no opening on northerly side. T-shaped building (only footings remain of head of T) about 14 ft. s of other building. Stem of T about 43 ft. long, 25 ft. wide. Four windows on easterly side, one door on northerly side, westerly wall nearly gone. For complete archaeological description see *Georgia's Disputed Ruins*, edited by E. Merton Coulter (Chapel Hill: University of North Carolina Press, 1937), pp. 203–13, where it is proved fairly conclusively that these are ruins of a sugar mill, not a Spanish mission. Erroneously listed as Santo Domingo Mission of Talaje in previous catalog. 1 sheet (1934); 2 ext. photos (1934); 3 ext. photos (1936); 2 data pages (1936).

Santo Domingo Mission of Talaje. See *Elizafield Plantation Sugar Works.*

Campbellton

See *Fairburn Vicinity.*

Carters
Murray County (107)

Carter's Quarters GA-173. Carters, w side of Old Hwy. 411, 1 mi. s of junction with Ga. Hwy. 282. Original part of house faces s. Wood frame with clapboarding, flush siding under porch, fieldstone foundation wall laid without mortar. Original structure rectangular, three-bay front, two

stories, gable roof, two end chimneys. One-story lean-to across back, one-story porch across front with scalloped frieze board and six chamfered posts, unequally spaced. Two entrance doors on front. Exquisitely simple stairway with square pickets, design of handrailing and newel post subtly interrelated. Mantel with segmental arched opening, pilasters, and center panel, similar to one in the Vann House* at Spring Place. Original part of house plantation plain style, built by John Martin (who was half-Cherokee) in what was then (very early 19th C.) Indian Territory. Numerous additions over the years including two-story ell, larger than original house, with two-story porch built ca. 1938 facing the highway. 4 ext. photos (1934); 2 int. photos (1934); 3 data pages (1934). Illustrated on p. 9.

Clinton
Jones County (85)

Hamilton-Johnson House (Johnson House) GA-1123. SE side of Madison St. (facing NW) between Washington St. and Wayside Rd. Frame with clapboarding, flush siding under porch. Three-bay front, rectangular, with wings to the rear. Gable roof (roof of entrance porch flat), at least two ext. end chimneys. Three-bay, one-story entrance porch with square tapered Doric-type wooden columns; ends of porch latticed, probably after house was built. Typical porch railing with very light rectangular pickets set vertically; round handrail. Six-panel entrance door with fanlight, framed by pilasters that match porch columns. Probably central hall plan. Excep-

tionally fine French scenic wallpaper (dating from 1821) of the pattern Le Jardin Français (multicolor) by the French firm Zuber and Co. was in parlor. The same room had paneled wainscot and an Adam-type mantel with reeded pilasters and reeded panels over, and a plain center panel. 1937 photo shows a wooden picket fence with wooden gate. Indigenous, simplistic Federal elements. Built ca. 1824. Restored ca. 1957 and remodeled with extensive additions to the rear, which then became the entrance front, the house thereafter facing the Milledgeville-Eatonton Hwy. instead of Madison St. Destroyed by fire 1963. 4 ext. photos (1936); 2 int. photos (1936); 1 data page (1936). Illustrated on p. 66.

Jade-Barron House. See *Mitchell-Barron House.*

Johnson House. See *Hamilton-Johnson House.*

Lowther Hall GA-14-59. s side of Monticello Rd., between Milledgeville-Eatonton Rd. and U.S. Hwy. 129. Faced NW. Frame with clapboarding, flush siding under porch, wood shingle roof. Five-bay front, rectangular, wing attached by breezeway on sw side. Two stories over raised basement. Hipped roof, two int. chimneys, corbelled and stuccoed. Exquisite small entrance porch with paired fluted Doric columns, flat roof with sheaf-of-wheat balustrade. Doorway to this roof similar to but not identical with main entrance doorway; both had six-panel doors with sidelights of intricate design and elliptical fanlight over door and sidelights. Lattice work of porch railing and tracery of side- and fanlights of both doors present crisp and delicate composition. Three-bay, one-story porch (probably of later date) with unroofed extensions each side, across rear of house.

Central hall plan, rear part of hall with stairway larger than front, and separated from it by an elliptical arch resting on clustered pilasters. Circular stairway with rectangular pickets and round handrail. Plaster cornices, some with acanthus leaves, foliated plaster ceiling medallions. Adam-type mantels of varying designs, illustrated with molded or fluted pilasters, and panels with simple oval or diamond motifs, or with carved sunbursts. Wellhouse in the form of a very small Doric prostyle distyle temple stood on N side and slightly to front of house. Picket fence, exceptionally graceful gates, gateposts with urns, the gates and posts installed 1910, having been removed from a neighboring house.

Traditional Federal style, front similar to many New England houses of a decade earlier. Architect probably Daniel Pratt. Destroyed by fire in 1942. 7 sheets (1934); 3 ext. photos (1934); 1 ext. photo (1936); 3 int. photos (1934); 6 int. photos (1936); 2 data pages (1936). Illustrated on p. 90.

Mitchell-Barron House (Jade-Barron House) GA-155. E corner (facing SW) of Washington and Madison Sts. Frame with beaded clapboarding, flush siding under porches. 45'3" (five-bay front), L-shaped. Two stories, gable roof (main roof spraddle gable, roof of ell salt-box type). Two ext. end chimneys, one int. chimney, all originally brick with stucco. Two-tiered five-bay full-width porch with fluted Doric columns first floor, fluted Ionic columns sec-

ond floor. Face of Ionic capitals hand carved, scrolls turned. Bays unequal, spaced according to unequal bays of house. Second-story porch railing with light rectangular pickets appears original; heavier first-floor railing of later date. Double-tiered back porch following both inside faces of L-shaped house; square wooden posts on first floor, solid turned Doric-type posts on second floor. Delicate frieze with blocks (cut to cove shape on three sides) immediately under cornice, similar to that of the Belcher-Hunter House★ in Savannah. At entrance, double doors with sidelights and transom, each door one panel wide, four unequal panels high. Central hall plan. Scenic wallpaper in parlor. Wellhouse with granite floor and well box with projecting granite supports for the windlass. Handhewn posts with mortised braces to the roof framing. Roof framing nailed on, not original.

House built in stages. Original unit 1810, brought to its present form (indigenous with Federal details) ca. 1822, minor changes since that time. Exceptionally well designed for climate, provides important link between plantation plain style and fully developed Greek Revival. 2 ext. photos (1936); 11 ext. photos (1980); 4 int. photos (1980); 1 data page (1936). Illustrated on p. 49.

Cobbham
McDuffie County (95)

Few House. See *Few House*, Thomson Vicinity.

Columbus
Muscogee County (108)

Alexander House (Alexander-McGahee-Woodall House) GA-153. 1543 Second Ave., facing E. Brick, stucco on brick under portico, 49'4" (five-bay front) × 38'6" plus projecting front portico and full-width rear porch, one-story raised cottage with gable roof and gable parapets. Greek Doric tetrastyle front portico (sixteen ft. wide), hipped roof, four fluted columns with academic entablature complete with triglyphs, sloping mutules, and guttae, five-bay back porch with shed roof, four end chimneys flush with ext. walls; central hall, two rooms each side. Greek Revival style, mid 19th C. Changes: back porch enclosed, int. adapted to serve as headquarters for senior citizens groups. 2 ext. photos (1936); 1 data page (1936).

Alexander-McGahee-Woodall House. See *Alexander House*.

Bank of Columbus GA-292. 1048 Broadway. Cast iron and brick, 50'2" (seven-bay Broadway front) N side × 138'6" (nineteen-bay front first floor, twenty bays second and third, Eleventh St. front) W side. Street fronts cast iron, other walls brick. Three stories, flat roof. All bays arched, first-floor arches spring directly from engaged Corinthian columns; second- and third-floor arched openings framed by Corinthian half-columns with entablatures. Heavy bracketed cornice third floor. Corner columns and pilasters square. Entrance at Eleventh St. (width of two standard bays) with curved, open top pediment; entrance doors with arched transom and arched sidelights within pseudo-arched recess. 19th C. Renaissance Revival style, ca. 1860, erected by William H. Young. Int. completely renovated. Now occupied by First National Bank (Broadway Branch). 1 ext. photo (1980). Illustrated on p. 153.

Billings House (Swift Mansion) GA-114. 303 Twelfth St. Stucco on brick, T-shaped with stem toward front. End of stem not including porch 21 ft. (two-bay), overall 49 ft. (four-bay front), two stories, modified hipped roof converging to small deck, lean-to at rear, one int. chimney, two chimneys flush with outside walls, two-story-high porch conforming to T-shape of house; stem of T consists of one room (open on three sides) plus porch, behind that room is a cross hall with two entrances, one each side of the projecting room. Outbuildings still standing include a frame cottage (before 1853), a brick carriage house and stables (1866), and a garçonniere (1866). Built in 1857, originally brick. Roof was almost flat with cast-iron cresting; columns were Doric. After a fire (1898) pitch of roof was increased, cresting removed, brick stuccoed, original Doric capitals changed to Corinthian order, and lean-to added. At same time hall was refurbished with natural-finish woodwork, including paneled walls, beamed ceiling, and new staircase. 2 ext. photos (1936); 1 data page (1936).

Bowers House. See *The Elms.*

Calhoun-Griffin House (Mott House) GA-163. Front Ave. at Fourteenth St. within Fieldcrest Mills complex. Brick, Flemish bond. Rectangular, one wing with chamfered corners, 62' (five-bay front)

plus 15' (one-bay) wing × 49'4", two-and-a-half stories, mansard roof with dormer windows and cupola, iron railing around flat part of roof and over entrance porch, four int. chimneys flush with outer walls, classic Greek Ionic tetrastyle entrance porch (one story) with fluted columns, and entrance doorway with Doric columns in antis; central hall floor plan. Main body of house has all the characteristics of the Developed Federal style; roof, cupola, and ironwork on roof are Second Empire style. Built ca. 1839, remodeled several times, first time shortly before Civil War, second time ca. 1892, and last during 20th C., when it was converted to offices. 2 ext. photos (1936); 1 data page (1936).

Cargill House. See *The Lion House.*

Cook-Thomas House. See *Rosemont.*

Judge Crawford House (Mrs. Crawford Jenkins' Boarding House) GA-1142. 209 Thirteenth St. First floor stucco on brick, second floor frame with clapboarding, flush siding under porches, rectangular (five-bay front), two stories, hipped roof, two-tiered octastyle porch, first-story columns stucco on brick, square, columns on second story round, tapered, of Tuscan inspiration. Porch rail with wooden pickets crisscrossed to form diamond pattern, mid 19th C. Destroyed ca. 1954. 1 ext. photo (1936); 1 data page (1936).

Dinglewood GA-293. 1429 Dinglewood Dr. Brick with stucco, rectangular (five-bay front), two-story central portion surrounded by one-story porches and rooms, front

porch (seven bays) with curved (three-bay) projection at center, porch returns down each side and terminates with projecting rooms at rear, back porch between projecting rooms. Six int. chimneys, four of them at ext. walls. Paired roof brackets, arched windows, paired square columns supporting decorative three-centered arches, open-arms entrance steps with elaborate wooden balustrade (heavy turned balusters) terminating with posts topped by cast-iron urns, entrance doorway with heavy paneled doors framed by Corinthian columns in antis and Carrara marble statues that are an integral part of the design; central hall plan, original marble mantels, gold-leaf overmantel mirrors, ornamental plaster work, and walnut doors. Italian workmen did most of the finish work; two houses built for them to live in while the work was underway are still on the grounds. Italianate (Tuscan villa) style, built for Joel Early Hurt in 1859; Barringer and Morton, architects. Rear porch enclosed and the porte-cochère added in the 1920s. Originally had its own private gas and waterworks systems. 1 ext. photo (1980); 1 int. photo (1980). Illustrated on p. 145.

Downing House GA-1141. 815 Broadway, facing E. Frame with clapboarding. Shape not ascertainable from photos. Porch with unusual cast-iron railings and post insets, held in place with wood framing. Mid 19th C.? Destroyed ca. 1950. 3 ext. photos (1936); 1 data page (1936). Recorded in 1936 as Ironwork on Downing House.

Eldorado (St. Elmo) GA-129. 2808 Eighteenth Ave., facing W. Stucco on brick, 54 ft. (three-bay front), two stories over semiraised basement, hipped roof, four ext. chimneys, two-story-high peripteral Doric porch (one story high at rear) with entablature reduced to little more than a light architrave with balustrade over, exquisite cast-iron balcony rail; entrance and balcony doorways with fan and sidelights. Divided central hall with circular stairway, two rooms each side. Transitional, Federal–Greek Revival, 1828–33. Two separate roof structures, one over body of house and a higher one over house and porch indicate that porch was probably added. Glassed-in rooms on s side may be original, other rooms stuck between columns are later additions, after 1934. Outbuildings include interesting brick dovecote. Famous visitors to the house included James K. Polk, Millard Fillmore, Henry Clay, and Winfield Scott. The original name, El Dorado, was changed to St. Elmo because Augusta J. Evans, the author of the novel *St. Elmo*, spent much of her childhood and part of her later years in this house. The house described in the novel, however, was quite different. 2 sheets (1932); 3 ext. photos (1934); 2 ext. photos (1936); 1 int. photo (1934); 1 photo (sketch of façade) (1934). Illustrated on p. 85.

The Elms (Bowers House) GA-1103. 1846 Buena Vista Rd., facing NNE. Frame with clapboarding, novelty siding under porch, rectangular central portion with bay-front additions each side and with rear ell, central part 51' (five-bay front), projecting wings 25'9'' (three-bay front) each, one story, three-bay central portion of five-bay Doric front porch projects with pediment, other roofs (except minor additions in rear) hipped, four int.

chimneys, two int. chimneys at outer walls. Side wings (higher than central unit) with arched windows and unusually large roof brackets; original plan central entrance hall with coved ceiling room behind, rooms each side, wings connect with porch and with rooms that flank entrance hall, marble floor in entrance hall, marble mantels with original gold-leaf mirrors over in flanking rooms. Murals painted in 1868 by an itinerant painter decorate walls and ceilings of entrance hall and ceilings of two other rooms. Original part Greek Revival, built ca. 1844; wings are Italianate, built 1868. 2 ext. photos (1934); 2 data pages (1934).

Fontaine House GA-140. SE corner Front Ave. and Eleventh St. Brick with stucco under porch, rectangular (five-bay front), two stories, hipped roof with decorative cast-iron cresting at eaves, two-story-high hexastyle Ionic front porch, fanlight entrance with engaged columns; divided central hall with circular stairway. Mid 19th C. Destroyed 1945. 3 ext. photos (1934); 1 ext. photo (1936); 4 int. photos (1936); 1 data page (1936).

Gunby House GA-119. 4900 Hamilton Rd., facing sw. Frame with clapboarding, plaster under porch, 54 ft. (five-bay front) × 45 ft. (53 ft. including front porch), one story, pyramidal roof, one int. chimney, three end chimneys at ext. walls, hexastyle Doric front porch, fluted columns; central entrance hall on axis with doorway (folding doors) to dining room at rear, cross hall between, Corinthian Tower-of-the-Winds columns between entrance hall and int. hall. Greek Revival, mid 19th C. (before 1846). Back porch later enclosed, minor additions to rear.

May have been prototype for similar cottages recurring in Alabama. 2 ext. photos (1934); 2 data pages (1934).

Hoxey-Cargill House. See *The Lion House.*

Ironwork on Downing House. See *Downing House.*

The Lion House (Cargill House) GA-1132. 1316 Third Ave., facing w. Frame with clapboarding, scored plaster under porch, basement brick with stucco scored, 52'6'' (five-bay front), two stories over raised basement, truncated pyramidal roof converging to small deck, four int. chimneys at ext. walls. Front portico full width of house, Tower-of-the-Winds-type Corinthian columns two stories high, entrance with pilasters topped by consoles, the architrave decorated with Greek-type carving with anthemion motif, two-story lean-to at rear (probably originally one-story porch), cast-iron lions on each side of entrance porch give house its name; central hall, two rooms each side, Corinthian Tower-of-the-Winds screen columns divide hall, impressive int. doorways with casing splayed in the Egyptian manner and with plain heavy cornices with Greek acroteria over, curved stairway. Greek Revival, ca. 1840; Stephen Decatur Button of Philadelphia, architect. Changes: general deterioration, int. adapted to apartments, porch at rear enclosed, asbestos siding applied over clapboarding. 4 ext. photos (1934); 1 int. photo (1936); 1 data page (1936).

May's Folly GA-294. 527 First Ave. Frame with clapboards, double octagon shape, the front octagon with 16 ft. sides, the rear one with 10 ft. sides, one story, pitched roofs (the front one pitched to a small deck and elaborate center chimney), projecting front porch has flat roof; two center chimneys, decorative iron and jigsaw woodwork; ingenious int. arrangement of rooms and closets. Probably designated as ornamented octagonal cottage when remodeled in early 1860s by Leander May. Originally simple rectangular cottage built by Alfred Iverson in 1829–30. Rear portion remodeled in 1920s, restored with modifications in 1971. 1 ext. photo (1980). Illustrated on p. 158.

Mott House. See *Calhoun-Griffin House.*

Muscogee Mills GA-110. SW corner Front Ave. and Fourteenth St., now part of Fieldcrest Mills complex. Brick; lower part next to river is stone. Wooden bell tower; covered walkways steel, processing tower steel with asbestos siding. Irregular shape resulting from being rebuilt at least once and from various remodeling and additions. Units vary from one to five stories, roofs flat, gable, stepped gable, modified stepped gable, hipped, and pyramidal; scattered chimneys. Picturesque (whether viewed from river or from street) accretion of primarily 19th C. industrial buildings, details include delicate wooden bell tower, patterned brickwork, and a former entrance with heavily paneled door, carved transom bar, and sunburst wooden tympanum in arch over; plan irregular. Muscogee Mills built 1867 on site of Coweta Falls Factory, which had been burned during Civil War. Some walls and possibly aforementioned entrance door may have survived and been incorpo-

rated into the new mill; they appear older than 1867 date would indicate. Low part along Front Ave. is a part of 1867 mill, adjoining five-story unit has date 1882 inscribed in the gable parapet, other units were added at intermediate and later dates, mostly late 19th C. Brick tower in the foreground of the 1936 photo has been removed. 1 ext. photo (1936); 1 data page (1936). Illustrated on p. 186.

Pease House GA-1135. NE corner Broadway and Ninth Sts. Raised basement walls stucco on brick, main floor frame with clapboarding, novelty siding under porches, H-shape (seven-bay front) one-story raised cottage, flat or low pitched roof behind parapet, cast-iron verandas over stuccoed brick piers, heavy classic entablature suggests that iron treillage may have replaced earlier columns, curving horseshoe entrance steps are cast iron. Mid 19th C. Demolished 1940. 2 ext. photos (1934); 1 ext. photo (1936); 1 photo (sketch of façade) (1934); 1 data page (1934).

Rankin House GA-112. 1440 Second Ave., facing W. Brick, two-story rectangular main central unit 54'2'' (five-bay front) with one-story wings projecting to rear and both sides, main roof truncated, pyramidal, converging to small deck, other roofs hipped, veranda (hipped) roof concave, four chimneys flush with ext. walls, cast-iron front veranda full width of house with cast-iron balcony over, cast-iron cresting over veranda posts and at midpoint of central bay, cast-iron fringe (cornice drop) at eaves, cast-iron ventilators under eaves between Italianate paired roof brackets, entrance

with Corinthian columns in antis, brick (2½'' × 8¼'' × 4'') hard with sharp corners, precisely laid with 3/16 in. joints; divided central hall, two rooms each side, double stairway merging into single stairway above landing, original marble mantels of different colors and designs. Outbuildings include brick carriage house and lattice gazebo, all possibly of later date than the house. Cast-iron fence and gates (of later date) and two cast-iron bird baths. Mid 19th C.; Lawrence Wimberly Wall, architect. Restoration architect, Edward W. Neal. 1 ext. photo (1936); 1 int. photo (1936); 1 data page (1936). Illustrated on p. 148.

Redd House GA-138. Redd Ave., between Twenty-Second and Twenty-Third Sts. Stucco on brick, rectangular, projecting center portion, projecting bay windows on side, several porches, five-bay front downstairs, three-bay front upstairs, gable roof with parapets (some crenellated), cast-iron cresting at roof of two porches. Two stories, two main int. chimneys, Gothic-style porches with octagonal columns and fretwork, oriel window over entrance porch, finials at peak of gables, turrets at corners. Plan said to be adapted from one in *Godey's Lady's Magazine.* House begun 1858; finished after Civil War. Destroyed ca. 1957. 1 ext. photo (1936); 1 data page (1936). Illustrated on p. 132.

Rosemont (Cook-Thomas House) GA-111. 629 Twentieth St., facing s. Frame with clapboarding, plastered under porch, 54'8'' (three-bay front) × 40' (four-bay side), plus front porch and lean-to at rear, two stories, hipped roof, four ext. chimneys (stucco on brick), seven-bay front porch, central bay two stories, projecting. Cast-iron porch railings and roof cresting, square paneled columns with composition or carved wreaths over; double front doors, each with heavy raised panels; sidelights and transom with etched glass in grapevine pattern; divided central hall, two rooms each side, circular stairway, unusually large and handsome six-panel doors. Built ca. 1847. Lean-to enlarged and changed. Int. hall, minor changes. Other rooms remodeled for offices. 1 ext. photo (1936); 1 data page (1936).

St. Elmo. See *El Dorado.*

Springer Opera House GA-295. 105 Tenth St., facing s. Brick, 145' (thirteen-bay front) × 150', three stories, hipped roof. Pressed-metal bracketed cornice, pressed-metal pediments over windows of upper floors. Five-bay, two-tiered porch or marquee with cast-iron columns first floor, cast-iron filigree columns, railing, frieze and brackets second floor; concave hipped metal roof. Two entrance doors with pilasters and a common entablature lead to foyer. Auditorium 65' × 68'6", ceiling 60 ft. Two curving balconies supported by Corinthian columns. Proscenium arch with original decorated border, flanked by three tiers of boxes. Mid to late Victorian commercial style, built 1871; Daniel M. Foley, architect. Converted to movie theater in 1930s, closed 1959. Restoration begun 1964, designated State Theater of Georgia by Gov. Jimmy Carter in 1970. 1 ext. photo (1980). Illustrated on p. 196.

Swift House. See *Billings House.*

Columbus Vicinity
Muscogee County (108)

Gunby House. See *Gunby House,* Columbus.

Slave Cabin, Old Bass Plantation GA-1150. On w side of Lumpkin Rd., .5 mi. s from intersection with Victory Dr. Log, rectangular, (one-bay front), one story, gable roof, one ext. end chimney, one room plus (later?) shed room. Indigenous, mid 19th C. Demolished in 1960s or earlier. 2 ext. photos (1936); 1 data page (1936).

Covington
Newton County (109)

Carr House. See *Carr-Watterson House,* Oxford.

The Cottage. See *Neal-McCormick House.*

Downs House. See *Neal-McCormick House.*

Milner-Neal-Ramsey House (Spence-Harris House) GA-130. 5129 Floyd St. Wood frame with clapboarding, rectangular, wings projecting toward front, portico between and advancing beyond wings. First-floor, five-bay front, second-floor, one-bay front. Main body of house two stories with hipped roof, wings one story with gable roofs. Four end chimneys, two int. chimneys. Two-story-high Greek Ionic portico, balcony beneath with wooden pickets in lattice design. Main entrance and entrance to balcony have sidelights, fanlights, and unorthodox pediments. Main part of house

(Milner) mid 19th C. Remodeled and portico added (Ramsey) ca. 1933. Portico, balcony, and parts of doorways were from a Neal house which stood on e side of Church St. between Conyers and Reynolds Sts. 1 ext. photo (1937); 1 data page (1936).

Neal-McCormick House (Downs House, The Cottage) GA-124. 2149 Floyd St., facing s. Wood frame with clapboarding, flush siding under porch, five-bay front, one story over raised basement. Pyramidal roof, four end chimneys. Modified Greek Doric hexastyle porch across front, similar but smaller distyle porch at back. Pilasters at corners of house, continuous entablature. Front entrance recessed, front and back entrances with sidelights and transom framed by pilasters with entablatures. Central hall plan, two rooms each side. Greek Revival, 1852. Outstanding example of successful synthesis of indigenous and Greek Revival architecture. 2 ext. photos (1934); 2 data pages (1934). Illustrated on p. 112.

Spence-Harris House. See *Milner-Neal-Ramsey House.*

Covington Vicinity
Newton County (109)

Salem Camp Ground GA-128. e side of Ga. Hwy. 162, .5 mi. n of intersection with Brown Mill Rd., which is about 6 mi. e of juncture of Brown Bridge Rd. with Clark St. in Covington. Tabernacle: wood, post and truss construction, clapboarding in gables and over braced part of posts. Rectan-

gular, 70' (five-bay front) × 100',
open shed with gable roof. Exposed hand-hewn mortised and
tenoned structural members. Built
1854; Moses Mann and Slider Pres-
nal, builders. Roof, rafters, and intermediate bracing are replacements or were installed later.
Concrete piers under posts not
original. 2 ext. photos (1936); 2
int. photos (1936); 1 data page
(1936).

Crawfordville

Taliaferro County (133)

Liberty Hall GA-158. Alexander
H. Stephens Memorial Park, facing s. Frame with clapboarding,
board-and-batten siding on wing,
wood shingle roof. 47'10" (five-
bay front) × 35'10", two stories,
hipped roof on main body of house
and on front porch, gable roof on
wing and rear ell. Two int. chimneys in main part of house, end
chimneys on wing and ell. One-
story, five-bay porch across front.
Square tapered columns, simple
wooden railing with square pickets. Four-panel entrance door with
sidelights; central hall plan, two
rooms each side. One original
outbuilding (restored), two outbuildings reconstructed. Grounds
enclosed by picket fence. Early
19th C., remodeled 1872. Old
photo (Georgia Department of Archives and History) shows front
with only three bays downstairs,
four upstairs, end chimneys, and
a much smaller three-bay porch
with pediment. Home of Alexander H. Stephens, vice-president
of the Confederate States of America. House museum. 4 ext. photos
(1936); 1 data page (1936).

Cumberland Island

Camden County (20)

Dungeness GA-2160. s end of Cumberland Island, facing NE. Stone,
irregular shape, multibayed, two-
and-a-half stories, hipped roof with
flaring eaves, numerous chimneys.
Square tower with bracketed balcony surrounding top floor. Three-
(four-?) story semicircular bay
window left of entrance. Many
windows: square-head and arched,
single and grouped. Reputedly
twenty-five to thirty-five rooms.
Wood frame guest and recreation
house with indoor swimming
pool. Built in 1884 by Thomas
Carnegie on site of old Dungeness, which had been built by
Gen. Nathanael Greene on the
site of an Indian midden, and was
destroyed to clear the site for the
later Dungeness. Guest house
built by Carnegie's widow ca.
1890. Dungeness destroyed by
fire 1959. Ruins of chimneys and
parts of masonry walls remain.
Guest house dilapidated and rot-
ting. 6 ext. photos (1958); 3 data
pages (1958).

*General Nathanael Greene Cot-
tage* GA-2161. Near Dungeness. s
end of Cumberland Island, facing
NE. Tabby, rectangular, four-bay
front, one-and-a-half stories, gable
roof with dormers, shed roof on
porch, one int. chimney. Five-
bay front porch across front, two
entrance doors, two rooms first
floor. Built ca. 1800. Two doors
sw side later converted to windows. Porch and dormers possibly
later. Thought to have been built
as gardener's cottage. 4 ext. photos (1958); 2 data pages (1958).

Dahlonega

Lumpkin County (94)

Court House. See *Dahlonega
Courthouse Gold Museum.*

*Dahlonega Courthouse Gold Mu-
seum* (Lumpkin County Courthouse) GA-181. Town square, main
entrance, facing SE. Brick, rectangular, five bays each side, two stories flush with ext. walls. Cornice
and raking cornices with mutules,
two oblique oval ventilators in
each pediment, lintels over windows and archivolts over doors
stuccoed. One entrance with double doors and fanlights each side,
main entrance (with fan- and sidelights) on second story under portico. Portico with rugged heroic
columns of Tuscan persuasion on
SE side; first story of portico (with
twin stairways to second-floor entrance) enclosed with brick. Workmanship of portico and its brick
enclosing walls appears crude
compared to the rest of the building. Courtroom on second floor.
Portico vernacular version of
Greek Revival, rest of building
Federal style, traditional phase.
Built 1836–38; Ephraim Clayton,
builder. Portico probably added
mid 19th C. Int. first floor remodeled several times, brick floor
being covered with wood floor
during one of the remodelings.
Restored as gold museum 1965–
66. Oldest surviving public building in region. 1 ext. photo (1936);
1 data page (1936).

Lumpkin County Courthouse.
See *Dahlonega Courthouse Gold
Museum.*

Old Hotel GA-180. E corner of
U.S. Hwy. 19 and Chestatee St.,
facing town square to NW. Wood

frame with clapboarding, apparently with flush siding under porches, rectangular, at least twelve bays on the front downstairs and thirteen upstairs, two-and-a-half stories with gable roof. Arched dormer windows with pilasters and open-bed pediment. Two-tiered veranda across front, first-story columns square with chamfered corners, second-story columns turned and with brackets. Several doors opening on each story, some with sidelights and transom. According to 1936 account, dormer windows opened to an attic, not a half-story, and there were originally elliptical head doorways in the end walls. Built ca. 1830; porch work probably changed before 1936. Used as hotel for many years, then as girls' dormitory for North Georgia College. Destroyed by fire 1948. 1 ext. photo (1936); 1 data page (1936).

Darien Vicinity
McIntosh County (96)

Altama GA-235. Entrance to plantation w side of Ga. Hwy. 99, 7.5 mi. s of Darien, .1 mi. s of intersection with U.S. Hwy. 95. Brick or tabby with stucco, original part rectangular (center bay recessed slightly, not affecting roof line), two stories. First-story walls with five openings on front; second-story walls with three. Hipped roof, four int. chimneys. First-floor windows, except those under porch, arched and set within blind arches. Three-bay, one-story front porch with masonry piers and arches stuccoed. Unusual for area in that it was built close to the ground. Developed Federal style, 1857. Many additions at

rear, one apparently three stories, the third floor with shingle siding. James Hamilton Couper, owner and architect. Additions apparently 20th C. Destroyed 1959. 1 ext. photo (1936); 1 data page (1936). Recorded in 1936 as in Glynn County.

Ashantilly Plantation GA-282. Entrance E side of Ga. Hwy. 99, 1.7 mi. N of intersection with U.S. Hwy. 17 in Darien. House faces ESE. Tabby with stucco, rectangular with wing on s side. Three-bay front, two and one-half stories, gable roof with two chimneys at rear, one end chimney on wing. Quoins at corners, cornice with terra cotta molding. Arched entrance with fanlight. House built ca. 1820; extensively repaired and to some extent remodeled shortly after the Civil War. Original house had a flat roof, a porch with marble columns, and wings each side connected by open passageways. Repairs and changes included reducing size of windows, enclosing open passageways, substituting hipped roof for flat one, and substituting one-story three-bay porch with square wood columns for original one with marble columns. Nearly destroyed by fire in 1937, but most of tabby walls remained. Rebuilt in 1939 with gable roofs and dormers, larger windows, and a changed and enlarged southern wing. Porch and northern wing not restored. Despite vicissitudes and locale, there is a pervasive Regency quality about the house and grounds which is due in part to the unity of the house and site. Designed primarily as a winter residence, breezes and humidity were not major factors, and the house was set much closer to the

ground than was customary in the area. 9 ext. photos (1936); 1 int. photo (1936); 2 data pages (1936).

Epping House GA-234. Ridgeville, NW corner of Ga. Hwy. 99 and Cow's Horn Rd., facing E of Ridgeville on Ga. Hwy. 99, 3 mi. N of Darien. Wood frame with clapboarding, rectangular, with wings. Five-bay front, two stories, gable roofs with wide eaves, three end chimneys. Two-tiered, five-bay porch across front, porch with square chamfered posts and scroll-saw brackets, balustrade with scroll-saw banisters. Windows on porch with hinged panels that open beneath. Entrance with sidelights and transom, central hall with two rooms each side. Indigenous with Victorian trim, built mid 19th C. Scroll-saw work may be later. Separate kitchen and servants' house destroyed since 1936. 3 ext. photos, including kitchen and servants' house (1936); 1 data page (1936).

Negro Cabin GA-283. w side of U.S. Hwy. 17, between Riceboro and Darien; precise site not ascertainable. Wood frame with clapboarding, wood shingle roof, 18 ft. square, rear ell, three-bay front, one story, gable roof, one end chimney built of mud. Porch with hipped roof and heavy square columns across front. According to 1936 account, the small house had a central hall, two rooms each side, and separate kitchen and dining room connected by a passage; in plan a mansion in miniature. Grounds enclosed by fence with split palings. Demolished ca. 1940, when the whole area was cleared and planted in pines. 2 ext. photos (1936); 1 data page (1936). Illustrated on p. 162.

Thicket Sugar Mill and Rum Distillery GA-271. E side of a dirt road which curves southward, 1 mi. SE of its junction on the E side of Ga. Hwy. 99, this junction .6 mi. N of intersection of that highway with Blue Haul Rd. in Ridgeville. Ridgeville 3 mi. N of Darien. Ruins of three major buildings, traces of other minor buildings, cisterns, and a large chimney. Remaining portions tabby, some with brick trim. Southerly building octagonal, about 46 ft. in diameter within which are walls of an octagonal room 24 ft. in diameter. Main entrance was by way of a ramp on W side. Typical of early 19th C. sugar mills in the area.

N of the octagonal building was a T-shaped building, probably for boiling and curing sugar. N of that building was a rectangular building, about 30 ft. wide and more than 90 ft. long, with an ell on the long side. Ruins of some int. partitions remain. This building was probably a combination rum distillery, storage building, and plantation commissary. Parts of the wall of this building are nearly full height and have a dentil-like frieze of brick at top; also an arched doorway with a brick archivolt. Bits of china and cast iron, nails, and other late 18th or early 19th C. artifacts that were intermixed with the tabby aggregate prove that the buildings are early 19th C., not 16th C. Spanish missions, as previously listed.

Built ca. 1816 as outbuildings on the Thicket Plantation. For fuller description see *Georgia's Disputed Ruins*, edited by E. Merton Coulter (Chapel Hill: University of North Carolina Press, 1937), pp. 111–32. 4 ext. photos (1934); 3 ext. photos (1936); 1 int. photo (1936); 4 data pages (1936). Recorded in the 1930s as Tolomato Mission. Illustrated on p. 67.

Tolomato Mission. See *Thicket Sugar Mill and Rum Distillery.*

Davisboro Vicinity
Washington County (152)

Jordan Cabin GA-164. Jordan-Pierson Plantation, NW side (facing S) of Ga. Hwy. 231, 1.2 mi. SW of Davisboro. Hewn logs, rectangular, three-bay front, one story, gable roof, originally two end chimneys. Open passageway through center, one room each side. Indigenous dog-trot cabin, probably late 18th C. 1 ext. photo (1972). Illustrated on p. 20.

Eatonton
Putnam County (119)

Paschal-Sammons House GA-27. E side of Maple Ave., facing W, .25 mi. S of intersection with Jefferson Ave. Frame with clapboarding, rectangular with ells and additions at rear. Four-bay front, main roof gable, other roofs hipped, shed, flat, and concave gable. Two int. chimneys, two int. end chimneys. Three-story entrance tower at front with flanking porch on one side, and a two-story window alcove on the other. Small entrance porch in front of tower.

Pilasters at corners of house, and classic entablature with dentils on sides. Bracketed cornices in front. Scroll-saw brackets on porch columns. Original style apparently Greek Revival, mid 19th C. Remodeled into Italian Villa style ca. 1860. 1 ext. photo (1972). Illustrated on p. 146.

Putnam County Courthouse GA-28. Town square, facing NNW.

Brick with wood, cast-stone, and metal trim, rectangular with projecting end pavilions front and rear, projecting center pavilions on sides. Nine-bay front, two stories, roofs both flat and gable types, the flat roofs with parapets. Octagonal center cupola with octagonal dome and lantern, the dome has clock faces on four sides. Heroic tetrastyle Corinthianesque porticos front and rear, square brick columns with cast-stone capitals and bases. Recessed side entrances with curved broken-top cast-stone pediments. Double windows with transoms over, the transom muntins arranged in lattice design; iron pickets of porch railings arranged in similar lattice design. Cross axial corridors, second-story courtroom with bull's-eye clerestory windows. 20th C. Classical Revival style, 1905; J. W. Golucke and Co., architects. 1 ext. photo (1972). Illustrated on p. 217.

Eatonton Vicinity
Putnam County (119)

Rock Eagle Mound GA-29. Rock Eagle State Park, W side of U.S. Hwy. 441, 7 mi. N of public square in Eatonton. Stones mounded to represent figure of eagle or vulture, the head facing SE. Underlayment a mixture of humus and red and yellow clay of a type not found in vicinity. Length 102 ft., wingspread 120 ft. A similar mound, likewise in Putnam County, faces NE; has a wingspread of 132 ft. Date unknown, generally placed about the time of Christ. 1 ext. photo (1980). Illustrated on p. 4.

Elberton Vicinity
Elbert County (53)

Richard B. Russell Project. Encompassing the largest physical area of any HABS undertaking in Georgia, this 1980 recording project documented buildings and farm complexes that will be removed with the construction of the Richard B. Russell Dam and Reservoir on the Savannah River, in Georgia and in South Carolina. Among the Georgia sites and properties recorded are the following.

Heardmont Vicinity

Dye-White Farm GA-31. 20th C. farm complex owned by a locally prominent black family. 1 sheet (1980); 18 photographs (1980); 18 data pages (1980).

Middletown Vicinity

Grogan House (Eureka) GA-33. Large frame house supported on granite piers. Built ca. 1873. 7 sheets (1980); 25 photos (1980); 23 data pages (1980).

Pearl Vicinity

Beverly Plantation (William Allen House) GA-34. Two-story frame house with two-tiered front portico. Built ca. 1790 with later additions. Federal style, one of earliest remaining houses in region. 1 sheet (1980); 35 data pages (1980).

Ruckersville Vicinity

Alexander-Cleveland House GA-30. Two-story frame house with later additions. Built ca. 1791. With Beverly, one of oldest houses in area. 6 sheets

(1980); 21 photos (1980); 50 data pages (1980).

Martin Anderson Farm GA-35. Early 20th C. farm complex. 1 sheet (1980, including R. J. Anderson farm); 18 data pages (1980).

R. J. Anderson Farm GA-32. Early 20th C. farm complex. 1 sheet (1980, including Martin Anderson farm); 15 photos (1980); 11 data pages (1980).

Fairburn
Fulton County (61)

Campbell County Courthouse at Fairburn GA-187. 45 E. Broad St., facing NNW. Brick, rectangular, first-floor, one-bay front, second-floor, three-bay front. Two stories, gable roof, temple form except that there are pediments on the sides as well as front and rear. Two-story-high tetrastyle modified Doric portico with brick pediment. Bracketed cornice, segmental arched windows. First-floor entrance has double doors with arched top panels and an arched transom over. Curving steps each side of first-floor entrance lead to second-story entrance, which has a single door three panels wide, the top panels arched; arched transom over. Stone steps with decorative iron railing. First floor has central corridor with offices each side, second floor has one room. Greek Revival with Italianate details, built 1871. Used as Campbell County Courthouse until 1952, when Campbell County was incorporated into Fulton County. Headquarters Campbell County

Historical Society, Inc., since 1975. 1 ext. photo (1980).

Fairburn Vicinity
Fulton County (61)

Beaver House GA-1155. NW side of Cochran Rd., facing SE, about a hundred yards NE of juncture with Church St. in Campbellton. Entrance to Campbellton via Church St. on NE side of Ga. Hwy. 92, about 9 mi. NW of intersection of that highway with Ga. Hwy. 14 in Fairburn; .1 mi. NW of intersection of Ga. Hwys. 91 and 154. House frame, flush siding and wainscot under porch, flush siding in porch pediment. L-shaped, four-bay front, one story, hipped roof, three end chimneys. Front porch simplified version of a tetrastyle Greek Doric portico with fluted columns, no capitals. Window with sidelights on one side of porch, two windows on other. Double entrance doors with sidelights and transom, central hall plan. Greek Revival, mid 19th C. Porches on rear since enclosed; additions to rear and to NE side. Window sash on SW side changed from nine-over-nine type to six-over-six. 1 ext. photo (1936); 1 data page (1936).

Old Campbell County Courthouse GA-154. Campbellton, E corner of Church St. and Cochran Rd. (facing SW), site marked by monument. Entrance to Campbellton via Church St. on NE side of Ga. Hwy. 92, about 9 mi. NW of intersection of Ga. Hwys. 92 and 14 in Fairburn, .1 mi. NW of intersection of Ga. Hwy. 92 with Ga. Hwy. 154. Brick, Flemish bond, rectangular, five-bay front, two stories, hipped roof with pediment in front. Arched entrance with double doors and fanlight over; brick archivolts and lintels stuccoed. Arched ventilator in pediment. Traditional Federal style, ca. 1828. Dismantled 1914. 1 ext. photocopy (1910); 1 data page (1936). Illustrated on p. 190.

Frederica. See *St. Simons Island, Town of Frederica.*

Griffin
Spalding County (128)

Bailey-Tebeault House GA-1148. 433 Meriwether St. Frame with clapboarding, horizontal boards and battens under portico (the half-inch-thick battens probably added to conceal cracks), central two-story rectangular unit 59 ft. (five-bay front) with one-story wings projecting to sides and rear, two-story tetrastyle portico on front, one-story Doric porches on front side of both projecting wings. Doric portico with pediment, other roofs hipped, four int. end chimneys in two-story part, two int. chimneys in wings. Pilasters at rear of portico and at corners of house; double doors at entrance with sidelights and transom, balcony with turned wood balusters, supported by carved wooden consoles; central hall plan, two rooms plus wings each side, circular stairway. Servants' house and two other outbuildings evidently built at same time as house; also kitchen, which was moved and connected to back porch at a later date. Back porch since enclosed. Otherwise ext. practically unchanged. Central hall and rooms on one side unchanged; other rooms changed to accommodate needs of funeral

home. Built 1859–62. 4 ext. photos (1936); 1 data page (1936).

Drewry House. See *Eason-Drewry House.*

Eason-Drewry House (Drewry House) GA-1147. 303 N. Thirteenth St. Frame with clapboarding, 46'6" (five-bay front) × 36'2", plus porch, two stories with hipped roof, two-story-high front porch with square wooden columns lighter than customary for time and place, and with simple moldings at cap and base, flat trim (with molding at edge) cut to pediment shape over entrance doors and over windows; ext. distinguished by its simplicity. Central hall plan, two rooms each side. Modified Greek Revival, built ca. 1850. Demolished, 1974. 1 ext. photo (1936); 1 data page (1936).

The Reverend Obediah C. Gibson House. See *Lewis-Mills House.*

Lewis-Mills House (The Reverend Obediah C. Gibson House) GA-1149. 406 N. Hill St. Stucco on brick, 56'3" (five-bay front) × 46' (four-bay side), two stories, main roof hipped to small deck, projecting front tetrastyle portico with gable roof and square colossal Doric columns, stucco over brick. Two int. chimneys. Front door, rear door, and balcony door have simple rectangular sidelights and transoms, wooden balcony; central hall plan, two rooms each side. Greek Revival. Built ca. 1852. A two-story wing has been added to the rear, probably during 19th C. Rear porch has been removed. Portico floor lowered to ground level in 1974, a landing with stairs on each side

added at entrance to accommodate changes in level. House museum. 1 ext. photo (1936); 1 data page (1936).

Nichols House GA-1146. 225 N. Thirteenth St. Frame with clapboarding. Rectangular (five-bay front) with projecting portico, main roof hipped, gable roof over portico, two int. chimneys, two-story-high tetrastyle portico with four square wooden Doric columns with extra moldings applied under capitals, antae at corners of house, dentils under tenia, wooden balcony with square pickets over entrance. Modified Greek Revival, mid 19th C. Demolished 1971. 1 ext. photo (1936); 1 data page (1936). Illustrated on p. 112.

Haddock Vicinity
Jones County (85)

Blount House. See *Gordon-Banks House*, Newnan.

Heardmont Vicinity
Elbert County (53)

Dye-White Farm. See *Richard B. Russell Project*, Elberton Vicinity.

High Shoals
Walton County (149)

Casulon GA-1110. sw side of County Rd. 298, facing NE, .3 mi. s of County Rd. 298 at intersection with Ga. Hwy. 186, this intersection 1.3 mi. w of Ga. Hwy. 186 at junction with County Rd.

188 in High Shoals. Frame with clapboarding, rectangular, one-story wings toward rear. Five-bay front, two stories with hipped roof, four end chimneys on original part of house. Five-bay, two-story-high porch with Corinthian-inspired polygonal tapered columns, bracketed capitals, the scroll-saw brackets a carpenter's version of acanthus leaves. Three-panel double doors at entrance with transom and sidelights, and heavily molded casings with entablature. Transom with inverted fan design. Central hall plan, two rooms each side. Hall doors with molded casings and corner blocks with star-shaped insets. Mantels with pilasters, sunbursts, and fluted coronae.

Boxwood parterre garden with picket fence in front, stone walls at sides. Pickets one-and-a-quarter in. square, gate posts with urn-shaped finials. Surviving outbuildings include well house, drying house, tool house, blacksmith shop, corn crib, two of the slave-houses, and traces of garden gazebo. House built by Joseph Moss in 1821, evidently in the traditional Federal style. Greek Revival porch was probably added by James W. Harris in mid 19th C. Overseer's house was moved to form a wing toward rear of house in late 19th C.; solarium was added to SE side in the 1920s. 3 int. photos (1936); 5 ext. photos (1936); 1 data page (1936). Illustrated on pp. 65, 108, 168.

Hoschton Vicinity
Barrow County (7)

Cochran House. See Cochran House, Braselton Vicinity.

Isle of Hope
Chatham County (26)

Fort Wimberly GA-2126. Wormsloe Plantation Historic Site (state park), entrance located on w side of Skidaway Rd., .1 mi. s of junction with Fallowfield Dr. Fourteen-inch-thick tabby walls (which would not have withstood cannonading), the fort proper is rectangular with projecting bastions at each of the four corners and a gate on N side. s wall, between bastions, served as an ext. wall of the fortified dwelling within. Dwelling (tabby ext. walls, wood partitions) was 24 ft. on N and s sides, 32 ft. on E and W sides, with a chimney on w side. Walls of fort were apparently 8 ft. high. Built by Captain Noble Jones, ca. 1740–44 on site of an older wooden fort. Brick buttresses apparently added at a later date. Parts of walls of fort remain, as well as its foundations and the foundations of the house; also the well. For complete description see Captain Jones's Wormslow, by William M. Kelso (Athens: University of Georgia Press, 1979). Museum. 2 ext. photos (1934); 2 data pages (1934). Illustrated on pp. 14, 15.

Rice Mill GA-2126. Wormsloe Plantation. Entrance to Wormsloe w side of Skidaway Rd., .1 mi. s of junction with Fallowfield Dr. Wood frame with clapboarding, rectangular with at least one wing. Two stories with gable roof and large freestanding square tapered chimney. One-story shed across side photographed. Indigenous, built early to mid 19th C. Demolished ca. 1945. 1 ext. photo (1934). Recorded in 1934 as Wormsloe. Illustrated on p. 46.

Slave Cabin and Wellhead GA-2126. Wormsloe Plantation. Entrance to Wormsloe w side of Skidaway Rd., .1 mi. s of Fallowfield Dr. Cabin wood frame with clapboarding, rectangular, four-bay w side (front?), five-bay E side, gable roof, one int. chimney. Shed porch across most of E side, small entrance porch with shed roof on w side. Two rooms plus attic. Indigenous, built before the Civil War, date unknown. Porches added or replaced after 1934.

Wellhead rectangular, wood frame with vertical board siding, the upper part slatted to permit ventilation. Gable roof, pseudo-arched opening. Indigenous, date unknown. 1 ext. photo of cabin (1934); 1 int. photo of cabin (1934); 1 ext. photo of wellhead (1934). Recorded in 1934 as Wormsloe. Illustrated on p. 163.

Wormsloe. See Fort Wimberly, Rice Mill, Slave Cabin and Wellhead.

Jefferson
Jackson County (79)

Bell-Maddox House GA-11. NE corner Sycamore and College Sts. Originally faced College St. and the public square (WSW); before 1936 turned to face Sycamore St., at the same time being moved back to free street frontage.

Frame with clapboarding, flush siding under porch. Generally rectangular, but with offsets in front and rear walls indicative of additions. Two stories, gable roof sloping to front and rear, the older part having the higher ridge. At least two int. chimneys, stuccoed. Thirteen-bay (one end bay enclosed) double-tiered veranda across front, unifying the irregular façade behind. Plain square columns of Doric proportions and with varying intercolumnations; delicate balustrade with plain vertical rectangular pickets. Indigenous adaptation of Greek Revival style. Mid 19th C. Built as a residence, converted to a hotel by means of additions. Apparently built in three stages, all pre–Civil War. Destroyed ca. 1960. 1 ext. photo (1936); 1 data page (1936).

Ethridge-Stanton House. See *Johnson House.*

Harrison Hotel GA-157. SW corner Lee and Washington Sts., facing SSE. Frame with clapboarding, flush siding under porch; rectangular, rear ell, two stories, gable roof, at least three int. chimneys; seven-bay, two-story porch across entire front, square tapered full-height wooden columns, Doric type; simple balustrade with rectangular pickets both floors, unusual entablature with wooden panel frieze. Greek Revival columns on indigenous structure, built ca. 1835, additions ca. 1845. Demolished 1955 or 1956. 1 ext. photo (1936); 1 data page (1936).

Johnson House (Ethridge-Stanton House) GA-184. 186 Lee St., facing SSE. Wood frame with clapboarding, flush siding under porch. 32'6'' (three-bay front) × 28'6''. Two stories, gable roof with integral lean-to front and back (spraddle gable roof), three ext. chimneys, two end chimneys; three-bay, two-story-high front porch with square tapered full-height wooden columns of Doric inspiration. Chinese-Chippendale lattice-type railing on balcony over entrance. Three-vertical-panel door with sidelights framed by pilasters; flat panel between

doorway and balcony (pierced by transom and decorated with small applied diamond-shaped panels) substitutes for entablature. Central hall plan. Indigenous version of Greek Revival. Built ca. 1836. Original wood shingle roof covered with metal before 1937, recovered with composition shingles after 1937. House moved from 178 Lee St., brick chimneys topped with concrete units before 1936. Porch floor changed to concrete, column bases to brick, and asbestos siding applied after 1937. 1 ext. photo (1935); 1 ext. photo (1936); 1 data page (1936). Illustrated on p. 100.

Pendergrass Store GA-16. NW corner Sycamore and College Sts., facing SSE. Frame with clapboarding, flush siding under portico and in pediment. 30'6'' (three-bay front) × 63'6'', rectangular, two stories, gable roof, one int. chimney at ext. wall stucco on brick, two-story-high prostyle tetrastyle portico with square tapered Doric-type wooden columns, oversize windows (twelve panes over nine) with heavy raised panel shutters each side of entrance. One large room each floor with service rooms at rear. Greek Revival, 1858 (date still on gutter in 1936). Service rooms at rear added shortly after completion of building. Wood shingle roof changed to composition, wooden porch floor changed to concrete, stucco on brick foundation changed to stone after 1936. 1 ext. photo (1935); 1 ext. photo (1936); 1 data page (1936).

Presbyterian Church GA-17. 177–79 Washington St., facing ENE. Frame with clapboarding, novelty siding in pediment, flush siding under porch. 48'7'' (five-bay front) × 57'8''. One-story, gable roof with classic pediment. Recessed

porch, distyle in antis with round fluted Greek Doric columns (wooden) flanked by anterooms with corner pilasters; auditorium with gallery. Greek Revival style, built ca. 1858. Gallery removed after Civil War, replaced 1972. Spire struck by lightning and removed ca. 1940. Other 20th C. changes include addition of Sunday school rooms, substitution of concrete for wooden porch floor, and stained glass replacing clear glass windows. Church was originally built for Baptists and Presbyterians, who held services on alternate Sundays. 1 ext. photo (1936); 1 data page (1936).

Jekyll Island
Glynn County (64)

Horton House Remains GA-2150. Main Rd., N end of Jekyll Island, facing N. Tabby, 41'6'' (five-bay front) × 18', two stories, two int. end chimneys. Holes for joists indicate two-tier porch originally across S side. Foundations indicate central hall plan, one room each side. Built before 1742 for Major William Horton. Burned 1742 by Spanish. Rebuilt with wood frame additions by Christophe Poulain du Bignon, late 18th C. Additions and int. probably destroyed before 1886. Remaining fabric much repaired since; walls stuccoed late 19th C. 2 sheets (1958); 3 ext. photos (1958); 2 int. photos (1958); 3 data pages (1958). Illustrated on p. 23.

Rockefeller Cottage (Indian Mound) GA-2164. 331 Riverview Dr., facing NNW. Frame, shingle siding, rectangular, wings side and rear, five-bay (six on second floor) front, two and one-half stories, gable roof with hipped roof dormers, two end chimneys, twelve int. chimneys, porch front, w side, and rear, second tier over part of front. Porte-cochère at entrance. Porch and porte-cochère with Doric columns on pedestals, balustrade with turned balusters. Oversize bay window at sw corner, smaller semicircular bay over; also several oriel windows. Central hall plan with open-well stairway, tiffany window over landing. Anonymous type, original part built by Gordon McKay in 1892. Kitchen with maids' rooms over added ca. 1905. Greatly enlarged, new porches built, and porte-cochère added by William Rockefeller after 1910. House museum. 4 sheets (1976). Illustrated on p. 225.

Kennesaw Mountain
Cobb County (34)

Kolb House GA-299. SE side (facing NW) of Powder Springs Rd., sw, about 100 yds. sw of intersection with Cheathem Hill Rd., S.W., and Callaway Rd., S.W. Squared hewn logs, rectangular, three-bay front, one story, gable roof and four end chimneys. Stone stoop at front, entrance with sidelights and transom, porch across rear (SE side). Central hall plan, two rooms each side, attic rooms over. Indigenous, 1836. Originally a dog-trot cabin, the ends of the trot later enclosed and the logs covered with clapboarding. Several additions. Restored to approx. 1864 state by the National Park Service in 1963. Excellent example of typical early north Georgia farmhouse. 9 ext. photos (1963). Illustrated on p. 46.

Knoxville
Crawford County (40)

Crawford County Courthouse GA-151. Public square, facing N. Brick with stucco. 42'4'' (five-bay front) × 53'3'' (six-bay sides). Rectangular, wing one side. Two stories, hipped roof with flaring eaves, four chimneys flush with ext. walls. Second floor with pilasters between bays and at corners, entablature over simplified Doric order. Granite steps with cast-iron rail each side of stoop leading to main entrance at second floor. Double doors with transom over. Main floor has entrance hall with chamber each side; courtroom full width at rear. Bottom floor has central corridor with doors front and back. Built ca. 1851. Service room added to w side 1961. Building restuccoed 1967. Original stucco was scored, even over pilasters; new stucco is not. New stucco has been carried over capitals of pilasters and over moldings of entablature, making these elements bolder and coarser than formerly, and eliminating dentil band in frieze. Blinds have been removed, as have tops of two chimneys. Metal awning has been installed over entrance. 3 ext. photos (1936); 1 data page (1936).

Lafayette
Walker County (148)

Marsh House (Marsh-Warthen House) GA-150. 308 N. Main St., facing s (facing side yard, Charleston style). Wood frame with clapboarding, flush siding under porch. Rectangular, five-bay front, two stories, pyramidal roof with railing near peak. Two int. chimneys, one end chimney, bracketed cornice, two-story-high, three-bay porch across front. Square tapered Doric-inspired columns. Double entrance doors with sidelights and transom, balcony over. One-story, one-bay porch at rear with paired Ionic columns and with doorway similar to that at the front. Central hall plan, two rooms each side. Greek Revival, ca. 1836. Wings added E side late 19th C. Columns on rear porch may not be original. Lattice wellhouse demolished since 1936. 3 ext. photos, including wellhouse (1936); 1 data page (1936). Illustrated on p. 162.

La Grange
Troup County (143)

Beall-Dallis House. See *Heard-Beall-Dallis House.*

Cameron House GA-121. 1105 Vernon St., facing N. First floor brick with stucco, second floor frame with clapboarding, 50' (five-bay front) × 38' (four-bay side), two stories, hipped roof, four ext. chimneys, double-tiered hexastyle porch with stucco on brick columns first floor, wooden columns second floor, bottom-story porch floor cut flagstone; four-room central hall plan; unusual mantel with three-quarters round paired pilasters with horizontal reeding. Built ca. 1853. Porches removed before 1936. 1 int. photo (1936); 1 data page (1936).

Culberson House. See *Culberson-Atkinson House.*

Culberson-Atkinson House (Culberson House) GA-116. 609 Country Club Dr. Frame with clapboarding, flush siding under porch, 48' (five-bay front) × 34' (four-bay side), two stories, hipped roof converging to cupola, four ext. chimneys, tetrastyle front porch two stories high with balcony over entrance, fluted columns with square abacus only for cap, balcony with sheaf-of-wheat railing spanning three openings; four-room central hall plan. Ca. 1840; designed and built by Charles C. Bailey. Originally built in rural Troup County; moved to 207 Broad St. before 1936; moved to present location 1963, at which time the porch floor was lowered to ground level, steps and landing added within porch, cupola was heightened and louvers installed. 2 ext. photos (1936); 1 data page (1936).

Edwards House (Old Edwards House) GA-118. 203 Broad St., facing N. Frame with clapboarding, flush siding under portico, rectangular 47 ft. (five-bay front), two stories, gable roof, two ext. end chimneys. Two-story-high Ionic tetrastyle front portico with fluted columns, unusually skillful adaptation of Greek prototype capitals to wood construction; face of capitals is hand carved, between faces the wood volute is machine turned. Doors with sidelights and arched fanlights at entrance and balcony; central hall plan. Transitional, late Federal, early Greek Revival, built ca. 1835; architect probably Collin Rodgers. Marked similarity to Boddie House★, La Grange vicinity. House dismantled and rebuilt on Greenville Rd., La Grange vicinity in 1956. Demolished ca. 1975. 2 ext. photos (1936); 1 data page (1936).

Heard-Beall-Dallis House (Beall-Dallis House) GA-117. 206 Broad

St., facing S. Frame with clapboarding, 49'2'' (three-bay front), two stories, very low slope hipped roof with lean-to at rear, four int. chimneys at outer walls, semiperipteral two-story-high porch, balcony over entrance, fluted Doric columns (six in front, four each side), delicate dentil band with unusually long dentils under cornice, the rhythm reiterated by wooden balusters of balcony, which spans three openings; four-room central hall plan, front rooms higher than those in rear. Greek Revival style. Older part of house (two-story, each two-room central hall plan) was built ca. 1820, rooms to front and porch added a few years later. Additions and minor changes to rear at various times thereafter. Kitchen moved and attached to house by a passageway ca. 1888. Most of the original mantels replaced then or shortly afterward. Boxwood bordering front walk planted before 1860. 1 ext. photo (1936); 1 data page (1936).

Huntley House GA-122. 302 Broad St., facing S. Frame with clapboarding, novelty siding under porch (three bays wide), two stories, gable roof, four end chimneys, two-story-high tetrastyle front porch with modified Doric columns. Indigenous Greek Revival, mid 19th C. Razed ca. 1940. 1 ext. photo (1936); 1 data page (1936). Illustrated on p. 100.

The Magnolias (Render House) GA-14-62. 612 Hines St., facing N. Frame with clapboarding, flush siding under portico, 50 ft. (five-bay front) with projecting Ionic tetrastyle portico with fluted columns, their capitals skillfully adapted to wood construction, face of capitals hand carved, be-

tween faces the wood volute is machine turned; one-and-a-half stories, gable roof, four chimneys, double entrance doors with fan- and sidelights; four-room central hall plan, doorway at rear of hall duplicate of front door. Transitional Federal–Greek Revival, built ca. 1833 for Joseph D. McFarland. Architect probably Collin Rodgers; Wagner, builder. Room and porch added to one side; ell with porch plus very deep overhang supported by square wooden columns resting on small monolithic granite piers added to rear in 1880. Scroll-saw work and late Victorian details of additions contrast pleasantly with older part. Mantels and window sash changed early 20th C. 5 sheets (1934); 2 ext. photos (1934); 2 data pages (1934). Illustrated on p. 69.

The Oaks (Todd House) GA-14-100. 1103 Vernon St., facing N. Frame with clapboarding, flush siding under porches, 50'6'' (five-bay front) × 38'4'' (plus porches) deep, two stories in front, two stories plus raised basement in rear, truncated pyramid roof with widow's walk, four int. chimneys at outer walls, two-story-high hexastyle porch at front with fluted columns, modified Doric order, antae with alternating squared and convex ribs at junction with body of house. Three-story tiered porch at rear, bottom (basement) story with square columns (stucco on brick), upper stories with square tapered wooden columns. Unusually heavy louvered blinds, extra wide (double door opening 6'5'') entrance doorway with sidelights and transom; four-room central hall plan, four marble mantels. Greek Revival, built ca. 1844. Philip Green, architect. Parts of back porches have been enclosed, and a kitchen (possibly moved from another position) attached to original porch. Boyhood home of Lamar Dodd, 20th C. painter. 9 sheets (1934); 3 ext. photos (1934); 3 data pages (1934). Illustrated on p. 119.

Render House. See *The Magnolias.*

Todd House. See *The Oaks.*

La Grange Vicinity
Troup County (143)

Boddie House GA-1143. N side of Greenville Rd., facing s (Ga. Hwy. 109). 7 mi. E of La Grange town square, in front of county milepost 22. Frame with clapboarding, flush boarding under portico, rectangular with rear wing; 48'5'' (five-bay front), two stories, gable roof, three ext. end chimneys, one ext. chimney on side of lean-to, projecting two-story-high front portico, Ionic tetrastyle with fluted columns. Unusually skillful adaptation of Greek prototype capitals to wood construction, faces of capitals are hand carved, between faces the wooden volutes are machine turned. Doors with sidelights and arched fanlights at entrance and at balcony, which is of wood with sheaf-of-wheat wooden railing. Central hall plan, originally four rooms downstairs, two upstairs; changed to four over four before Civil War. Plainness of stairway contrasts with other millwork; joint in upstairs flooring near stairway indicates that it might not have been built as originally planned. Adam-type mantels with sunbursts, wainscot with original paint simulating grained wood with raised panels

and with black moldings in one room. Original locks stamped "Wm. IV R." Transitional: late Federal, early Greek Revival. Built 1833–36; architect probably Collin Rodgers. Marked similarity to Edwards House★ in La Grange. Second-story lean-to rooms added, and first-floor lean-to rooms enlarged ca. 1844; 20' × 40' dining room at back may have been added at the same time. Kitchen (possibly the original detached kitchen) added to dining room early 20th C. Fireplace removed from side of dining room, replaced with sliding glass doors mid 20th C. Owned continuously by descendants of first owner. 9 ext. photos (1936); 3 int. photos (1936); 1 data page (1936). Illustrated on pp. 70, 71.

Lexington
Oglethorpe County (111)

Baldwin-Cox-Chedell House (Cox-Chedel-Johnston House) GA-175. 120 Church St., facing SSW. Frame with beaded clapboarding, rectangular with rear ell, 50'4'' (first-floor, five-bay, second-floor, six-bay front), two stories, truncated pyramidal roof (steeper than customary for the period) with concealed gutters, four end chimneys, one int. chimney in ell. Windows nine-over-nine first floor, nine-over-six second floor, 8'' × 10'' panes. Two-story-high hexastyle porch with round fluted columns that have round stone bases and square capitals. A reeded triglyph carries through architrave and frieze over each column; frieze is paneled between triglyphs. Entrance with sidelights and transom framed by pilasters with entablature. Divided central hall, stairs in front

part, two rooms each side.

Carriage house, wood frame with clapboarding, square, two stories, second story a dovecote, smaller than first story and separated from it by a hipped skirt roof. Roof of second story pyramidal with finial at apex.

Original house only one room deep, early 19th C., probably built by William Baldwin. Doubled in size and Greek Revival porch added by Swepson Cox or Dr. Chedell mid 19th C. Carriage house destroyed mid 20th C. 1 ext. photo of house (1937); 1 ext. photo of carriage house (1936); 1 data page (1936).

Cox-Chedel-Johnston House. See *Baldwin-Cox-Chedell House.*

Cox-Steward-Knox Place. See *Pigeon House on Cox-Steward Farm,* Lexington Vicinity.

Gilmer House GA-78. NW corner of Gilmer St. and unnamed dirt road, the first road S of Boggs St. Frame with clapboarding, L-shaped, first-floor addition on one side, two small second-story additions, one over first-floor addition, the second over entrance porch. Main body of house had five-bay front, was two stories, the principal roof gable type (the two sides with different pitches) but hipped at corner of L. Three end chimneys. Three-bay, one-story entrance porch, combination-type columns with scroll-saw work in center, scroll-saw brackets, and scroll-saw work in frieze; turned banisters. Two-story-high fluted Doric columns support rear porch, which follows L shape of house. Entrance door with sidelights and full elliptical fanlight. Built early 19th C., greatly enlarged by Gov. George

Gilmer ca. 1840. The entrance door appears to have been traditional Federal style, the back porch Greek Revival, the front porch American Victorian, the small additions, including the projecting bay over the front porch, of no particular style. Demolished ca. 1972. 3 ext. photos (1934); 2 data pages (1934).

James-Willingham-Watkins House (Willingham-Wadkins House) GA-176. 222 Church St., facing ssw. Frame with clapboarding, rectangular, rear ell, curved bay addition on E side. Five-bay front, two stories, hipped roof with concealed gutters, three int. chimneys, one end chimney on bay. Two-story-high porch with round fluted wooden columns, stone bases, and square capitals, the capitals in two parts, each with dentils. Frieze paneled between reeded triglyphs that carry over frieze and architrave. Entrance door with sidelights and transom, framed by pilasters with entablature; balcony with sheaf-of-wheat railing. Doorway to balcony similar to entrance doorway. Central hall plan. Built ca. 1830 by Robert P. James, remodeled and Greek Revival porch added ca. 1850 by Willis Willingham. Sidelights, transoms, and window sash changed to single type, two-story bay added early 20th C. by Thaddeus Watkins. 1 ext. photo (1936); 1 data page (1936).

Moore-Young-Platt House (Judge Platt House) GA-18. 102 Church St., facing ssw. Frame with clapboarding, 52'5'' (five-bay front), rectangular with rear ell. Two stories (over raised basement in rear) with hipped roof. Two-story-high hexastyle porch with round fluted columns, square abacus and

suggestion of an echinus. Simplified entablature. First-story full-length windows opening onto porch. Entrance with elliptical fanlight over door and sidelights. Central hall plan, two rooms each side. Parlor with foliated ceiling medallions, cornice with beaded, foliated, and egg-and-dart moldings. Molded window and door trim with rosette corner blocks. Mantels of unusual design, one with three small colonnettes in frieze over paired colonnettes below, center panel with sunburst. First part built late 18th C. by Moore, enlarged ca. 1830 by George Young, and Greek Revival porch added by Judge Platt in mid 19th C. 1 ext. photo (1936); 2 int. photos (1936); 1 data page (1936).

Oglethorpe County Courthouse GA-194. Town square, facing N. Brick with granite trim, irregular shape, front five structural bays, ten openings first floor, five second floor. Two stories, hipped roof, six end chimneys, two (later?) int. chimneys. Entrance tower center of front façade with continuous round brick turrets at the four corners, terminating with conical pinnacles at the top; two front turrets rest on squat granite columns with round rusticated abaci. The tower rises in five stages: the first and second stages open, one bay wide; the third open, two bays wide; the fourth with two windows, and the fifth with a clock. Conical spire. Recessed two-tiered porch with one arch each side of tower at first floor, two arches each side second floor. East side has recessed porch with one wide arch first floor, four narrow arches second floor. All arches have rusticated stone voussoirs. Diverse window and sash types: some with transoms,

some arched, some curved with curvature of wall, some sash with one light, some with as many as thirty-six. Double entrance doors with transom and windows each side. Central hall plan. Richardsonian Romanesque, 1886–87; Wheeler and Parkins, architects; McAfee and Bondurant, builders. Courthouse built of locally manufactured brick and of wood and granite from Oglethorpe County. 1 ext. photo (1980). Illustrated on p. 204.

Saims-Bacon House. See *Saims House,* Lexington Vicinity.

Willingham-Wadkins House. See *James-Willingham-Watkins House.*

Lexington Vicinity
Oglethorpe County (111)

Pigeon House on Cox-Steward Farm (Cox-Steward-Knox Place) GA-172. sw side of abandoned dirt road, .1 mi. NW of its junction with County Rd. 156, this junction .7 mi. NE of junction of County Rd. 156 and U.S. Hwy. 78, which is 7 mi. SE of courthouse in Lexington. Frame with clapboarding, raised one story off ground. Pyramidal roof with finial and with flaring eaves. Supported by four wooden posts with braces at top, the braced portion covered with vertical tongue-and-grooved beaded boards; the rest of the base enclosed with diagonal lattice work. House had large door with pilasters and pediment one side. Classic frieze and cornice with two dentil bands, the lower one with triangular dentils; holes for pigeons below frieze. Probably mid 19th C. Demolished mid 20th C. Separately photographed was the old farm bell, which had been turned upside down, placed on a pedestal, and put to use as a flower pot. 2 ext. photos (1936); 1 data page (1936). Illustrated on p. 174.

Judge Platt House. See *Moore-Young-Platt House*, Lexington.

Saims House (Saims-Bacon House) GA-171. sw corner of Upson St. and unnamed dirt road, .2 mi. N of Church St. Frame with clapboarding, wood shingle roof, rectangular if porch is included. Five-bay front, one story, gable roof spraddle type, at least three end chimneys. Porch across front with N end enclosed, leaving three open bays. Square columns with Greek Revival proportions, concealed beam over so that cornice and porch ceiling are unified. Latticework between foundation piers. Double entrance doors with sidelights and transom, apparently central hall plan with two rooms each side. Typical mid 19th C. plantation style cottage, Greek Revival influence apparently limited to the proportions of the columns. Demolished mid 20th C. 1 ext. photo (1936); 1 data page (1936).

Louisville

Jefferson County (82)

Slave Market GA-14-2. Public square. Hand-hewn timber with wood shingle roof, 22-ft. square open pavilion, three bays each side. One story, pyramidal roof with belfry. Timber posts, 9 in. square, with mortised braces to beam over. Belfry with clapboard-

ing and louvers in pointed arch frames. Exposed hand-hewn roof framing, late 18th C., not documented. Braces were originally mortised at a lower level; could have been raised to allow headroom for a taller generation, or bottom of posts may have rotted, thus lowering height of building. Posts now rest on a concrete floor. Bell, cast in France in 1772 by François Gourbillon, used to assemble settlers in case of Indian attack. Belfry was possibly added after building was in use; its pointed arches and delicate roof line suggest later date. 1934 photo shows it surmounted by lamp, which has since been replaced with weathercock. Original floor was probably flagstone or earth, or possibly brick.

Building antedates city of Louisville and was erected at juncture of Georgetown and Savannah trails, where there was an Indian trading post. It was originally called the Market House, but slaves were sold here; it also became the official place for sheriff's sales and was for a number of years used as a community market house. 1 sheet (1934); 2 photos (1934); 3 data pages (1934). Illustrated on pp. 86, 87.

Macon

Bibb County (11)

Andrews House GA-141. 110 Third St., facing NW. Frame with clapboarding, stucco under porches, brick foundation piers with wood lattice between. Rectangular (five-bay front), projecting rear wings, one story, hipped roof capped by low rectangular louvered tower. Apparently six chimneys, two at ext. walls. Pilasters at corners of

house. Five-bay front porch with wrought-iron columns and railings of delicate and restrained design; peristyle courtyard at rear (facing SE) with Doric-type square wooden columns. The ventilating tower on the roof had similar though much shorter columns with louvers between. Entrance and rear door with sidelights and transom over, floor-length windows with louvered blinds on front porch; both floor-length and standard windows on peristyle. Evidently central hall plan. Greek Revival, 1856–57; demolished ca. 1949. Superb example of architectural expression deriving from climate and local methods of construction, while adhering to Greek Revival tenets. 4 ext. photos (1936); 1 data page (1936).

Baber House (Clinic Hospital) GA-190. 577 Walnut St., facing sw. Brick with stucco, scored. 54-ft. five-bay front, three-bay side; two stories over raised basement (basement partially concealed by retaining wall in front), hipped roof with center pediments in front and in back, four end chimneys flush with ext. walls. Elliptical arched recessed entrance with landing approached by horseshoe steps with wrought-iron railing. House crowned by entablature with cable molding under cornice and Greek fret incised into frieze. Lozenge-shaped tie rod heads, four in front and three on the sides, an integral part of the composition of the façade. Double entrance doors with additional set of louvered doors. Divided central hall plan with elliptical arch resting on paired columns, circular stairway with skylight over at rear of hall. Symmetrically molded window and door trim with carved foliated corner blocks.

Iron fence with anthemion-crested pickets with Greek key at base alternating with pointed pickets, the fence mounted on a low granite-capped wall. Traditional Federal style, completed 1830. Remodeled ca. 1920, at which time the horseshoe stairs were changed and present entrance porch added. Entrance door and fanlight are replacements, original fanlight having been removed before 1920. Int. remodeled to meet hospital requirements. Wings and addition to rear were added at various times between 1920 and 1937; connecting link to SE wing constructed after 1937.

At one time walled gardens extended to river at rear. Originally built by Dr. Ambrose Baber, who had his office in the yard. Home of Confederate General Howell Cobb 1862–68. Distinguished visitors included Confederate President and Mrs. Jefferson Davis, Confederate Generals P. G. T. Beauregard and Joseph E. Johnston. 6 ext. photos, 2 taken before 1920 (1936); 3 int. photos (1936); 6 data pages (1937).

Birdsey House. See *Coleman-Solomon House.*

Callaway House (Macon Hospital) GA-189. SW side of Pine St., facing NE, between New and Spring Sts. Brick with stone lintels, window sills, and steps. Rectangular, five-bay front, two stories, evidently low-pitched hipped roof, int. chimneys. Pilasters at corners and full Greek Doric entablature completely around house. One-story Greek Doric entrance porch with paired fluted columns; no pilasters at juncture with house. Entrance door with sidelights and transom, apparently central hall plan.

Greek Revival, ca. 1844; Elam Alexander, architect-builder. Eight-panel entrance door removed before photo was taken; entrance porch probably had pilasters that were likewise removed. Demolished 1972. 1 ext. photo (1936); 2 data pages (1936).

Canning House. See *Cannon Ball House.*

Cannon Ball House (Canning House) GA-142. 856 Mulberry St., facing NE. Frame with clapboarding, flush siding under porch. Thirty ft. (three-bay front), two stories, hipped roof, three chimneys at ext. walls. Two-story-high prostyle tetrastyle Greek Ionic porch with fluted columns, unfluted Doric antae. Balcony over central window supported by cast-iron brackets. Balcony and porch railings metal and twisted wire. Entrance door with two vertical panels, sidelights, and transom. Side hall plan, principal rooms with plaster cornices, foliated center medallions, and marble mantels. Two-story brick servants' house, walled garden. Greek Revival, 1854. Pediment-shaped parapet was destroyed during a storm; one wing, formerly on NW side, was moved to SW side before 1936. Int. blinds added after 1937. House was damaged by cannonading during the Civil War, hence its name. House museum. 1 ext. photo (1936); 1 data page (1936).

Chapman House (Poe House) GA-139. 841–45 Poplar St., facing SW. Brick, 50 ft. (five-bay front), L-shaped . Two stories over raised basement (basement partially concealed by retaining wall in front), hipped roof, three end chimneys flush with ext. walls. Balcony with cast-iron railing across front,

center part of balcony projecting to form roof of three-bay entrance porch with fluted cast-iron Corinthian columns. Cast-iron step and porch railings, marble entrance steps. Brick pilasters capped with concave brackets appear to help support balcony. Eight-panel entrance door with sidelights and transom. Central hall plan, hall divided by elliptical arch with circular stair at rear. Eight-panel int. doors with symmetrically molded trim, carved floriated corner blocks. Servants' house: brick, four-bay front, L-shaped, gable roof.

Federal style, ca. 1840. Remodeled into low-rent apartments, int. cut up. Front, rear, and NW sides painted. 3 ext. photos (1936); 2 int. photos (1936).

Christ Church Rectory. See *Rectory of Christ Church.*

Clinic Hospital. See *Baber House.*

Coleman House. See *Cowles-Bond House.*

Coleman-Solomon House (Birdsey House) GA-165. 2056 Vineville Ave., facing NE. Frame with clapboarding, flush siding under porches. Seven-bay, H- or U-shaped, hipped roof with balustrade, two stories. Giant order reentrant porch with fluted Greek Doric columns, unfluted pilasters at corners. Porch and balcony have wooden balustrades. Apparently central hall plan. Greek Revival, 1843; Elam Alexander, architect-builder. Extensively remodeled before 1937, when projecting wings were added and former prostyle porch changed to follow shape of remodeled house. Remodeling by Richard Drinn, architect-builder. Demolished 1963. 1 ext. photo (1936); 1 data page (1936).

Cowles-Bond House (Coleman House) GA-1124. 988 Bond St., facing sw. Brick with unpainted stucco scored, metal roof. 54' (five-bay front) × 40'8", rectangular, wings at sides and rear. Hipped roofs (flat at eaves, with concealed gutters) with deck and cupola; main roof and deck with balustrades. Four end chimneys flush with ext. walls in main body of house, four chimneys in wings, all brick with stucco. Two-story-high Doric porch three sides, columns brick (presumably) with stucco, unfluted. Eight columns across front, six each side. Wings and appendages to rear a medley of Greek Revival and Italianate styles. Pilasters across front of house, but not on sides. Heavy four-panel oak entrance door carved in high relief with fauna, flora, and scrolls. Fanlight and arched sidelights, both with etched and painted glass. Balcony with cast-iron railing with arch motif over entrance. Balconies with similar railings on each wing, the motif also repeated in the design of the cast-iron ventilators under the porch.

Central hall plan, the hall divided by paired Doric columns supporting an elliptical arch, and terminated by three-story spiral stairway with light coming from dome above. Eight-panel int. doors with symmetrical molded trim and foliated corner blocks. Plaster cornice moldings in hall and adjoining rooms, ceiling medallion in hall. Twin rooms of elongated octagonal shape in wings on each side, each with elaborate egg-and-dart plaster cornices with foliated frieze beneath, and floriated ceil-

ing medallions. Rose-tan marble mantel with arched opening in one of these rooms, both rooms with floor-length windows opening onto balcony. Parquet floors in all principal first-floor rooms. Kitchen and various service rooms are integral with the wings to the rear of the house.

Italianate servants' house. Other outbuildings include a cooling house, brick with stucco, and a picturesque combination carriage house and barn, frame with board-and-batten siding and a louvered tower. On s side toward front of house is the most fanciful of Victorian summer houses designed in the "Oriental style." Main part of house built 1836–40; Elam Alexander, architect-builder. Servants' house and most of the wings and appendages were added in 1850. Italianate doorway and balcony probably replaced a simpler entrance, and the one-story back porch was also probably enclosed at that time. Bathrooms projecting over the enclosed porch are post–Civil War additions. Minor changes made recently to accommodate the functions of a private school. Most of the mantels have been removed for safekeeping.

Confederate President and Mrs. Jefferson Davis and daughter, Winnie, were entertained at a ball held here in their honor in 1887. 1 ext. photo (1934); 2 data pages (1936). Illustrated on p. 169.

Cowles House. See *Cowles-Sams House.*

Cowles-Sams House (Cowles House) GA-14-27. 4596 Rivoli Dr., facing s. Brick with stucco, five-bay front, rectangular, wings toward rear. One story, hipped roof over porch, main roof gable with flat and sloping end parapets, four

end chimneys flush with ext. walls and combined with parapets. Classic Greek Ionic tetrastyle entrance porch with unfluted columns and pilasters. Porch entablature (complete with dentil band and egg-and-dart moldings) aligns with stucco band that carries over uncapped pilasters between front windows and at frontal corners of house; stucco lintels and keystones over windows. Six-panel entrance door with sidelights and pilasters, full-width elliptical fan over. Central hall plan. Plaster cornices and ceiling medallions, mantels with ornaments in gold leaf. Jeffersonian Federal, ca. 1830; Elam Alexander, architect-builder. Moved from about 539 Walnut St. (where it faced sw) in 1948. w wing added 1885; e wing 1948. Roof changed from standing-seam metal to composition, and roof balustrade removed 1948. First owner later built Cowles-Bond House★ in Macon, using the same architect-builder. 3 sheets (1934); 6 ext. photos (1934–36); 2 data pages (1936). Illustrated on p. 68.

Emerson-Holmes Building GA-195. 566 Mulberry St., facing ne. Brick with stucco, 23'9" (three-bay front), rectangular. Three stories, shed roof with false gable in front, one chimney in party wall. Originally three unequal arched openings at first floor, the wider center arch elliptical. Arched door with 4-in. thick stiles. Second floor with cast-iron balcony supported by console stone brackets, three floor-length arched windows above which are arched (top and bottom) glass panels with console stone brackets and hood molds over. Ornate cast-iron attic ventilators and raking cornice with modillions. Lower floor commercial (originally dental offices). Second floor two int. halls with skylights and arched doorways; one hall with entrance stair, the other with delicate curving stairway to third floor. Two second-story chambers at rear opening on roof of first floor; one chamber over these on third floor. Halls and salon to front are two stories high. Front chamber, or salon, full width of int. (21'3'') and 30 ft. long with elliptically vaulted ceiling, approximately as high as the room is wide. This room entered by arched sliding doors 14½ ft. high, one leaf opening to each hall. Walls with sunken panels framed by heavy moldings; coffered ceiling. Third-floor chamber gets through ventilation by way of elaborately framed ventilator grilles which open to the upper part of the hall. Italianate, 1856; James B. Ayers, architect. Original marble mantels, pier mirrors, glass chandeliers, and silver doorknobs have been removed, as has cast-iron balcony on front. Entrance to apartment has been changed from int. to ext. one. Large shop window has replaced two of street-floor arched windows or doors. 1 ext. photo (1937); 4 int. photos (1936); 1 data page (1936). Illustrated on p. 144.

First Presbyterian Church GA-274. 682–90 Mulberry St., facing NE. Brick with stucco scored, tucked jointing. Copper roof, copper-clad spire. 65'8'' including buttresses, three-bay front, five-bay sides. One story over raised basement, gable roof with sloping parapet ends, dormer windows. Projecting tower with square base, octagonal belfry with louvers, octagonal spire with copper finial. Octagonal buttresses each corner, pilaster-type buttresses on side walls.

Arched windows with geometric tracery. Corbel projection at top of walls, simple corbel pattern on side walls, trefoil pattern on front and rear walls. Front steps granite, T-shape in plan with stem toward church. Parapet-type wall in front of steps, the wall height changing with ogee curves. Entrance under tower, high arched opening, double doors (4' × 8' each) with equal-size panels over, semicircular transom at top with wood tracery and center quatrefoil. Doors and panels of same pattern. Shafts of clustered colonnettes and pilasters at face of opening carry through as archivolts when they reach the arch, no capitals. Wheel window over arch.

Vestibule with groin-vaulted ceiling under tower. Four-aisle auditorium with original pews. Plaster walls with heavy cove at top; four exposed scissors trusses. End wall plain except for arched reredos with organ pipes and small arched window over. Romanesque Revival, 1858. Additions to rear; auxiliary building in same style on SE side. Dormer windows added late 19th C., giving light via stained-glass panels in the ceiling. Original apse with windows screened by organ pipes. Clear glass has been replaced with stained glass, and int. louvered shutters removed. Two chimneys within end wall have been removed. 1 ext. photo (1981). Illustrated on p. 135.

Holt House GA-144. 1229 Georgia Ave., facing SSW. Frame with clapboarding, basement brick with stucco scored. 52'8'' (five-bay front), rectangular, low-pitched hipped roof, four end chimneys within ext. walls, two stories over raised basement. Two-story-high hexastyle Greek Doric front

porch with fluted wooden columns, side porch with similar columns of formed sheet metal. Horseshoe entrance steps with wrought-iron railing (the pickets curved outward toward the top) with spiral volutes and ball-capped newels. Six-panel entrance door with sidelights and transom, pilasters each side with scroll brackets supporting wooden balcony. Porch and balcony with wooden balustrades, the porch balustrade curving outward between columns. Floor-length windows on porch. Central hall plan, the hall with varicolored marble floor. White marble mantels. Greek Revival, ca. 1840; Elam Alexander, architect-builder. Remodeled ca. 1884, at which time the side porch was added, the original metal porch railing was replaced by the present wooden balustrade, and the marble floor was installed. It is likely that the large-paned window sashes were installed at that time, that the chimneys were recapped, and that some changes were made in the balcony and its supports. House originally had a pediment-shaped parapet in front, and round silver balls (replaced by brass ones) on the front-step newels. 1 ext. photo (1936); 1 data page (1936).

Johnston-Hay House GA-275. 934 Georgia Ave., facing NE. Brick with thin coat of red stucco with narrow white convex (tucked) mortar joints meticulously indicated, these joints not always coinciding with the real mortar joints beneath. This coating worn away except in protected areas. Standing-seam metal roof. Five-bay front, rectangular, with lower irregular rear wings. Two-and-a-half stories over raised basement, plus two-story octagonal cupola.

Flat roof with balustrade over front porch, other roofs hipped. Six corbelled chimneys (with chimney pots) flush with ext. walls. Seven-bay, one-story Corinthian porch, the three center bays curving out to form a convex unit. Fluted wooden columns on pedestals, wooden balustrade. Curving open-arms marble entrance steps with marble balustrade. Windows of two main floors arched, those of second story arched and pedimented. Ocular windows on top floor. Ornate entablature with scroll-type brackets. Octagonal cupola with console buttresses. Heavy (6-in.-thick stiles) arched double entrance door, elaborately carved in high relief, with etched glass panels and silver-plated hardware. Central hall plan, the hall with marble floor and arched double doors opening into adjoining rooms. One set of doors both arched and curved. Doors of varying types of wood, including oak and rosewood. Design of door and window frames varies, all ornate and most with hand-carved details. Open-well three-flight stairway with heavy mahogany balustrade, stained- or painted glass window at middle flight, niche (on landing) that is actually a camouflaged door leading to a secret room. Elaborate plaster ceilings, medallions, and cornices. Tiffany stained-glass window of later date in dining room. Copper water-storage tank in attic to furnish pressure for running water. Italianate (Tuscan villa) style, built 1855–60; T. Thomas and Son, New York City, architects.

William Makepeace Thackeray visited owner, William B. Johnston, while house was under construction and found him living in one of his servant's houses. Part of the Confederate treasury is

said to have been stored for a while in the secret room. House museum. 1 ext. photo (ca. 1978); 1 int. photo (1978). Illustrated on pp. 142, 143.

Dr. Miller House. See *Raines House.*

Napier-Small House (Small House) GA-143. 156 Rogers St., facing E. Frame with clapboarding, flush siding under porch. 54'6" (five-bay front), two stories, truncated hipped roof, four end chimneys within ext. walls. Heroic hexastyle Greek Doric porch across front, end columns square, unfluted, other columns round, fluted, all columns wooden. Full entablature over porch with inverted laurel-wreath ornaments instead of traditional triglyphs and mutules; entablature without architrave or ornaments around rest of house. Entrance door with sidelights and transom, framed by pilasters and entablature; balcony over, supported by additional pilasters with console brackets. Central hall plan. Greek Revival, ca. 1847; Elias Carter, architect (?). House originally on N side of Vineville St. between Rogers and Corbin Sts., facing S. Moved to present location before 1936, when windows, entrance door, and mantels may have been changed. House formerly sat on a high basement. A pediment-shaped parapet with central and end acroteria has been temporarily removed from above porch. 1 ext. photo (1936); 1 data page (1936).

Old State Bank GA-168. 451 Walnut St. Brick with stucco scored. Two-bay street front, entrance on side. Rectangular, built against Slade House of same HABS number. Gable roof with pediment,

at least one int. chimney, large eighteen-light windows with louvered blinds. Singularly pleasing proportions. Built ca. 1827. Demolished ca. 1940. 1 ext. photo (1936); 2 data pages (1936).

Poe House. See *Chapman House.*

Raines House (Dr. Miller House) GA-145. 1183 Georgia Ave., entrance facing SSW. Frame with clapboarding, flush siding under porches. Greek cross shape, each arm one bay wide. Two stories (central octagonal tower three stories) over raised basement. One-story porches, bay windows. Central tower has peaked roof with balustrades; cross arms have gable roofs with pediments; porches and bay windows have flat roofs with balustrades. Four int. chimneys with tall shafts projecting above tower. Pilasters with bowtel cap molding but no abacus at each ext. corner; Ionic entablature over. One-story, five-bay, quarter-circle Greek Ionic entrance porch between two of the projecting arms. Polygonal central hall plan. Three-story spiral stairway with clerestory widows, floriated ceiling medallion in color. Greek Revival with some Italianate details. Built 1848; Elam Alexander, architect-builder. Plans adapted from those of W. H. Ranlett, published in *The Architect* (New York, 1847–49), plates 31–35. Entrance porch changed to its present circular form and woodwork in central hall changed, both before 1936. Two-story unit in angle of cross at rear probably not original, minor changes in rear porch. 1 ext. photo (1936); 2 int. photos (1936); 1 data page (1936). Illustrated on pp. 158, 159.

Rectory of Christ Church GA-1100. 211 Third St., facing SE. Frame with clapboarding. Three-bay front, rectangular, wing on NW side. Two-story hipped roof, at least one chimney at ext. wall. Heroic tetrastyle porch with fluted Greek Doric columns, unfluted antae, simplified entablature. Reduced version of porch, one story high and two bays wide, was repeated on wing. Entrance door with sidelights and transom. Greek Revival, mid 19th C. Originally at 538 Walnut St., facing N. Moved to Third St. ca. 1925. Demolished ca. 1949. 1 ext. photo (1936); 1 data page (1936).

Slade Houses GA-168. 453 Walnut St., facing SW. Main house brick, Flemish bond, six-bay rectangular. Gable roof with end parapets. Apparently four end chimneys flush with end walls. Double house with two fanlight entrance doors, one with a small one-bay modified Doric entrance porch with square columns; the other of later vintage, with a three-bay porch with turned columns. Each unit side hall type, the halls being toward the center and adjacent. Carpenter version of Adam mantel with paired colonnettes. Two-story brick servants' house with gable roof and ext. stair. Old State Bank Building (with the same HABS number) built flush against SE side. Probably early 19th C. Both entrance porches probably added after house was built. Demolished ca. 1940. 3 ext. photos (1936); 1 int. photo (1936); 2 data pages (1936).

Small House. See *Napier-Small House.*

State Bank. See *Old State Bank.*

Madison

Morgan County (106)

Boxwood (Kolb-Pou-Newton House) GA-183. 357 Academy St., facing NW; also faces Old Post Rd. Frame with narrow (3¼-in. exposed face) clapboarding. Rectangular, one wing on NE side. 50'6'' (five-bay, second story six-bay, front) × 45'7''. Two and one-half stories, the half-story windows in the oversized frieze of the entablature. Hipped roof with unusually wide eaves, five int. chimneys. Doric type pilasters at corners. Small entrance porch on SE (Old Post Rd.) front with Doric columns in antis, steps on three sides. Five-bay porch with pagoda-type roof across Academy St. front, delicate columns and frieze with lattice inset, scroll-saw brackets, and sheaf-of-wheat railing. Full-length windows open to porch. Both entrances with sidelights and transoms of red Venetian glass with grapevine pattern in clear glass; corner panes blue with same pattern. Wide central hall with rounded open-well stairway recessed to one side, leaving hall unobstructed. Connecting parlors with matching marble mantels on SE side of hall, one of the parlors still furnished with the gold-leaf mirrors, furniture, draperies, and carpet installed when the house was built.

In the kitchen (not an outbuilding), the original cast-iron stove remains. The house was provided with running water, a bathroom, and more than ample closets.

Both fronts are approached through formal gardens with boxwood-bordered flower beds, the pattern unchanged. Picket fences separate the gardens from the street. Outbuildings include a servants' house, frame with board-and-batten siding, rectangular, two stories, gable roof, barge boards with scroll-saw design; also a square smokehouse of similar construction, but one story, and with pyramidal roof.

Greek Revival with Italianate and Victorian details, built for James Kolb in 1845–51. Architect unknown, but house was precut in Augusta and the parts brought to Madison by oxcart. 3 photos of gardens (1936); 1 int. photo (1936); 1 data page (1936). Illustrated on pp. 123, 170.

Kolb-Pou-Newton House. See *Boxwood.*

Thurleston GA-182. 847 Dixie Ave., facing S. Wood frame with clapboarding, 52 ft. (five-bay front). Rectangular, irregular additions toward rear. Two and one-half stories, gable roof, two end chimneys within ext. walls, two end chimneys flush with ext. walls, one int. chimney. Front façade with four fluted Doric-type pilasters, full entablature with triglyphs and modillions, three gables with frieze and architrave repeated under raking cornice. Deck full width of house. Double entrance doors with sidelights and transom framed by pilasters with entablature. Balcony over entrance. Central and cross halls. Unusual mantel with three-quarter reeded columns with exaggerated entasis. Projecting frieze over columns has pointed arch openings on three sides, revealing finial within. Center panel in frieze has sunburst with concave disc at center, and a sphere in the center of the disc. Oldest part of house 1818; two front rooms and hall 1848; deck before 1936. Wooden balcony over entrance was replaced by metal balcony after 1937. Other additions, changes at various times. Architect for 1848 addition said to have been English, name unknown. 1 ext. photo (1936); 1 int. photo (1936); 1 data page (1936).

Marietta

Cobb County (34)

Bostwick-Fraser House (Fraser-Couper House) GA-1107. 199 Fraser St. (also 325 Atlanta St.), facing w. Frame with clapboarding, flush siding under central part of porch, brick wing. Rectangular, rear ell and side wing, two stories, first floor with three-bay front, second story with five bays. Gable roof with three end chimneys, one-story lean-to across back with brick wing attached on s end. Windows with small (8" × 10") panes except in French doors, which are apparently replacements for first-story windows opening on the porch. Entrance and balcony doors with sidelights and transoms. Central hall plan. Apparently built early 19th C., the windows changed to French doors and the Greek Revival porch added mid 19th C., possibly in 1844, the date generally given as the year of construction. 2 ext. photos (1936); 1 data page (1936).

Fraser-Couper House. See *Bostwick-Fraser House.*

Marietta Vicinity

Cobb County (34)

Covered Bridge over Sope Creek GA-185. About 100 yds. s of present Paper Mill Rd. Bridge, which is 2 mi. E of intersection of Paper Mill Rd. with Roswell St., which is 3 mi. E of Roswell St. and U.S. Hwy. 75 intersection in Marietta. Wood frame, board-and-batten siding, coursed rubble piers, gable roof. Town lattice construction with heavy hand-hewn timbers, wooden pegs. Antebellum (?). Destroyed after 1936, though parts of stone piers remain. 1 ext. photo (1936); 1 data page (1936).

Marshallville

Macon County (97)

Frederick-Wade House GA-146. N side of w Main St., facing s down McCaskill St. Frame with clapboarding, flush siding, paneled wainscot under porch. 50'4" (five-bay front), rectangular with irregular additions toward the rear. Main roof hipped; both gable and hipped roofs on additions. Four ext. end chimneys, corbelled. Two-story-high, five-bay front porch with square Doric-type wooden columns across front. Ornate double entrance door with stained glass, heavy moldings, and raised panels in a variety of shapes and sizes. Stained-glass fanlight over door, stained-glass sidelights against, but not a part of, the doorway. Balcony with turned wooden balusters is supported by curvilinear wooden brackets. One-light window sash. Central hall plan. Victorian iron fence. Built ca. 1840. Moved from nearby site in 1929, when entrance doorway, windows, balcony, and int. were much changed. Old photo shows plain sidelights, transom, and balcony, and a wooden picket fence. 1 ext. photo (1936); 1 data page (1936).

McCaskill-Rumph House GA-149. w side of McCaskill St., facing E, .3 mi. from W. Main St. Brick (made on site), 53'6" (five-bay front), rectangular, two stories, pyramidal roof, two int. chimneys with sunken panels and corbelled tops. Five-bay, two-story porch with full-length fluted wooden Doric columns across front, paneled antae at junction with house, Ionic entablature. Balustrade with turned wooden balusters both stories, the balusters of the first floor being unusually bold (5¼ ins. square at the base) and resting directly on floor. Entrance door with arched top panels, bottom panels square with concave corners; sidelights and segmental arched transom over, framed by pilasters and cornice. Central hall plan. Greek Revival with some Italianate details, built ca. 1855. 1 ext. photo (1936); 1 data page (1936).

Slappey House GA-147. s side of Main St., facing N onto Bryan Hill Rd. Frame with clapboarding, 52'3" (five-bay front), rectangular, rear wings. Two stories, hipped roof, five end chimneys within ext. walls. Five-bay two-story-high porch with fluted wooden Doric columns and paneled antae at junction with house. Ionic entablature around two-story part of house. Balcony across five bays, balustrade with turned wooden balusters on balcony and porch, those on porch being heavier (5¼ ins. at base) and resting directly on floor. Porch and balustrade are markedly similar to those of nearby McCaskill-Rumph House★. Full-length windows on porch. Double entrance doors, each with an elongated octagonal upper panel and an octagonal lower panel. Sidelights with transom over, framed with pilasters and cornice. Two small one-bay, one-story entrance porches at each side of house. Central hall plan with cross hall at back. Unusual two-flight stairway, lower flight being in cross hall, upper flight in central hall. Greek Revival with Italianate details. Ca. 1860; may have been completed after Civil War. One-story part at back appears to have been a separate house, moved against main body of the house. Porch on w side has been enclosed by glass. Stairway has possibly been changed; if so this was probably done about the turn of the century. 1 ext. photo (1936); 1 data page (1936).

Marshallville Vicinity
Macon County (97)

Felton House GA-169. McCaskill St. Extension 3.2 mi. from intersection with Main St. in Marshallville, sw corner (facing N), intersection with road leading to Ga. Hwy. 22 and McCaskill St. extension. Frame with clapboarding, flush siding under porch. Five-bay front, rectangular with rear ell, two stories, one-story lean-to and ell at rear. Main roof gable. Three ext. chimneys stuccoed, one int. chimney. One-bay, two-tiered front porch with pediment, heavy square wooden columns, lighter pilasters. Double entrance doors, similar to traditional six-panel type except that the two top panels are combined into one horizontal panel. Sidelights and transom, sidelights not included in frame, but placed against it, top of sidelights aligned with top of transom. Single door with similar sidelights and transom to second-story porch. Cen-

tral hall plan. Indigenous, semiclassical porch and doorway, ca. 1830. Sidelights may be an early addition; columns are obviously replacements, probably of four (instead of present two) lighter columns at each story. Balusters also appear to be of later date. According to one account, there was formerly a one-story porch across front, but flush siding and pilasters indicate that original porch was narrower two-story type. A separate kitchen was moved against house, creating ell at back. 1 ext. photo (1936); 1 data page (1936).

Rumph House GA-160. On NE side of unnamed county road, facing ssw, the site .3 mi. NW of road's intersection with County Rd. 32, which is 1.5 mi. NE of fork-type intersection of County Rd. 32 with Ga. Hwy. 127 (E. Main St. Ext.). This fork is .5 mi. E of intersection of that street with Hwy. 49 in Marshallville. Frame with clapboarding, flush siding under porches. Five-bay front, probably rectangular. Two stories, hipped roof, at least two end chimneys. One-bay, two-story-high entrance porch with plain square Doric-type wooden columns. Balcony behind supported by similar but smaller columns. Double entrance doors (four unequal panels per door), sidelights two lights wide, pilasters each side of door and of sidelights, elliptical fanlight over cornice. Door to balcony single type with molded casing instead of pilasters, but otherwise doorways are duplicates. Balcony had sheaf-of-wheat railing. Said to have been built ca. 1840, but details indicate an earlier date. Two-story-high porch, probably antebellum, was apparently added after house was built; before that, en-

trance must have been similar to entrance to Lowther Hall★ in Clinton, Ga. Demolished ca. 1955. 3 ext. photos (1936); 1 data page (1936).

Stage Coach Inn GA-148. s side of Bryan Hill Rd., 2.6 mi. from its intersection with W. Main St. in Marshallville. Frame with clapboarding, fieldstone foundation piers, wood shingle roof. Two stories with gable roof, lean-tos front and back (plantation plain style). At least two end chimneys. Ends of porch were enclosed; open dog trot through house. Hand-hewn framing, mortised and tenoned. Hand-cut boarding for floors, walls, and ceilings; no plaster. Unpainted wood throughout. Indigenous type, built 1810. Destroyed by fire ca. 1965. 2 ext. photos (1936); 1 data page (1936). Illustrated on p. 46.

Midway
Liberty County (90)

Midway Congregational Church GA-44. NE corner of junction of Ga. Hwy. 38 with U.S. Hwy. 17, facing s. Frame with wide (7⅛-in. face) beaded clapboarding, foundation brick with stucco, 40′4″ (five-bay front) × 60′5″. One story with balcony, gable roof at front with eaves returned at base of gable, hipped roof at rear. Square tower rising from roof, open hexagonal belfry. Bull's-eye ventilators in gable and in tower. Windows as in a two-story building because of balcony. Main entrance with double doors, single door at side of main entrance leads to balcony. Meetinghouse plan with U-shaped gallery. Original box pews. Post-colonial, built 1792 to replace 1756 building burned by British. Church first had doors on N, S, and W sides, the pulpit then on E (long) side. Pulpit moved to N side in 1849, doors on N and W sides closed, and gallery enlarged. Cemetery laid out in 1756, greatly enlarged and partly enclosed by a masonry (brick with stucco) wall 1800–13. Numbers of outstanding Georgians were connected with church and buried in cemetery. 2 sheets (1934); 1 ext. photo (1934); 2 int. photos (1934); 1 photo of cemetery (1934); 3 data pages (1934). Illustrated on p. 44.

Milledgeville
Baldwin County (5)

The Bell House. See *Old Parsonage.*

Brown-Sanford House (Stetson-Sanford House) GA-136. NW corner W. Hancock and N. Jackson Sts., facing SSW. Frame with clapboarding, flush siding under porch. Thirty-eight-ft., five-bay front by three-bay side. Two stories, gable roof, four end chimneys. Two-story, three-bay Palladian porch with Doric pilasters first floor, Ionic pilasters second floor, rectangular (not original) fluted columns first floor, round fluted Doric columns second floor (may have been original first-floor columns). Six-panel entrance doorway with sidelights and full elliptical fanlight with eagle at its pivotal center. Similar doorway to second-story porch. Off-center hall front to back. Hall divided by elliptical arch. Freestanding elliptical stairway in rear part of hall. Unusually graceful Adam-type mantels with carved wooden ornaments.

Traditional Federal style, built ca. 1820, John Marler, architect-builder. Originally located E side of Williamson St., between Montgomery and Hancock Sts., where it faced WNW. Moved to present location and restoration begun 1966. Original deep colors, marbleizing, wood graining, and gilding are features of restoration. Palladian porch unusual for its time. House museum. 6 ext. photos (1936); 2 data pages (1936). Illustrated on p. 65.

The Cedars GA-191. 131 N. Columbia St., facing WSW. Frame wtih beaded siding except under porch, where flush siding is used. Pavilion projecting to form portico, wings of unequal size each side. Irregular plan, 56'10'' (five-bay front), one side two bays deep; other side four bays deep. Two stories, gable roof, three ext. chimneys. Two-story, one-bay portico, attenuated full-length reeded Ionic columns with carved wooden capitals and matching pilasters. Decorative wooden fan in tympanum. Balcony supported by wrought-iron brackets attached to columns. Entrance door with sidelights and full elliptical fanlight; balcony door with sidelights and fan over door only, Palladian style. Off-center hall with curving stairway of unusual grace. Milledgeville Federal style, portico a type that appears to be unique to this area. Ca. 1825; Daniel Pratt (?), architect-builder. 3 ext. photos (1936); 1 int. photo (1936); 1 data page (1936). Illustrated on p. 56.

Central Building, State Hospital. See *Powell Building.*

Conn House. See *Stovall-Conn House.*

Governor's Mansion. See *Old Governor's Mansion.*

The Homestead (Williams-Ferguson House) GA-134. SE corner Washington and Liberty Sts., facing NNW. Frame with clapboarding, flush siding under portico. Rectangular, five-bay front, four-bay sides, two stories over raised basement, gable roof, four end chimneys. One-bay, two-story portico with full-length attenuated Tuscan (solid wood) columns with matching pilasters; balcony extending to and partly supported by columns. Entrance door with elliptical fan; similar door to balcony. One-story shed porch with one end enclosed across back. Central hall plan. Adam-type mantel with engaged columns and carved wooden sunbursts. Milledgeville Federal; 1818. Architecture typical of the period except for the two-story porch, which appears to be the first of a type unique to this area. 3 int. photos (1936); 1 data page (1936). Illustrated on p. 64.

Johnson-Ennis House. See *Rockwell.*

Lockerly (Tucker-Hatcher House) GA-1151. 1500 S. Wayne St., facing NW. Brick with stucco scored, 58' (five-bay front) × 43'2'', full-width front and back porches. Two stories over raised basement, hipped roof, four end chimneys flush with ext. walls. Hexastyle Greek Doric porch, heroic order, across front; one-story Greek Doric porch, one end enclosed, across rear. Central hall plan. Trim for doors and windows with shouldered architraves and batten profiles. Walnut doors, mahogany stair railing, marbleized risers. Greek Revival, ca. 1839. 1 ext. photo (1937); 1 data page (1936).

Milledgeville State Hospital. See *Powell Building.*

Old Governor's Mansion GA-156. 120 S. Clark St., facing wsw. Brick with stucco, granite trim. 79' (seven-bay front) × 61' (five-bay sides). Two stories over raised basement, hipped roof with pediment over portico, four end chimneys flush with ext. walls. Tetrastyle Greek Ionic portico, heroic order. Unfluted columns, simplified entablature. Entrance door with two vertical panels with enriched moldings, the door framed by pilasters with entablature. Central rotunda with coffered domed ceiling and skylight. Side corridor with stairway. Heavy plaster cornice moldings and ceiling medallions. Greek Revival, 1838; Charles B. Cluskey (?), architect; Timothy Porter, superintendent of construction. Except for removal of blinds, ext. is little changed, a cupola added at a later date having been removed. Minor changes have been made to main floor, which was restored in 1967, as was basement kitchen, with its large fireplace and Dutch oven. Second floor has been converted into an apartment for president of Georgia College at Milledgeville. Mansion was used as governor's residence from 1839 to 1868. Portions open to the public. 1 ext. photo (1934); 5 int. photos (1936); 1 int. photo (1980); 3 data pages (1936). Illustrated on pp. 104, 117, 120.

The Old Parsonage. See *The Parsonage.*

Old State Capitol GA-137. E. Greene St., also E. Franklin St., between S. Wayne and S. Elbert Sts. Four entrances, originally facing the four streets, principal entrance facing NNE onto Greene St. Brick with stucco. Main body of building 49'6" (Greene St. and Elbert St. fronts) × 145'2" at basement level; the towers project beyond the central block at each of the four corners. Three-bay front (Greene and Franklin Sts.) with eleven-bay fronts toward Elbert and Wayne Sts. Two stories over raised basement, flat roofs with crenellated parapets. Greene St. and Franklin St. entrance porches with pointed arches, principal windows of second story are Gothic arch type with hood moldings; other windows straight top with label moldings. Central tower with crenellated parapet and corner pinnacles. Axial cross corridors.

Matching Gothic-style gates on Greene St. and Franklin St. sides brick with stucco, crenellated parapet, three pointed-arch openings. Large center opening for vehicles, flanking openings for pedestrians.

Original building 1807; Maj. Gen. Jett Thomas, master builder. Corner towers and other changes ca. 1833; Joseph Lane, architect. Porticoes added 1850. Gates built ca. 1865 under supervision of Federal Army Col. B. W. Frobel. Int. and parts of ext. destroyed by fire in 1941; rebuilt with int. changes 1942. Served as Georgia State Capitol Building from 1807 to 1868. Used variously as day school, office building, and courthouse from 1869 to 1879, and for Georgia Military College (originally Middle Georgia Military and Agricultural College) since that time. Probably as old as any surviving Gothic Revival public building in the United States. 2 ext. photos (1936); 2 ext. photos (1937); 1 data page (1936). Illustrated on pp. 42, 125.

The Parsonage (Bell House) GA-192. 140 N. Columbia St., facing ENE. Frame with clapboarding, standing-seam metal roof. Main body of house rectangular (five-bay front), wings at rear. One-story hipped roof, two int. chimneys with corbel tops. Three-bay porch across front, fluted Doric columns and only the suggestion of an architrave. Complete entablature around main body of house. Full-length windows on porch, entrance doorway slightly recessed, full-length sidelights and transom. Central hall plan. Greek Revival, mid 19th C. Apparently only minor changes. 1 ext. photo (1936); 1 data page (1936). Illustrated on p. 122.

Powell Building (Milledgeville State Hospital) GA-1156. State Hospital grounds; NW corner Broad St. and Swint Ave., facing SSE. Brick with stucco, seven-bay rectangular central block, wings. Three stories plus attic story, hipped roof with parapet over central block only. Greek Ionic portico, tetrastyle, heroic order, unfluted columns three stories high and resting on pedestals. Center unit with pilasters between bays, attic story with lunettes, dome with lantern, belt courses each floor, flat arch windows. Three-story wings, semicircular arched windows with archivolts and impost blocks. Ionic entablature around central block and wings. Double entrance doors with balcony over. Rotunda with axial cross halls. Greek Revival, 1856; Scholl and Fay, architects. Wings added before 1937. 1 ext. photo (1937); 1 data page (1936).

Rockwell (Gov. Johnson–Ennis House) GA-135. 165 Allen Memorial Dr., facing SSE. Frame with clapboarding, flush siding under portico and in tympanum. Central block rectangular, five-bay front, four-bay sides, two stories, one-story wings, all over raised basement. Six end chimneys within ext. walls. Two-story-high Greek Ionic portico with two sets of paired columns. Lunette with fanned louvers in tympanum. Convex-front cantilevered balcony with Greek fret at edge of floor, cast-iron railing. Entrance doorway with double doors, leaded sidelights and full elliptical fanlight. Similar doorway at balcony. Interior doorways, paneled casing with anthemion ornaments, frieze with fret and anthemion motifs and cornice. Eight-panel doors.

Servants' house, frame with clapboarding and with gable roof, but much changed; attractive wellhouse with pyramidal roof and with segmental arches remain, as does handsome cast-iron fence mounted on low brick wall at front of lawn. Woodwork from dining room has been removed and installed in the Winterthur Museum in Wilmington, Del. Transitional Federal–Greek Revival, 1834; Joseph Lane, architect. Built for Herschel Johnson, governor of Georgia (1853–57) and Confederate senator. 1 ext. photo (1936); 2 int. photos (1936); 1 data page (1936). Illustrated on p. 84.

State Capitol. See *Old State Capitol.*

Stetson-Sanford House. See *Brown-Sanford House.*

Stovall-Conn House (Conn House) GA-132. 141 S. Wilkinson St., facing ENE and SSE. Frame with clapboarding, beaded siding first floor. Oldest part apparently L-shaped;

many irregular additions to northerly and westerly sides. Wilkinson St. (ENE) side three bays downstairs, five upstairs; Greene St. (SSW) side five bays. Two-story-high porch on two street sides of house has fluted columns, their capitals being a naive version of the Ionic order. Seven columns each side, total thirteen. Wilkinson St. doorway (principal entrance now) with sidelights, symmetrically molded trim with corner blocks and center tablet over door. Irregular plan; rooms at various levels. Older rooms at front have plaster walls and wood paneled ceilings. Large room in one-story part at rear has a plastered tray ceiling with center medallion, a type common in old Bermuda houses, but rare in Georgia.

Indigenous, Federal and Greek Revival styles. Oldest part (apparently one story) probably very early 19th C. Second story and porch thought to have been added ca. 1825. Most of the other additions between 1825 and 1860. 1 ext. photo (1936); 1 data page (1936).

Tucker-Hatcher House. See *Lockerly.*

Williams House. See *John Williams House.*

Williams-Ferguson House. See *The Homestead.*

Williams-Orme-Crawford House. See *John Williams House.*

John Williams House (Williams-Orme-Crawford House) GA-133. 251 S. Liberty St., facing ENE. Frame with clapboarding, 52'3'' (five-bay front) × 35'10'' (four-bay sides) plus one-story lean-to at

back. Two and one-half stories, gable roof with one dormer, four ext. end chimneys. Two-story-high portico with two slender solid wooden Tuscan columns with matching pilasters. Cantilevered balcony with curved corners, wooden handrail, and wrought-iron pickets. Entrance doorway with leaded sidelights and full semicircular fanlight; balcony doorway similar except fanlight elliptical. Decorative wooden fan in tympanum of portico, large lunette with fan muntins in N gable, same shape window with double-hung sash and sidelights in S gable.

Central hall with rounded stair, Adam-type mantels with carved sunbursts. Milledgeville Federal style, ca. 1830; Daniel Pratt (?), architect-builder. 5 ext. photos (1936); 3 int. photos (1936); 1 data page (1936). Illustrated on p. 57.

Milledgeville Vicinity
Baldwin County (5)

Boykin House GA-170. NE side of Ga. Hwy. 24 E, 9.5 mi. SE of Milledgeville City Hall; 6.9 mi. SE of Ga. Hwy. 24 E fork with Ga. Hwy. 22 E. Drive from highway to house .4 mi. House faces SSW. Frame with clapboarding, flush siding in tympanum of portico. Rectangular, five-bay front, two stories, two rooms deep downstairs, one room deep upstairs. Gable roof second floor, shed roof first floor. Two chimneys, int. at first-floor level, exposed at rear of second story. Two-story, one-bay portico with full-length fluted Doric columns and pilasters. Modified entablature without frieze, but with band of cone-shaped guttae immediately under cornice. Entrance doorway with sidelights and full semicircular fanlight; door to second-story porch similar except that fanlight is elliptical. Central hall with simple open-well stairway. Unusually fine wood and plaster work: Adam-type mantels with carved wooden fleurated motifs, one mantel flanked by concave arched niches framed with fluted wooden pilasters and foliated plaster arch moldings; window and door frames have symmetrically molded trim with foliated corner blocks; panels have concave corners and wave moldings under windows; plaster ceiling cornices with acanthus-leaf frieze. Milledgeville Federal, ca. 1830; Daniel Pratt (?), architect-builder. Stairway may not be original. One mantel removed. Much of the plaster work damaged. 2 ext. photos (1936); 1 ext. photo (1937); 9 int. photos (1936); 2 data pages (1936). Illustrated on p. 58.

Gov. Johnson–Ennis House. See *Rockwell*, Milledgeville.

McComb's Mount. See *Mount Nebo.*

Mount Nebo (McComb's Mount) GA-14-4. N side of Laurel Lake Rd. (County Rd. 90782) facing S, 4.1 mi. N of intersection with Ga. Hwy. 24 E, this intersection 2 mi. E of Milledgeville City Hall. Frame with clapboarding, standing-seam metal roof, rectangular, five-bay front. Two-story central pavilion with one and one-half story wings, gable roofs, arched dormer windows on wings. Salt-box type roof on wings. Four end chimneys, one int. chimney. Two-story, three-bay portico full width of central pavilion; lower floor with slender fluted Doric columns, second

floor with slender fluted Ionic columns. Recessed rear porch with segmental arches.

Entrance with unusual double glass doors, each door four panes wide and six panes high, the outer panes very narrow, the top and bottom panes very short. Single wooden panel below meeting rail. Fanlight over doors and louvered blinds each side. Similar door to second-story porch. Divided central hall, the front (reception) hall larger than the stair hall behind it. Graceful elliptical stairway, Adam-type mantels with carved wooden sunburst ornaments.

Gateposts and part of wall (stucco on stone) still remain and have been restored or repaired since 1964. Traditional Federal style, 1823. Destroyed by fire 1940. 4 sheets (1934); 3 ext. photos (1934); 1 int. photo (1934); 3 data pages (1934). Illustrated on pp. 39, 40.

Polhill-Baugh House GA-1154. NW side of Ga. Hwy. 243, facing ESE, 6 mi. S of intersection with Hancock St. in Milledgeville. Frame with board-and-batten siding, rectangular, five-bay front, one story, spraddle roof, two int. chimneys, five-bay porch across front. Double entrance doors, central hall, two rooms each side. Plantation cottage type with square Greek Revival type columns, ca. 1840. 1 ext. photo (1981). Illustrated on p. 74.

Westover GA-14-31. SE side of Pine Lodge Rd. (formerly Meriwether Rd.) facing NW, .4 mi. N of intersection with Ga. Hwy. 212 W, which is 3 mi. W of intersection of Ga. Hwy. 212 and Ga. Hwy. 22 W, which is 2.4 mi. W of intersection of Ga. Hwy. 22 W and North Columbia St. in Milledgeville.

Frame with clapboarding, L-

shaped, 55′4″ (five-bay front). Two stories, hipped roof except at portico, three end chimneys. Two-story portico, tetrastyle, Roman Doric. One-story porch on NE side, another on SE side, both modified Doric. Entrance doorway with etched sidelights and semicircular fanlight; similar doorway to second-story porch. Central hall plan with three-story, free-standing circular stairway, elaborate ceiling medallion centered over round stairwell. Ornamental plaster cornices with grapevine motif in ceiling plane, and acanthus leaves at the wall. Windows with fluted pilasters (some Ionic, some Corinthian), entablatures, and panels under windows, all grained, the carvings highlighted with gold. Marbleized baseboards and Adam-type mantels with fluted pilasters and sunbursts.

Magnificent gardens enclosed by a picket fence, extended to street. Much of the planting and one brick garden house still remain. Federal style (late, with Jeffersonian influence) ca. 1822; Daniel Pratt, architect and master builder. Ballroom (squaring the L shape and possibly replacing a porch) added ca. 1850. Porch and kitchen added behind ballroom. Destroyed by fire ca. 1942; replaced by a modified version of the original. 5 sheets (1934); 4 ext. photos (1934); 5 int. photos (1934); 3 data pages (1936). Illustrated on pp. 59, 88.

Middletown Vicinity
Elbert County (53)

Grogan House (Eureka). See *Richard B. Russell Project*, Elberton Vicinity.

Monroe

Walton County (149)

Briscoe-Selman House GA-1137. 343 McDaniel St., facing NE. Frame with clapboarding, flush siding on front center bay. Rectangular, irregular wings toward rear, five-bay front, two stories; roof part gable, part hipped, part shed, and part flat. Four end chimneys, one int. chimney. Double entrance doors with sidelights and full elliptical fanlight over; door to balcony similar. Corner stiles at front of house capped with carved Ionic type scrolls subtly interrelated in design with moldings of stile. Two-story-high porch extending across front and part of way down sides; round fluted columns resting on unusually high piers, widely spaced, six in front, four on SE side, three on NW side. Main body of house central hall plan, two rooms each side. Mantels with Federal-type motifs used in unorthodox but successful manner.

Original part of the house traditional Federal, ca. 1832; was one room deep and apparently had a two-tiered porch the width of the center bay. Greatly enlarged with successive additions over the years; the colonnaded porch added ca. 1900. 2 ext. photos (1936); 1 int. photo (1936); 1 data page (1936).

Davis House. See *Davis-Edwards House.*

Davis-Edwards House (Davis House) GA-1138. 238 N. Broad St., facing W. Frame with clapboarding, flush siding under porch. L-shaped, five-bay front, two stories with gable roof and three end chimneys, the chimneys brick with stucco scored. Three-bay, two-tiered portico with square

wooden columns and a frieze that continues across the front of the house. Frieze has unusually short triglyphs formed of four adjacent half-round moldings applied vertically. One-story porches with shed roofs on N side and E side, E porch enclosed at the end. Double entrance doors with sidelights and transom; similar entrance to second-story porch, except that some of the transom panes have been painted to imitate etched glass. Central hall plan, one room each side. Chamber on S side has plastered walls and ceiling with ceiling medallion. Other rooms have ceilings of flush boards; some rooms have walls of flush boards. All rooms have wainscot, all doors have four vertical panels and a transverse panel at lock rail. Brick outbuilding with large fireplace and with part of wall torn out for use as a garage. Greek Revival, 1845; builder and first owner Josiah A. Clark, who sold it to Charles A. Davis before completion. First story of porch was extended and an extra pediment added between first and second stories of the porch ca. 1880; various rooms added 1880–1930. Restored to original form 1971–79, Joseph A. Aycock in charge of restoration. Outstanding example of successful combination of indigenous and modified Greek Revival architecture. 1 ext. photo (1936); 1 ext. photo (1981); 1 data page (1936). Illustrated on p. 111.

Montrose Vicinity

Laurens County (88)

White Hall GA-159. SE side (facing N) of Ga. Hwy. 26, .1 mi. NE of Laurens–Bleckley County line. Frame with clapboarding, flush

siding under porch, T-shaped (rectangular including porch), five-bay front, one story, hipped roof, two int. chimneys, three end chimneys. Porch three sides, dying against projecting rooms at rear. Square porch columns of Greek Revival proportions resting on piers in front of porch; ten across front, four down sides, porch railing with turned balusters behind. Double entrance doors with transom and sidelights. Central hall plan. Ancient cedar trees remain. Modified Greek Revival, 1820?; built by Joseph McKee White; Sessions, architect. Transom with radiating muntins installed in 1960s to replace older one of simpler design, at which time Adam-type plaster and woodwork was installed, carport added, and breezeway between house and kitchen enlarged and enclosed. Particularly gracious example of integration of indigenous and Greek Revival architecture. 1 ext. photo (1980). Illustrated on p. 110.

Nacoochee Valley

White County (156)

Crescent Hill Baptist Church GA-162. N side (facing S) of Ga. Hwy. 17, .3 mi. W of intersection with Ga. Hwy. 75. Frame with clapboarding, flush siding in porch gable, stone piers with wood lattice between. Original part 24'3" (three-bay front) × 42'. One story, gable roof, one end chimney (not original). Steeply pitched pyramidal spire with dormer louvers resting on square belfry over vestibule, the spire braced to the corners of the belfry by decorative wooden mini-buttresses. Metal-covered ball and wrought-iron finial cap spire. Three-bay porch with pointed arches resting on column capitals in the form of a tulip or lotus blossom. Lattice-type windowpanes, those in front pointed-arch type, those on sides with triangular tops. Meeting-house plan with vestibule and balcony; balcony supported by columns with lattice inset. Board-and-batten walls, the battens fitted to a cornice board of pointed arches, thus forming a series of lancet-like panels. Exposed rafters and trusses. Gothic Revival, ca. 1872. 20th C. addition to rear. Built as Presbyterian church. 1 ext. photo (1981). Illustrated on p. 191.

Nichols-Hardman House GA-167. N side (facing S) of Ga. Hwy. 17, .125 mi. E of intersection with Ga. Hwy. 75. Frame with clapboarding, flush siding under porch, metal roof, stone piers with wood lattice between. Piers rest on solid rock outcropping. Rectangular, three-bay front, two stories, pyramidal roof with cupola, two int. corbelled chimneys stuccoed, bracketed cornice. Two-story square bay windows each side of entrance, two-story splayed bay windows on sides of house. Main porch front and two sides with oblique corners and with projections reflecting bay-window projections. Clustered columns, scroll-saw balusters. Segmental arched-top windows, paired. Arched entrance, double doors with sidelights carrying over in form of a transom arched at bottom and top. Central hall plan, open-well stairway curved at corners. Doors and stair-railing walnut. Black marble mantels, elaborate plaster cornice and ceiling medallions. Washstands with lavatories inset and original fixtures in bedrooms and in bath. Original

acetylene light fixtures and chandeliers since electrified. Outbuildings include a fanciful gazebo atop an Indian mound directly across highway from house, remains of two fountains, a greenhouse, a spring house, detached kitchen, smokehouse, acetylene house, servants' house, carriage house, corn crib, and horse barn, all designed to be in keeping with surroundings and with house. Original furnishings intact, even straw matting upstairs, window valances, and most of the books. Italianate (Tuscan villa) style ca. 1873. 3 ext. photos (1981). Illustrated on pp. 6, 188, 189.

Newnan
Coweta County (39)

Gordon-Banks House (Blount House) GA-1125. Originally located W side (facing E) on Bowman's Mill Rd., 1.1 mi. S of intersection with Ga. Hwy. 22 in Haddock. Now located S side U.S. Hwy. 29, 1.6 mi. W of courthouse in Newnan. House was reversed when it was moved, entrance is now from side that was at rear, and portico (facing S) is now at rear, overlooking private terraces, lawn, and lake.

House frame with clapboarding, flush siding in pediment, five-bay front (now rear), rectangular, gable roof, two int. chimneys. One-bay, two-story portico with attenuated Doric columns, fluted. Matching pilasters at corners of house and under porch. Porch pediment steeper than classic prototype; porch frieze omitted. Double six-panel doors (equal panels) with sidelights and full semicircular fanlight at first floor of portico; doorway at balcony similar except that fanlight is

elliptical. Divided central hall plan, stairway part larger than former entrance part; two parts of hall separated by fluted pilasters with elliptical arch ornamented with acanthus leaves. Circular freestanding stairway with rectangular balusters. Exquisite Federal-type mantels of varying designs throughout, one with flanking niches with decorative plaster shells. Details for woodwork and plasterwork primarily from Asher Benjamin. Original colors throughout: white walls, woodwork a combination of grained or marbleized work with contrasting colors. Gilded details such as stair brackets, acanthus leaves on arch, carved corner blocks of door frames, mantel ornaments, and pilaster capitals, gold color repeated in brass mounts of contemporaneous furnishings. Graining, marbleizing, color combinations approach the fine arts category.

Milledgeville Federal style, construction begun 1828; Daniel Pratt, architect-builder. Moved and restored 1969. Original flankers destroyed before 1900; new flankers and entrance porch replacing original back porch erected 1969. House was used as headquarters by Gen. Francis P. Blair of Sherman's army in 1864. Probably the most exquisite doorway and most authentic colors of the Federal period to be found in Georgia. 3 ext. photos (1934); 2 ext. photos (1936); 4 int. photos (1934); 13 int. photos (1936); 3 data pages (1936). Illustrated on pp. 60, 61, 62, 63.

Oxford
Newton County (109)

Carr-Waterson House (Carr House) GA-126. 1105 Wesley St.,

facing E. Wood frame with clap-boarding, novelty siding under porch and in pediment, rectangular, rear ell, five-bay front, two stories, gable roof, three end chimneys. Two-story-high Greek Ionic portico, balcony with wooden railing in lattice designs. Main entrance door and door to balcony Palladian type. Central hall plan, one room each side. Late Federal style, ca. 1836; Collin Rodgers, architect (?). Originally located N side of Corley St. between West and Spring Sts. in Covington, where it faced S. Converted into apartments and stripped of much of its int. woodwork mid 20th C. Moved to Oxford and restored in 1975, when rear ell was greatly enlarged, stairway changed to accommodate second floor of ell, and replacements for missing mantels installed. 5 ext. photos (1936); 2 data pages (1936).

Few Literary Society Hall GA-198. Campus, Emory at Oxford, facing w. Brick with stucco scored, pediment wood frame with flush siding. Rectangular, one-bay front, two stories, prostyle tetrastyle temple form with two-story, heavy square columns (brick with stucco) of Doric inspiration. Recessed entrance with sidelights and transom, the recess framed by pilasters with entablature. Vestibule with stairs to second floor, which consists of a vestibule and one large meeting room. Greek Revival, 1852; William Galloway and George B. Carpenter, builders. Original windows with wood sash and sidelights replaced by metal windows; four end chimneys (flush with ext. walls) removed; stairway and first-floor plan changed since 1936. 2 ext. photos (1936); 1 data page (1936). Illustrated on p. 108.

Old Emory Church GA-125. W side (facing E) of Wesley St. between W. Clarke and W. Soule Sts. Wood with clapboarding, rectangular, wings toward rear, two-bay front, one story, gable roof, front gable pediment type, belfry with louvers and pyramidal roof. Pilasters at corners of church; twin entrances, each with double doors with transoms and each framed by pilasters with entablatures. Meetinghouse plan with gallery on three sides and in wings. Greek Revival, 1841; belfry added later. Wings added and chancel remodeled 1878. 1 ext. photo (1936); 1 data page (1936). Illustrated on p. 101.

Phi Gamma Literary Society Hall GA-197. Campus, Emory at Oxford, facing E. Brick with stucco, rectangular one-bay front, one-story prostyle tetrastyle temple form on semiraised basement that is completely above ground in the rear. Two chimneys flush with ext. walls, pilasters at corners and in center of each side. Portico with antae and two Ionic columns. Tympanum faced with beaded boards run diagonally to meet at center line of tympanum. Entrance has double doors with sidelights and transom framed by pilasters with entablature. Vestibule with meeting room behind. Greek Revival, 1851. Windows with wood sash replaced by metal sash since 1936. 1 ext. photo (1936); 1 data page (1936).

Panola Vicinity

De Kalb County (45)

Latimer-Felton House. See *Latimer-Felton House*, Atlanta Vicinity.

Pearl Vicinity

Elbert County (53)

Beverly Plantation. See *Richard B. Russell Project*, Elberton Vicinity.

Plains

Sumter County (131)

Billy Carter Service Station GA-243. 216 W. Church St., facing N. Main body of station frame with novelty siding, rectangular, four-bay front, one story, gable roof, one int. chimney; annex at rear with asbestos siding, gable roof. Flat roof metal canopy supported by metal posts at front. Sloping canopy similarly supported over grease rack on w side; storage room with galvanized sheet metal roofing used as siding behind grease rack.

Gasoline pumps, vending machines, and benches under front canopy. Wall clock, long stopped at 1:26, over window. Two entrance doors: the one for employees opening behind bar on int., the one for customers opening in front of it. Interior with L-shaped bar and stools, merchandise on wall behind bar, photos and posters decorate other walls.

20th C. vernacular. Main body built ca. 1935 as playroom for a residence, and moved to this location in 1954. Additions, at various times 1954–78. Once owned by President Carter's brother Billy, the station was the scene of much campaigning by "the good ole boys of Plains" during 1976 presidential election. 2 ext. photos (1979). Illustrated on p. 236.

Jimmy Carter House GA-244. 209 Woodland Dr., facing E. Brick veneer, one wing and carport board-and-batten siding. Central block rectangular, irregular rambling wings, rear ell. Nine-bay (some double or triple) front including wings, one story, gable roof and one int. chimney. Recessed entrance with double flush doors with sidelights. Floor-length multipaned windows in principal rooms at front; glassed-in porch overlooking patio at rear. Entrance hall with brick floor combined with carpeted reception room, opening onto living room with fireplace, bookshelves, and exposed truss ceiling. w wall of this room all glass sliding doors which open onto glassed-in porch. From entrance hall through glass walls of living room and porch there is a view of patio and surrounding woods.

Carport with bedroom over connected by covered walk roofed with translucent plastic. Small one-room child's playhouse in rear. Grounds wooded and natural except for driveway, patio, and comparatively small irregular lawn area near the house. No swimming pool.

Anonymous or ranch-house style, built 1961–62. Carport enclosed, porch and new carport added 1974. Hugh W. Gaston, A.I.A., architect for original part and for additions. 6 ext. photos (1979). Illustrated on p. 227.

Plains Vicinity

Sumter County (131)

Jimmy Carter Boyhood Home GA-245. N side (facing ssw) of Lebanon Cemetery Rd. (County Rd. 92), 1.5 mi. sw of its intersection with Church St. (Ga. Hwy. 280). Frame with clapboarding, chim-

neys, piers under front-porch columns, part of foundation walls faced with small uncoursed fieldstone. Latin cross shape, three-bay front, one story, main roof hipped, projections with gable roofs, dormer for attic ventilation with shed roof. Two int. chimneys. Wide eaves with exposed rafters. Porch across front with short square wooden columns resting on high stone piers. Plan similar to divided central hall type with three rooms each side, but front hall and the room on w side are combined.

Commissary or store in side yard; frame with clapboarding, rectangular, one-bay front. Gable roof (gable toward front) with sheds each side. Porte-cochère with hipped roof at front, its roof resting on two short columns on high stone piers like those of the house.

House anonymous style reflecting bungalow influence, ca. 1910. Front porch since screened, metal awnings added. Present grass lawn was swept yard during Carter's childhood. Jimmy Carter lived there from 1928 to 1946. 2 ext. photos (1979); 1 ext. photo of commissary (1979). Illustrated on p. 224.

Ridgeville

McIntosh County (96)

Epping House. See *Epping House,* Darien Vicinity.

Rincon

Effingham County (52)

Jerusalem Church GA-242. Ebenezer Community, se side (facing

NW) of Ga. Hwy. 275 at its eastern termination at the Savannah River; this site 5.5 mi. E of junction of Ga. Hwy. 255 with Ga. Hwy. 21; this junction 3 mi. N of intersection of Ga. Hwy. 21 and Fourth St. in Rincon. The church brick, English bond, 58'9" (three-bay NW front) × 69'. One story with balcony. Gable roof at front, hipped roof at rear, flared eaves, square tower (frame with clapboarding) rising from roof in two stages; upper one has pyramidal roof with finial and weathervane. Clock in gable. Brick openings for window and door frames have segmental arches; windows as in a two-story building because of balcony. Double entrance doors with transoms on NW, SW, and SE sides. Meetinghouse plan with gallery NW side, no vestibule. Colonial, built 1767–69, tower probably added several years later. Floor of hand-made clay tile later covered with terrazzo. Additions to SE sides since 1934. Form of church markedly similar to Midway Congregational Church★ at Midway, and to the 1749 building (since destroyed) of St. Paul's Church★ in Augusta. Jerusalem (Lutheran) Church and Cemetery are the most conspicuous remains of the colonial town of Ebenezer, founded by the Salzburgers. 2 ext. photos (1934); 2 int. photos (1934); 2 data pages (1934). Illustrated on p. 17.

Rock Springs

Walker County (148)

Carter's Quarters. See *Carter's Quarters,* Carters.

Rome

Floyd County (58)

Thornwood GA-152. 105 Shorter Ave., facing N. Wood frame with clapboarding, novelty siding under porches. Rectangular, three-bay front, two stories over raised basement, gable roof with pediment each end, three int. chimneys. Pilasters at corners and between bays front and rear; double windows front and rear. One-story, three-bay Greek Doric porches with flat roofs on each of the four sides. Double entrance doors, front and back, side and corner lights, and transom, the front entrance recessed. Central hall plan, two rooms each side. Open-well stairway about midway of hall, with another open-well stairway leading from first landing to second landing, which opens to roof of rear porch, and also supports flight of stairs leading to attic, an arrangement that produces a dramatic expression of space and light. Greek Revival, mid 19th C. E porch partially enclosed, probably after house was built. Part of E porch extended as wing since 1936. Int. and basement changed to adapt to primary school usage; fire escapes added since 1936.

Symmetrically crowning a hill, with Greek orders whose proportions have been maintained without overwhelming the house, the design is one of the most successful adaptations of Greek architecture in Georgia. 3 ext. photos (1936); 1 data page (1936).

Roswell

Fulton County (61)

Barrington Hall GA-1105. 60 Marietta St., facing N. Wood frame with clapboarding, rectangular, three-bay front, two stories, gable roof with pediments and a lookout, two end chimneys. Two-story-high modified Greek Doric porch three sides; six columns in front, the pediments and five columns on each of lateral sides. Central hall plan (divided by an arch with columns), two rooms each side plus rooms in one-story ell across back. Attic rooms have sliding windows. Brick dairy and icehouse. Elaborate gates with wooden pickets and brick piers mark termination of Mimosa St. and beginning of wide front walk, which, like street, is on axis with central hall. Gates and boxwood parterre gardens on E side of house were designed about the time of its building. Greek Revival, 1839–42; Willis Ball, architect; Barrington King, first owner. 1 ext. photo (1936); 2 data pages (1936).

Bulloch Hall GA-14-13. Western termination of Bulloch Ave., facing E. Wood frame with clapboarding, flush siding under porch. Rectangular, three-bay front, two stories, gable roof, four end chimneys. Prostyle tetrastyle temple form with lean-to across back. Portico two stories high, simplified Greek Doric, ceiling of which aligns with bottom of architrave. First-story windows opening on porch are floor length. Entrance with sidelights and transom. Central hall plan, divided by an arch and two columns, with two rooms each side plus rooms in one-story ell. Most of millwork copied or adapted from Asher Benjamin. Greek Revival, 1840; Willis Ball, architect. Martha Bulloch was married to Theodore Roosevelt, Sr., in this house; they were the parents of President Theodore Roosevelt and the grandparents of Eleanor Roosevelt. 3 sheets (1934); 4 ext. photos (1934); 1 int. photo (1934); 2 data pages (1934). Illustrated on p. 106.

Lewis House (Holly Hill) GA-1104. 632 Mimosa Blvd., facing ESE. Wood frame with clapboarding, rectangular, three-bay front, one and one-half stories over raised basement, gable roof with dormers on rear, four end chimneys within ext. walls. Main roof extends over porches front and back. Porches across front and back, each five bays with gable over three center bays, modified Greek Doric, entablature completely around house. Triple full-length windows open onto porches. Entrance has double doors with transom over. Central hall plan, two rooms each side. Indigenous type raised cottage adapted to Greek Revival, built 1840–45. Added closet protrudes onto back porch; basement porch under back porch since enclosed. 1 ext. photo (1936); 2 data pages (1936).

Methodist Church. See *Old Methodist Church*.

Mimosa Hall GA-1102. 123 Bulloch Ave., facing S. Brick with stucco scored, porch pediment frame with clapboards, rectangular, three-bay front, two stories with one-story ell across back, gable roof, four end chimneys flush with ext. wall. Prostyle tetrastyle temple form with two-story-high modified Greek Doric portico, round unfluted columns brick with stucco, moldings adapted to local craftsmanship. First-floor windows that open onto porch are floor length and framed by pilasters with entablatures. Eight-panel entrance door with sidelights and transom, also framed by pilasters with entablature. Central hall plan, two rooms each side plus rooms in ell. Most architectural details copied or adapted from Asher Benjamin. Lattice wellhouse with classic doorway. Greek Revival, 1847; Willis Ball, architect. An earlier house on the site named Dunwoody Hall, built of wood, burned the night of the housewarming. Rebuilt with brick and stucco, it was named Phoenix Hall, this name later changed to Mimosa Hall. The two principal rooms on w side of the hall were combined into one room, baths added, and an antique door from a New York mansion substituted for the original front door by the architect Neel Reid before 1936. 4 ext. photos (1936); 2 data pages (1936).

Old Methodist Church GA-193. Built at fork of Alpharetta and Green Sts. (about 200 ft. behind fork) facing s down Alpharetta St. Brick, 43'4'' (two-bay front) × 65'3'', one story, gable roof with pediments. Ornate and unusual entablature around building and following raking cornice; dentil band on cornice, double dentil band on architrave. Semicircular ventilators in pediments. Meetinghouse plan. Built ca. 1859; Jim Stewart, Aaron Butler, and J. A. Gunter, builders. Abandoned as a church and doors changed before 1937. Pilasters have been added, steel windows have replaced the original ones, doors were again changed and building stuccoed since 1937. 1 ext. photo (1936); 1 data page (1936).

Ruckersville Vicinity
Elbert County (53)

Alexander-Cleveland House, Martin Anderson Farm, R. J. An-

derson Farm. See *Richard B. Russell Project*, Elberton Vicinity.

St. Marys
Camden County (20)

Orange Hall GA-14-16. 311 Osborne St., facing E. Wood frame with clapboarding, flush siding under porches and in pediments, foundation brick with stucco scored and with quoins at corners. 56'4'' (five-bay front) × 62'4'' including porches. Two stories over raised basement, gable roof with pediments front and rear, two int. chimneys, temple form. Three-bay, two-story-high front portico with attenuated Greek Doric columns, simplified and reduced entablature, balustrade with octagonal tapered balusters that resemble miniature Doric columns. Three-bay, two-tier porch in antis at rear. First-floor windows that open onto porch are floor length, entrance with sidelights and transom framed by pilasters with entablature and a flat pediment with acrotera. Rear door similar except without pediment. Ext. and int. doors with two vertical panels. Central hall plan, two rooms each side. Molded trim with corner blocks, some of the blocks carved with representations of magnolia blossoms. Windows with louvered blinds on ext., folding paneled shutters on int. Kitchen with brick floor in basement. Picket fence front and sides. Greek Revival; ca. 1850. Much of the stucco of the foundation wall was gone by the time the 1934 photos were taken; more has fallen off since. All but center bay of rear porch enclosed since 1934. 12 sheets (1934); 3

ext. photos (1934); 2 int. photos (1934); 3 data pages (1934). Illustrated on pp. 113, 114, 115, 118.

St. Marys Vicinity
Camden County (20)

New Canaan Sugar House GA-14-18. w side of Ga. Hwy. 40 SP, 3 mi. N of intersection with Ga. Hwy. 40 in St. Marys. Tabby walls, roughly T-shaped, 122' 9'' long, the head of the T (to N) 72'9''. N side (probably the main entrance) five bays. s chamber two stories, rest of building one story; both one- and two-story sections same total height, about 13 ft. N end (head of T) divided into three sections by low walls, and probably used for curing and storing. s of this in stem of T was the boiling room, which had open sheds on E and w sides. Piers for sheds, irregularly spaced, still stand. At end of stem to s was two-story mill proper. The grinding is thought to have been in the lower story, operated by an animal-powered rotating lever on the second floor. Built ca. 1825; only tabby walls and piers remain. For more detailed description see *Georgia's Disputed Ruins*, edited by E. Merton Coulter (Chapel Hill: University of North Carolina Press, 1937), pp. 148–60. 2 sheets (1934); 4 ext. photos (1934); 2 int. photos (1934); 3 data pages (1934). Recorded erroneously in 1934 as Santa Maria Mission.

Santa Maria Mission. See *New Canaan Sugar House*.

St. Simons Island

Glynn County (64)

Cannons Point Kitchen Remains
GA-2159. Cannons Point Plantation, N end of island at Cannons Point. Brick fireplace with segmental arch over, ovens with either segmental or barrel vaults. Probably early 19th C. Originally part of the detached kitchen of the Cannons Point Plantation house of the Couper family. Only ruins remain. 1 ext. photo (1958).

Fort Frederica. See *Fort Frederica*, St. Simons Island, Town of Frederica.

Hamilton Plantation Slave Cabin and Barn GA-219. w side of Arthur Moore Dr. between King's Way and Sea Island Rd. Cabin is tabby, rectangular, three-bay front, one and one-half stories, gable roof with dormers, one end chimney. Barn is tabby, two stories, first story has one-bay front, second story has two-bay front, gable roof. Both probably built ca. 1825. Cabin remodeled before 1936. 1 ext. photo cabin (1936); 1 ext. photo barn (1936); 1 data page (1936).

Rest House GA-255. 812 Ocean Blvd. Tabby, 32' × 16'5''. Apparently one story with gable roof, the ends of which may have been truncated. Probably built early 19th C. Only ruins of walls remained when photographed in 1934. Original use of building unknown. Ruins incorporated into residence in 1936. 1 ext. photo (1934); 2 data pages (1934).

Retreat House GA-220. sw side of cul-de-sac which terminates Retreat Ave. Frame with clapboarding, rectangular, additions to rear.

Original part one and one-half stories, apparently with a spraddle roof, dormer windows, and two end chimneys. Five-bay porch with wooden jalousies across front. Plantation cottage type, similar to Wild Heron★ near Savannah. Built ca. 1790. Additions included two-story annex larger than original house. Burned 1906. Photo of house before fire in *Historic Glimpses of St. Simons Island, Georgia* (St. Simons, Ga., 1973). Brick foundation and one chimney remained when HABS photos were made. John James Audubon visited here in 1831. 1 ext. photo (1936); 1 data page (1936).

Slave Hospital and Greenhouse, Retreat Plantation GA-21. sw side of cul-de-sac terminating at southern end of Retreat Ave. Hospital tabby with stucco scored, rectangular, three-bay front, gable roof, at least one int. chimney. Greenhouse tabby, rectangular, one-bay entrance side, one-slope roof. Both buildings illustrated in *Old Mill Days: St. Simons, Ga., 1874–1908* (St. Simons, Ga., 1976). Both buildings probably early 19th C.; both in ruins when HABS photos were made. 2 ext. photos hospital (1934); 1 ext. photo greenhouse (1934); 3 data pages (1936).

St. Simons Island, Town of Frederica

Glynn County (64)

Barracks Remains GA-2146. Tabby, 94'6'' square with a central courtyard. One story with a two-story battlemented tower in middle of N side. Probably had six chimneys. Built 1741–42, foundation and part of tower remain. Served as barracks for Gen-

eral Oglethorpe's regiment during fight of English colonists against Spanish; also used as prison and hospital for captured Spanish soldiers. 7 sheets (1959); 17 ext. photos (1958); 1 photocopy of ca. 1850 drawing (1958); 2 data pages (1958). Illustrated on p. 124.

Calwell House Remains GA-2147. Lot no. 3, N ward. Foundations tabby, rectangular, 27'1'' × 37'. Base of brick chimney with oven-fireplace complex in basement and foundation remain. Built ca. 1740. 3 sheets (1961); 12 ext. photos (1958); 4 data pages (1958). Illustrated on p. 12.

du Bignon House Remains. See *Parker–du Bignon House Remains.*

Fort Frederica. See *King's Magazine Remains.*

Foundation in Northeast Bastion GA-2157. Tabby, 12' × 16', plank floor. Probably built 1736. 1 ext. photo (1958).

Hawkins-Davison House Remains GA-2149. Lots no. 1 and no. 2, S ward. Brick with some tabby and some wooden walls, irregular L shape, duplex, each unit rectangular. Probably two and one-half stories or one and one-half stories over partially raised basement. Basement floors brick or tabby. Lot originally enclosed with wooden fence. Built 1736–38. Now ruinous, nothing left above ground. Probably remodeled twice before it was destroyed. 3 sheets (1959); 8 ext. photos (1958); 1 photocopy of conjectural drawing (1958); 5 data pages (1958). Illustrated on p. 12.

Houston House Bins Remains GA-2155. Lot no. 3, S ward. Brick, rectangular, 9'6'' × 4' × 3' deep, overall dimensions. Walls brick, floor tabby. Vertical slits 1'' wide × 1'' deep divide the bins into three equal parts; slits probably held wooden partitions. Built in 1740s. Stabilized 1958 with two top courses of modern brick. Below grade intact except for wooden (?) partitions. 2 ext. photos (1958); 2 data pages (1958).

Humble House Remains GA-2153. Lot no. 8. s ward. Walls and foundation tabby; 24' × 14'; two brick chimneys. Date unknown. 2 ext. photos (1958); 2 data pages (1958).

King's Magazine Remains GA-2162. Tabby, some brick vaults, 20' × 96', rectangular except that a center bay projects 6 ins. Built 1740–41. Portions remained above grade in 1903, when some walls and battlements were reconstructed. Stabilized 1956–57. Undocumented research indicates that walls were battlemented, but that battlements were nonfunctional. 2 sheets (1959); 9 ext. photos (1958); 1 photocopy of view ca. 1910 (1958); 1 photocopy of 1796 map (1958); 2 data pages (1936); 2 data pages (1958).

Levally House Remains GA-2154. Lot no. 9, s ward. Tabby foundations, 14'3'' × 25'. One end chimney. Foundation plans indicate two rooms. Date unknown; nothing above grade. 1 sheet (1959); 3 ext. photos (1958); 2 data pages (1958).

Mackay House Remains GA-2148. Lot no. 6, N ward. Tabby foundations, 32'6'' × 22'4½''. At least one brick chimney. Built ca. 1740; nothing above grade. 3 sheets (1958); 9 ext. photos (1958); 2 data pages (1958).

Moore House Remains GA-2163. Lot no. 20. Brick, rectangular. Built before 1743. 3 sheets (1959). Illustrated on p. 13.

Parker–du Bignon House Remains (du Bignon House Remains) GA-2152. Lot no. 7. Brick and poured tabby; ext. walls of portions stuccoed and scored. H plan 60' × 90' overall. Tabby or brick enclosure wall at rear of lot. Built 1797; remodeled early 19th C. Nothing remains above grade. 2 sheets (1959); 9 ext. photos (1958); 3 data pages (1958).

South Storehouse Remains GA-2156. Fort Frederica. Foundations and first story flint and brick, timber above, tile roof, 18'6'' × 60'. Built 1739; foundation walls reconstructed in brick 1957. 2 sheets (1959); 2 ext. photos (1958); 2 data pages (1958).

Welch House Remains GA-2151. Lot no. 5, s ward. Foundations tabby, 50'8'' × 22½''. Central chimney. House may have been duplex; evidently destroyed by fire. 3 sheets (1959); 8 ext. photos (1958); 2 data pages (1958).

Sapelo Island
McIntosh County (96)

Spalding Sugar Mill GA-2129. sw part of island on Spalding Sapelo Island Plantation, near Barn Creek Landing. Tabby, originally with stucco and stucco quoins; foundation cobblestones. Octagonal, approximately 45 ft. in diameter, circular inner chamber 28'9'' inside diameter. Two stories, ca. 1810. Auxiliary buildings included boiling and curing houses destroyed or incorporated into later

plantation buildings. This was the first of the tabby sugar mills in the area. For fuller description see *Georgia's Disputed Ruins*, edited by E. Merton Coulter (Chapel Hill: University of North Carolina Press, 1937). 1 ext. photo (1934); 3 data pages (1934). Erroneously recorded in 1934 as Spanish Fort.

Spanish Fort. See *Spalding Sugar Mill*.

Savannah
Chatham County (26)

Anderson-Leslie House (Leslie House) GA-1173. 4 W. Oglethorpe St., facing s. Brick, basement brick with stucco, marble trim. Rectangular (five-bay front), three stories over raised basement, flat or low-pitched roof with parapet, four end chimneys flush with ext. wall, five bays (N bay enclosed), one-story side porch (E) with brick piers, cornice at base of parapet, corbelled belt course at third-story floor level, first-story windows floor length, marble entrance stoop with marble steps each side, simple wrought-iron railing, balcony with cast-iron brackets and railing over entrance. Entrance doorway with sidelights and transom. Central hall plan. Built 1836, enlarged 1867. Original house probably three-bay front, side hall plan, two stories over raised basement. Porch and interior radically altered in later years for commercial purposes. 3 ext. photos (1966); 2 int. photos (1966).

Anderson-Preston House (House, 14 E. Oglethorpe St.) GA-1174. 14 E. Oglethorpe St., facing s.

Brick with stucco scored, irregular shape (three-bay front), three stories over raised basement, hipped roof, belt course at third-story windowsill level, belt courses at second-story windowsill level and second-story floor level with relief sculpture between, two-story oriel window w side of entrance, double windows with balcony E side of entrance, above the double windows is a single full-length second-story window with balcony. Entrance stoop with curving marble steps one side. Unorthodox plan with elaborate and complicated Queen Anne style stairway. Built for John Anderson 1853; remodeled and enlarged by William Preston, architect, 1892. 3 ext. photos (1966); 1 int. photo (1966).

Arnold House GA-289. 128 E. State St., corner Abercorn St. Originally faced Abercorn St. (ESE); after additions and remodeling the entrance faced State St. (SSW). Oldest part frame with clapboarding; addition brick with stucco scored. Original part rectangular with two bays toward State St., two-and-a-half stories, gambrel roof with dormers. Addition rectangular, three-bay front, two stories over semiraised basement, flat roof with parapet, corbel cornice at base of parapet. Full-length windows in original part. Elaborate int. plaster cornice with rinceau design. Brick garden wall with combination corbel and sawtooth brick coping. Original part post-colonial, built late 18th or early 19th C., addition 1852–53. Windows in older part probably changed at time of addition. Demolished 1950. 1 ext. photo (1936); 1 int. photo (1936); 1 data page (1936).

John Ash House (House, 114 W. Hull St.) GA-1175. 114–16 W. Hull St., facing S. Brick. Basement, side, and rear walls brick with stucco, stone steps and windowsills, rectangular double house (six-bay front), two and one-half stories over raised basement. Gable roof with dormers and end parapets, six end chimneys flush with ext. walls. Windows of w half only are floor length with cast-iron guards first floor, cast-iron balcony second floor. Stoop with stairs each side, two entrances, each having double doors with fanlights. Arched window under w side of stoop, oval window under E side. Side hall plans. Traditional Federal, Adamesque, 1817. w side apparently remodeled mid 19th C. 3 ext. photos (1966); 2 int. photos (1966).

Bank GA-14-2131 (see also *Newspaper Office*). 19 E. Bay St., facing NNE. Marble veneer, rectangular, three-bay front, two stories, gable roof with parapet. Center entrance with double doors and arched transom over; second entrance with single door, sidelight one side, and transom. Metal railings on each side of both entrances. Built ca. 1822, remodeled ca. 1936, at which time the original brick with stucco walls were veneered with marble, window was replaced by second entrance, new windows and doors were installed, chimneys removed, metal balcony added over center door, and metal railings added. Int. remodeled many times. 1 ext. photo (1934); 1 data page (1934).

Barclay-Wetter House (Wetter House) GA-2136. 425 W. Oglethorpe St. Brick with stucco, apparently rectangular, wing one side. Five-bay front, three stories over raised basement. Hipped roof with bracketed cornice, wing with gable roof with parapets. First-floor windows arched, some French type. Double entrance doors part glass with semicircular transom. Two-tiered cast-iron veranda on three sides; roof of second story apparently used as deck. Veranda had paired cast-iron columns, seven bays in front, five on side. Arches over each bay, pointed arches over smaller bays and between columns. Cast-iron frieze. Cast-iron railings with medallions, relief portraits of famous poets and statesmen. Apparently central hall plan. Side yard enclosed with high wall with blind arcade and with cast-iron cresting (rinceau design) on top. Built ca. 1822 by Anthony Barclay; remodeled and enlarged 1857 by the owner-architect, Augustus Wetter. Ironwork added at that time. Demolished ca. 1950. 3 ext. photos (1934); 4 ext. photos (1936); 2 data pages (1936). Illustrated on p. 147.

Battersby-Anderson House. See *Battersby House.*

Battersby House (Battersby-Anderson House) GA-254. 119 E. Charlton St., entrance facing NNE. Brick with stone trim, basement brick with stucco. Rectangular, two bays plus side-porch bay with doorway, two stories over raised basement, flat roof with parapet, one int. chimney, one chimney flush with ext. wall. Entrance door from sidewalk to E porch, Charleston style. Street front with dentil cornice at base of parapet, windows with sidelights and pediment-shaped stone lintels, cast-iron balconies at first-floor windows, unusually handsome

wrought-iron bracket light by entrance. Two-tiered porches on E
and W sides. E porches overlook
garden; walls under these porches
stuccoed, louvers between columns. W porches since partially
enclosed; an elaborately carved
bracket curiously substitutes for a
first-floor end column. High brick
wall with corbel and sawtooth
coping surrounds garden. Two-
story brick carriage and servants'
house on alley at rear. Mid 19th
C. pattern of garden still preserved.
Greek Revival, 1852. Minor
changes. 1 ext. photo (1936); 1
data page (1936).

Belcher-Hunter House (MacKay
House) GA-2138. 125 E. Congress
St., facing NNE. Frame with clapboarding and wood quoins, brick
basement story. Rectangular,
seven-bay front, five-bay (E) side,
two stories over raised basement,
hipped roof, two int. chimneys.
Cornice with brackets coved on
three sides, Greek fret on architrave. Two entrances, principal
entrance with eight-panel door,
full semicircular fanlight and sidelights and a Palladian window with
semicircular wrought-iron balcony over. Entrance off-center,
with two bays E side, four bays W
side. Exquisite Adam-type mantels, doorways, plaster cornices.
One anomalous mantel with
simulated bamboo colonnettes,
Gothic arcade motif on frieze,
and center panel with pastoral
scene, all executed in the delicate
late 18th C. manner. Traditional
Federal, Adamesque, built between 1797 and 1803. Basement
later remodeled for commercial
use. End bays W side may have
been added or may have been
porch later enclosed. Entrance
foyer and int. details (Adam
mantel) now installed at Telfair
Academy. Gift of Thomas P.

Saffold and Mrs. B. F. Bullard.
Demolished ca. 1940. 5 ext.
photos (1936); 17 int. photos
(1936); 1 data page (1936). Illustrated on pp. 36, 37.

Timothy Bonticou Double House
GA-1176. 418–20 S. State St., facing SSW. Frame with random width
(exposed face varying from less
than 7″ to more than 10″)
beaded clapboarding. 40′6″ (four-
bay front) × 15′4″, rectangular
with rear ell. Two stories, hipped
roof, shed roof over ell, one int.
chimney. Two entrance doors.
Second-story windows in front
are single sash, six-light, sliding
type. Other windows double
hung, fifteen-light downstairs,
twelve-light upstairs. Originally
two apartments, first-floor rooms
plaster with paneled wainscot,
mantels with simple pilasters and
shelf. Second-story rooms with
sloping ceilings, batten doors.
Built 1854–61 at 419–21 E.
Broughton Lane, where it faced N.
Moved to State St. and restored
1971. 6 sheets (1962); 2 ext.
photos (1962); 2 int. photos
(1962); 6 data pages (1962). Illustrated on p. 165.

Branch of United States Bank.
See *United States Bank.*

Christian Camphor House GA-
1177. 122 E. Oglethorpe Ave., facing S. Frame with clapboarding,
rectangular, four-bay front, one-
and-a-half stories over raised basement, salt-box roof with dormers,
one int. end chimney. Colonial,
built ca. 1760–67. Raised on high
foundation 1871, balcony remodeled 1907. 1 ext. photo (1980).
Illustrated on p. 16.

*Carriage House for 127–129 Ab-
ercorn St.* See *Mary Marshall
Houses.*

*Carriage House for 330 Abercorn
St.* See *Hamilton House.*

*Carriage House for Mercer-
Wilder House.* See *Mercer-Wilder
House.*

*Carriage House for Abram Minis
House.* See *Abram Minis House.*

*Central of Georgia Administra-
tion Building* GA-213. 22 W.
Broad St., facing E. Brick, rectangular (nine-bay front), two stories,
flat or low slope roof, at least seven
int. chimneys, two-story-high
Doric hexastyle portico, pilasters between bays, full entablature with widely spaced triglyphs
around portico and building. Portico ceiling paneled, panel over
entrance with design in color featuring monogram and date 1856.
Part glass double entrance doors
with transom over. Central hall
plan. Greek Revival, 1856. 4 ext.
photos (1962); 1 int. photo (1962);
3 data pages (1962).

*Central of Georgia Railroad
Bridges* GA-213. Both bridges
across W. Boundary St., the older
one about 20 yds. N of its intersection with W. Hull St., the second one about 100 yds. N of the
first. Both bridges brick, four
arched spans. S side of first bridge,
which has elliptical arched vaults
spanning 30 ft., is integral with
retaining wall at side of Hull St.
This wall extends eastward along
Hull St. and parallel to railroad
tracks until it joins and ties in
with railroad station. The bridge
has one blind bay W of spans,
then crowstepped to grade. Faces
of arches have projecting brick
extrados; soffits of vaults stuccoed; recessed niches on face of
bridge between arches. Brick guard
railing with stone coping over
corbel table of blind arches with

brackets under; brick corbel table and dentils under this. Romanesque revival, built 1852. Second bridge with 48-ft. spans, segmental arched vaults. Brick extrados with projecting header courses over; sloping (battered) walls between vaults with string course below spring line; string course elaborated into pediment on end face of walls between vaults. Buttresses between center arches, paterae between others. Stone coping with rounded edges and corbel table under. Sloping flankers each end of bridge. Built 1858; Schwab and Miller probably engineers for both bridges. 4 ext. photos (1936); 1 data page (1936). Illustrated on p. 136.

Central of Georgia Railroad Station GA-213. 301 W. Broad St., facing E. Overside brick with granite stoop, steps, belt courses, and windowsills; marble and metal cornices. Rectangular (nine-bay front), two stories, gable roof. Façade includes a central five-bay pavilion with pilasters between bays, the pilasters repeated at the corners and between every other bay elsewhere. Windows and doorways arched. Double entrance doors with transoms in each end bay of the pavilion.

Train shed on rear of building. Shed brick, rectangular, approximately 380' (twenty-five bays) × 70'. Gable roof with open clerestory-type ventilator running the length of the ridge. Each side of shed arcaded; arches on N side (except at gate) semienclosed, with arched top brick panels in lower part; arches S side with handsome wrought-iron gates except two E bays enclosed for services and two W bays enclosed for baggage room. Eaves overhang 5 ft. each side, supported by cast-iron brackets. Exposed trusses,

the top chords of timber, the compressive struts of cast iron, and the tensile members of wrought iron.

Station begun 1861, finished 1876. Shed built 1861. Both designed by Augustus Schwab, engineer. 2 ext. photos (1962); 2 int. photos (1962). Illustrated on p. 137.

Central of Georgia Train Shed. See *Central of Georgia Railroad Station.*

Champion-McAlpin House GA-288. 230 Barnard St., facing WNW. Brick with stucco, slate and metal roof, rectangular with projecting enclosures at sides of former rear porch. Five-bay front, three-bay sides plus porch enclosure, two-and-a-half stories over semiraised basement, mansard roof with pedimented dormers, four int. chimneys, simplified Corinthian entablature, belt course at each floor. Two-story-high porch with four Tower-of-the-Winds Corinthian columns in antis; square antae at corners. Curved steps at each end of porch. Central hall plan, the hall divided into three parts separated by square columns, the middle space with an ocular opening in the ceiling. Stairway in side hall. Hall floor black and gray marble. Ornamental plaster moldings and ceiling medallions, black marble mantels with original black iron grate frames, original gold-leaf mantel and pier mirrors and window cornices. Lot enclosed by combination cast- and wrought-iron fence on stone base at front, and by lattice brick wall at rear. Greek Revival, ca. 1840–44; Charles B. Cluskey, architect.

Remodeled ca. 1895, at which time rear porch was enclosed and incorporated into house, and another rear porch, a half-story, and

mansard roof added. Stair, originally in side hall that opened onto center part of main hall, was moved to side hall at rear. Stucco, once colored reddish brown, now softly streaked and mellowed. 4 ext. photos (1936); 5 int. photos (1936); 2 data pages (1936).

Dr. Charlton House. See *Rahn House.*

Chippewa Square Monument GA-1179. Chippewa Square, bounded by Hull, Perry, and Bull Sts. Bronze statue of Gen. James Oglethorpe, portrayed in full dress uniform with sword in hand, facing S toward the menacing Spanish colonies. Statue is 9 ft. high, mounted on marble pedestal inscribed on three sides with excerpts from the charter for the Georgia colony. Pedestal is in turn mounted on marble base with four lions rampant, one at each corner, on which appear respectively the Oglethorpe coat of arms and the great seals of the colony of Georgia, the state of Georgia, and the city of Savannah.

Erected 1910; Daniel Chester French, sculptor; pedestal and base designed by Henry Bacon. 3 ext. photos (1966).

Christ Church GA-236. 28 Bull St., facing WNW. Brick with stucco, basement with banded rustication. Rectangular, three-bay front, six-bay sides. One story over raised basement, gable roof, one int. chimney. Temple form with Greek Ionic hexastyle portico, and with two towers located at rear corners. Doric pilasters at corners of building and between bays on sides. Complex but comfortable and attractive system of stone steps and landings lead to portico. Heavy cast-iron railings. Three entrances, double doors with cornices supported by console brackets. Meetinghouse plan with vestibule and gallery on three sides. Arched chancel, Corinthian pilasters and entablature, coffered ceiling. Greek Revival, 1837; designed by James Hamilton Couper, planter and amateur architect. Church bell cast by Paul Revere and Sons, Boston, 1819. Building gutted by fire 1897, rebuilt with some interior changes the following year. Steps, originally a straight flight, changed before 1936. Chancel changed from apse-type to square end since 1937. Photos include one of a painting of the preceding church building, which was brick, rectangular with center entrance tower, three-bay front, gable roof. Octagonal lantern with engaged columns at corners, arched louvers, and domed roof with finial. Nave had arched windows with louvered blinds, buttresses at sides. Probably meetinghouse plan, one story with gallery on three sides. Built 1811, demolished 1837. Christ Episcopal Church founded 1733; first building erected on site 1750. 2 ext. photos of present church (1936); 1 int. photo of present church before chancel changed (ca. 1870); 1 ext. photo of 1837 painting of former church (1936); 2 data pages (1936); 1 data page (1937).

Clark House GA-214. 107 E. Oglethorpe Ave., facing NNE. Brick, Flemish bond; basement brick with stucco scored. Stone trim. Rectangular, 27'2'' (three-bay front). Two and one-half stories over raised basement, gable roof with dormer window and parapets, brick corbel table at base of parapet, two chimneys flush with ext. walls. Six-panel entrance door with leaded fan and side-

lights. Stone entrance steps with wrought-iron railing and lantern stand. Side hall plan. Apparently built as a twin to house at 109 Oglethorpe, which now has a third story. Traditional Federal, built 1820–21. 2 ext. photos (1936); 1 data page (1936).

Charles B. Cluskey Embankment Stores GA-1180. s side of ramp (facing N) leading from E. Bay St. to River St., opposite 104–10 E. Bay St. Brick, trapezoidal, 66' (front consisting of four major bays, one small bay, and four very small windows) × approximately 32' on eastern end and 48' on western. Structure consists of four parallel vaulted rooms and a narrow storage (?) room; each vaulted room with an 8-ft.-wide arched opening, a small window on N side and a light well at rear. Narrow room has small rectangular door on N side. Earth fill behind N wall and over vaults; the top planted and forming part of Emmett Park. Brilliant exploitation of structure to provide useable space, to reduce amount of fill needed, and to serve as retaining wall. Built 1840; Charles B. Cluskey, architect. Except for doorway to narrow room, there are no closures for openings. Remains of hinges indicate that there were originally doors for the arched openings. 3 sheets (1962); 2 ext. photos (1962); 1 int. photo (1962); 2 data pages (1962).

Cunningham House. See *John Hunter House.*

Customs House GA-215. 1–3 E. Bay St., facing NNE. Smooth-faced granite, 110' (eleven-bay front) × 52' (five-bay sides), two stories over raised basement, hipped roof except at portico. Hexastyle Co-

rinthian portico with monolithic Tower-of-the-Winds columns without bases, modified entablature carrying around building, Doric pilasters under portico and at corners of building. Three pairs of entrance doors, each pair with heavy paneled outer doors and half-glass inner doors. Center lobby terminating in apse, central flight of stairs dividing at landing into double flight of geometrical stairs with cantilevered marble steps and gilded metal railings, all similar to famous stairway designed by Robert Adam at Home House, London. Cast-iron fence mounted on low granite wall surrounds the property. Greek Revival, cornerstone laid 1848, building completed 1853. John S. Norris, New York, architect. Minor int. changes. 2 ext. photos (1936); 1 data page (1936).

Davenport House GA-14-8. 324 E. State St., facing ssw. Brick with brownstone trim, standing-seam metal roof. 46' (five-bay front) × 37'. Two and one-half stories over raised basement, gable roof with dormers and gable parapets, four end chimneys flush with ext. walls. Horseshoe steps, wrought-iron railing with scrollwork medallion. Six-panel entrance door with sidelights and full elliptical fanlight over. Central hall plan (two rooms each side), rear (stair) part of hall wider than front, and separated by an elliptical arch supported by Ionic columns. Open-well stairway with rounded returns. Rich plaster cornices with acanthus leaf, leaf and tongue, and rinceau motifs. Traditional Federal, completed 1820; Isaac Davenport, builder and first owner. Restored after 1954; opened as house museum 1963. 5 sheets (1934); 3 ext. photos (1934); 2 ext. photos (1936); 2 int. photos (1934); 2 data pages (1936). Illustrated on p. 41.

Denis Houses GA-2143. 25–27 Lincoln St., facing ESE. Frame with clapboarding, brick basement, standing-seam metal roof. Rectangular, six-bay front, two and one-half stories over raised basement, gable roof with dormers, lean-to on back, flat roofs on entrance porches. One central chimney. Duplex, two small one-bay entrance porches with square wooden columns. Wrought-iron stair and porch railings, arched entrance to basement under porches. Side hall plan. Built 1819–20; demolished ca. 1947. 1 ext. photo (1934); 2 data pages (1934).

Dent House. See *Stephen B. Williams House.*

Dickerson House GA-280. 203 E. York St., facing NNE. Brick with stone trim, 34 ft. (three-bay front), rectangular, three stories over raised basement, flat roof, parapet with decorative cast-iron ventilators, entablature with brick dentils at base of parapet. Flagstone stoop at entrance with stone steps on side, combination wrought- and cast-iron railing. One-panel entrance door with frosted glass sidelights and transom. Side hall plan. House is half of six-bay front double house. Two-story brick carriage and servants' house facing alley at rear. Built 1853. Int. alterations for apartments in upper floors, offices in basement. 1 ext. photo (1936).

Doorway, 115 W. Oglethorpe Ave. See *Thomas Gardner House.*

Eppinger-Lane House (House, 211 W. Perry St.) GA-1181. 404 E. Bryan St., facing S. Frame with clapboarding, rectangular, five-bay front, two stories over raised basement, gable roof changing to shed type (very low slope) at rear, two int. end chimneys, small entrance porch with square columns, side steps. Six-panel entrance door with fanlight, central hall plan. Built for John Eppinger Estate, 1821–23, at 211 W. Perry St. Moved 1969. 3 ext. photos (1966); 2 int. photos (1966).

Factor's Warehouse GA-2144. N side of River St., between street nos. 1 and 30. Rubble stone with brick at corners and around openings, standing-seam metal roof. Rectangular, five-bay front, three stories, gable roof with end parapets. Two doorways set in segmental arched openings, both with double batten doors, one pair square head, the other pair (apparently older) arched with diagonal boards and long strap hinges. Corbel brick cornice with brick dentils. Rubble stonework skillfully integrated with brickwork. Foundation built 1744, date inscribed on stone. Upper part of building may originally have been of wood; building probably burned and rebuilt more than once. Building as photographed thought to have been rebuilt in 1870s. Demolished ca. 1950. 1 ext. photo (1934); 1 data page (1934).

First African Baptist Church GA-276. Montgomery St., occupying block between Bryan and St. Julian Sts., facing ESE. Brick, basement brick with stucco. Three-bay front (60′5″) by five-bay sides, rectangular, projecting tower at front and apse at rear. One story over raised basement. Gable roof, its pediment repeated in miniature at front of tower. Square belfry with louvers framed by pilasters with pediments on each of the four sides. Octagonal lantern with octagonal spire over belfry; urns top corners of belfry. Brick entablature with brick dentils around church. Blind arches at each bay, the ones on the sides framing square-head windows, two in front framing double entrance doors with console-supported cornices with windows above. Entrance landings with side steps of stone and with cast-iron railings flank tower; entrance to basement (offices and Sunday school rooms) in base of tower.

Meetinghouse plan, vestibule, auditorium with gallery on three sides supported by slender Corinthian columns and entablature. Stained-glass windows. Originally Rationalist Federal style, 1859–61. Changes include addition of tower in 1888. Original windows probably clear glass with louvered shutters. Present tower a replacement of 1888 one, which was destroyed by a hurricane in the early 20th C. Steeple formerly rose in seven stages, all square except the top one, which was octagonal with an octagonal roof. Int. and main body of church are classical, but steeple was a unique combination of classical and unorthodox elements, oddly suggestive of a Japanese pagoda. Church was organized in 18th C. 2 ext. photos (1936); 1 data page (1936). Illustrated on pp. 84, 187.

First Baptist Church GA-1182. 223 Bull St., facing E. Cast stone, 60′ × 102′ (five-bay front), one story over semiraised basement. Temple form with gable roof, prostyle hexastyle Corinthian portico, entrances at each of three center bays, double doorways with cornices, window over each. Pilasters at corners and between each bay, windows on sides arched.

Meetinghouse plan with vestibule and auditorium, gallery over vestibule, choir loft behind pulpit. Greek Revival, 1833; Elias Carter, architect. Remodeled 1922; Henrik Wallace, architect. 2 ext. photos (1966); 3 int. photos (1966).

Fort Wayne GA-23. E end of block bounded by E. Bay St., Island Expressway, and Broughton St. Brick wall encompasses area on N, E, and S sides, the "corners" curved in a quarter circle. Buttresses up to 6 ft. wide and projecting up to 5½ ft. at approximately 25 ft. on center on N, NE, and E sides. Height about 24 ft. at highest point. Arched opening and chamber within on eastern side. Walls may have been erected on foundation of old fort, but appear to be retaining, not fortress, walls.

First fort on site was constructed of earth and wood in 1736, reinforced in 1779. Rebuilt 1808–12. According to records of Georgia Historical Society, fort was "entirely destroyed" in 1842. Existing brick walls are quite old; they could have been built when Bay St. was extended in 1840s, or when Savannah Gas Co. opened their plant in 1850. Interesting brick industrial buildings with Gothic Revival details from that era remain on site. Some of these have been converted into prestigious apartments. 1 ext. photo (1936); 1 data page (1936).

Joseph F. Gammon Houses (Houses, 118–124 E. Harris St.) GA-24. 118–124 E. Harris St., facing SSW. Double house, brick with stone trim, six-bay front, rectangular, three stories over raised basement, flat roof with parapet, two int. chimneys, brick cornice with dentils. Doric entrance porches with combination cast- and

wrought-iron railings, six-panel entrance doors with sidelights and transom. Square columns between door and sidelights, entablature between door and transom. Side hall plan, principal rooms with plaster cornices and medallions, black marble mantels. Two-story brick carriage and servants' house facing rear alley. Built 1852. Rear porches since enclosed. 1 ext. photo (1936); 1 data page (1936).

Thomas Gardner House (House, 115 W. Oglethorpe Ave.) GA-249. 115 W. Oglethorpe Ave., facing NNE. W half of double house, brick with stucco scored, 27'2" (three-bay front) × 42'3". Three stories over raised basement, gable roof with end parapets, two end chimneys flush with ext. wall. Flagstone landing with stone steps, wrought-iron railings. Six-panel entrance door with sidelights and full elliptical fanlight. Fluted pilasters between door and sidelights; half pilasters at outer jamb; delicate transom bar with incised Greek frets. Side hall plan. Traditional Federal style with marked Adam influence, early 19th C. Int. much changed. Landing and steps of adjoining twin house (the two sets were originally unified) removed. Int. and ext. dilapidated. 1 ext. photo (1936); 1 data page (1936). Recorded in 1936 as Doorway, 115 W. Oglethorpe Ave.

Gibbons Block GA-2130. Bounded by Congress, St. Julian, Whitaker, and Barnard Sts., rectangular, 60' (three major bays, each consisting of two sub-bays) × 185' (eight major bays, each consisting of two sub-bays). Three stories, flat roof with parapet. Quoins at corners, Corinthian pilasters, giant order, separate major bays. Minor

bays at first floor separated by square columns. Large windows or half-glass doors filled space between columns and between columns and pilasters, giving bottom floor the open effect of 20th C. commercial buildings. Standard double-hung windows with carved stone lintels at second and third floors. Full Corinthian entablature with parapet over. Traditional Federal style, 1820. Various units remodeled at various times. Much of cornice and all but two of original pilaster capitals missing; remaining wooden capitals and carved stone lintels badly eroded by time. Windows have been changed, signs erratically placed, and major bays and different floor levels painted different colors, thus destroying the unity of what must have been a classically beautiful building successfully designed for commercial use. 3 ext. photos (1934–36); 1 data page (1936).

Gibbons Servants' and Carriage House (Reid Servants' and Carriage House) GA-2137. Behind 118 E. State St. Brick faced with cut and striated sandstone, slate roof. Central block with wings; central block one bay, two stories. Wings one story. Hipped roof with parapet on central block, gable roofs with end parapets on wings. Recessed porches adjacent to central block in each wing, with two square stone columns in antis. Segmental arched openings with recessed surrounds of smooth stone around windows and doors. Rational Federal style, 1820. Demolished ca. 1940. 3 ext. photos (1934, 1937); 1 data page (1936). Illustrated on p. 86.

Gordon Row (Row Houses) GA-2145. 101–129 W. Gordon St.,

facing NNE. Brick with stone trim, basement brick with stucco. Fifteen units, each 20 ft. wide, three bays per unit, three stories over raised basement. Low slope shed roof with parapet in front, two chimneys between units. Each unit with stone-floored stoop, curving stone steps to one side, steps and stoop with ornate cast-iron balustrade. Full-length windows first floor with delicate cast-iron balustrades. All windows double hung but with wide center mullion to give appearance of casement windows. One-panel entrance doors with sidelights and transom; square columns between door and sidelights, entablature between door and transom. Entrance to basement under stoop. One-story porch at rear. Side hall plan. Brick, two-story carriage and servants' houses opening on alley at rear; high brick walls separate rear gardens. Built 1853. Units now in various stages of repair, most having been restored. Some units since stuccoed or painted; blinds missing from some units. 3 ext. photos (1958). Illustrated on p. 152.

Green-Meldrim House GA-222. 327 Bull St., facing ssw toward street, which has since been closed. Brick with stucco, stone trim. Rectangular with service wing on w side, 64′ (five-bay front) × 56′. Flat roof with crenellated parapet, four end chimneys flush with ext. walls. Cast-iron entrance porch with imitation Gothic stone columns and tracery flanked by delicate cast-iron verandas with pagoda-type roofs. Veranda terminates on w side at two-story porch, but continues around E (Bull St.) side. Bay window with crenellated parapet and Gothic tracery over entrance porch, simi-

lar but smaller oriel windows over E veranda.

Entrance consisting of paired arched doors with arched sidelights, all set within recessed Tudor arch. Three sets of doors at entrance: ext. pair wooden with arched panels, hinged; center pair with glass panels, sliding type; int. pair sliding, louvered. Central hall plan, double parlors E side; chambers on w side divided by cross hall with freestanding marble stairway with wrought-iron railing and domed skylight over. Central hall terminated with bay window. First-floor rooms with tile floors, elaborate floriated plaster cornices and medallions, wall niches with foliated archivolts, marble mantels with naturalistic flowers carved in high relief and arched cast-iron grate frames. Gold-leaf pier and mantel mirrors, window cornices. Folding louvered int. blinds at oriel windows, gliding type at other windows. Windowpanes unusually large (up to 40 in.) for the time; those on N side (facing directly on Harris St.) translucent. One large bathroom, second floor, designed in Greek Revival style.

Two-story wing w side contained servants' rooms, kitchen, carriage house, and stables. Garden on E side of house surrounded by cast-iron fence with motifs matching porch treillage. Victorian Gothic, begun 1853, finished 1861; John S. Norris (?), architect. Stucco removed after 1934. House purchased by St. John's Episcopal Church in 1943, and w wing converted into rectory, with a covered walk connecting to church. House served as Sherman's headquarters from Dec. 22, 1864 until Feb. 1, 1865. 24 sheets (1962); 1 ext. photo (1934); 5 ext. photos (1936); 4 ext. photos (1962); 7 int.

photos (1936); 1 int. photo (1962); 1 photocopy of drawing of int. (ca. 1884); 1 data page (1936); 6 data pages (1962). Illustrated on pp. 122, 131.

Nathanael Greene Monument GA-1183. Johnson Square, which is bounded by Bull, Bryan, and Congress Sts. Marble obelisk mounted on a pedestal that rests on a platform of two steps. N and s faces of shaft and of pedestal wider than E and w faces. Copper plaque with inscription on N face of pedestal, copper plaque with relief figure of General Greene on s side. Proportions of platform, base, and obelisk unified and harmonious. Overall height 50 ft. Cornerstone laid 1825 by Lafayette. Rational Federal style, completed 1830; William Strickland, architect. General Greene's remains reinterred beneath monument in 1902. 3 ext. photos (1966). Illustrated on p. 76.

Habersham House (The Pink House) GA-238. 23 Abercorn St., facing ENE. Brick with stucco, rectangular with wing and rear ell. Five-bay front, two stories, gable roof with end parapets (flat roof with parapet on wing), two end chimneys. Quoins at corners, Palladian window over entrance, broken top pediments on console brackets over other windows, Tuscan entrance porch with paired columns, intricately paneled entrance door flanked by paired fluted Doric halfcolumns with lattice panel between, fanlight. Central hall plan. Built ca. 1789. Remodeled and enlarged ca. 1812, when it was used as a branch bank. Entrance porch added ca. 1820. Pediments over windows probably mid 19th C. Stucco originally scored. Part of house converted to use as a "tea room" before 1936. Int. changed in the years since to accommodate the demands of the restaurant and lounge which now occupy the building. 7 ext. photos (1934, 1936); 2 data pages (1936).

Hamilton-Turner House. See Samuel P. Hamilton House.

Samuel P. Hamilton House (Hamilton-Turner House) GA-1184. 330 Abercorn St., facing w. Brick with stucco scored and with quoins, rectangular with projecting center pavilion and with side and rear wings. Two and one-half stories over semiraised basement, mansard roof with cresting, dormers and central tower; lower slope of mansard roof covered with green slate in hex pattern. One int. chimney, four end chimneys. Cornice with paired pendant brackets. Decorative hoods over windows. Some windows arched, some full length, some with balconies, all with one-pane sash. Entrance porch with two square paneled columns with matching pilasters, arches between. Arched doorway with double doors. Central hall plan, principal doors arched, windows with int. blinds.

Matching carriage house, rectangular, one-bay front. Pseudo mansard roof at front, so that front is one story with dormer; rest of building two stories with low-slope shed roof, no chimney. Front with triple window with fanlight.

Second empire style, built 1873; J. D. Hall, architect. Originally brick, later stuccoed. Int. converted into apartments. Carriage house converted to residence, the triple windows replacing the former door, and the dormer window replacing a door to the loft. 5 ext. photos (1966); 3 int. photos (1966). Illustrated on p. 195.

Hampton-Lillibridge House, No. 1 GA-1185. 507 E. Julian St., facing N. Frame with clapboarding, four-bay front, two-and-a-half stories over raised basement, gambrel roof with dormers and widow's walk, two int. end chimneys, small entrance porch with shed roof and side steps. Postcolonial, built ca. 1796 at 310 E. Bryan St., facing s. Moved and restored in 1962. 4 sheets (1962); 4 ext. photos (1962); 8 data pages (1962).

Hampton-Lillibridge House, No. 2 GA-1186. 312 E. Bryan St. with end toward street, s. Wood frame with clapboarding, three-bay front, two-and-a-half stories, gambrel roof with dormers, two small entrance porches. Postcolonial, built ca. 1796. Two-tier porch on w side since enclosed; house converted to duplex with later entrance at end of enclosed porch, and small porches added each entrance. Demolished 1962. 2 ext. photos (1962); 2 int. photos (1962).

Harbor Beacon GA-232. 600 block, N side of Bay St., E end of Emmett Park. Cast iron with octagonal granite base; lantern sheet-metal and glass. Cast-iron post octagonal at base, diminishing and changing to a variety of rounded forms embellished with representations of leaves and naturalistic motifs as it ascends, culminating with calix of leaves immediately under lantern. Erected 1858 as beacon light for mariners navigating the Savannah River. 1 ext. photo (1934); 1 data page (1934).

Houses, 127–129 Abercorn St. See Mary Marshall Houses.

House, 330 Abercorn St. See Samuel P. Hamilton House.

Houses, 312 and 314 E. Broughton St. GA-240. Facing ssw. Double house, frame with clapboarding, six-bay front, apparently rectangular, three stories over raised basement, gable roof flared at eaves, one int. chimney. Front façade had bracketed cornice, pedimented windows first and second stories, full-length windows first story. Doric entrance porches with side steps, two slender columns, and roof balustrades. Eight-panel entrance doors with sidelights and full elliptical fanlights. Side hall plan. Traditional Federal-style entrance doorways, mid-Victorian cornice. Probably mid 19th C.; possibly earlier with mid 19th C. renovations. Demolished ca. 1940. 2 ext. photos (1936); 1 data page (1936).

Houses, 118–124 E. Harris St. See Joseph F. Gammon Houses.

House, 14 E. Oglethorpe St. See Anderson-Preston House.

House, 18 E. Oglethorpe St. See William Williams House.

Houses, 103–109 E. President St. GA-1187. Facing N. Brick with stone trim, three stories over raised basement, flat or low slope roof with parapet, corbelled brick modillion cornice, similar belt course at third-story window-sill level. Three-unit apartment house, each unit with wooden stoop with side steps. Mid 19th C. Wooden stoops and steps probably replacements. Demolished ca. 1970. 3 ext. photos (1966); 2 int. photos (1966).

House, 203 E. York St. See Dickerson House.

House, 114 W. Hull St. See John Ash House.

House, 115 W. Oglethorpe Ave.
See *Thomas Gardner House.*

House, 211 W. Perry St. See *Eppinger-Lane House.*

Houston-Screven House GA-246. 32 Abercorn St. Frame with clapboarding, rectangular with center pavilion, two-and-a-half stories, apparently a mansard roof with dormers, and apparently two chimneys. Modillion cornice, wood quoins, cast-iron veranda on side. Flagstone entrance stoop with stone steps each side, wrought-iron railings. Frontispiece entrance with fanlight, half-columns, and broken-base pediment. Central hall plan, the hall divided into entrance hall with wider stair hall behind. Entrance hall had paneled wainscot, pilasters, and groin-vaulted ceiling. Open-well rounded stairway with Palladian window over. Traditional Federal, Adamesque, built between 1784 and 1796; Adrian Boucher (?), architect. Demolished 1920. 1 ext. photo (1937 copy); 2 int. photos (1936 copies); 1 data page (1936). Illustrated on p. 38.

John Hunter House (Cunningham House) GA-257. 101 E. Oglethorpe, facing NNE. Brick Flemish bond, basement brick with stucco scored, stone windowsills, lintels, and belt course. Western half of double house, each unit 30' (three-bay front) × 42'4'' plus additions. Three stories over semiraised basement, low slope or flat roof, two int. chimneys shared with adjoining unit. Marble entrance porch with two Ionic columns, modified entablature, and roof balustrade. Italianate entrance arched and with two sets double doors, outer set heavily paneled and fitting into jambs when open;

inner set with etched glass panels. Side hall plan. Marble mantels, int. shutters that fold into window jambs. Traditional Federal, 1821–22. Third floor may be mid 19th C. addition. Oriel window added w side 1892. Marble porch may be replacement of earlier wooden porch, as on the other unit. 1 ext. photo (1934); 1 data page (1934).

Independent Presbyterian Church GA-237. sw corner Oglethorpe Ave. and Bull St., facing ESE. Granite with quoins, wooden trim, and slate roof. Rectangular, one story, gable roof. Gibbes-type steeple with projecting granite tower, three-stage octagonal wooden belfry, and octagonal spire. Round clock faces and arched pediments at top of tower are repeated with vitality in round and arched windows of belfry; windows seem to be ascending from the tower. Engaged Corinthian columns at corners of two lower stories of belfry, Corinthian pilasters at corners of top story. Tetrastyle Roman Doric portico with classical entablature and tympanum fan in relief. Meetinghouse plan with vestibule. Auditorium with gallery on three sides, and with oval domed ceiling supported by four Corinthian columns. Clear glass arched windows with int. louvered blinds. Parvis paved with flagstone brought by oxcart from New Jersey. Traditional Federal, Adamesque, built 1819; John Holden Greene, architect. Burned 1889; rebuilt 1890 from measured drawings of original building, drawings by W. G. Preston, architect for rebuilding. Original church was of frame construction; no other major changes. 4 ext. photos (1936); 3 int. photos (1936); 2 int. photos (1962); 2 data pages (1936). Illustrated on p. 32.

Kerr House (Tobias House) GA-256. 18 W. Harris St., facing ssw. Brick, basement brick with stucco scored horizontally, marble trim. Marble steps and marble-bordered stoop. Row house, two-bay front with slightly projecting entrance bay. Three stories over raised basement, shed roof with parapet in front, two int. chimneys. Marble entablature, marble belt course at first floor, windows with sidelights (except those above entrance) and with pediment-shaped lintels; first-floor windows full length with iron balcony. Entrance stoop with side steps, combination cast- and wrought-iron railings. Double entrance door with molded trim and corner blocks. Side hall plan, marble mantels. Half of double house. Greek Revival, built 1842–43; Charles B. Cluskey (?), architect. 2 ext. photos (1934); 1 data page (1934).

LePage House GA-259. 112 W. Hull St., facing ssw. Frame with clapboarding, foundation brick with stucco. Stone stoop with stone steps one side. Wrought-iron railing with three medallions and exquisitely worked scrolls. Simple entrance with transom and sidelights with rectangular panes. Probably erected before 1832; demolished ca. 1952. 2 ext. photos (1936), 1 data page (1936).

Low House GA-210. 329 Abercorn St., facing ESE. Brick with stucco, rectangular, five-bay front, sides four bays plus porch, two stories over raised basement. Low slope pyramidal roof, four end chimneys flush with ext. walls. Wide eaves with Italianate wooden brackets, five-bay three-tiered rear porch with full-length square columns, jalousies between columns on upper floors. Cast-iron balconies front and s sides, side balcony has delicate cast-iron columns and frieze, and pagoda-type roof. Double-hung windows with wide center muntins to give appearance of casement windows. First-floor windows full length. Stone frontispiece entrance with pediment and Tower-of-the-Winds Corinthian columns in antis; recessed doorway, heavily studded double doors with transom and sidelights, the latter flanked by Corinthian pilasters. Central hall plan, double parlor one side. Int. doorways with simplified pediments and pilasters repeating Tower-of-the-Winds motif. Black marble mantels, handsome stairway with curved returns. Cast-iron fence front and sides, high brick wall, stuccoed, enclosing rear garden.

Remodeled carriage house and servants' quarters (two stories, brick with stucco) at rear; Victorian parterre gardens in front. Greek Revival, built 1849; John S. Norris, architect. Baths since added behind jalousies of rear porch. The stucco, now painted, was formerly a brick color with a patina of soot and age in pleasant contrast with the painted wood and metal work. An outstanding design, expressive of its time, locale, and climate.

Robert E. Lee and William Makepeace Thackeray were guests at this house. Here, in 1912, Juliette Gordon Low organized the first Girl Scout troop in America. The carriage house is used by local council as their headquarters. 3 ext. photos (1936); 2 int. photos (1936); 1 data page (1936). Illustrated on p. 116.

Lufburrow House (Ravenel House) GA-2139. 116 E. McDonough St., facing SSW. Brick (oversize, thickness 2¾" to 3½", length 8½" to 9½") with brownstone trim. Rectangular central block, one-story wing. Three bays wide (four bays including wing, which is flush with front), two stories over raised basement, hipped roof on main part, shed roof with end parapet (toward street) on wing. Two chimneys between wing and main body of house, these flush with ext. walls of second story; one int. chimney. Brick cornice with large and prominent brick dentils. Concrete deck on E side, over sidewalk. Rear porch, now enclosed. Stone entrance landing and side steps with elegantly simple wrought-iron railing. Recessed entrance with fanlight and one-piece stone archivolt. Side hall plan. Brick carriage house. Side and rear yards enclosed with high brick wall. Traditional Federal, simplistic, built ca. 1830; Matthew Lufburrow, architect-builder. Singular restraint and simplicity. 1 ext. photo (1934). Illustrated on p. 53.

McAlpin House. See *Champion-McAlpin House.*

MacIntosh House GA-22. 110–111 E. Oglethorpe Ave., facing SSW. Brick with stucco, 31 ft. (five-bay front), three stories, shed roof sloping to rear, two chimneys flush with ext. walls. Italianate brackets under eaves at front, full-width cast-iron balcony at second story, entrance stoop with side steps, cast-iron railing. Two-panel (vertical) entrance door with transom over. Central hall plan with separate stair hall at rear. Built before 1783; third floor and balcony added mid 19th C. Int. remodeled many times. Home of Gen. Lachlan MacIntosh 1782–1806. George Washington stayed here on his visit to Savannah in 1791. 1 ext. photo (1936); 1 data page (1936).

Mackay House. See Belcher-Hunter House.

Mary Marshall Houses GA-1188. 127–129 Abercorn St., facing E. Brick with sandstone trim, rectangular, six-bay front, four stories, nearly flat roof with parapet, four end chimneys. Corbelled modillion brick cornice, corbelled modillion brick belt course at windowsill level third floor. Cast-iron balcony across front at second floor. Double house with two entrances, two side halls. Cast-iron fence on stone base at front. Matching carriage house, one bay wide, two stories. Built 1859. Rear porches since enclosed; two- and four-story wings added to rear. 5 ext. photos (1966); 2 int. photos (1966).

Mercer-Wilder House GA-1189. 429 Bull St., facing E. Brick with banded stone base, stone steps; stone, wood, and cast-iron trim. Rectangular, three-bay front, two stories over raised basement, very low slope or flat roof with very wide bracketed eaves, one int., four end chimneys. Ornate cast-iron cornices over arched windows, some of which are paired, some full-length, with cast-iron balconies. Three-tiered porch across back. Corinthian entrance porch with two sets of paired columns, recessed arched doorway. Central hall plan with skylighted circular stairway in side recess. Elaborate Italianate wood and plaster work.

Rectangular carriage house extending full width of lot with carriage entrance facing Whitaker St. Brick with brownstone trim, low slope or flat roof. Cast-iron fence on stone base surrounds front of house; high brick wall and carriage house enclose rear garden.

Italianate, begun ca. 1860 by Gen. Hugh Mercer; John S. Norris, architect. Vandalized by Federal troops and plans lost before completion. Rebuilt for John R. Wilder according to restoration plans by Muller and Bruyn, who were familiar with the original plan. Completed ca. 1866. 5 ext. photos (1966); 2 int. photos (1966); 2 data pages (1965). Illustrated on p. 141.

Mickve Israel Synagogue GA-1190. 428 Bull St., facing w. Brick with stucco, cruciform shape, three-bay front, one-story basilican type with gable roof, shed roofs below clerestory. Central entrance tower with Gothic porch, large pointed arch window over. Two-stage tower, buttress with finials at corners; belfry with onion-dome roof. Round windows in clerestory, other windows pointed-arch type. Buttresses with finials between structural bays. Interior with nave, apse, side-aisles, transepts. Plaster vaulting. Gothic Revival, 1876–78; Henry G. Harrison and J. D. Foley, architects. Additions at rear. 4 ext. photos (1966); 2 int. photos (1966). Illustrated on p. 192.

Abram Minis House GA-281. 204 E. Jones St., facing s. Brick with stone trim, five-bay front, two-and-a-half stories over raised basement, hipped roof with dormers, four end chimneys. Brick frieze with dentils, wooden cornice with modillions. One-story porch E side, floor-length windows with balconies each side of entrance. Stone stoop, open-arms stone steps with cast-iron railing. Recessed entrance with shouldered

architrave stone frame with cornice with shell motif. Central hall plan; marble mantels.

Carriage house brick with stucco, apparently L-shaped, two stories with gable roof. Balcony with wrought-iron railing and steps. Very heavy cast-iron fence in front, high brick wall at sides and rear. Italianate, 1859–60; Stephen Decatur Button, architect. Stucco removed and carriage house demolished ca. 1972. 5 ext. photos (1966); 3 int. photos (1966).

Isaac Minis House GA-28. 202 W. Hull St., facing ssw. Brick with scored stucco, slate roof, 48'2" (three-bay front) × 40'2". Two stories over semiraised basement, gable roof with parapet, bracketed wood cornice at base of parapet, four end chimneys flush with ext. walls. Stone entrance landing with stone steps each side, wrought-iron railings with volutes at curtail steps, wrought-iron gate to basement under landing. Recessed arch entrance with sidelights and full fanlight, Greek Doric halfcolumns between door and sidelights. Full-length triple windows flanking entrance, French doors with wrought-iron balconies over those windows; exquisite wrought-iron medallions in railings. One-story rear porch, later enclosed. Central hall plan. Traditional Federal, built 1830–31; demolished ca. 1938. 4 sheets (1934); 3 ext. photos (1934); 1 ext. photo (1936); 1 int. photo (1934); 2 data pages (1936).

Newspaper Office GA-2131 (see also *Bank*). 17 E. Bay St., facing NNE. Marble veneer, rectangular, three-bay front, two stories, gable roof, two entrance doors, the western one with a semicircular tran-

som. Built early 19th C. Remodeled several times; extensively remodeled ca. 1935, when marble veneer was installed over brick and stucco walls, semicircular transom of w entrance replaced a fanlight and central entrance (formerly with fanlight) was combined with the enlarged E window. See photographs and data pages listed in *Bank* entry.

Old Branch of the United States Bank. See *United States Bank*.

Owens-Thomas House. See *Richardson-Owens-Thomas House.*

The Pink House. See *Habersham House.*

Rahn House (Dr. Charlton House) GA-286. 220 E. Oglethorpe, facing ssw. Brick with brownstone trim, 30 ft. (three-bay front), two-and-a-half stories over raised basement, gable roof with dormers and parapet, dentil-type corbel table at base of front parapet, two end chimneys flush with ext. wall. Brownstone belt course at main floor, brownstone lintels (pediment type at first and second floors) over windows. One-bay entrance porch with square columns, stone steps one side; wrought-iron railing with pickets and scroll designs. Door to basement under porch. One-panel entrance door with enriched moldings and sidelights. Side hall plan, double parlors with sliding doors between. Plaster cornices, black marble mantels. Built ca. 1853. Doors to basement 20th C. replacements; many int. changes. 1 ext. photo (1936); 1 data page (1936).

Ravenel House. See *Lufburrow House.*

Reid Servants' and Carriage House. See *Gibbons Servants' and Carriage House.*

William Remshart Row Houses GA-1191. 102–112 W. Jones St., facing s. Brick with sandstone trim, end walls stuccoed, one-story wing to E is imitation brick. Rectangular, four units three bays wide, one unit three bays wide at basement floor, one bay wide on upper floors (total thirteen-bay front main floors). Three stories over raised basement, shed roof with parapets, brick dentil band at base of parapet, stoops with steps one side, combination cast-and wrought-iron railings, sandstone steps and trim. Side hall plans. No. 104 still has brick carriage and servant's house at rear. Built 1853. No. 102 may originally have been tiered porches. Porches enclosed and many additions at rear. 3 ext. photos (1966); 2 int. photos (1966).

Richardson-Owens-Thomas House GA-14-9. 122–24 Abercorn St., facing WNW. Brick with stucco, basement tabby with deeply incised horizontal jointing. Slate roof. 60′4′′ (five-bay front) × 50′6′′ (five-bay sides), plus projecting semioctagonal wings at rear. Two stories over semiraised basement, hipped roof with parapet with recessed panels, two int. chimneys. Belt course in form of a cornice with dentils and frieze at second-floor level; cornice in form of simplified molding at base of parapet. Quoins at corners first floor; pilasters at second floor. N (State St.) façade with recessed panels instead of windows at dining room (except for horizontal sash, which admits indirect light that side). Rear (E façade) with porch recessed between wings, the

porch with two Ionic cast-stone columns; room of frame construction with flush siding over porch. Center pavilion with paired pilasters on s (President St.) façade; balcony first floor, E side of pavilion. Roof of balcony concave with cast-iron cresting and fringe. Cast-iron Corinthian columns with delicate cast-iron railing. Balcony supported by unique acanthus-leaf consoles. Elliptical blind arches over second-story windows, arches repeated on front (w façade), which likewise has center pavilion. Entrance porch with bombé front and four cast-stone Greek Ionic columns flanked by curving stone steps with wrought-iron railings. Double paired entrance doors within apsidal recess, the outer pair three-panel wooden doors curving with the wall; the inner pair part glass. Door with sidelights and full elliptical fanlight to roof over entrance porch. Architectural elements orchestrated for effect rather than for structural expression. s façade has rhythmic power emphasized by staccato details. Front is lyrical, with undulating and polyphonic curves. Unsymmetric placement of balcony on s façade has led to speculation that a second one was originally intended for balance; this would, however, have weakened the unique relation between this side and the front.

Central hall plan, but with front and back halls separated by service stairs, and front hall subdivided by Corinthian columns with gilt capitals. Columns frame central flight of symmetrically divided grand staircase. Stair treads and mahogany handrailings are inlaid with brass; balusters are cast iron. Second-story hall, bisected by stairwell, is divided into two parts connected by a bridge,

the floor of which curves upward at center. Plasterwork throughout is elegant, restrained, and based on classic motifs. Drawing room on s side of foyer has a flat domical ceiling with a center floriated medallion encircled by a Greek fret, the fret repeated at edges of the dome; pendentive fans in corners of the room. Mantel is white marble with mythological figures, and is flanked by arched niches.

Dining room (N side of hall) with curved E end and concave niche in N wall, the concavity emphasized by convex wall treatment over and by indirect natural lighting. Cresting similar to a series of antefixae between frieze molding and ceiling. Int. oval windows in rear rooms to provide cross ventilation.

Front enclosure wall of tabby with cast-stone balustrade and decorative urns, iron fence at sides. Rear yard enclosed with high tabby wall on two sides; carriage and servants' house at rear. English Regency, begun 1816, finished 1819; William Jay, architect; John Retan, builder. House designed by Jay while in England. Minor changes only. Second story of rear wings and room over rear porch are early additions. SE chamber (now furnished as bedroom) was originally combined with rear entrance hall. Carriage and servants' house have been remodeled into apartments. Lafayette stayed here during his visit to Savannah in 1824. House museum. 8 sheets (1934); 3 ext. photos (1934); 7 ext. photos (1936); 5 int. photos (1934); 5 int. photos (1936); 2 data pages (1936). Illustrated on pp. 77, 78, 82, 83, 91.

Roberts House. See *Oliver Sturges House.*

Row Houses. See *Gordon Row.*

St. John's Episcopal Church GA-1192. 329 Bull St. Brick with stucco, stone trim. Rectangular with projecting central entrance tower and projecting chancel. Three-bay front, one story, gable roof. Buttresses at corners and between bays, tower buttresses with finials. Open pointed arches at base of tower; tower square, spire octagonal. Lancet windows. Narthex with balcony over; three aisles in nave; hammer-beam ceiling. Carved paneling in chancel. Gothic Revival, 1852–53; Calvin N. Otis, architect; Calvin Fay, supervising architect; Daniel L. Cohen, builder. Bells installed in 1854, stained-glass windows in 1886 and 1938. 1 ext. photo (1980). Illustrated on p. 129.

St. Vincent's Academy GA-1193. 207 E. Liberty St., facing N. Brick with stucco scored, rectangular with five projecting pavilions on front, ell on rear (sixteen-bay front). Two stories over raised basement, flat or low slope roof with parapets. Pavilion parapets crenellated but with center pediment; pediment of center pavilion surmounted with cross. Pilasters between bays. Two entrance porches each with two sets paired square columns, parapets similar to those of pavilions. Marble plaque with inscription in frieze of each porch, the inscription including dates: 1845 for western part; "enlarged" 1855 for eastern. High wall, brick with stucco scored, on w side and part of rear. Iron fence in front; gates and stair railing part wrought and part cast iron, with wrought-iron lanterns outstanding. Built 1845; Charles B. Cluskey, architect. Enlarged 1855 and 1869. 20th C. addition on E side. 3 ext. photos (1966); 2 int. photos (1966).

Savannah Cotton Exchange GA-1194. 100 E. Bay St., facing Factors' Walk, s. Brick and terra cotta, rectangular (three-double-bay front), three stories above bridge on Factors' Walk side, six stories in rear on River St. side. Bull St. Ext. continues under building. Hipped roof with dome, parapet with pediment and balustrade in front. First two floors with pilasters and entablature; central bay arched. Third floor similar to an attic story, the façade possibly inspired by Roman triumphal arches. Pilaster capitals and relief sculpture brick and terra cotta, brick red monochromatic. Oversize double entrance doors heavily paneled, panels varying in size, shape, and arrangement. Entrance to walk and bridge two stories above "moat," but approximately level with Bay St. Walks; bridge with elaborate wrought-iron railings. Eclectic or late Victorian with classical motifs unconventionally combined. Built 1886; William G. Preston, architect. 3 ext. photos (1966); 2 int. photos (1966). Illustrated on p. 205.

SAVANNAH VICTORIAN HISTORIC DISTRICT GA-1169. Bounded N by Gwinnett St., E and W by Price and Montgomery Sts., s by Anderson St. Plan of district an extension of the old Savannah plan, but without its system of parks. District developed mainly during the late 19th and early 20th C., largely as an area of comparatively modest one- and two-family residences. Though predominantly Queen Anne, most popular styles of those years were represented, as were technological advances from oil lamps to electric lights, from water pumps to indoor plumbing, and from horse-drawn vehicles to automobiles. With the advent of the automobile and easy access to suburbs, original residents moved away and were replaced by low-income tenants. Residences were subdivided into apartments; overcrowding and urban blight resulted. In the early 1970s the Savannah Landmark Rehabilitation Project was formed with the express purpose of rehabilitating the area, restoring the period architecture, and encouraging an influx of higher-income groups without displacing the current residents. The aim is a historic district with residents of economic and ethnic diversity. The plan has progressed, and is being implemented with the cooperation of the Historic American Buildings Survey, the Georgia State Historic Preservation Office, the Savannah-Chatham County Metropolitan Planning Comission, the City of Savannah Community Planning and Development Department, and the Historic Savannah Foundation. 1 sheet (1979); 227 photos (1979); 27 photocopies (various dates); 27 data pages (1979). Illustrated on pp. 248, 249, 253. Some of the buildings that were documented in detail follow.

313 East Bolton Street GA-1169 K. Frame with clapboard siding, 31' (five-bay NW front) × 52'6'', one story, gable roof with standing-seam tin roofing. Porch extends across front, supported by four chamfered square posts, decorative sawed scrollwork between posts, deep molded cornice with scroll brackets, central front door with plain surrounds. Central hall plan; vinyl-covered hardwood floors, narrow tongue-and-groove paneling on walls and ceilings, wooden fireplace mantels. Built

1885; John Joseph McMahon, builder. Rear lean-to added. 1 sheet (1979); 2 ext. photos (1979); 4 data pages (1979).

321 East Bolton Street GA-1169 L. Frame with clapboard siding, irregular shape, 26′11″ (N front) × 64′6″, two-and-a-half stories, intersecting hip roofs with gable ends, elaborate sawed bargeboards, deep denticulated eaves with brackets. One-story front porch with square chamfered posts, turned balusters and spindle frieze; enclosed two-story rear porch. Front entrance has paneled double doors topped by stained-glass transom, corniced window frames. Side hall plan; entrance foyer has encaustic tile floor inlaid with original owner's initials. Hardwood floors, plaster walls and ceilings with decorative medallions, sliding double doors between main rooms, wooden fireplace mantels with tile surrounds and hearths, built-in bench and bookcase in drawing room; Queen Anne style details. Built for John J. O'Neil in 1899. 1 sheet (1979); 5 ext. photos (1979); 3 int. photos (1979); 5 data pages (1979).

103 East Duffy Lane GA-1169 R. Frame pier-and-beam construction with clapboard siding, 31′3″ (three-bay S front) × 20′1″, two stories. Gable roof with diamond-patterned asphalt shingles, three pairs of hinged garage doors on S, second-floor entrance on N, second-story wooden entry stoop with plain square posts and balusters, plain cornice. Three-car garage on ground floor, central hall plan on second floor, narrow wooden board flooring, plaster walls and ceilings with picture molding, plain doorway and window surrounds. Built ca. 1900–

20. 1 sheet (1979); 4 data pages (1979).

404-410 East Duffy Street GA-1169 T. Frame with clapboarding, 60′4″ (six-bay S front) × 55′1″ with rear ell additions. Two stories, hip roofs with deep bracketed molded cornice; double gallery on front with decorative wooden balusters and turned posts supporting flat roof, two wide front doorways. Side hall plan, apartments, hardwood floors, corner block doorway moldings. Built 1894; upper decks added ca. 1916. 2 sheets (1979); 3 ext. photos (1979); 4 data pages (1979).

525–529 East Gwinnett Lane GA-1169 I. Frame with clapboard siding, each unit measures 16′ (S front) × 26′9″ with rear kitchen ells (8′3″ × 16′7″), one-and-a-half stories, gable roof, one-story stoops supported by plain square wooden posts. Side hall plan, hardwood floors, walls are plastered above and beaded vertical boarding below, wooden paneled doors, corner fireplaces. Built ca. 1898–1916. 1 sheet (1979); 4 data pages (1979).

224 East Henry Street GA-1169 U. Frame with clapboard siding, 25′6″ (three-bay S front) × 46′ with projecting front polygonal bay (5′ × 10′), three stories. Mansard roof covered with polychrome slates and pierced by segmental-arched dormers, one-story entrance porch with square columns and sawed scrollwork infill, bracketed cornice and frieze. Side hall plan, apartments, pine floors, painted plaster walls and ceiling, heavily molded doorway and window surrounds, arched fireplace mantels with fluted pilasters and brackets; Second Empire details.

Built 1881; John O. Smith, prominent Savannah carpenter and builder. Converted from single-family residence to apartments. 1 sheet (1979); 2 ext. photos (1979); 1 int. photo (1979); 6 data pages (1979).

521 East Henry Street GA-1169 W. Frame with clapboarding, 23′5″ (N front) × 40′6″, two stories. Gable roof with deep box cornice and returns, one-story porch across front supported by large chamfered square columns, pointed-arched attic vent in front pediment. Main doorway framed by side panels and three-light transom. Side hall plan, wooden and vinyl floor, plaster walls; modest neoclassical details. Built 1898. 1 sheet (1979, including plan); 2 ext. photos (1979); 4 data pages (1979).

115 East Park Avenue GA-1169 Q. Frame with clapboarding, two stories, five-bay N front with projecting porch, gable roof with outside end chimneys, boxed eaves, porch across front with round wooden posts and balusters. Central hall plan, sheetrock over lath wall surfaces, hardwood floors, paneled wooden doors, wooden fireplace mantels. Built 1868, one of earliest houses in Victorian District. 1 sheet (1979); 1 ext. photo (1979); 4 data pages (1979).

300–306 East Waldburg Street GA-1169 N. Frame with clapboard siding, rectangular, five-bay S front, nine-bay W side, two stories. Shallow hipped roof with vented wooden parapet, two brick chimneys, double-tiered two-story porch with square brick piers built across front, four transomed apartment entrances, plain window surrounds, wide flat eaves. Side hall plan, apartments, enclosed stairway, oak board flooring, plaster walls and ceilings, wooden raised panel doors, oak fireplace mantels with white tile surrounds, original electrical fixtures. Built ca. 1900. 2 sheets (1979); 3 ext. photos (1979); 3 data pages (1979); field records.

414–416 East Waldburg Street GA-1169 O. Brick, two stories, 51′ (four-bay s façade) × 34′ with ell (14′6″ × 30′) to rear of 214 E. Waldburg, gable roof covered with terra cotta tiles, shallow hipped roof with standing-seam tin roofing, irregular gable ends. One-story porch across s front, supported by round wooden Corinthian columns on marble bases resting on brick pedestals, turned wooden balusters; two second-story polygonal bays with conical dome roofs, main doorways with marble lintels and sills and topped by transom. Side hall plan, apartments, hardwood floors, plastered walls, transomed doorways; neoclassical and Flemish details. Built for Dr. Thomas Waring, 1900. 2 sheets (1979); 5 ext. photos (1979); 4 data pages (1979).

213 West Bolton Street GA-1169 B. Frame with clapboard siding, L-shaped, 29′4″ (five-bay N front) × 53′3″ with rear kitchen ell (13′2″ × 21′11″). One story, intersecting gables with standing-seam tin roofing, porch (16′7″ × 5′11″) built into front ell with square chamfered posts and gingerbread brackets, deep eaves with carved decorative bargeboards. L-shaped plan; hardwood floors, painted plaster walls and ceilings, paneled doors topped by leaded stained-glass transoms, stained-glass skylight, floor-length parlor windows with wide architraves, wooden

fireplace mantels framed by plain frieze and pilasters; Victorian Gothic details. Built for William B. Sturtevant, 1868; Anselm Atkins, stained-glass designer. 1 sheet (1979); 2 ext. photos (1979); 5 data pages (1979).

217–219 West Bolton Street GA-1169 C. Brick and frame with clapboard siding, 26′ (three-bay NW front) × 45′. Two stories with fully exposed basement, gable roof with standing-seam tin roofing, box cornice with gable returns, tall brick chimney with denticulated cornice at E, raised entrance porch approached by metal steps from E and supported by square columns. Double main doorway topped by transoms, enclosed triple-deck rear porches. Side hall plan, hardwood floors, sheetrock wall surfaces over lath, plain wooden fireplace mantel. Built for L. Wilson Landershine, bookkeeper, 1870. 1 sheet (1979); 1 ext. photo (1979); 4 int. photos (1979); 4 data pages (1979).

101–25 West Duffy Street GA-1169 F. Frame with clapboard siding, 23′3″ (front façade) × 63′3″, two stories. Gable roof with standing-seam tin roofing, deep bracketed cornice, two-story front bay with lancet-arched windows, two-tiered front porch with tongue-in-groove decking and plain square columns, mansard skirt between first and second story. Side hall plan, hardwood floors, sheetrock ceiling surfaces, plaster walls, wooden fireplace mantels with plain frieze and pilasters; Victorian Gothic details. Built for Burrell L. Boulineau, 1867. 4 sheets (1979); 11 ext. photos (1979); 1 int. photo (1979); 4 data pages (1979).

215 West Gwinnett Street GA-1169 A. Frame with clapboarding, 28′6″

(front N façade) × 54′4″, two stories. Hipped roof, enclosed E porch, w porch with square posts supporting spindled frieze, two-story N polygonal bay with hexagonal roof. Side hall plan with double parlors to E of hallway, sliding doors between parlors, wooden floors, plastered walls, plaster ceiling medallions; Italianate details. Built for Charles Dorsett, real estate developer, 1885; E porch enclosed 1893. 2 sheets (1979); 2 ext. photos (1979); 1 int. photo (1979); 1 photocopy of 1893 photo; 5 data pages (1979).

210–212 West Henry Street GA-1169 H. Frame with clapboard siding, 40′4″ (three-bay s front) × 52′8″, two-story main block with one-story rear addition, gable roof with standing-seam tin roofing, covered entry stoops supported by turned wooden columns, two-light transom over main doorway, bracketed eaves. Side hall plans, apartments, stairway with turned spindles, wooden floors, paneled plaster walls, sliding doors between parlors, wooden fireplace mantels; modest Italianate details. Built for George O. Penton, 1883; converted from single-family residences to apartments ca. 1920. 1 sheet (1979); 2 ext. photos (1979); 4 data pages (1979).

119 West Park Avenue GA-1169 E. Brick with wooden trim, L-shaped, 42′9″ (five-bay N front) × 35′2″ with rear addition, one story with fully exposed basement level. Low hipped roof with standing-seam metal roofing, box cornice and brick dentils, central entrance porch, iron steps with turned balusters approaching landing from w, main doorway framed by sidelights and transom, brick water table across front at first floor. Central hall plan, hardwood floors, painted plaster walls, paneled doors with wide-shouldered surrounds, wooden fireplace mantels with plain frieze and pilasters in all rooms; classical details. Built ca. 1852–66; two-story rear ell added. 1 sheet (1979); 3 ext. photos (1979); 5 data pages (1979).

207 West Waldburg Street GA-1169 D. Frame with clapboarding, two stories, 24' (two-bay N front) × 73'6''. Hipped roof with molded cornice and beaded concave frieze, two-story polygonal bay, one-story entry stoop with round columns on square plinths supporting flat canopy, front doorway framed by sidelights and transom. Side hall plan, apartments, wooden floors, plaster cornice in front parlor, wooden fireplace mantels, decorative dining-room ceiling medallion; Victorian details. Built for Joseph E. Fulton, realtor, 1886. 1 sheet (1979); 1 ext. photos (1979); 4 data pages (1979).

Scarborough House. See Scarbrough House.

Scarbrough House GA-2127. 41 W. Broad St., facing ESE. Brick with stucco, stucco below main-floor level with heavy banded rustication. T-shaped, 62 ft., three-bay front, central bay emphasized by slight projection and higher parapet. Two stories over semi-raised basement, low-pitched roof with parapet, two int. chimneys, two chimneys flush with rear wall of second story. Belt courses consisting of modified frieze and cornice at second floor and at base of parapet. Porches each side of

rear wing, S side porch with cast-iron Corinthian columns with vertical slots (presumably for louvers), and elaborate cast-iron railing. Entrance porch has side walls with arched openings, the front with archaic Greek Doric columns in antis, the porch flanked by arched windows set in arched recesses. Landing in front of entrance porch with segmental arch under and with steps each side; heavy cast-stone balusters. Diocletian window with double glass doors centered over entrance porch. Entrance with cast-stone architrave trim, modified (Regency style) pediment, and a double set of paired doors, the outer leaves four-panel wooden type, the inner leaves three glass panels and a bottom panel of wood.

Two-story atrium-type entrance hall with four classic Greek Doric columns supporting peripheral balcony; clerestory-type skylight over. Parlors each side with curved end walls and arched windows. Two symmetrically placed doors at rear of hall lead to ballroom with porches each side and two fireplaces on W wall. Behind the ballroom is a shallow room shaped like a porch and extending across rear of house to connect the two side porches. Side and rear yards enclosed by high walls, brick with stucco. Arched carriage gateway to side yard is flanked by paired columns similar to those of the entrance porch and supporting simplified entablatures with attic stories over.

Transitional Federal, 1819; William Jay, architect. Third floor was added and stairs changed during 19th C. Third floor removed and house restored 1975–76. Original skylight may have had solar screening and provision for ven-

tilation. French doors in ballroom may have had arched fanlights to match parlor windows. In its conceptual stage, room behind ballroom may have been an open porch. One original white marble mantel remains; other mantels are replacements. President Monroe stayed here during his visit to Savannah in 1819. House museum. 22 sheets (1962); 3 ext. photos (1934); 2 ext. photos (1936); 2 ext. photos (1962); 1 int. photo (1936); 16 data pages (1962). Illustrated on pp. 79, 80.

Smets House GA-258. 2–4 E. Jones St., facing SSW. Brick (accurately manufactured and precisely laid with narrow joints) with stone trim, first floor stuccoed with banded rustication. Rectangular, five-bay front, three stories, low pitched pyramidal roof culminating with cupola; four int. chimneys, the chimney tops emerging at the corners of the cupola and appearing to be corner buttresses. Three-story porch at rear; cast-iron balcony with concave roof, cast-iron frieze, columns, railings, and brackets on Bull St. side. Double entrance doors with sidelights and transom, central hall plan with open-well stairway, int. doors with modillion cornices and pediments, delicate circular stairway leading from third floor to cupola. Built 1853; John S. Norris (?), architect. Victorian entrance doors and one-light sash probably not original. Int. remodeled many times for various uses. Upper floors vacant; first floor used for offices. 1 ext. photo (1934); 1 data page (1934).

Archibald Smith's Factors' Building (Van Schaick Warehouse) GA-

1195. 202–206 E. Bay St., facing
s. Brick with stucco scored, rectangular nine-bay (three structural
bays) front, four stories, gable roof
with stepped end parapets, parapets between major bays. One int.,
two end chimneys. Front with
classical wooden cornice and with
three entrances to fourth floor.
Cantilevered walk in front connected to Bay St. level by bridge;
entrances third and second floors
connecting by bridges to intermediate levels. Entrances River
St. side to first floor. Crossarm
heads of tie rods conspicuous feature of end walls. Typical Factors'
Walk building with offices upper
floor opening to Bay St., entrances
to warehousing space (lower floors)
River St. side. Built 1823. Fourth
floor still used as offices; first
floor for various shops. Field
records only (1962).

Sorrel House (Sorrel-Weed House)
GA-2140. 6 W. Harris St., facing
ssw. Brick with stucco scored,
rectangular with projecting enclosures at sides of rear porch,
three-bay front, two stories over
raised basement, nearly flat roof
with parapet of varying heights
and with pediments three sides;
four end chimneys flush with ext.
walls. Two-story rear porch with
end "garden" rooms; one-story
porches each side, these porches
with ends enclosed, but with a
louvered arched opening toward
street. Entrance porch with two
Greek Doric columns in antis,
combination cast- and wrought-
iron railing. Two flights of stone
steps lead to landings each side of
porch. Central hall plan with circular stairway, double parlors one
side. Plaster ceiling moldings and
medallions, marble mantels. Cast-
iron fence on stone base in front;

two-story (brick with stucco) carriage and servants' house in rear.
Greek Revival, 1841; Charles B.
Cluskey, architect. Commercial
buildings have been built against
Bull St. side of house since 1937.
8 ext. photos (1936); 6 int. photos
(1936); 1 ext. photo, gate (1936);
3 data pages (1936).

Sorrel-Weed House. See *Sorrel
House.*

Spencer-Woodbridge House. See
George B. Spencer House.

George B. Spencer House (Spencer-Woodbridge House) GA-2133.
22 Habersham St., facing wnw.
Frame with beaded siding, brick
addition to rear. Rectangular, five-
bay front (34'4") by four-bay sides;
original part two-bay sides. Two-
and-a-half stories, original part
gable with dormers, shed roof on
addition. Two int. chimneys. One-
story porch across rear, one-bay
simplified Doric entrance porch.
Central hall plan. Mantel with
shouldered architrave, and with
dentil band over frieze. Paneled
overmantel with extruded corners.
High brick wall around side
and rear yards; small front yard
paved with brick to street. Post-
colonial, 1790–1804. Entrance
porch may not be original, but
built before 1934. Additions at
end of and over rear porch before
1934. 1 ext. photo (1934); 2 ext.
photos (1936); 1 int. photo (1936);
1 data page (1936).

Oliver Sturges House (Roberts
House) GA-25. 26 Abercorn St.,
facing E. Brick, Flemish bond,
basement walls stuccoed, marble
steps, brownstone trim. 30'6"
(three-bay front), rectangular, rear
ell, three stories over raised base-

ment, gable roof with end parapet, two end chimneys flush with
ext. walls. Small entrance porch
with two slender unfluted Doric
columns and two fluted Corinthian pilasters, mutule cornice
with beaded molding. Entrance
doorway and window over have
sidelights and full elliptical fanlights. Rear ell with octagonal
end at second floor, dentil brick
cornice. Side hall plan. Iron fence
around front yard, high brick wall
around rear. Traditional Federal,
Adamesque, built 1813. Third
floor added 1835. Originally northern half of double house. Original
fan, sidelights, and some mantels
removed. Now used as offices for
Morris Newspaper Corporation.
22 sheets (1962); 3 ext. photos
(1936); 1 data page (1936); 13 data
pages (1962).

William Taylor Store GA-1196.
204 W. Bay St., facing s. Stone and
brick, brick primarily at corners
and around openings. E part rectangular, w part roughly rectangular, wider at rear than front. Front
wall continuous, rear wall broken
where smaller w unit adjoins E
unit. Bay St. side three stories,
River St. side four. Gable roof
(hipped at E end) with parapets.
One int., three end chimneys.
Three entrances top floor Bay St.
side, each with arched opening
and double batten doors, each
connecting with Bay St. level by
bridges. Similar entrances second
and first floors. Main entrances
River St. side at bottom floor. Top
floors of w unit converted to residence; top floors of E unit to restaurant and lounge. Lower floors
both units utilized by various
shops. Built 1818, rebuilt after
1885 fire. 4 sheets (1962); 3 ext.
photos (1962); 3 int. photos

(1962); 1 photo of old site map (1962); 10 data pages (1962). Illustrated on p. 95.

Telfair Academy GA-217. 121 Barnard St., facing E. Brick with stucco, rectangular, larger rectangular addition at rear, three-bay front, two stories over semiraised basement. Flat roof with parapet, three end, one int. chimney. Corners offset, high attic story. French windows with cast-iron balconies first floor. One-story tetrastyle Corinthian entrance porch with Diocletian window over; arch repeated under porch. Details of Corinthian capitals notably crisp, free, and open. Central hall two stories high with skylight. Ends of double room on N side of hall curved, windows curve with walls; two rooms on S side, the front one octagonal. Marble mantels, some with mythological scenes on center panel by John Frazee. Mantel in W wing from Belcher-Hunter House★, gift of Thomas P. Saffold and Mrs. B. F. Bullard. Transitional Federal style, built for Alexander Telfair in 1820; William Jay, architect. Remodeled and enlarged for museum ca. 1880; Detlef Lienau, architect. 2 ext. photos (1936); 2 int. photos (1936); 1 data page (1936). Illustrated on pp. 81, 83.

Tenement Houses GA-2134. 421–423 E. York St., facing N. Brick with stucco, rectangular (six-bay front), one story over semiraised basement, gable roof with flared eaves and end parapets, three int. chimneys, two front stoops with side steps with wrought-iron railings. Shed porch at rear with end louvered. Duplex, each side apparently with central hall. Traditional Federal style, simplistic, 1831 (?). Demolished before 1945.

1 ext. photo (1934); 1 data page (1934).

Tobias House. See Kerr House.

Trinity Church GA-212. 127 Barnard St., facing ENE. Brick with stucco, rectangular, temple form, 65'2" (three-bay front, five-bay sides), one story, gable roof with pediment, recessed with two Corinthian columns in antis. Bays each side with panel delineated by groove in stucco and with antae at corners; pilasters between side bays. Double entrance doors framed by pilasters with console brackets and entablature, doors with raised panels framed by moldings set in pattern with extruded corners. Meetinghouse plan with balcony on three sides and recess for pipe organ behind chancel. Recess with Corinthian columns in antis and original organ pipes; later pipe organ in gallery. Greek Revival, 1848–50; John B. Hogg, architect. 1 ext. photo (1936); 1 data page (1936).

Troup Trust (McDonough Row) GA-1197. 410–424 E. Macon St., facing S. Brick walls, sandstone trim, rectangular (twenty-four-bay, eight-unit front); end unit to W faces Habersham St. (five-bay front). Three stories with flat or low-pitched roof, fire parapets between units. Chimneys not visible. Bracketed cornice with brick dentil course below. Windows and doors with pediment-shaped sandstone lintels on front sides. Second-story windows in front are floor length, those in end unit toward W opening onto balconies with twisted iron railings. Four-panel entrance doors (top panel arched) with sidelights and transom. Italianate. Four-unit apartment to E built 1872 for John

McDonough; four-unit apartments to W built 1855 for Edward Kennedy. J. J. Dooley, architect. Apparently all apartments originally had balconies. 3 ext. photos (1966); 2 int. photos (1966).

United States Bank GA-291. E side of Drayton St., occupying block between St. Julian and Bryant Sts., facing WNW. Brick with stucco, rectangular, seven-bay front, one story, flat roof with parapet. Greek Doric hexastyle porch with modified entablature and with a parapet that is higher over end bays than at center. Porch parapet is higher throughout than parapet on rest of building. Unfluted pilasters at corners of building and between bays. Arched windows. Transitional Greek Revival with some Federal details. Built in 1818; William Jay, architect. Remodeled and second story added ca. 1900. Demolished 1924. Views of this bank were published in the *Commercial Directory of the United States* (Philadelphia: J. C. Kayser and Co., 1823), p. 34, and in the *History and Topography of the United States of America*, by J. H. Hinton (London: Hinton, Simpkins, and Marshall, 1831), vol. 2, pl. 71. A view was also included in a series of ceramic works called *Beauties of America*, produced in England before 1830 by John and William Ridgeway. 1 ext. photocopy (1831). Recorded in the 1930s as Old Branch of United States Bank. Illustrated on p. 82.

Van Schaick Warehouse. See Archibald Smith's Factors' Building.

Waring House GA-2142. 127 W. Oglethorpe St., facing N. Brick, basement brick with stucco. Rectangular, six-bay front, three stories over raised basement, apparently hipped roof with four end chimneys. Wide bracketed cornice. Two entrance doorways, the principal one (in center of what appears to have been original five-bay front) with sidelights and full elliptical fanlight; engaged columns between door and sidelights. Triple window with fanlight opening onto balcony over entrance. Arched doorway with double doors in end bay that may have been porch. Original part traditional Federal, Adamesque, 1816; additions Italianate, mid 19th C. Additions apparently included third floor and an additional bay on E and S sides. Demolished ca. 1940. 1 ext. photo (1934); 3 ext. photos (1936); 1 data page (1936).

Wayne-Gordon House GA-211. 10 E. Oglethorpe St., facing S. Brick with stucco scored, rectangular, two semicircular bays at rear, five-bay front, three stories over raised basement, hipped roof, two rear, two end chimneys. Top floor with bracketed cornice and quoins at corners and around windows, former cornice at second floor serving as belt course at window-sill level of third floor. Second-floor windows set in blind arches. One-story porch E side. One-story tetrastyle Doric entrance porch with steps each side. Central hall plan, two rooms each side, N side of rear rooms curved. Curving stairway with arched window with bull's-eye glass over. Principal rooms have plaster cornices with classical motifs, fleurated center ceiling medallions, black marble mantels, molded window and door trim with carved corner blocks and center panels. Rear yard enclosed with high walls or service buildings. Transitional Federal, 1820; attributed to William Jay. Third floor added and

minor changes executed 1886; Detlef Lienau, architect. Service buildings remodeled for offices ca. 1956. Birthplace of Juliette Gordon Low, founder of the Girl Scouts of America. 3 ext. photos (1936); 6 int. photos (1936); 2 data pages (1936).

Wetter House. See *Barclay-Wetter House.*

Stephen B. Williams House (Dent House) GA-1198. 128 W. Liberty St., facing S. Frame with clapboarding, rectangular, five-bay front plus enclosed porch. Two and one-half stories over raised basement. Hipped roof over front part, another hipped roof over the rear part, valley between. Casement-type dormer windows, two int. chimneys. Small entrance porch with two slender Doric columns and flanking wooden steps. Entrance with sidelights and full elliptical fanlight. Central hall plan, two rooms each side; stairs divide into two flights at landing, one ascending toward front, the other toward rear. Marble mantels apparently mid 19th C. Built ca. 1835, remodeled and enlarged ca. 1851. House was apparently one room deep originally. Side porch since enclosed; single panes of glass have replaced original fan and sidelights. 3 ext. photos (1966); 2 int. photos (1966).

William Williams House GA-1199. 18 E. Oglethorpe St., facing S. Wood frame with clapboarding, rectangular (three-bay front). Three and one-half stories over raised basement. Gable roof with dormers, changing to shed type at rear. Two int. end chimneys, two-tiered Victorian porch on E side. Windows with pediments, first-floor windows in front are floor length.

Small entrance porch with side steps. Double entrance doors, paneled, side hall plan. Built 1826; raised and remodeled 1873, when side porch and much gingerbread were added. Apparently, rear was originally an open porch. Ext. restored and int. recycled for office use by Medden-Gilmore, realtors, 1969. 3 ext. photos (1966); 2 int. photos (1966).

Savannah Vicinity
Chatham County (26)

Fort Pulaski GA-2158. Cockspur Island. Entrance to drive N side U.S. Hwy. 80, 14 mi. E of intersection with Montgomery St. in Savannah. Brick with special hard-baked brick, brownstone, or granite around openings and at vital points. Five-sided fort; long side toward W; parallel short sides to N and S; diagonal sides forming a point toward E. Casemated walls 25 ft. above water, 7½ ft. minimum thickness. One entrance or "sally port" on W side, approached by drawbridge. Vaulted structures within, inner face of all but W wall being a series of ovoid arches. Because of soil conditions, the brickwork was constructed on a mat of wooden pilings; reverse arches mirroring those above grade were used below grade. Parts of moat are extended to form a V to W, thus forming a triangular area surrounded by water and adjacent to ext. side of W wall of the fort.

Built 1829–47; designed by Gen. Simon Bernard. Gen. Robert E. Lee, then Lieutenant Lee, supervised construction for about a year of that time. Occupied by Confederate troops from January 3, 1861 to April 11, 1862, when the new guns of the Federal troops demolished sections of the walls, thereby making such "impregnable" fortresses obsolete. Established as a national monument in 1924; administration transferred to the National Park Service in 1939. 5 ext. photos (1935); 2 ext. photos (1936). Illustrated on p. 180.

The Hermitage GA-225. N side of U.S. Hwy. 80, 2.8 mi. w of intersection with Bull St. in Savannah. Faced S. Brick with stucco, rectangular, symmetrical wings with oblique corners. Six-bay front, one story over raised basement, hipped roof with parapet, six int. chimneys, two end chimneys. Matching Corinthian tetrastyle entrance porches front and back, the entablatures continued around the house. Curving steps each side of porches; arched loggias beneath. Off-center hall serves as entrance front and back; stairs in side hall.
Row of slave houses forming a forecourt bordered approach to house. These were brick, rectangular, three-bay front, one story, hipped roof, one end chimney.
Main house Greek Revival, ca. 1830; Charles B. Cluskey (?), architect. Demolished 1965. Outstanding for its grounds and for grace of house. 3 sheets (1930); 5 ext. photos (1934); 2 data pages (1936). Illustrated on pp. 72, 73, 164.

Wild Heron Plantation GA-253. N side of Grove Point Rd., 1 mi. E of intersection with King George Rd., this intersection .3 mi. S of King George Rd. intersection with Ga. Hwy. 204, which is 13.5 mi. S of Hwy. 204 intersection with De Renne Ave. in Savannah. House faces S. Frame with clapboarding, flush siding under front

porch. Rectangular, five-bay front, one-and-a-half stories over raised basement, spraddle roof with shed roof dormers, three end chimneys. Full-width porches front and back. Front porch with light hexagonal columns and beaded ceiling joists. Two front rooms, one larger by width of back hall than the other; rear hall with one room each side. Wainscot of two very wide boards. Plantation cottage type, colonial, built ca. 1756 by Col. Francis Harris. Restored in 1930s, when additional basement rooms were built, some plastering of main floor replaced with paneling, and modern conveniences installed. Probably oldest surviving wooden house in Georgia. 2 ext. photos (1936); 3 data pages (1936). Illustrated on p. 17.

Shoals Vicinity

(Glascock County)
Hancock County (71)

Thomas Cheely House GA-1119. NW side (facing E) of County Rd. S-1098, 2 mi. w of Shoals, .5 mi. w of Hancock–Glascock County line (Ogeechee River). Frame with clapboarding, body of house L-shaped, rectangular including porches. Five-bay front, two stories, gable roof, three end chimneys. Two-tier, three-bay porch, Doric columns first story, vernacular version Ionic columns second story. Dog trot, first floor with arches each end, one room S side, two rooms N side. Second floor divided into two sections; S (boys') section reached by curving porch stairway, N (girls') section reached by stairway from master bedroom. Vernacular Federal, ca.

1825. Louvers at rear of dog trot added later, probably before 1861. 1 ext. photo (1980). Illustrated on pp. 50, 51.

Sparta

Hancock County (71)

Dr. Terrell House. See *Terrell House.*

Hancock County Courthouse GA-228. Town square, facing N. Brick with stone quoins, archivolts, window headers, and sills. Shape roughly similar to Greek cross, but with projecting center pavilions each side. Main block five-bay front; nine bays including wings. Main block two stories, wings two-and-a-half stories. Roof types hipped, mansard, helm, domical, and gable. Four int. chimneys. Square cupola terminating with octagonal dome; clocks on four sides. Second-story windows (for courtroom) of central block very high, arched, and with relieving arches over. Bracketed cornices. Six-bay, one-story porch at front with turned wooden columns, open segmental arches, and cast-iron cresting. Cross-axial corridors. Second Empire style, 1881–83; Parkins and Bruce, architects. 1 ext. photo (1972). Illustrated on p. 193.

Judge Little House. See *Rossiter-Little House.*

Rossiter-Little House (Judge Little House) GA-188. 223 Broad St., facing SSW. Frame with clapboarding, flush siding under porch. Central block 30'4" (three-bay front) with projecting wings 18'2" (one-bay front). One and one-half stories, central block with spraddle roof and dormer windows, the wings with gable roofs. Two exposed end chimneys, two end chimneys within ext. walls, one int. chimney. Three-bay front porch across central block, terminating at wings. Columns and frieze with Chinese lattice-design insets. Full-length windows on porch. Six-panel entrance door with transom. Central hall plan. Original part built before 1812, possibly late 18th C. Wings and front porch built before 1860, windows on porch probably enlarged at same time. Rear ell added later. Dormer windows in front enlarged and changed before 1937. Porch probably had balustrade, probably sheaf-of-wheat design. This removed before 1937. 3 ext. photos (1937); 1 int. photo (1936); 1 data page (1936). Illustrated on p. 157.

Sayre-Shivers House GA-179. 118 W. Broad St., facing NNE. Frame with clapboarding, granite block basement, square granite posts for piers under entrance porch. 52 ft. (five-bay front), four-bay sides. Two stories over raised basement, low slope hipped roof, four end chimneys (stuccoed) within ext. walls. Entablature with plain cornice, frieze, and architrave around house. Flat-roofed entrance porch, combination of Tuscan and Doric orders, two sets of paired fluted columns, sheaf-of-wheat railing, center ceiling medallion. One-story porch across rear of house. Six-panel entrance door with sidelights and transom with delicate wooden tracery in curved and straight forms. Narrow pilasters with entablature framing doorway between door and sidelights.

Central hall plan, double parlor one side. Rear door with sidelights and transom similar to front door. Open-well stairway, curving

at return. Reeded trim with foliated corner blocks, also foliated center blocks over double doors and over entrance door. Int. shutters that fold into jambs of sidelights and windows; windows also have ext. louvered blinds. Plaster cornice moldings and foliated ceiling medallions. Black marble mantels with Ionic colonettes and fireplaces with the original iron firebacks.

Greek Revival. Begun 1829, finished 1839. Back porch enclosed and wings added to rear in 1920s. House originally had fence repeating sheaf-of-wheat design of porch railing, and extensive formal gardens to front, side, and rear. 3 ext. photos (1936); 5 int. photos (1936); 2 data pages (1936). Illustrated on p. 121.

Terrell House (Dr. Terrell House) GA-186. 839 Jones St., facing ESE. Frame with clapboarding, rubble stone foundation, monolithic tapered granite piers under front porch. L-shaped, 56'6" (five-bay front) with ell to rear. Two stories, low slope hipped roof with balustrade, two int. chimneys stuccoed. Modillion cornice. Palladian window in center bay, second floor. Five bays, flat roof, one story, Roman Ionic porch with turned wooden balusters across front. Double six-panel entrance doors flanked by Greek Ionic half-columns (no entablature) with sidelights beyond columns; elliptical fanlight over doors. Similar door at rear. Wide (12-ft.) central hall plan, stairs in a separate area so that axial view is uninterrupted when both sets of doors are open. Extremely fine plaster work: cornices with egg-and-dart motif and with Greek key motif in soffits; repetitive ceiling molding has quarter circles with fan design at

int. corners. Principal chamber has square ceiling panel with center foliated medallion, fan motif of cornice repeated in transition from square frame to round medallion. Large, full-length (thirty-two-light) windows and marble mantels in first-floor front rooms. Stone kitchen and milk house in rear. Remains of classic carriage house in side yard.

House traditional Federal style, ca. 1820; stone kitchen thought to be much older, possibly 18th C. Front porch was originally a small entrance porch with open decks each side. Both front and back porches have been enlarged, probably before 1860. Originally there was a large conservatory, a series of formal gardens, and an artificial pond large enough for "a sail in a row boat" (see Mary Ann Mansfield to Giles Mansfield, Oct. 22, 1838, files, Georgia Historical Society, Savannah, Ga.). 3 ext. photos (1936); 3 int. photos (1936); 3 data pages (1936).

Spring Place
Murray County (107)

Vann House GA-174. NE corner intersection U.S. Hwy. 76 and Ga. Hwy. 225, facing N. Flemish and English bond brick with stucco under porches, rectangular (three-bay front), two stories, gable roof, two end chimneys. Modillion cornice, stucco pilaster strips between bays front and rear. Three-bay, two-story front porch with grouped square columns, lattice design railing; one-bay, two-story porch with similar details N side. Double entrance doors with sidelights and fanlight at front and rear; double doors to second-story porch with fanlights. Central hall plan, one room each side. Complex open-well stairway with improbably cantilevered landing. Large fireplaces with intricately designed and painted mantels. Fireplace in E room (first floor) 5 ft. wide. Fireplace in W room has flamboyant Georgian overmantel with arched panels, pulvinated frieze, colonettes, and stylized Cherokee rose motifs. Plaster walls white, woodwork including wainscot and ceilings painted in colors that had symbolic meaning to Cherokees and that present an exotic combination of hues. Built 1805, restored 1958, restoration of porches conjectural; Henry Chandler Forman, restoration architect. Original owner, James Vann, was half Cherokee. President James Monroe and John C. Calhoun, secretary of war, were entertained here in 1819. House museum. 7 sheets (1953); 2 ext. photos (1934); 1 ext. photo (1936); 6 ext. photos (1962); 2 int. photos (1934); 10 int. photos (1962); 1 data page (1936); 4 data pages (1964). Illustrated on pp. 8, 67.

Talbotton

Talbot County (132)

Bailey House (Hill-Leonard House) GA-1108. w side of Washington Ave. (Ga. Hwy. 41) 1 mi. s of Talbotton Square. Frame with clapboarding, flush siding under front porch, rectangular, 42 ft. (five-bay front) with ell, two stories, pitched roof, three ext. chimneys, one int. chimney. Two-story-high tetrastyle front porch, fluted columns with abacus only for capital, similar porch with three columns on s side of ell; balcony over entrance. Central

hall plan, stairs recessed to one side so that hall can be unified with porch of ell, row of columns on one side and porch wall on other seeming to be a continuation of hall. Greek Revival style, built 1837. Second-floor gallery added to ell porch late 19th C. Kitchen and breakfast room added to ell early 20th C.; possibly original detached kitchen moved next to house and renovated at the time. 3 ext. photos (1936); 1 data page (1936).

Episcopal Church. See *Zion Episcopal Church.*

First Methodist Church (Methodist Church) GA-1126. w side of College Ave., between Washington Ave. and Clark St. Brick, stucco on brick under portico, 50'2'' (two-bay front) × 70' plus portico (9'8''), one story over raised basement, gable roof, two ext. chimneys, one of which may not be original, hexaprostyle temple with stucco on brick cylindrical untapered columns, widened like a pipe collar for capital, square bases. Octagonal domed tower over portico, two entrance doorways, each with double doors; main floor one room with balcony, center medallion for chandelier. Greek Revival, 1857. 20th C. changes include concrete steps and floor for portico, asbestos shingles applied over tympanum and over base of tower, new altar railing and retable; also installation of partitions in basement. 1 ext. photo (1936); 1 int. photo (1936); 1 data page (1936).

Hill-Leonard House. See *Bailey House.*

Dr. Leonard House. See *Rebel Ridge.*

Maxwell House GA-1140. w side Jackson Ave., between Van Buren St. and Jackson Ave., facing E. Frame with clapboarding, plaster under porch, rectangular (five-bay front), one story with hipped roof, two int. chimneys, hexastyle porch across front, decagonal columns, modified Doric with only a suggestion of an echinus and with unusual column bases, repeating shape of columns. Entrance with etched glass sidelights and transom. Greek Revival, mid 19th C. Burned ca. 1945. 1 ext. photo (1936). Illustrated on p. 109.

Methodist Church. See *First Methodist Church.*

Rebel Ridge (Dr. Leonard House) GA-1118. SE side of U.S. Hwy. 80 E, .75 mi. N of square. Frame with horizontal boarding, flush boarding front and sides, clapboarding at rear, rectangular (five-bay front with four-bay sides), two-story-high octastyle peristyle porch with seven columns on each side, fluted columns with octagonal echinus and square abacus. Front entrance with paired sidelights and transom; may originally have been folding doors with sidelights and transoms, as are balcony doors and rear entrance, balconies over front and rear entrances. Central hall four-room plan; the spacious halls becoming breezeways or dog trots when the doors are folded back. Greek Revival, 1837; David Shelton, builder and first owner. 4 ext. photos (1936); 2 data pages (1936).

Straus–Le Vert Memorial Hall GA-1136. w side of College Ave., between Polk and Clark Sts. Frame with clapboarding, two-story rectangular central unit with one-story wings, rear sides of which are flush with rear of central unit (wings may be of later date), central unit 40' (three-bay front) × 60' plus portico. Gable roof on central unit, hipped roof on wings, one int. chimney. Two-story-high portico, semiperipteral, with the entablature curiously carried beyond the terminus of the columns, six fluted columns across the front, four down each side, all with Ionic capitals of naive design. Transverse entrance hall with stairways at either end. Second int. hall on first floor with one room each side, large room at rear. Upstairs, transverse hall is repeated, rest of floor being one large room or auditorium. Greek Revival, mid 19th C. Extensively repaired in 1965 with some changes in room arrangement of first floor. 1 ext. photo (1936); 1 data page (1936).

Zion Episcopal Church (Episcopal Church) GA-1139. Frame with flush vertical siding, rectangular, projecting tower with porch under, 35' (three-bay front) × 54' (four-bay sides), gable roof, no chimney. Lancet windows with clear glass and with louvered blinds. Gothic Revival details have little relation to structure (attenuated buttresses do not coincide with int. trusses) but act as counterpoint to sophisticated simplicity of the rest of the church. Vertical siding was probably stained or left unpainted; it is now painted brown like weathered wood. Narthex and auditorium with balcony along rear and sides. Pipe organ (Pilcher, installed in 1850) is located in balcony, to rear. Walls, ceilings, floors, doors, and trim are heart pine, unpainted. Walls random-width vertical boards, some 15 ins. wide. Ceiling supported by six exposed scissors trusses. Box pews are

pine, trefoil pointed-arch design of paneled ends stained. Altar furnishings are of native walnut. Original oil lamp still hangs in center, and other than candles provides the only artificial illumination. The one grave in churchyard has Gothic-type stone marker of rare distinction. Church was built ca. 1850, and apparently is little changed since that time. 3 ext. photos (1936); 1 data page (1936). Illustrated on p. 128.

Thomasville
Thomas County (138)

Thomas County Courthouse GA-216. Town square facing NE, Broad St. Brick with stucco scored, rectangular with projecting pavilions front and rear. Seven bays, two stories over raised basement, hipped roof with gable (pedimented) pavilions and porticos, central dome. Entablature around building, pilasters at corners. Two-story-high tetrastyle porticos each side of rear pavilion. Segmental arched windows and cornices except in pavilions. Front pavilion three bays wide with semicircular windows, entrance with double doors and fanlight. Built 1858 in Greek Revival style; John Wind, architect. Remodeled 1888, columns removed, portico enclosed and converted to pavilion as at present, a pavilion or wing added to rear, and segmental window cornices installed; Eaves and Ware, contractors. Clock added to cupola 1909. One-story wings squaring bottom floor, 1918 and 1922. Two-story annex and porticos added to rear, 1937; Prince Jinright, architect. 8 sheets (1969); 6 data pages (1969).

Thomson Vicinity
McDuffie County (195)
Columbia County (37)

Few House GA-1153. Cobbham Community. E side (facing NNE) of Ga. Hwy. 150, 4.5 mi. NE of intersection with U.S. Hwy. I-20; 8 mi. NE of Thomson, McDuffie County. Frame with clapboarding, rectangular (five-bay front), two stories, hipped roof, four end chimneys. Five-bay, two-story-high porch across front, slender square tapered columns. Entrance with sidelights and transom, balcony over. Central hall plan, two rooms each side. Picket fence around front yard. Family graveyard with markers dating to 18th C. Original part of house built late 18th or early 19th C.; enlarged and remodeled mid 19th C., when Greek Revival porch was added, roof was truncated and had a lookout, and brick paved courtyard was installed between kitchen and house. Roof changed and lookout removed late 19th C. Destroyed by fire 1977. 2 ext. photos (1936); 1 data page (1936).

Old Rock House GA-277. NW side of Stephen Hunter Rd., facing SE, 1.5 mi. W of junction with Howell Young Rd., which changes to Twin Oaks Rd.; that junction 1.3 mi. W of junction of Twin Oaks Rd. with Ga. Hwy. 223, which is .7 mi. W of junction of Ga. Hwys. 223 and 17 in Thomson. Fieldstone with stucco scored (walls 2 ft. thick), rectangular, five-bay front, one story over semiraised basement, gable roof, two end chimneys. Five-bay front porch, two adjacent entrance doors opening into separate rooms. Two front rooms, one with stairs to attic, both with oversize fireplaces and hewn wooden lintels. Smaller rooms across back, one with unique corner fireplace with triangular fire chamber. Traces of plaster remain on int. of stone walls. Counters formed in attic rooms where chimney diminishes, also in rear room under window adjoining doorway. Some window jambs splayed. Partition walls frame with horizontal boards. Exposed beaded joists. Built ca. 1785. Mortise holes for rafters in front cornice indicate that original porch was smaller, slightly wider than opening for the two front doors. Exterior stuccoed in 1920s. Sole remaining building of the Quaker settlement of Wrightsboro. 1 ext. photo (1981).

Toccoa Vicinity
Stephens County (109)

Jarrett Manor. See *Travelers Rest.*

Travelers Rest (Jarrett Manor, Jarrett House) GA-14-5. N side of Riverdale Rd., facing w, .25 mi. N of intersection with Hwy. 123, which is 6 mi. NE of Hwy. 123 intersection with Hwy. 17 in Toccoa. Frame with clapboard, flush siding under porch, handsplit wooden shake roof, stone foundation. 91' (ten-bay) front × 18' (40'4'' including 12'4'' front porch, 10' rear shed room). Original part 50'6'' front. Two-story plantation plain style with one-story porch in front, one-story porch and rooms at rear, daylight basement room at N end. Gable roof on two-story part, shed roofs on one-story part; two int. chimneys, three end chimneys (the end chimney on N side stone with brick shaft above second floor,

other chimneys brick except for stone foundation). Nine-bay porch across front with solid (10'' × 10'') columns tapered above railing. Observation holes (for Indians) in gables. Original part dog trot or central hall plan, additional rooms open onto porch or into adjacent rooms. Basement room (kitchen) has plaster on stone walls, flagstone floor; other rooms wooden floors, wooden ceilings, wood panel (horizontal or vertical) walls. Doors either batten or six-panel type, except main entrance door nine-panel type. Large mantels with Federal-type moldings and pilasters, stairway with delicately carved brackets. Braced frame construction with 12'' × 12'' sills, 12'' × 12'' L-shaped corner posts; rafters mortised into each other (no ridge board), evidently fitted on ground and marked with Roman numerals.

Weave house (frame with clapboarding on raised basement) attached by bridge to N end of house; basement used for cultivating silk worms. Two servants' houses, one frame with clapboarding, one with board-and-batten siding. Foundations only for milkhouse and for smokehouse.

Indigenous type, plantation plain style, the original part probably built between 1816 and 1825, addition ca. 1835. N chimney and stone foundation of the kitchen possibly date back to earlier 18th C. structure; there is evidence that an Indian structure previously occupied this site. The original open dog trot was enclosed, and stairway changed at time of the addition. Woodwork unpainted inside and out until 20th C., when walls and ceilings of some rooms were painted. Restoration begun ca. 1965, still in progress. House

museum. 4 sheets (1934); 3 ext. photos (1934); 3 data pages (1934). Illustrated on p. 25.

Toomsboro Vicinity
Wilkinson County (160)

Jackson House GA-278. E side (facing SW) of Ga. Hwy. 112, 3 mi. N of intersection with Ga. Hwy. 57 in Toomsboro. Wood frame with clapboarding, flush siding under porches, rectangular, five-bay front, two stories, gable roof, two end chimneys. Lean-to across back; five-bay, one-story porch across front with square columns resting on brick piers in front of porch floor. Central hall plan, plantation plain style, early 19th C. 1 ext. photo (1972). Illustrated on p. 47.

Warm Springs
Meriwether County (100)

Roosevelt's Little White House GA-279. Ga. Hwy. 85W, .5 mi. S of Warm Springs, within city limits. Frame with clapboarding, rectangular, 54 ft. (five-bay front), projecting Doric tetrastyle portico, one story, gable roof, one int. chimney; contemporaneous irregular plan adapted to traditional symmetrical façade. 1932 version of Greek Revival cottage. Built 1932; Henry J. Toombs, architect. Outbuildings include a guest house built in 1933 and a museum added to the complex in 1961. Used as a second residence by Franklin D. Roosevelt during his terms of office as president. House museum. 1 ext. photo (1980). Illustrated on p. 218.

Warthen Vicinity
Washington County (152)

Harrison House GA-2121. sw side (facing NNW) of unnamed dirt road, 1 mi. SE of intersection with Ga. Hwy. 15, this intersection .1 mi. s of Hancock–Washington County line. Log covered with asbestos siding, rectangular, rear ell. Three-bay front, two stories, primary roofs gable, front porch and lean-to roof shed type. Two end chimneys stuccoed. Two-tier, five-bay porch across front. Hand-hewn framing, porch columns, and porch balusters; exposed framing beaded. Central hall plan. Probably early 19th C. Asbestos siding, stucco, ells added later. Original dog trot enclosed; other int. changes. Rare indigenous log house of a type that may have been prototype for Greek Revival mansions. 1 ext. photo (1972). Illustrated on pp. 48, 49.

Washington
Wilkes County (159)

Abbot-Toombs House (Toombs House) GA-13. 216 E. Robert Toombs Ave., facing N. Frame with clapboarding, flush siding under porch. 47′2′′ (three-bay front) × 29′, plus wings at rear and sides. Two stories over raised basement, main roof hipped, roofs of front porch and w wing flat, other roofs gable. One int. chimney, four int. end chimneys, stuccoed. Heroic tetrastyle Greek Doric front porch with fluted columns, balustrade with turned balusters. Four-panel entrance door with sidelights and transom framed by pilasters with entablature; balcony over with rectangular pick-

ets in vertical and lattice design; balcony doorway similar to entrance. First-floor windows at porch full length, all windows at porch framed with pilasters and entablatures. Central hall plan with rear cross hall connecting to wings. Original part with small pane windows and delicate Federal-type entablature; porch and main façade Greek Revival. Other additions a mixture of indigenous and eclectic Victorian styles. Four outbuildings. Original part built ca. 1797 facing w for Dr. Joel Abbott. Enlarged, remodeled to face N ca. 1810. Greek Revival portico, w wing, and details added ca. 1837 by Robert Toombs; E wing late 19th C. House presently being restored. Home of Robert Toombs, Confederate general, U.S. and Confederate statesman 1837–1885, except for two years spent in exile. House museum. 2 ext. photos (1934); 2 data pages (1936). Illustrated on p. 107.

Alexander House. See *Gilbert-Alexander House.*

Bennett House. See *Pope-Tupper House.*

Gilbert-Alexander House (Alexander House) GA-1145. 117 Alexander Dr., facing s. Brick, E wing and a shed addition frame with clapboarding. Rectangular, non-symmetrical wings each side. Central unit 32′10′′ (three-bay front) × 46′5′′; two stories. Gable roof on central unit, hipped roof on wings, two int. chimneys, two end chimneys. Central unit dentil cornices and Palladian window in pediment; three-bay, two-tiered porch with square tapered columns and balustraded roof deck. Side hall plan, arch separating entrance part from main stair hall;

secondary stairs in each wing. Mantels with reeded pilasters and sunbursts. Outbuildings include a carriage house (1800–1808), a brick kitchen (1808), a smoke-house ca. 1825, a servants' house ca. 1835, and a barn ca. 1845. The central portion of the house (traditional Federal) was built in 1808, w (brick) wing ca. 1828, E wing shortly thereafter. Front porch and shed addition mid 19th C. 3 ext. photos (1934); 1 int. photo (1934); 1 int. photo (1936); 2 data pages (1936).

New Haywood GA-2122. 201 W. Robert Toombs Ave., facing s. Frame with clapboarding, irregular shape. First floor two bays plus corner bay window; second story three bays plus bay window. Two stories, hipped roof with projecting gables, shed roof on porch, reverse ogee roof on cupola. Three int. chimneys, two int. end chimneys. Wraparound porch on front and w side, turned posts and balusters, open frieze with spools. Scroll-saw brackets. Two-story octagonal bay (SE corner) with gazebolike cupola over. Entrance door with leaded stained-glass panel and leaded clear glass transom. Irregular plan. Outbuildings include wellhouse with storage room, two servants' houses. Queen Anne style. Built by Theoderick Morrison Green ca. 1890. 1 ext. photo (1980). Illustrated on p. 200.

Peacewood (Wingfield-Cade House) GA-19. 120 Tignall Rd., facing s. Frame with clapboarding, 48′6′′ (five-bay front) × 38′10′′ with wing E side. Two stories, hipped roof, one int. chimney, two end chimneys. Two-story-high hexastyle porch across front, round fluted columns with abacus only as capitals, fluted pilasters and balustrade with turned balusters. Entrance with sidelights and transom framed by pilasters and entablature; balcony with wooden railing and similar entrance over. Central hall plan, two rooms each side. Original part, evidently a plantation plain style house, was built for Thomas Wingfield in late 18th C. Present form evolved in several stages, major additions by Jesse Callaway in 1830s. Greek Revival porch probably added by Francis G. Wingfield in 1850s. Attached kitchen, E side, added by Capt. W. G. Cade after the Civil War. Outbuildings include old separate kitchen, two-room privy, overseer's house (now guest house), wellhouse, dairy with "dry well" for cooling, and milk barn, all antebellum. One of the few houses with picket fence remaining around front yard. 4 ext. photos (2 of outbuildings) (1936); 1 data page (1936). Illustrated on p. 175.

Pope-Tupper House (Bennett House) GA-1158. 101 W. Robert Toombs Ave., facing S. Wood frame with clapboarding, 42' × 35'9" (five-bay front), two stories over raised brick basement. Hipped roof over house proper, roof of porch slopes toward house and connects to that roof, forming gutter at junction. Two int. chimneys. Heroic peripteral Doric porch with six fluted columns across front, five on each side. Twin L-shaped flights of steps lead to a common landing in front of porch; lattice work with arched opening under landing; lattice work under steps. Entrance with sidelights and full elliptical fanlight; balcony over with similar doorway. Central hall, two rooms each side. Mantels with slender pilasters, center

panels, and sunbursts. Body of house traditional Federal style, built by William H. Pope ca. 1832. Greek Revival porch added by Henry Allen Tupper ca. 1860. Lattice under porch steps removed since 1940. 1 ext. photo (1940).

Presbyterian Church GA-115. 206 E. Robert Toombs Ave., facing N. Frame with clapboarding, wood shingles in pediment and on spire. 32'6" (three-bay front) × 58'6", one story, gable roof, flat roof over porch. Church tower with square base, octagonal belfry, and conical spire. Three-bay porch with fluted Doric columns, paneled entablature. Double entrance doors with sidelights and full elliptical fanlight. Meetinghouse plan with vestibule and auditorium, clear glass arched windows with blinds. Auditorium built 1825, vestibule, steeple and pulpit added ca. 1836; porch late 19th C. Classrooms added 1940. 4 ext. photos (1936); 1 data page (1936).

Toombs House. See *Abbot-Toombs House.*

Wingfield-Cade House. See *Peacewood.*

Washington Vicinity
Wilkes County (159)

James C. Daniel House GA-2123. W side of Bartram Trace (also called Rayle Rd.), 1.4 mi. N of junction with Ga. Hwy. 44, which is 11.2 mi. SW of junction of Hwy. 44 and Robert Toombs Ave. in Washington. Rectangular, brick, five-bay front, two stories over raised basement, gable roof, two int. end chimneys. Stuccoed wedge-shaped lintels over windows. Three-panel

double entrance doors with fanlight and stuccoed archivolt. Central hall plan, one room each side, open-well stairway continuous to attic room. Log house (smokehouse?) behind. Traditional Federal, simplistic style, ca. 1815. Stoop and front steps not original. 1 ext. photo (1980); 1 int. photo (1980). Illustrated on pp. 52, 53.

Watkinsville
Oconee County (110)

Eagle Tavern GA-1127. SE corner Main and Third Sts., facing WSW. Frame with beaded siding. Rectangular, 36' (five-bay front first floor, four bays second floor) × 18'. Two stories, gable roof, one end chimney. Windows nine lights over nine downstairs, nine over six upstairs, raised panel shutters. Two front doors, one leading to tavern area, the other to a store. Sleeping quarters on second floor. Walls, floors, ceilings of wide boards. Indigenous, of a type that could be 18th C., but documentary evidence suggests about 1820. Additions more than doubling its size and including a two-story veranda before 1860. Additions removed and original part restored 1969. House museum. 1 ext. photo (1936); 1 data page (1936).

Waynesboro
Burke County (17)

Munnerlyn House GA-2120. 541 Liberty St., facing ENE. Wood frame, rectangular with two projecting wings in front. Gable roof, four end chimneys on core of house, five chimneys on wings. House appears to have been plantation plain style with lean-to in front and one-story wings annexed. Built ca. 1780, demolished ca. 1936. A plaque on the site reads in part "to honor George Washington who lodged here May 17–18, 1791." 1 ext. photo (1934); 2 data pages (1936).

West Point
Troup County (143)

Booker House. See *White Hall.*

White Hall (Booker House) GA-161. Avenue E between Third and Fourth Sts. Frame with clapboarding, novelty siding under porch, rectangular, 51 ft. (three-bay front), two stories with one-story shed rooms at rear, two-story part 20′2″ deep plus porch, gable roof. Kitchen connected to shed rooms by breezeway, two ext. end chimneys, one ext. chimney at outer wall of lean-to. Front porch two stories high, Ionic hexastyle full width of house, with fluted columns on brick pedestals and Doric entablature. Windows with sidelights under porch, entrance with sidelights and transom, balcony with decorative wire

railing over; central hall plan, circular stairway, parlor with center medallion and plaster cornice with egg-and-dart moldings. Greek Revival, 1857–58; Urpe, builder. Two-story ell with separate stairway added 19th C. Breezeway connecting kitchen converted to carport; old kitchen changed to storage room in 20th C. 1 ext. photo (1936); 1 data page (1936). Illustrated on p. 102.

Whitesville Vicinity
Harris County (73)

John Davidson House GA-1144. W side of Ga. Hwy. 219, facing SSE, 3.5 mi. N of intersection with Monument Rd. in Whitesville. Frame with clapboarding, flush siding under portico, rectangular with rear ell, three-bay front, two stories, gable roof, at least two end chimneys. Two-story-high one-bay portico, solid wooden columns with vernacular version Ionic capital, cornice with mutules. Double entrance doors with sidelights and fanlights; balcony over with similar doorway. Central hall plan, one room each side. Milledgeville Federal style, ca. 1845. Destroyed by fire ca. 1951. According to previous HABS data, the house was patterned after the

Fontaine House (destroyed) in Beallwood, and built from lumber cut and brick made on the plantation. 2 ext. photos (1936); 1 data page (1936).

Woodbine Vicinity
Camden County (20)

Refuge Plantation GA-248. N side of County Rd. S-1850, facing S, 2.8 mi. W of intersection with U.S. Hwy 17, which is 4.1 mi. N of Hwy. 17 intersection with Third St. in Woodbine. Frame with clapboarding, rectangular, detached auxiliary buildings connected by covered ways rear and side. Five-bay front, one-and-a-half stories, spraddle roof with dormers, two int. chimneys. Seven-bay front porch with chamfered columns resting on low piers in front of porch floor; balustrade with plain vertical pickets around porch, behind columns. Central hall plan. Large fireplace with crane and cooking utensils in detached kitchen, fireplace still used for cooking in 1936.

Built ca. 1775. Indigenous, plantation cottage type. Demolished ca. 1970. 2 ext. photos (1936); 1 int. photo (kitchen) (1936); 1 data page (1936). Illustrated on p. 21.

Glossary of Architectural Terms

Abacus. The flat slab which forms the top part of a classical column capital.

Acanthus. A plant with scalloped leaves which served as a model for the stylized foliage of a Corinthian capital. The motif was later much used on interior cornices and ceiling medallions.

Acroterion. An ornament placed at the peak or the lower ends of a pediment.

Aedicule. A framework consisting of columns or pilasters on each side, with an arch or an entablature over. Formerly a frame for a shrine.

Ancones. Console brackets on either side of a doorway, supporting an entablature or other feature.

Anta. A pilaster used in conjunction with columns of a different order.

Antefixae. Blocks, usually sculptured, used at the end of a row of roof tiles to close and to decorate the openings.

Anthemion. An ornamental motif based on the honeysuckle flower and leaves.

Antis, in. Descriptive of a classical recessed porch with columns.

Apse. A circular or angular alcove, terminating a church sanctuary.

Arcade. A range of arches.

Arch. A span supported at each end and curving upward toward the center. When of masonry, the arch is formed of a number of wedge-shaped units called voussoirs.

Architrave. The lowest of the three principal horizontal divisions of a classic entablature. See *Order.*

Architrave Trim. See *Casing.*

Archivolt. The arched projections or moldings on the face of an arch.

Arris. The sharp edge produced by the meeting of two surfaces, usually used to denote the juncture of the flutes of a Greek Doric column.

Art Nouveau. A style of decoration, popular during the late nineteenth and early twentieth centuries, based on flowing, sinuous forms frequently derived from the structure of various parts of plants.

Ashlar. Stone masonry, the units of which are laid in precise regular courses.

Atlantes. Supports in the form of carved male figures. See also *Caryatids.*

Baluster. An upright support for a handrail.

Balustrade. The combination of balusters and handrail. Banisters.

Banded Rustication. Masonry or imitation masonry in which the horizontal joints are deeply cut and emphasized.

Bargeboard. A nonsupportive end gable rafter or board (usually decorative) which is attached to the roof sheathing at some distance from the gable wall. A verge board is similar, but is placed flush against the gable wall.

Basilican Church. A church building with a nave with clerestory windows, the nave flanked by side aisles with lower ceilings.

Bastion. A projecting angular or circular strong point in a defensive wall, as in the wall of a fort.

Batten. (a) A narrow board or molding, parallel to and covering the crack between adjoining (usually vertical) boards. (b) A board attached and perpendicular to two or more boards, the term usually denoting a door so constructed.

Battlement. A parapet consisting of alternate uprights (merlons) and open spaces (embrasures). In ancient times, the merlons served as defensive shields, the embrasures for fighting off attackers.

Bay. (a) Any opening in an exterior wall. (b) One of a number of structural subdivisions (such as vaults or the units formed by posts, two beams, and joists) which together form a building.

Bay Windows. An angular or curved projecting group of windows.

Bead. A small circular molding, sometimes integral with a wider molding or a board.

Belfry. The upper (open or louvered) story of a steeple, usually constructed for bells.

Belvedere. A lookout tower on the roof of a building.

Blinds. Window shutters with louvers.

Blind Arch. See *Wall Arch.*

Bolection Molding. A molding to cover the joint of adjoining surfaces that are not in the same plane.

Bombé. A curve that changes from straight or concave at the ends to convex at the center.

Bond. In brickwork, the pattern in which bricks are laid. See *Common Bond, English Bond, Flemish Bond.*

Brise Soleil. A sun shield that permits the passage of breezes.

Buttress. A wall projection that strengthens the wall or resists a thrust from within.

Byzantine. A style of architecture developed chiefly in the fifth and sixth centuries in the Byzantine Empire, characterized by arches, domes, mosaics, relief carving, and decorative masonry.

Cames. Lead muntins. Frequently used in fan and sidelights, also with stained glass.

Cantilever. A projecting structural member supported at one end only.

Capital. The head of a column or pilaster; that part of a capital above the shaft. See *Order.*

Caryatid. A support in the form of a carved female figure. See also *Atlantes.*

Casement Window. A window with sash hinged at the side.

Casing. The trim or enframement for a window or door opening. When molded trim is used, the

casing is often called architrave trim.

Catenary Arch. An arch that follows the form of a catenary curve (exemplified by the curve of a chain when suspended between two points). A catenary arch has structural advantages in resisting thrusts.

Cavetto. A concave molding.

Ceiling Oculus. A circular opening in a ceiling.

Chamfer. A bevel that changes the right-angle corner of a unit to a diagonal surface.

Chinese Lattice. Lattice work arranged in a more intricate, Chinese inspired, pattern than normal lattice work. Much used in adaptations of Chinese designs.

Clapboard. Overlapping horizontal boards used as siding or weatherboarding.

Clerestory (also clearstory). High windows occurring above adjacent roofs.

Colonnade. A range of columns.

Colossal Order. See *Giant Order.*

Columbia Cottage. See *Plantation Type Cottage.*

Column. A supporting post, the term generally used when the post has a capital and base or other architectural features.

Composite Order. A hybrid order in which the upper part of the capital is Ionic, the lower part Corinthian.

Concave Roof. A roof, the upper side of which is concave, the lower side convex, as though the rafters had sagged. Also called a pagoda roof. *See diagram following glossary.*

Console. A scroll-like form, one end concave, the other convex.

Corbel. Projections, usually masonry, in which upper courses project beyond lower ones.

Corinthian Order. See *Order.*

Corner Blocks. Square blocks, fre-

quently carved, used at the corner of window or door frames. When used, the casing butts against the blocks instead of being mitered.

Cornice. (a) The upper projecting part of an entablature. *(b)* A projecting eave or series of moldings at the top of a building. *(c)* The molding or moldings at the juncture of wall and ceiling.

Corona. The flat horizontal band that forms a part of a classical cornice.

Course. A horizontal row of masonry units.

Crenellations. Battlements, the term usually designating that the battlements are decorative, not defensive. See also *Battlements.*

Cresting. A series of ornaments carried along the top of a wall, cornice, or roof.

Crockets. Decorative features projecting from the angles of spires, gables, pinnacles, canopies, etc., of Gothic buildings.

Crow Steps. A parapet that rises in a series of steps, most often used at gable ends.

Cruciform Plan. A plan shaped like a cross.

Cupola. A small structure built at the top of a tower or above a roof and used as a lookout. In the strict sense of the term, such a structure with a domical roof.

Curtail Step. The lowest of a flight of steps, wider than the others and with curved ends.

Cusp. Projecting points formed by intersecting Gothic window tracery.

Cyma Recta. A double-curved molding, concave above, convex below.

Cyma Reversa. A double-curved molding, convex above, concave below.

Cymatium. The topmost molding of a classical cornice.

Dado. *(a)* The portion of a classical pedestal between its base and cornice. *(b)* The space between a chair rail and the base board. *(c)* A waist-high wainscot.

Deck. A roofless porch.

Dentils. A decorative row of small blocks.

Diaper Pattern. A pattern, usually lozenge shaped, repeated over a surface.

Diocletian Window. A semicircular window divided into three parts by two vertical mullions.

Distyle. Descriptive of a classical porch with two columns.

Dog-leg Stair. A two-flight stairway, one flight ascending and one descending from a landing, the flights adjacent to each other without an open space (or well) between.

Doric Order. See *Order.*

Dormer Window. A vertical window, with its own roof and side walls, projecting above a sloping roof.

Double-hung Window. A window consisting of sashes that can be raised or lowered.

Drum. A vertical supporting wall for a dome, which is similar in plan to the base of the dome and usually has windows.

Echinus. The rounded molding immediately under the abacus of a Greek Doric capital.

Egg and Dart. A convex decorated molding with alternating egg- and dart-shaped motifs.

Ell. *(a)* A one-story lean-to wing. *(b)* A wing built at right angles to the main body of a building.

Elliptical Arch. An arch whose curve is elliptical.

Embrasure. A deeply recessed opening, frequently with splayed sides.

End Chimney. A chimney occurring at the end of a building.

Engaged Column. A column attached to a wall or pier.

English Bond. Brickwork in which the brick are laid so that header courses alternate with stretcher courses.

Entablature. The horizontal part of an order that occurs above the columns. See *Order.*

Entablature-type Parapet. A roof parapet the outer face of which serves as an entablature.

Entasis. The convex tapering of a column.

Escarpment. A steeply sloping bank erected at the base of a fortification.

Etched Glass. Glass with the surface treated to make it translucent, often in a pattern of part clear glass, part translucent. Also called frosted glass.

Extrados. The arched enframement of an arch; also the outer face of the voussoirs that make up a masonry arch.

Extruded Corner. A right angle or circular projection from the inner angle of a polygon or from an interior corner of a building.

Exterior End Chimney. An end chimney that projects beyond the exterior face of its adjoining wall.

Façade. The face or elevation of a building.

Fanlight. A window, usually over a door and arched, with radiating muntins suggestive of a fan.

Fascia. A plain horizontal band, the term frequently used to denote the horizontal bands of an architrave, or the face of a simple boxed eave.

Finial. The topmost ornament of a spire, gable, pinnacle, etc.

Flat Arch. A structural masonry arch formed of wedge-shaped voussoirs so shaped that the bottom of the arch is horizontal.

Flemish Bond. Brickwork with the brick laid so that the headers and stretchers alternate in each course, and so that the headers are centered immediately above and below the stretchers.

Floor-length Window. A window whose sill is at floor level. Also called a full-length window.

Floriated. Carved with floral ornaments.

Flush Siding. Wall siding applied so that the boards do not overlap, but are flush. Joints are usually shiplap. Often used under porches instead of clapboarding during the Federal and antebellum periods.

Fluting. A series of vertical concave grooves, primarily on the shafts of classical columns and pilasters.

Foliated. Carved with leaflike ornamentation.

French Door. A door most of which is glass.

Fret. A band of ornament based on geometrical patterns of straight lines.

Frieze. *(a)* An ornamented horizontal band along the upper part of a wall. *(b)* The middle horizontal division of an entablature. See also *Order.*

Frontispiece Entrance. An entrance with pilasters or columns at each side, and with an entablature (with or without pediment) over.

Frosted Glass. See *Etched Glass.*

Full-length Window. See *Floor-length Window.*

Gable. See *Roof.*

Gambrel Roof. See *diagram following the glossary.*

Giant Order. An order whose columns rise through two or more stories. Also called heroic order and colossal order.

Gibbs Surround. A window or door enframement the sides of which consist primarily of blocks arranged like quoins.

Gibbs-type Steeple. A steeple similar to those of churches designed by James Gibbs (English architect, 1682–1754) consisting of towers that ascend in several stages and feature classical motifs.

Gingerbread. Superfluous ornament, the term frequently applied to the fanciful decorations of late Victorian architecture.

Grained. A surface painted to simulate the grain of wood. Pine was often grained to simulate more exotic woods in the late eighteenth and the nineteenth centuries.

Greek Cross Plan. A plan in the shape of a Greek cross, i.e., with equal length arms.

Half Column. Half a column (approximately semicircular in section) attached to a wall or pier.

Half-hipped Roof. See *Jerkin-head Roof.*

Half-timbering. In medieval times a structural system consisting of a timber framed building, the interstices filled with masonry and usually stuccoed. The term also used to designate the later practice of applying boards to the face of a wall in imitation of half-timbered construction.

Hammerbeam Roof. A form of exposed roof construction in which brackets are used to reduce the unsupported span of the roof trusses.

Header. A brick laid so that the end appears in the face of brickwork; also the exposed end of the brick.

Heroic Order. See *Giant Order.*

Hexastyle. Descriptive of a classical porch with six columns.

Hip Roof. See diagram following glossary.

Hood Molding. A projecting molding on the face of a wall, usually over a door or window, designed to throw off water. Also called a label molding.

Horseshoe Steps. Curving steps symmetrically placed each side of a landing, the plan of the steps and landing similar to the shape of a horseshoe.

Ionic Order. See *Order.*

Interior Chimney. A chimney occurring wholly within the building.

Interior End Chimney. An end chimney within the exterior walls of a building.

Intrados. The soffit or undersurface of an arch.

Jamb. The inner surface between the interior and exterior casing of a door or window frame. Also called the reveal.

Jerkin-head Roof. A type of roof in which the upper part is hipped and the lower part gabled. Because of the hipped portion, the gable ends are truncated. Also called a half-hipped roof.

Joist. One of a series of framing members supporting a floor or ceiling surface.

Keystone. The topmost center voussoir of an arch.

Knop. A spherical-shaped section of a turned wood member, often seen in the spindles and balusters of decorative Victorian woodwork.

Label Molding. See *Hood Molding.*

Lancet Window. A narrow, sharply pointed, arched window.

Lantern. A small circular or polygonal structure with windows, the lantern occurring at the top of a roof, tower, or dome.

Lean-to. A subordinate structure with a shed roof which is built against a higher adjacent part.

Lights. When used in reference to windows, the windowpanes.

Lintel. A supporting horizontal member spanning an opening.

Loggia. A gallery behind an open colonnade or arcade, usually on the first floor and sometimes with galleries over.

Lookout. (a) A bracket for the support of a roof, a balcony, or other minor projecting part of an upper story. *(b)* An elevated structure, frequently on a roof, affording a widespread view.

Louver. A series of horizontal (unless otherwise noted) slats, usually sloping or adjustable, to exclude sun, rain, or vision, and to permit passage of air.

Lunette. (a) A semicircular opening. *(b)* A small, round or arched-top window in a vault or a roof.

Machicolation. A projecting gallery (of a fortified structure) with holes in the floor through which missiles or molten material could be dumped on an enemy below.

Mansard Roof. See diagram following glossary.

Marbleized. A surface painted to simulate marble.

Meetinghouse Plan. The plan of a church with a plain rectangular sanctuary.

Merlons. The solid portions of a battlement.

Metope. The plain or decorated surfaces between the triglyphs of a Doric frieze. See *Order.*

Miesian. Descriptive of architecture similar to that designed by Ludwig Mies van der Rohe (1886–1969), which was distinguished for its simplicity and elegance.

Modillion. A series of brackets, usually scroll form, supporting a cornice or the upper part of a cornice.

Mullion. A vertical member between adjacent windows.

Muntins. Members that support and separate the panes of glass within a door or window.

Mutules. Blocks occurring on the underside of the cornice, centered over the triglyphs and metopes of a Doric entablature.

Narthex. The vestibule of a church.

Nave. The main part of the interior of a church.

Nook Shaft. A shaft in the angle of a pier, wall, window, or door jamb.

Novelty Siding. Boards with a continuous horizontal concave groove on the face of the upper part, and a rebate on the back of the lower part, the rebate to receive the thin part of the concave groove of the board beneath. When in place, the boards are in a vertical plane and the horizontal joints emphasized by the concave grooves.

Octastyle. A classical porch with eight columns.

Oculus. A round window. See also *Ceiling Oculus.*

Ogee. A curve made up of a convex and a concave part. See *Cyma.*

Open-arms Steps. A flight of steps curving outward toward the bottom, so that the balustrade has the form of a pair of open arms.

Open-topped Pediment. A pediment, usually occurring over a door or window, in which the sloping sides are returned before reaching the apex.

Open-well Stair. A stairway consisting of two or more flights, arranged so that there is an open space or well between the flights.

Order. A combination of a column with a base (usually), a shaft, and a capital, and of an entablature with an architrave, a frieze, and a cornice. The basic classical orders are the Tuscan, the Doric, the Ionic, and the Corinthian. *See diagram following glossary.*

Oriel Window. A bay window that is cantilevered or supported by brackets or by means other than a foundation.

Overdoor. A framed panel, the framework unified with a door frame beneath.

Overmantel. A framed panel, the framework unified with a mantel beneath.

Pagoda-type Roof. See *Concave Roof.*

Palladian Opening. An arched opening flanked by smaller square-head openings. Also called a Venetian opening or a Serliana.

Parapet. A low wall, placed as protection from a sudden drop such as at the sides of a bridge or the edge of a roof. Roof parapets are also built as fire stops and for the sake of appearance.

Patera. A flat circular or oval ornament, sometimes carved into the form of a rosette or with designs on the surface.

Pavilion. A projecting subdivision of a larger building, often emphasized by a pediment.

Pediment. In classical architecture, the gable occurring above an entablature. It has a cornice carried along the sloping edges. Pediments may be used over a wall or a portico, and may be used decoratively over doors, windows, or other features.

Pergola. An arbor, usually constructed of a double row of supports with an open framework between.

Peripteral. Descriptive of a building surrounded by a single row of columns.

Peristyle. A range of columns surrounding a building; also a range of columns surrounding an open court.

Perron. An exterior landing approached by a single or double flight of steps. The term generally is used only when the feature is impressive.

Piazza. (a) An open space surrounded by buildings. *(b)* A porch or gallery, the term more often used in this sense in Georgia.

Pilaster. A rectangular column, projecting slightly from a wall.

Pinnacle. A small turretlike termination at the top of a spire, buttress, or other feature of Gothic architecture.

Pitch. The slope, usually of a roof.

Plantation Plain Style. Originally descriptive of a weatherboarded plantation house with a simple gable roof and brick or clay chimneys. The term now applied to similar houses which are two stories, basically one room deep, and which have a porch with a shed roof across the front. It is in the latter sense that the term is used herein.

Plantation Type Cottage. A one- or one-and-a-half story cottage with porches front and back, and with a spraddle roof. Minor variations in the roof may occur, but are noted, i.e., a plantation type cottage, the shed roof of the front porch not integral with the main roof; or a plantation type cottage, the porches recessed under the main gable roof. The terms *Columbia cottage* and *Sand Hills cottage* signify plantation type cottages which admit such variations without their being noted.

Plinth Block. A block at the base

of a door frame, chimney piece, etc., against which the skirting is butted.

Pointed Arch. An arch composed of two segmental curves that meet at the apex of the arch.

Porch. A space adjacent to a building, with roof and floor, but open or partially enclosed on the sides.

Porte-cochère. A porch under which vehicles may be driven to provide covered access into a building.

Portico. A porch with classical columns and a pediment.

Prostyle. Descriptive of a building with a portico at the front.

Pseudo-arch. A lintel, curved at the ends to resemble an arch.

Pulvinated. Convex in profile, the term usually applied to a frieze whose face is convex.

Puncheon. A split log or heavy slab with a smooth face.

Quatrefoil. In window tracery, a panel divided into four round or leaf-shaped openings.

Quatrefoil Column. A column, the section of which is quatrefoil in shape.

Quoins. Blocks of stone or imitation stone placed at the corners of buildings, usually laid so that the long sides and the short ends alternate vertically.

Raking Cornice. A cornice that slopes with the edge of a sloping roof.

Rafter. One of the series of framing members which support a roof.

Reeded. Descriptive of a surface shaped to resemble a series of adjacent parallel convex strips.

Reredos. A wall or screen, usually decorated, behind an altar.

Return. A molding or other member which continues, but at an angle to its original direction, usually returning toward a wall

or other background.

Reveal. See *Jamb.*

Ridge. The horizontal apex of the junction of two sloping roofs.

Rinceau. An ornamental motif, usually consisting of a series of scroll-like forms.

Riser. The upright part of a step, between treads.

Rococo. A florid, delicate style of ornamentation, usually featuring naturalistic motifs.

Roof. (a) The ceiling of a church when the structure is expressed or exposed. *(b)* The covering of a building including the surface and adjacent framing. *See diagram following the glossary for the types most used in Georgia.*

Rubble Masonry. Irregular stones, generally not laid in courses.

Rustication. Masonry, usually stone or imitation stone, cut to emphasize texture or to accentuate the joints.

Salt Box. See diagram following glossary.

Sanded Paint. Paint mixed with sand to simulate the texture of stone.

Sand Hills Cottage. See *Plantation Type Cottage.*

Sash. The sliding glazed frames of a double-hung window.

Sawtooth Design. A pattern resembling the teeth in a saw, frequently applied to brickwork in which a course of brick is laid diagonally to the face of a wall so that the ends project like saw teeth, also to a roof with a series of sloping skylights which in profile present a saw tooth pattern.

Scroll-saw Work. Flat woodwork (brackets, balusters, etc.) cut into fanciful designs with a scroll or jig saw.

Segmental Arch. An arch whose curve is segmental.

Serliana. See *Palladian Opening.*

Shaft. The part of a classical column between the base and the capital. See *Order.*

Sheaf-of-Wheat Design. A latticelike pattern apparently consisting of two cross pieces arranged like an x, and a central vertical piece. The overall shape is similar to that of a sheaf of wheat. A block is sometimes used at the crossing, and appears to be binding the pieces together.

Shed Roof. See *Roof.*

Shouldered Trim. An enframement, the upper part of which projects slightly, like shoulders.

Shutter. A solid cover, hinged at the side, for windows.

Sidelights. Glass panels installed in a doorframe at each side of the door. Sometimes used to describe very narrow windows each side of and adjacent to a much wider window.

Sill. (a) The lowest member of the framing for a building. *(b)* The lowest member of a window or door frame; also the horizontal masonry member occurring under window frames in masonry walls.

Skirting. The molding or combination board and molding at the base of an interior wall.

Soffit. The underside of an architectural member, such as the underside of an eave or of the head of a door or window frame.

Spindle. A decorative turned member, similar to a slender baluster. Often used repetitively in porch friezes and in space dividers in Queen Anne style structures.

Spire. A tapering roof surmounting a steeple.

Spraddle Roof. See diagram following glossary.

Spring Line. The point at which

the vertical lines of an arched opening change to a curve.

Steeple. A church tower including the upper stages and the spire.

Stretcher Course. Brick laid so that the lengthwise side of the brick is exposed.

String Course. A projecting element forming a band across the face of a building.

Stud. One of a series of upright members forming the framework for the walls of a wooden frame building.

Sunburst. A flat, usually elliptical, ornament with a design in relief of rays emanating from a center.

T-Astragal. The T-shaped molding attached to the side of one leaf of a double door to act as a stop for the other leaf.

Temple Form. A form similar to that of a Greek temple with a plain rectangular plan, and a gable roof with pediments at each end.

Terra Cotta. Made of baked clay as is brick, but cast in various, usually ornamental, patterns.

Tetrastyle. Descriptive of a classical porch with four columns.

Tiered Porch. A porch of two or more stories.

Tithing. A term used to describe the residential blocks of colonial Savannah. Each ward contained four tithings of ten lots each.

Tower. (a) A structure that is much higher than its length or width. *(b)* The lower part of a church steeple.

Tower-of-the-Winds Order. A variation of the Corinthian order in which the capital is simplified, and the scrolls and acanthus leaves of the upper part of the capital replaced by a range of water leaves.

Transom. A horizontal, glazed window above a door or window.

Tray Ceiling. A ceiling that slopes downward at the edges, like a tray with slanting sides, inverted.

Tread. The upper, horizontal part of a step.

Trefoil. A panel of window tracery, divided into three round or leaf-shaped openings.

Triglyph. A rectangular block, projecting slightly and usually having vertical grooves, alternating with the metopes of a Doric frieze.

Turned Work. A round member, often of varying thickness, turned on a lathe.

Turret. A small slender tower, usually part of a larger structure or substructure.

Tuscan Order. A classical order, similar to the Doric, but simpler; usually more massive than the Roman Doric, less massive than the Greek Doric, and more adaptable to varied types of structure than either.

Two-story-high Porch. A one-story porch whose height is equal to two interior stories.

Two-story Porch. A porch of two stories.

Two-tiered Porch. A porch of two stories.

Tympanum. The space enclosed between an arch and a horizontal lintel; also the triangular surface bounded by the sloping and horizontal cornices of a pediment.

Vault. An arched ceiling or roof.

Venetian Opening. See *Palladian Opening.*

Veranda. A long gallerylike porch, the roof of which is supported by light, usually metal, posts.

Verge Board. The finish board covering the juncture of the wall and the roof of a gable. The board follows the slope of the roof and fits snugly against the wall. See also *Bargeboard.*

Vestibule. An entrance hall, usually shallow, and acting as a link between the outer door and the interior rooms of a building.

Volute. A spiral scroll, the principal feature of an Ionic capital. Smaller versions also appear on composite and on most Corinthian capitals.

Voussoir. One of the wedge-shaped units of which a masonry arch is composed.

Wainscot. Wood paneling, the term most often applied to paneling on the lower part of a wall.

Wall Arch. An arch that is not open, but that forms a pattern or a shallow recess in a wall.

Water-table. A projecting ledge, molding, or string course along the side of a building designed to throw off water.

Weatherboarding. Wall siding of overlapping horizontal boards.

Weathering. A sloping surface on sills or on the tops of buttresses, buttress offsets, or chimney shoulders.

Winders. Steps radiating from a center.

Withes. (a) A vertical division, one unit wide, in masonry construction. *(b)* Masonry walls within a chimney with separate flues.

Roofs

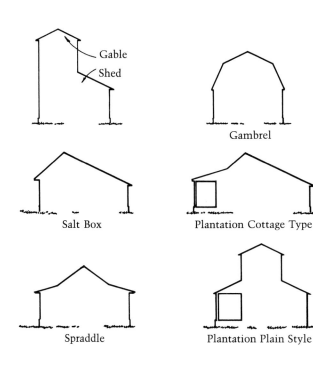

Gable

Shed

Gambrel

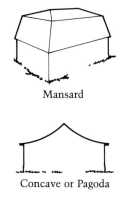

Mansard

Salt Box

Plantation Cottage Type

Concave or Pagoda

Spraddle

Plantation Plain Style

Hip

Orders

Corinthian

Ionic

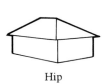

Roman Doric,
Denticular

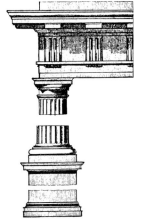

Roman Doric, Mutular

Appendixes

National Register of Historic Places

Georgia, January 1, 1980

Atkinson County

Willacoochee Vicinity. *McCranie's Turpentine Still.* w of Willacoochee on U.S. Hwy. 82.

Baldwin County

Milledgeville. *Atkinson Hall, Georgia College.* Georgia College campus.
————. *Central Building, State Lunatic Asylum.* Broad St.
————. *Former Governor's Mansion.* 120 S. Clark St.
————. *Milledgeville Historic District.* Bounded by Irwin, Thomas, and Warren Sts. and Fishing Creek.
————. *Old State Capitol (Georgia Military College).* Greene St.
Milledgeville Vicinity. *Barrowville.* E of Milledgeville on Ga. Hwy. 22/24.
————. *Maj. Francis Boykin House.* 10 mi. SE of Milledgeville off Ga. Hwy. 24.
————. *Old State Prison Building.* 3 mi. w of Milledgeville on Ga. Hwy. 22.
————. *Samuel Rockwell House.* 165 Allen Memorial Dr.
————. *John Rutherford House.* 550 Allen Memorial Dr.
————. *Storehouse, State Lunatic Asylum.* Broad St. and Lawrence Rd.

————. *Thalian Hall.* Allen Memorial and Ivey Drs.
————. *Woodville.* 3 mi. s of Milledgeville on Ga. Hwy. 243.

Banks County

Commerce Vicinity. *New Salem Covered Bridge.* 6 mi. N of Commerce on Ga. Hwy. S992 over Grove Creek.
Homer Vicinity. *Kesler Covered Bridge.* 10 mi. N of Homer on County Line Rd. over Middle Fork Broad River.

Barrow County

Bethlehem Vicinity. *Kilgore Mill Covered Bridge and Mill Site.* 3.5 mi. SW of Bethlehem across Apalachee River/county line.
Winder. *Winder Depot.* Broad and Porter Sts.

Bartow County

Cartersville. *Roselawn (Sam Jones House).* 244 Cherokee Ave.
Cartersville Vicinity. *Etowah Mounds.* 3 mi. s of Cartersville on Ga. Hwy. 61.
————. *Etowah Valley District.* Along Etowah River and drainage areas.

————. *Rebecca Latimer Felton House.* N of Cartersville off U.S. Hwy. 411.
————. *Valley View.* Euharlee Rd., SW of Cartersville.

Berrien County

Nashville. *Berrien County Courthouse.* Town Square.

Bibb County

Macon. *Capt. R. J. Anderson House.* 1730 West End Ave.
————. *Judge Clifford Anderson House.* 642 Orange St.
————. *Ambrose Baber House.* 577–587 Walnut St.
————. *Thomas C. Burke House.* 1085 Georgia Ave.
————. *Cannonball House (Judge Asa Holt House).* 856 Mulberry St.
————. *Central City Park Bandstand.* Central City Park.
————. *Christ Episcopal Church.* 538–566 Walnut St.
————. *Andrew J. Collins House.* 1495 Second St.
————. *Cowles House (Stratford Academy).* 988 Bond St.
————. *Jerry Cowles Cottage.* 4569 Rivoli Dr.
————. *Dasher-Stevens House.* 904 Orange Ter.
————. *Davis-Guttenberger-*

Rankin House. 134 Buford Pl.

———. *Domingos House.* 1261 Jefferson Ter.

———. *Emerson-Holmes Building.* 566 Mulberry St.

———. *Robert Findlay House.* 785 Second St.

———. *First Presbyterian Church.* 690 Mulberry St.

———. *Fort Hawkins Archaeological Site.* Fort Hill St.

———. *Goodall House.* 618 Orange St.

———. *Grand Opera House.* 651 Mulberry St.

———. *Green-Poe House.* 841–845 Poplar St.

———. *Hatcher-Groover-Schwartz House.* 1144–1146 Georgia Ave.

———. *Holt-Peeler-Snow House.* 1129 Georgia Ave.

———. *Johnston-Hay House.* 934 Georgia Ave.

———. *Sidney Lanier Cottage.* 935 High St.

———. *Lassiter House.* 315 College St.

———. *W. G. Lee Alumni House* (Bartlett House). 1270 Ash (Coleman) St.

———. *Macon Historic District.* Area around Mercer University and Walnut, Mulberry, Cherry, and College Sts.

———. *Dewitt McCrary House.* 320 Hydrolia St.

———. *Mercer University Administration Building.* Coleman Ave.

———. *Militia Headquarters Building.* 552–564 Mulberry St.

———. *Monroe Street Apartments.* 641–661 Monroe St.

———. *Municipal Auditorium* 415–435 First St.

———. *Munroe-Dunlap-Snow House.* 920 High St.

———. *Munroe-Goolsby House.* 159 Rogers Ave.

———. *Leroy Napier House.* 2215 Napier Ave.

———. *Ocmulgee National Monument.* 1207 Emory Hwy.

———. *Old Macon Library.* 652–662 Mulberry St.

———. *Old U.S. Post Office and Federal Building.* 475 Mulberry St.

———. *Railroad Overpass at Ocmulgee.* 1207 Emory Hwy.

———. *Raines-Carmichael House.* 1183 Georgia Ave.

———. *Randolph-Whittle House.* 1231 Jefferson Ter.

———. *Rogers, Rock House.* 337 College St.

———. *Rose Hill Cemetery.* Riverside Dr.

———. *Slate House.* 931–945 Walnut St.

———. *Small House* (Napier-Small House). 156 Rogers Ave.

———. *Solomon-Curd House.* 770 Mulberry St.

———. *Solomon-Smith-Martin House.* 2619 Vineville Ave.

———. *St. Joseph's Catholic Church.* 812 Poplar St.

———. *Villa Albicini.* 150 Tucker Rd.

———. *Willingham-Hill-O'Neal Cottage.* 535 College St.

Brooks County

Quitman Vicinity. *Eudora Plantation.* 3.5 mi. s of Quitman off Ga. Hwy. 33.

Bryan County

Ellabelle Vicinity. *Glen Echo.* 2 mi. E of Ellabelle on Ga. Hwy. 204.

Richmond Hill Vicinity. *Fort McAllister.* 10 mi. E of Richmond Hill via Ga. Hwy. 67.

———. *Kilkenny.* E of Richmond Hill on Kilkenny Rd.

———. *Richmond Hill Plantation.* E of Richmond Hill on Ford Neck Rd.

———. *Seven Mile Bend (Bryan's Neck).*

———. *Strathy Hall.* SE of Richmond Hill.

Savannah Vicinity. *Old Fort Argyle Site.* 15 mi. w of Savannah off Ga. Hwy. 204.

Butts County

Indian Springs. *McIntosh Inn.* Ga. Hwy. 42.

Jackson. *J. R. Carmichael House.* 140 McConough Rd.

Camden County

St. Marys. *Orange Hall.* 311 Osborne St.

———. *St. Marys Historic District.* Roughly bounded by Waterfront Rd., Norris, Alexander, and Oak Grove Cemetery.

St. Marys Vicinity. *High Point–Half Moon Bluff Historic District.* NE of St. Marys on Cumberland Island.

Carroll County

Burns Quarry. Burns Rd.

Carrollton. *Bonner-Sharp-Gunn House.* West Georgia College campus.

Catoosa County

Chattanooga, Tenn. Vicinity. *Chickamauga and Chattanooga National Military Park.* s of Chattanooga on U.S. Hwy. 27.

Fort Oglethorpe. *Fort Oglethorpe*

Historic District. U.S. Hwy. 27.

Ringgold. *Ringgold Depot.* U.S. Hwy. 41.

———. *Whitman-Anderson House.* 309 Tennessee St.

Ringgold Vicinity. *Stone Church.* E of Ringgold off U.S. Hwy. 76/41.

Chatham County

Nicholsonville. *Nicholsonville Baptist Church.* White Bluff Rd.

Port Wentworth Vicinity. *Mulberry Grove Site.* N of Port Wentworth.

Savannah. *Central of Georgia Depot and Trainshed.* W. Broad and Liberty Sts.

———. *Central of Georgia Railroad, Savannah Shops and Terminal Facilities.* W. Broad St. and Railroad Ave.

———. *Central of Georgia Railway Company Shop Property.* Between W. Jones St. and Louisville Rd.

———. *Isaiah Davenport House.* 324 E. State St.

———. *Federal Building and U.S. Courthouse.* Wright Sq.

———. *First Bryan Baptist Church.* 575 W. Bryan St.

———. *Fort Jackson.* Islands Expressway.

———. *Green-Meldrim House.* Macon and Bull Sts.

———. *W. B. Hodgson Hall.* 501 Whitaker St.

———. *Laurel Grove–South Cemetery.* Thirty-Seventh St.

———. *Juliette Gordon Low Birthplace.* 10 Oglethorpe Ave. E.

———. *Massie Common School House.* 207 E. Gordon St.

———. *Owens-Thomas House.* 124 Abercorn St.

———. *Savannah Historic District.* Bounded by E. Broad, Gwinnett, and W. Broad Sts. and the Savannah River.

———. *Savannah Victorian Historic District.* Bounded N by Anderson St. E by Price St. W by Montgomery St. S by Gwinnett St.

———. *William Scarbrough House.* 41 W. Broad St.

———. *Oliver Sturges House.* 27 Abercorn St.

———. *Telfair Academy.* 121 Barnard St.

———. *U.S. Customhouse.* 1–3 E. Bay St.

Savannah Vicinity. *Bethesda Home for Boys.* S of Savannah at Ferguson Ave. and Bethesda Rd.

———. *Fort Pulaski National Monument.* 17 mi. W of Savannah, Cockspur Island.

———. *Lebanon Plantation.* SW of Savannah.

———. *Wild Heron.* 15 mi. SW of Savannah off U.S. Hwy. 17.

———. *Wormsloe Plantation.* Isle of Hope and Long Island.

Chattahoochee County

Fort Benning. *Riverside (Quarters No. 1).* 100 Vibbert Ave.

Clarke County

Athens. *Bishop House.* Jackson St., University of Georgia campus.

———. *Camak House.* 279 Meigs St.

———. *Carnegie Library Building.* 1401 Prince Ave.

———. *Albon Chase House.* 185 N. Hull St.

———. *Church-Waddel-Brumby House.* 280 E. Dougherty St.

———. *T. R. R. Cobb House.* 194 Prince Ave.

———. *Cobb-Treanor House.* 1234 S. Lumpkin St.

———. *Cobbham Historic District.* Roughly bounded by Prince Ave., Hill, Reese, and Pope Sts.

———. *Ross Crane House.* 247 Pulaski St.

———. *Albin P. Dearing House.* 338 S. Milledge Ave.

———. *Dearing Street Historic District.* Roughly bounded by Broad and Baxter Sts. and Milledge Ave., and includes both sides of Finley St. and Henderson Ave.

———. *Downtown Athens Historic District.* Roughly bounded by Hancock Ave., Foundry, Mitchell, Broad, and Lumpkin Sts.

———. *Franklin House* (Old Athens Hotel). 464–480 E. Broad St.

———. *Garden Club of Georgia Museum-Headquarters House* (Founder's Memorial Garden). Lumpkin St., University of Georgia campus.

———. *Henry W. Grady House* (Taylor-Grady House). 634 Prince Ave.

———. *Dr. James S. Hamilton House* (Alpha Delta Pi Sorority House). 150 S. Milledge Ave.

———. *Lucy Cobb Institute Campus.* 200 N. Milledge Ave., University of Georgia campus.

———. *Gov. Wilson Lumpkin House* (Rock House). Cedar St., University of Georgia campus.

———. *Joseph Henry Lumpkin House.* 248 Prince Ave.

———. *Morton Building.* N. Hull and Washington Sts.

———. *Old North Campus, University of Georgia.* Bounded by Broad, Lumpkin, and Jackson Sts.

————. *Parrott Insurance Building*. 283 E. Broad St.

————. *President's House, University of Georgia* (Benjamin Hill House). 570 Prince Ave.

————. *James A. Sledge House*. 749 Cobb St.

————. *Thomas-Carithers House*. 530 S. Milledge Ave.

————. *Upson House*. 1022 Prince Ave.

————. *Ware-Lyndon House*. 293 Hoyt St.

————. *Wilkins House*. 387 S. Milledge Ave.

Whitehall. *White Hall*. Whitehall and Simonton Bridge Rds.

Clay County

Fort Gaines. *Dill House*. 102 S. Washington St.

————. *Walter F. George Dam Mound*. SE of Walter F. George Lock and Dam.

Fort Gaines Vicinity. *Fort Gaines Cemetery Site*.

————. *Toney-Standley House*. NW of Fort Gaines off Ga. Hwy. 39.

Clayton County

Fayetteville Vicinity. *Orkin Early Quartz Site*. E of Woolsey off Woolsey Rd. S of Flint River crossing.

Jonesboro. *Jonesboro Historic District*. Ga. Hwys. 54 and 3.

————. *Stately Oaks*. Jodeco Rd.

Rex. *Rex Mill*. Rex Rd.

Cobb County

Austell. *Israel Causey House*. 5909 Maxham Rd.

Kennesaw. *The General*. Big Shanty Museum off Cherokee St.

Mableton Vicinity. *Johnston's Line*. SE of Mableton off U.S. Hwy. 78 at Chattahoochee River.

Marietta. *Arnoldus Brumby House*. 472 Powder Springs St.

————. *Glover-McLeod-Garrison House*. 250 Garrison Rd. S.E.

————. *Northwest Marietta Historic District*. NW of town square, including parts of Kennesaw Ave., Church St., Polk St., and along the L&N Railroad tracks.

Marietta Vicinity. *Andrew J. Cheney House*. SW of Marietta at Powder Springs and Bankstone Rds.

————. *Gilgal Church Battle Site* (Federal Entrenchments). 9 mi. W of Marietta on Sandtown Rd.

————. *Kennesaw Mountain National Battlefield Park*. 2 mi. W of Marietta.

————. *William Gibbs McAdoo House*. SW of Marietta on Ga. Hwy. 5.

————. *Sope Creek Ruins*. E of Marietta on Paper Mill Rd.

Columbia County

Appling. *Kiokee Baptist Church*. Kiokee Rd.

Augusta Vicinity. *Stallings Island*. 8 mi. NW of Augusta in the Savannah River.

Winfield Vicinity. *Woodville*. SE of Winfield off Ga. Hwy. 150 on Dozier Rd.

Coweta County

Newnan Vicinity. *Gordon-Banks House*. S of Newnan on U.S. Hwy. 29.

Crisp County

Cordele Vicinity. *Cannon Site*. W of Cordele off Ga. Hwy. 230.

Dawson County

Dawsonville Vicinity. *Steele's Covered Bridge*. 7 mi. NW of Dawsonville on Ga. Hwy. 2275.

Decatur County

Bainbridge. *J. W. Callahan House*. 200 Evans St.

Bainbridge Vicinity. *Curry Hill Plantation*. 6 mi. E of Bainbridge on U.S. Hwy. 84.

De Kalb County

Atlanta. *Callanwolde*. 980 Briarcliff Rd. N.E.

————. *De Kalb Avenue–Clifton Road Archaeological Site*. De Kalb Ave.

————. *Emory University District*. N. Decatur Rd.

Atlanta Vicinity. *Druid Hills Historic District*. U.S. Hwy. 29/78.

————. *Soapstone Ridge*. S of Atlanta off River Rd.

Atlanta and Vicinity. *Druid Hills Parks and Parkways*. Both sides of Ponce de Leon Ave. between Briarcliff Rd. and the Seaboard Coast Line R.R. tracks.

Decatur. *Mary Gay House*. 524 Marshall St.

————. *Old De Kalb County Courthouse* (Civic Center). Court Sq.

————. *Swanton House*. 720 Swanton Way.

Lithonia. *The Seminary*. 6886 Main St.

Dooly County

Vienna. *Stovall-George-Woodward House*. 305 Union St.

Dougherty County

Albany. *Bridge House*. 112 N. Front St.

———. *Samuel Farkas House.* 328 W. Broad Ave.

———. *Municipal Auditorium.* 301 Pine Ave.

———. *Old St. Teresa's Catholic Church.* 313 Residence Ave.

———. *W. E. Smith House.* 516 Flint Ave.

———. *Union Depot* (Terminal Station). Roosevelt Ave. and N. Front St.

———. *U.S. Post Office and Courthouse.* 337 Broad Ave.

Douglas County

Atlanta Vicinity. *Sweet Water Manufacturing Site.* w of Atlanta off Interstate Hwy. 20.

Early County

Blakely Vicinity. *Kolomoki Mounds.* 8 mi. N of Blakely on U.S. Hwy. 27, Kolomoki Mounds State Park.

Hilton Vicinity. *Coheelee Creek Covered Bridge.* 2 mi. N of Hilton on Old River Rd.

Effingham County

Springfield Vicinity. *Ebenezer Townsite and Jerusalem Lutheran Church.* E of Springfield on Ga. Hwy. 275 at Savannah River.

Elbert County

Elberton. *William Allen House* (Beverly Plantation). 9 mi. E of Elberton on Ga. Hwy. 6.

Elberton Vicinity. *Ralph Banks Place.* N of Elberton off Ga. Hwy. 77.

———. *Ralph Gaines House.* N of Elberton on Ga. Hwy. 368.

Ruckersville. *Rucker House.* Ga. Hwy. 985.

Ruckersville Vicinity. *Alexander-Cleveland House.* 3.5 mi. NE of Ruckersville.

Fayette County

Fayetteville Vicinity. *Tandy King House.* s of Fayetteville on Ga. Hwy. 92.

Floyd County

Rome. *Chieftains.* 80 Chatillon Rd.

———. *U.S. Post Office and Courthouse.* W. Fourth Ave. and E. First St.

Rome Vicinity. *Berry Schools.* N of Rome on U.S. Hwy. 27.

Forsyth County

Cumming Vicinity. *Pool's Mill Covered Bridge.* NW of Cumming off Ga. Hwy. 369 on Pool's Mill Rd.

Franklin County

Kesler Covered Bridge. See Homer Vicinity, Banks County.

Carnesville Vicinity. *Cromer's Mill Covered Bridge.* 8 mi. s of Carnesville at Nails Creek.

Fulton County

Atlanta. *Ansley Park Historic District.* Ansley Park and environs.

———. *Atlanta and West Point Railroad Freight Depot.* 215 Decatur St. Destroyed.

———. *Atlanta University Center District.* Roughly bounded

by transit right-of-way, Northside Dr., Walnut, Fair, Roach, W. End Dr., Euralee, and Chestnut Sts.

———. *Atlanta Waterworks Hemphill Avenue Station.* 1210 Hemphill Ave. N.W.

———. *Atlanta Woman's Club Complex.* 1150 Peachtree St. N.E.

———. *Baltimore Block.* 5, 7, 9, 11, 13, 15, 17, 19 Baltimore Pl.

———. *Brookwood Hills Historic District.* Off Peachtree Rd. at Brighton and Huntington Rds.

———. *Bass Furniture Building.* 142–150 Mitchell St.

———. *Cabbagetown District.* Bounded by Boulevard, Pearl St., Memorial Dr., and railroad tracks.

———. *Candler Building.* 127 Peachtree St. N.E.

———. *Capital City Club.* 7 Harris St. N.W.

———. *Carnegie Library of Atlanta.* 126 Carnegie Way N.W.

———. *Church of the Sacred Heart of Jesus.* 335 Ivy St. N.E.

———. *Citizens and Southern Bank Building.* 35 Broad St.

———. *Cyclorama of the Battle of Atlanta.* Cherokee Ave., Grant Park.

———. *Degive's Grand Opera House.* 157 Peachtree St. N.E. Destroyed.

———. *Dixie Coca-Cola Bottling Company Plant.* 125 Edgewood Ave.

———. *English-American Building.* 74 Peachtree St.

———. *First Congregational Church.* 105 Courtland St. N.E.

———. *Fox Theater.* 660 Peachtree St. N.E.

———. *Georgia Institute of Technology Historic District.* 225 North Ave.

———. *Garrison Apartments.* 1325–1327 Peachtree St. N.E.

———. *Georgia State Capitol.* Capitol Sq.

———. *Grant Park Historic District.* Roughly bounded by Glenwood and Atlanta Aves.

———. *Habersham Memorial Hall.* Fifteenth St. w of intersection with Piedmont Ave.

———. *Joel Chandler Harris House* (Wren's Nest). 1050 Gordon St. S.W.

———. *Healey Building.* 57 Forsyth St.

———. *Hillyer Trust Building.* 140 Peachtree St.

———. *Hurt Building.* 45 Edgewood Ave. N.E.

———. *Inman Park.* Roughly centered between De Kalb Ave., Lake Ave., and Waddell St. centering along Edgewood and Euclid Aves.

———. *Martin Luther King, Jr., Historic District.* Bounded roughly by Irwin, Randolph, Edgewood, Jackson, and Auburn Aves.

———. *Victor H. Kriegshaber House.* 292 Moreland Ave. N.E.

———. *William P. Nicolson House.* 821 Piedmont Ave.

———. *North Avenue Presbyterian Church.* 607 Peachtree Ave. N.E.

———. *Oakland Cemetery.* 248 Oakland Ave. S.E.

———. *Odd Fellows Building and Auditorium.* 228–250 Auburn Ave. N.E.

———. *Peachtree Southern Railway Station.* 1688 Peachtree St. N.W.

———. *Edward C. Peters House.* 179 Ponce de Leon Ave.

———. *Piedmont Park.* Bounded by Tenth St., Southern Railway, and Piedmont Rd.

———. *Thomas H. Pitts House and Dairy* (Casa Loma). 3105 Cascade Rd. S.W.

———. *Rhodes-Haverty Building.* 134 Peachtree St. N.W.

———. *Rhodes Memorial Hall.* 1516 Peachtree St.

———. *Rufus M. Rose House.* 537 Peachtree St.

———. *Shrine of the Immaculate Conception.* 48 Hunter St. S.W.

———. *Tullie Smith House.* 3099 Andrews Dr. N.W.

———. *Southern Bell Telephone Company Building.* 51 Ivy St. N.E.

———. *Staff Row and Old Post Area*, Fort McPherson. NE corner of Fort McPherson.

———. *The Texas.* Cyclorama Bldg., Grant Park.

———. *Stone Hall, Atlanta University.* Morris-Brown College campus.

———. *Swan House.* 3099 Andrews Dr. N.W.

———. *Sweet Auburn Historic District.* Auburn Ave.

———. *Techwood Homes Historic District.* Roughly bounded by North Ave., Parker, Williams, and Lovejoy Sts.

———. *Henry B. Tompkins House.* 125 W. Wesley Rd. N.W.

———. *U.S. Post Office and Courthouse.* 76 Forsyth St.

———. *E. Van Winkle Gin and Machine Works.* Foster St.

———. *Western and Atlantic Railroad Zero Milepost.* Central Ave. between Wall St. and Railroad Ave.

———. *Stuart Witham House.* 2922 Andrews Dr. N.W.

Fairburn. *Campbell County Courthouse.* E. Broad and Cole Sts.

Fort McPherson. *Forscom Command Sergeant Major's Quarters.* Bldg. 532.

Roswell. *Barrington Hall.* 60 Marietta St.

———. *Bulloch Hall.* Bulloch Ave.

———. *Roswell Historic District.* Centers around town square going out along Mimosa Blvd., Bulloch Ave., Atlanta St., and E to mill along Roswell Creek.

Glynn County

Brunswick. *Brunswick Old Town Historic District.* Roughly bounded by First, Bay, New Bay, H, and Cochran Sts.

Brunswick Vicinity. *Brunswick Old Town.* Bounded s by First St. w by Bay and New Bay Sts.

———. *Fort Frederica National Monument.* 12 mi. N of Brunswick.

———. *Hofwyl-Broadfield Plantation.* N of Brunswick on U.S. Hwy. 17.

Jekyll Island. *Faith Chapel.* Old Plantation Rd.

———. *Horton–du Bignon House, Brewery Ruins, du Bignon Cemetery.* Riverview Dr.

———. *Jekyll Island Club.* Between Riverview Dr. and Old Village Blvd.

———. *Rockefeller Cottage.* 331 Riverview Dr.

St. Simons Island. *St. Simons Lighthouse Keepers Building.* 600 Beachview Dr.

Gordon County

Calhoun Vicinity. *New Echota.* NE of Calhoun on Ga. Hwy. 225.

Oakman Vicinity. *Freeman-Hurt House.* S of Oakman on U.S. Hwy. 411.

Grady County

Beachton Vicinity. *Susina Plantation* (Cedar Grove). w of Beachton on Meridian Rd.

Greene County

Greensboro Vicinity. *Penfield Historic District*. 7 mi. N of Greensboro on Ga. Hwy. 5925.

Gwinnett County

Dacula Vicinity. *Elisha Winn House*. 2 mi. SE of Hog Mountain on Ga. Hwy. 324.
Lawrenceville. *Old Seminary Building* (Lawrenceville Female Seminary Building). Perry St.
Lilburn Vicinity. *Thomas Wynne House*. N of Lilburn on U.S. Hwy. 29.

Habersham County

Clarkesville Vicinity. *Woodlands and Blythewood*. About 3 mi. N of Clarkesville on U.S. Hwy. 441.

Hall County

Buford. *Bowman-Pirkle House*. NE of Buford on U.S. Hwy. 23 on Friendship Rd.
Gainesville. *Brenau College District*. Academy, Prior, Washington, and Boulevard Sts.
———. *Federal Building and Courthouse*. 126 Washington St.
———. *Green Street District*. Both sides of Green St. from Green St. Pl. to Glenwood Rd.
Gainesville Vicinity. *Tanner's Mill*. S of Gainesville on Ga. Hwy. 3.

Hancock County

Devereux Vicinity. *Roe-Harper House*. 2 mi. W of Devereux off Ga. Hwy. 2133.

Jewell. *Jewell Historic District*. Ga. Hwys. 248 and 16.
Jewell Vicinity. *Cheely-Coleman House*. S of Jewell off Ga. Hwy. 123 at Ogeechee River.
———. *Shivers-Simpson House* (Rock Mill). N of Jewell on Mayfield Rd.
Linton and Vicinity. *Linton Historic District*. Town of Linton and its environs.
Mayfield Vicinity. *Camilla-Zack Community Center District*. Rte. 1.
Sparta. *Sparta Historic District*. Centered on courthouse square and out Ga. Hwy. 22 and Broad, Court, and Jones Sts.
Sparta Vicinity. *Glen Mary*. Linton Rd. S of Sparta.
———. *Rockby*. NE of Sparta off Ga. Hwy. 16.

Haralson County

Buchanan. *Haralson County Courthouse*. Courthouse Sq.

Harris County

West Point. *White Hall*. Off U.S. Hwy. 29.

Henry County

Hampton. *Hampton Depot*. E. Main St.

Houston County

Henderson Vicinity. *Davis-Felton Plantation*. NW of Henderson on Felton Rd.

Jackson County

Commerce. *Seaborn M. Shankle House*. 125 Cherry St.

Jasper County

Monticello. *Jordan-Bellew House*. Madison Hwy.
———. *Hitchcock-Roberts House*. N. Warren St.
———. *Monticello High School*. College St.

Jefferson County

Louisville. *Old Market* (Slave Market). U.S. Hwy. 1 and Ga. Hwy. 24.

Jenkins County

Millen Vicinity. *Birdsville Plantation*. NW of Millen.
———. *Camp Lawton*. N of Millen.

Johnson County

Wrightsville. *Grice Inn*. E. Elm St.

Jones County

Bradley Vicinity. *Cabaniss-Hanberry House*. NE of Bradley on Transquilla Rd.
Clinton. *Old Clinton Historic District*. 3 mi. W of Gray N of U.S. Hwy. 129.
East Juliette Vicinity. *Jarrell Plantation*. 6 mi. E of East Juliette off Dames Ferry Rd.
Round Oak Vicinity. *Cabiness-Hunt House*. SE of Round Oak off Ga. Hwy. 11.

Laurens County

Dublin. *Carnegie Library*. Junction of Bellevue, Academy, and Jackson Sts.

Dublin Vicinity. *Fish Trap Cut.*
Off Ga. Hwy. 19 5.5 mi. s of
Dublin on the Oconee River.

Montrose Vicinity. *Sanders Hill.*
s of Montrose off Interstate
Hwy. 16/Ga. Hwy. 404.

Liberty County

Midway. *Midway Historic District.* Junction of U.S. Hwy. 17
and Ga. Hwy. 38.

Midway Vicinity. *Fort Morris.*
About 10 mi. E of Midway
off Ga. Hwy. 38.

Riceboro Vicinity. *Woodmanston
Site* (LeConte Plantation). sw of
Riceboro off Barrington Rd.

South Newport Vicinity. *St. Catherines Island.* 10 mi. off Georgia coast between St. Catherines Sound and Sapelo Sound.

Lincoln County

Danburg Vicinity. *Chennault
House.* NE of Danburg at junction of Ga. Hwy. 44 and Ga.
Hwy. 79.

———. *Matthews House.* NE
of Danburg on Ga. Hwy. 79.

Lumpkin County

Dahlonega. *Dahlonega Courthouse Gold Museum* (Old
Lumpkin County Courthouse).
U.S. Hwy. 19.

———. *Fields Place–Vickery
House.* W. Main St. and Vickery Dr.

———. *Price Memorial Hall.* College Ave.

Dahlonega Vicinity. *Calhoun
Mine.* 3 mi. s of Dahlonega off
Ga. Hwy. 60.

Macon County

Andersonville Vicinity. *Andersonville National Historic Site.*
1 mi. E of Andersonville on Ga.
Hwy. 49.

Madison County

Danielsville. *Crawford W. Long
Childhood Home.* Old Ila Rd.

Marion County

Buena Vista Vicinity. *Fort Perry.*
N of Buena Vista off Ga. Hwy.
41.

McDuffie County

Thomson. *Hickory Hill* (Thomas
E. Watson House). Hickory Hill
Dr. and Lee St.

———. *Usry House.* 211 Milledge St.

———. *Thomas E. Watson House.*
310 Lumpkin St.

Thomson Vicinity. *Bowdres-Rees-
Knox House.* sw of Thomson
on Old Wrightsboro Rd.

———. *Thomas Carr District.* N
of Thomson near junction of
Ga. Hwy. 150 and Interstate
Hwy. 20.

———. *Old Rock House.* NW
of Thomson on Old Rock
House Rd.

McIntosh County

Cox Vicinity. *Fort Barrington.* NW
of Cox.

Crescent. *D'Antignac House.* Off
Ga. Hwy. 99.

Darien Vicinity. *Fort King
George.* E of U.S. Hwy. 17.

Meriwether County

Alvaton Vicinity. *White Oak
Creek Covered Bridge.* SE of Alvaton on Covered Bridge Rd.

Greenville. *Meriwether County
Courthouse.* Court Sq.

———. *Meriwether County Jail.*
Gresham St. and Ga. Hwy. 27A.

Greenville Vicinity. *Clarkland
Farms.* La Grange Rd.

———. *Harman-Watson-
Matthews House.* sw of Greenville on Odessadale/Durand Rd.

———. *Mark Hall.* sw of Greenville off Ga. Hwy. 18.

Warm Springs. *Warm Springs Historic District.* s of Ga. Hwy. 194
and w of Ga. Hwy. 85w.

Woodbury. *Red Oak Creek Covered Bridge.* N of Woodbury
on Huel Brown Rd.

Mitchell County

Camilla. *James Price McRee
House.*

Monroe County

Bollingbroke Vicinity. *Great Hill
Place.* w of Bollingbroke off Ga.
Hwy. 41.

Forsyth. *Hil'ardin* (Sharp-Hardin-
Wright House). 212 S. Lee St.

Macon Vicinity. *Montpelier Female Institute.* w of Macon.

Morgan County

Madison. *Nathan Bennett
House.* Dixie Ave.

———. *Bonar Hall.* Dixie Ave.

———. *Madison Historic District.* Roughly bounded on both

sides by U.S. Hwy. 441/129/278 at Ga. Hwy. 83.

Madison Vicinity. *Cedar Lane Farm.* N of Madison off Ga. Hwy. 83.

Murray County

Spring Place. *Vann House.* Junction of U.S. Hwy. 76 and Ga. Hwy. 225.

Muscogee County

Columbus. *Bullard-Hart House.* 1408 Third Ave.

——. *The Cedars.* 2039 Thirteenth St.

——. *Columbus Historic District.* Roughly bounded by Ninth and Fourth Sts., Fourth Ave. and the Chattahoochee River.

——. *Columbus Historic Riverfront Industrial District.* Columbus River from Eighth St. N. to Thirty-Eighth St.

——. *Columbus Ironworks.* 910 Front Ave.

——. *Dinglewood.* 1429 Dinglewood St.

——. *Robert E. Dismukes, Sr., House.* 1617 Summit Dr.

——. *First National Bank* (Bank of Columbus). 1048 Broadway.

——. *Goetchius-Wellborn House.* 405 Broadway.

——. *Gordonido.* 1420 Wynnton Rd.

——. *Gunboats C.S.S. Muscogee and Chattahoochee.* Fourth St. w of U.S. Hwy. 27.

——. *Hilton.* 2505 Macon Rd.

——. *Illiges House.* 1428 Second Ave.

——. *Joseph House.* 828 Broadway.

——. *Lion House* (Hoxey-Cargill House). 1316 Third Ave.

——. *McGehee-Woodall House.* 1534 Second Ave.

——. *Mott House.* Front Ave.

——. *Octagon House.* 527 First Ave.

——. *Peabody-Warner House.* 1445 Second Ave.

——. *Pemberton House.* 11 Seventh St.

——. *Rankin House.* 1440 Second Ave.

——. *Rankin Square.* Bounded by Broadway, First Ave., Tenth, and Eleventh Sts.

——. *William Henry Spencer House.* 745 Fourth Ave.

——. *Springer Opera House.* 105 Tenth St.

——. *St. Elmo.* 2810 St. Elmo Dr.

——. *Swift-Kyle House.* 303 Twelfth St.

——. *Walker-Peters-Langdon House.* 716 Broadway.

——. *Wells-Bagley House.* 22 Sixth St.

——. *John W. Woolfolk House.* 1615 Twelfth St.

——. *Wynn House.* 1240 Wynnton Rd.

——. *Wynnton Academy.* 2303 Wynnton Rd.

——. *Wynnwood* (The Elms). 1846 Buena Vista Rd.

Newton County

Covington. *Floyd Street Historic District.* Floyd St. from Elm to w of Sockwell St.

Oxford. *Orna Villa* (Alexander Means House). 1008 N. Emory St.

——. *Oxford Historic District.* College and residential district centered around Wesley St.

Oconee County

Watkinsville. *Eagle Tavern.* U.S. Hwy. 129.

——. *South Main Street Historic District.* S. Main St. and Harden Hill Rd.

Oglethorpe County

Crawford. *Crawford Depot.* U.S. Hwy. 78.

Crawford Vicinity. *Amis-Elder House.* W of Crawford on Elder Rd.

——. *Langston-Daniel House.* 5 mi. W of Crawford on U.S. Hwy. 78.

Lexington. *Lexington Historic District.* U.S. Hwy. 78.

Lexington Vicinity. *J. L. Bridges Homeplace.* N of Lexington on Ga. Hwy. 22.

Philomath. *Philomath Historic District.* Ga. Hwy. 22.

Smithsonia Vicinity. *Howard's Covered Bridge.* 3 mi. SE of Smithsonia on Ga. Hwy. S2164 over Big Clouds Creek.

Paulding County

Dallas Vicinity. *Pickett's Mill Battlefield Site.* NE of Dallas off Ga. Hwy. 92.

Pickens County

Tate Vicinity. *Tate House* (Pink Palace). E of Tate on Ga. Hwy. 53.

Pulaski County

Hawkinsville. *Hawkinsville City Hall–Auditorium* (Old Opera

House). Lumpkin and Broad Sts.

———. *Taylor Hall.* Kibbe St.

Putnam County

Eatonton. *Eatonton Historic District.* Most of town centered around courthouse and city hall.

Eatonton Vicinity. *Gatewood House.* 6 mi. NE of Eatonton off Ga. Hwy. 44.

———. *Rock Eagle Site.* N of Eatonton off Ga. Hwy. 300.

———. *Singleton House.* SW of Eatonton off Ga. Hwy. 16.

———. *Tompkins Inn.* N of Eatonton on U.S. Hwy. 441.

———. *Woodland.* NE of Eatonton on Harmony Rd.

Randolph County

Cuthbert. *Cuthbert Historic District.* Centered around U.S. Hwys. 82 and 27.

Richmond County

Augusta. *Academy of Richmond County.* 540 Telfair St.

———. *Augusta Canal Industrial District.* E Augusta along W bank of Savannah River from Richmond-Columbia Co. line S to corner of Tenth and Fenwick Sts.

———. *Augusta Cotton Exchange Building.* Reynolds St.

———. *Stephen Vincent Benet House* (President's Home, Augusta College). 2500 Walton Way.

———. *Brahe House.* 456 Telfair St.

———. *First Baptist Church of Augusta.* Greene and Eighth Sts.

———. *Fitzsimons-Hampton House.* Ga. Hwy. 28.

———. *Fruitlands* (Augusta National Golf Club). 2604 Washington Rd.

———. *Gertrude Herbert Art Institute* (Nicholas Ware House). 506 Telfair St.

———. *Gould-Weed House.* 828 Milledge Rd.

———. *Harris-Pearson-Walker House.* 1822 Broad St.

———. *Lamar Building* (Southern Finance Building). 753 Broad St.

———. *Meadow Garden.* 1230 Nelson St.

———. *Old Medical College Building.* Telfair and Sixth Sts.

———. *Old Richmond County Courthouse.* 432 Telfair St.

———. *Reid-Jones-Carpenter House.* 2249 Walton Way.

———. *Sacred Heart Catholic Church.* Greene and Thirteenth Sts.

———. *St. Paul's Episcopal Church.* Sixth and Reynolds Sts.

———. *Woodrow Wilson Boyhood Home.* 419 Seventeenth St.

Augusta Vicinity. *College Hill* (Walton-Harper House). 2216 Wrightsboro Rd.

Rockdale County

Conyers Vicinity. *Dial Mill.* NE of Conyers off Ga. Hwy. 138.

Screven County

Sylvania Vicinity. *Seaborn Goodall House.* N of Sylvania at junction of U.S. Hwy. 301 and Ga. Hwy. 24.

Spalding County

Griffin. *Bailey-Tebault House.* 633 Meriwether St.

———. *Hawkes Library.* 210 S. Sixth St.

———. *Hill-Kurtz House.* 570 S. Hill St.

———. *Hunt House* (Chapman-Kincaid-Hunt House). 232 S. Eighth St.

———. *Mills House.* 406 N. Hill St.

———. *Old Medical College Historical Area* (Middle Georgia Medical College). 223–233 E. Broadway St.

———. *Pritchard-Moore-Goodrich House.* 411 N. Hill St.

———. *Sam Bailey Building.* E. Poplar and Fourth Sts.

Griffin Vicinity. *Double Cabins* (Mitchell-Walker-Hollberg House). NE of Griffin on Ga. Hwy. 16.

Williamson Vicinity. *Old Gaissert Homeplace.* NE of Williamson on Ga. Hwy. 362.

Stephens County

Toccoa. *Schaefer-Marks House.* 316 E. Doyle St.

Toccoa Vicinity. *Traveller's Rest.* E of Toccoa on U.S. Hwy. 123.

Stewart County

Lumpkin. *Bedingfield Inn.* Cotton St.

Lumpkin Vicinity. *Singer-Moye Archaeological Site.* S of Lumpkin.

———. *West Hill.* S of Lumpkin on U.S. Hwy. 27.

Omaha Vicinity. *Roods Landing Site.* S of Omaha at confluence of Rood Creek and the Chattahoochee River.

Sumter County

Americus. *Americus Historic District.* Irregular pattern along Lee St. with extensions to Dudley St., railroad tracks, Rees Park, and Glessner St.

Talbot County

Talbotton. *Levert Historic District.* Roughly bounded by Washington Ave., railroad tracks, Madison and Smith Sts.
———. *George W. B. Towns House.* Ga. Hwy. 208.
———. *Weeks-Kimbrough House.* 1 mi. SE of Talbotton on U.S. Hwy. 80.
Talbotton Vicinity. *Zion Episcopal Church.* S of Talbotton on U.S. Hwy. 80.

Taliaferro County

Crawfordville. *Liberty Hall.* Alexander H. Stephens Memorial State Park.
Crawfordville Vicinity. *Colonsay Plantation.* ENE of Crawfordville off Ga. Hwy. 908.

Thomas County

Metcalf. *Metcalfe Historic District.* Roughly bounded by Magnolia, Hancock, Louis, and Williams Sts.
Thomasville. *Dr. David Brandon House* (Hayes House). 329 N. Broad St.
———. *Bryan-David House* (Cater House). 312 N. Broad St.
———. *Hardy Bryan House.* 312 N. Broad St.
———. *Burch-Mitchell House.* 737 Remington Ave.
———. *East Side School.* 120 N. Hansell St.

———. *Greenwood Plantation.* Ga. Hwy. 84.
———. *Augustine Hansell House.* 429 S. Hansell St.
———. *Lapham-Patterson House* (Scarbrough House). 626 N. Dawson St.
———. *Park Front* (Charles Hebard House). 711 S. Hansell St.
———. *Ephraim Ponder House.* 324 N. Dawson St.
———. *Thomas County Courthouse.* N. Broad St.
———. *Thomasville Historic District.* Irregular pattern extending N to North Blvd., S to Loomis, E to Hansell and W to Oak St.
———. *Wright House.* 415 Fletcher St.
Thomasville Vicinity. *Millpond Plantation.* S of Thomasville on Pine Tree Blvd.

Troup County

La Grange. *Bellevue* (Benjamin Harvey Hill House). 204 Ben Hill St.
———. *Ferrell-Holder House.* 1402 Vernon Rd.
———. *Heard-Dallis House.* 206 Broad St.
———. *McFarland-Render House.* 612 Hines St.
———. *Strickland House.* NW of La Grange on Glenn Rd.
La Grange Vicinity. *Liberty Hill.* NW of La Grange on Liberty Hill Rd.
———. *Nutwood.* N of Big Springs Rd. near Newsom Cemetery.
———. *Reid-Glanton House* (Hutchinson House). E of La Grange at junction of Ga. Hwy. 109 and Pattillo Rd.
———. *Rutledge House.* S of La Grange on Bartley Rd.
Mountville Vicinity. *Nathan Van Boddie House.* W of Mountville on Ga. Hwy. 109.

West Point Vicinity. *Long Cane Historic District.* N of West Point on U.S. Hwy. 29.

Twiggs County

Fitzpatrick Vicinity. *Myrick's Mill.* NE of Fitzpatrick on Ga. Hwy. 378.

Union County

Blairsville Vicinity. *Walasi-Yi Inn.* S of Blairsville on U.S. Hwy. 129.

Upson County

Thomaston Vicinity. *Auchumpkee Creek Covered Bridge.* 10 mi. SE of Thomaston off U.S. Hwy. 19 on Allen Rd.

Walker County

Chickamauga. *Gordon-Lee House.* 217 Cove Rd.
Kensington Vicinity. *Lane House.* E of Kensington off Ga. Hwy. 341.
Rossville. *John Ross House.* Lake Ave. and Spring St.
Rossville Vicinity. *Ashland Farm.* SW of Rossville off Ga. Hwy. 193.

Walton County

Kilgore Mill Covered Bridge and Mill Site. See Barrow County.
Good Hope Vicinity. *Casulon Plantation.* E of Good Hope off Ga. Hwy. 186.
Monroe. *Davis-Edwards House.* 238 N. Broad St.

Ware County

Waycross. *Waycross Historic District.* Roughly bounded by Plant Ave., Williams, Lee, Chandler, and Stephens Sts.

Warren County

Warrenton. *Roberts-McGregor House.* Depot St.

Washington County

Davisboro Vicinity. *Francis Plantation.* SE of Davisboro on Ga. Hwy. 2189.

White County

Cleveland. *Old White County Courthouse.* On Ga. Hwy. 115.

Whitfield County

Dalton. *Crown Mill Historic District.* U.S. Hwy. 41.

———. *Western and Atlantic Depot.* Depot St., w end of King St.
Dalton Vicinity. *Prater's Mill.* N of Dalton on Ga. Hwy. 2.

Wilkes County

Danburg. *Anderson House.* Ga. Hwy. 44.
Danburg Vicinity. *Willis-Sale-Stennett House.* N of Danburg off Ga. Hwy. 79 on Ga. Hwy. 1445.
Tignall Vicinity. *Pharr-Callaway-Sethness House.* N of Tignall on Ga. Hwy. 2193.
Washington. *Campbell-Jordan House.* 208 Liberty St.
———. *The Cedars.* 210 Sims St.
———. *East Robert Toombs Historic District.* E. Robert Toombs Ave. between Alexander Ave. and Grove St.
———. *Gilbert-Alexander House.* 116 Alexander Dr.
———. *Holly Court (Ficklen House).* 301 S. Alexander St.
———. *Mary Willis Library.* E. Liberty and S. Jefferson Sts.
———. *North Washington District.* Bounded by Jefferson and Court Sts., Poplar Dr. and U.S. Hwy. 78.
———. *Old Jail.* 103 Court St.
———. *Peacewood.* 120 Tignall Rd.
———. *Poplar Corner.* 210 W. Liberty St.
———. *Robert Toombs House.* 216 E. Robert Toombs Ave.
———. *Tupper-Barnett House.* 101 W. Robert Toombs Ave.
———. *Washington Presbyterian Church.* 206 E. Robert Toombs Ave.
———. *Washington-Wilkes Historical Museum* (Barnett-Slaton House). 308 E. Robert Toombs Ave.
———. *West Robert Toombs District.* W. Robert Toombs Ave. between Allison St. and Ga. Hwy. 44 and Lexington Ave.
Washington Vicinity. *Arnold-Callaway Plantation.* NW of Washington on U.S. Hwy. 78.
———. *Kettle Creek Battlefield* (War Hill). 9 mi. SW of Washington off Tyrone Rd.
———. *Thomas M. Gilmer House.* 5 mi. W of Washington on U.S. Hwy. 78.

National Historic Landmarks

Georgia, January 25, 1980

Baldwin County

Milledgeville. *Old Governor's Mansion.* 120 S. Clark St.

Bartow County

Cartersville Vicinity. *Etowah Mounds.* 3 mi. s of Cartersville on Ga. Hwy. 61.

Bibb County

Macon. *Carmichael House.* (Raines House). 1183 Georgia Ave.
———. *Johnston-Hay House.* 934 Georgia Ave.

Chatham County

Savannah. *Central of Georgia Railroad Depot.* 301 W. Broad St.
———. *Central of Georgia Railroad, Savannah Shops and Terminal Facilities.* W. Broad and Railroad Ave.
———. *Green-Meldrim House.* 327 Bull St.
———. *Juliette Gordon Low House.* 10 Oglethorpe Ave.
———. *Owens-Thomas House* (Richardson-Owens-Thomas House). 122-124 Abercorn St.
———. *Savannah Historic District.* Bounded by East Broad, Gwinnett, and West Broad Sts. and the Savannah River.
———. *William Scarbrough House.* 41 W. Broad St.
———. *Telfair Academy.* 121 Barnard St.

Clarke County

Athens. *Taylor-Grady House.* 634 Prince Ave.

Columbia County

Augusta Vicinity. *Stallings Island.* 8 mi. NW of Augusta in the Savannah River.

Early County

Blakely Vicinity. *Kolomoki Mounds.* 8 mi. NW of Blakely on U.S. Hwy. 27.

Floyd County

Rome. *The Chieftains.* 80 Chatillon Road.

Fulton County

Atlanta. *Fox Theater.* 660 Peachtree St. N.E.
———. *Joel Chandler Harris House.* 1050 Gordon St.
———. *Martin Luther King, Jr., Historic District.* Bounded roughly by Irwin, Randolph, Edgewood, Jackson, and Auburn Aves.
———. *State Capitol.* Capitol Square.
———. *Stone Hall, Atlanta University.* Morris-Brown College campus.
———. *Sweet Auburn Historic District.* Bounded by Courtland and Houston Sts., Auburn and Piedmont Aves.

Glynn County

Jekyll Island. *Riverview Drive and Old Village Boulevard.*

Gordon County

Calhoun Vicinity. *New Echota.* Ga. Hwy. 225, 4.2 mi. NE of intersection with Court St. in Calhoun.

Liberty County

South Newport Vicinity. *St. Catherines Island.*

Lumpkin County

Dahlonega Vicinity. *Calhoun Gold Mine.* 3 mi. s of Dahlonega, off Ga. Hwy. 60.

McDuffie County

Thomson. *Thomas E. Watson House*. Hickory Hill Dr. and Lee St.

Meriwether County

Warm Springs. *Warm Springs Historic District*. (Little White House). s of Ga. Hwy. 194 and w of Ga. Hwy. 85w.

Muscogee County

Columbus. *Columbus Historic Riverfront Industrial District*. River from Eighth St. N to Thirty-Eighth St.
———. *Octagon House* (May's Folly). 527 First Ave.
———. *Springer Opera House*. 105 Tenth St.

Richmond County

Augusta. *College Hill* (Walton-Harper House). 2116 Wrightsboro Rd.
———. *Commandant's House* (U.S. Arsenal). Augusta College Campus.
———. *Historic Augusta Canal and Industrial District* (Confederate States Powder Works Chimney and Sibley Mills). E Augusta along w bank of Savannah River from the Richmond-Columbia Co. line s to the corner of Tenth and Fenwick Sts.

Stephens County

Toccoa Vicinity. *Traveller's Rest*. Riverdale Rd., 6 mi. NE of Toccoa.

Thomas County

Thomasville. *Lapham-Patterson House* (Scarbrough House). 626 N. Dawson St.

Troup County

La Grange. *Belleview*. 204 Ben Hill St.

Walker County

Rossville. *John Ross House, Spring, and Lake*. Lake Ave. and Spring St.

Wilkes County

Washington. *Robert Toombs House*. 213 E. Robert Toombs Ave.
———. *Tupper-Barnette House*. 101 W. Robert Toombs Ave.

Historic American Engineering Record

Georgia, December 31, 1980

Chatham County

Savannah. *Central of Georgia, Brick Arch* (Central of Georgia Railroad Bridge). Across Boundary St. N of Hull St.

——. *Central of Georgia, Brick Arch Viaduct* (Central of Georgia Railroad Bridge). Across Boundary St. N of Hull St.

——. *Central of Georgia Railroad, Passenger Station and Train Shed.* W. Broad and Liberty Sts.

——. *Central of Georgia Railroad, Repair Shop.* W. Broad St. and Railroad Ave.

Muscogee County

Columbus. *Bibb Company* (Columbus Plant). First Ave. at Thirty-Eighth St.

——. *W. C. Bradley Company.* 1017 Front Ave.

——. *City Mills Company.* 9 Eighteenth St.

——. *Columbus Iron Works.* 910 Front Ave.

——. *Columbus Manufacturing Company.*

——. *Eagle and Phenix Mills.* 1200–1300 Front Ave.

——. *Empire Mills Company.* Across from Columbus Iron Works on Front Ave.

——. *Front Avenue Industrial District.* Along Front Ave.

——. *Hydroelectric Power Development at North Highlands.* Near Bibb Company on Chattahoochee River, 1.3 mi. N of City Mills Dam.

——. *Sol Loeb Warehouse.* Front Ave. near Columbus Iron Works.

——. *Muscogee Manufacturing Company.* Front Ave. and Fourteenth St.

——. *Power Station of the Columbus Railroad Company.* At City Mills Dam, Eighteenth St. and Chattahoochee River.

——. *Seaboard Air Line Railroad, Freight Depot.* Front Ave. near Columbus Iron Works.

——. *Water Power Development at the Falls of the Chattahoochee.* At the Chattahoochee River Falls through Harris and Muscogee Counties.

Richmond County

Augusta. *American Foundry.* 602 Eleventh St.

——. *Augusta Canal.* E Augusta along w bank of Savannah River from the Richmond-Columbia Co. line s to the corner of Tenth and Fenwick Sts.

——. *Augusta Canal Industrial District.* Same as above.

——. *Augusta Machine Works* (Augusta Lumber Company). Bounded by D'Antignac, Jackson, Adams, and Campbell Sts.

——. *Augusta Railway Company, West Power Station.* 301 Fifteenth St.

——. *Augusta Water Works.* 3 mi. NW of Broad St. on dirt ext. of Goodrich St.

——. *Crescent Grain and Feed Mill* (Southern Milling Company). 1015 Twiggs Rd.

——. *Cunningham's Flour Mill.* 639 Thirteenth St.

——. *Dartmouth Spinning Company* (Southerland Mill). 510 Cottage St.

——. *Enterprise Manufacturing Company.* Greene St. at Fifteenth St.

——. *Georgia Iron Works.* 620–640 Twelfth St.

——. *Globe (Blanche) Mill.* 605 Twelfth St.

——. *Hight and McMurphy* (Lombard Ironworks and Supply Company). 636 Eleventh St.

——. *John P. King Manufacturing Company.* 1701 Goodrich St.

——. *Pendleton and Boardman* (Lombard Ironworks and Supply Company). 636 Eleventh St.

——. *Russell and Simmons Factory.* Goodrich St.

——. *Shamrock Mill Site.* Between the Seaboard Coastline Railroad tracks and the Augusta Canal.

——. *Sibley Manufacturing Company.* Goodrich St., .25 mi. NW of intersection with Broad St.

Historic American Buildings Survey Sites

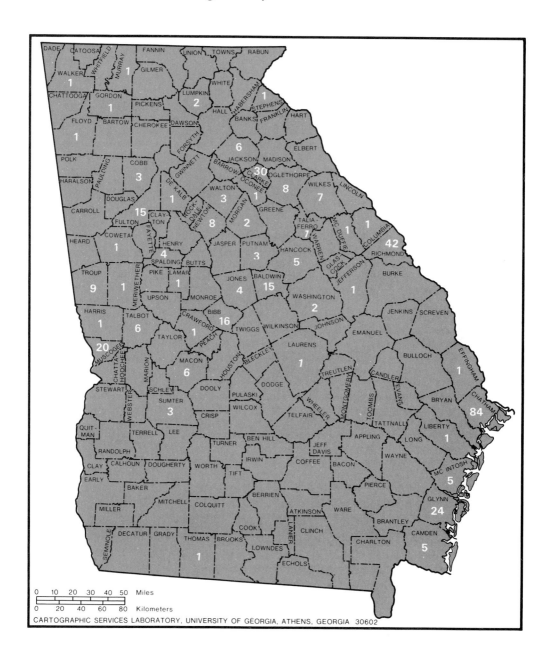

CARTOGRAPHIC SERVICES LABORATORY, UNIVERSITY OF GEORGIA, ATHENS, GEORGIA 30602

National Register of Historic Places Sites

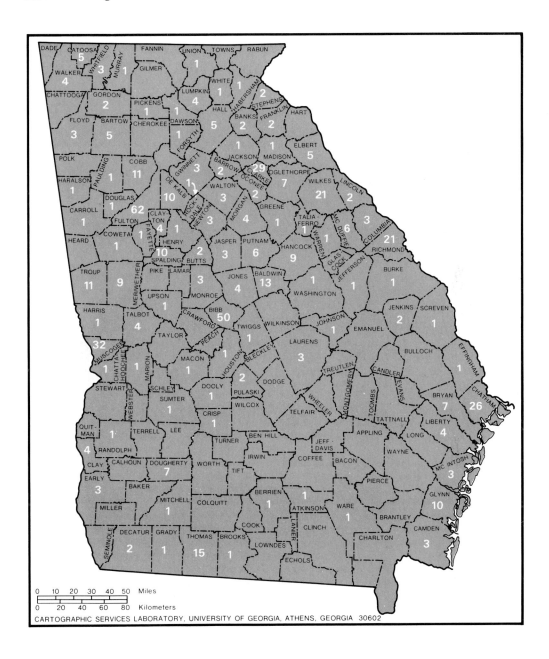

National Historic Landmarks Sites

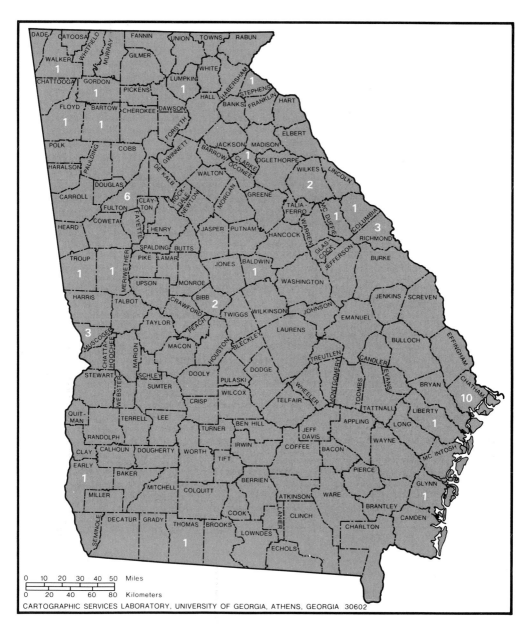

CARTOGRAPHIC SERVICES LABORATORY, UNIVERSITY OF GEORGIA, ATHENS, GEORGIA 30602

Note: Historic American Engineering Record sites are concentrated in three counties. There are 18 sites in Richmond County, 14 in Muscogee County, and 4 in Chatham County.

Illustration Credits

Page 4: Rock Eagle GA-29 HABS photograph by Kenneth Kay, 1980; drawing (not HABS) by Ken Paolini.

Page 5: Council Chamber drawing courtesy of the University of Georgia Libraries.

Page 6: Nacoochee Mound (Nichols-Hardman House GA-167) HABS photograph by Kenneth Kay, 1981.

Page 8: Vann House GA-174 HABS photograph by Jack E. Boucher, 1962.

Page 9: Carters Quarters GA-173 HABS photograph, 1934.

Page 11: Peter Gordon drawing courtesy of the University of Georgia Libraries.

Page 12: Hawkins-Davison House (GA-2149) drawing reprinted from the *Georgia Historical Quarterly*, vol. 40, no. 3 (September 1956). Calwell House Remains GA-2147 HABS drawing sheet no. 1.

Page 13: Moore House Remains GA-2163 HABS drawing sheet no. 3.

Page 14: Drawing of Fort Wimberly reprinted from *Captain Jones's Wormslow* by William M. Kelso (Athens: University of Georgia Press, 1979).

Page 15: Fort Wimberly GA-2126 HABS photograph, 1934.

Page 16: Christian Camphor House (GA-1177) photograph by Van Jones Martin, 1981.

Page 17: Wild Heron (GA-253)

photograph by Van Jones Martin, ca. 1974, from *The Architecture of Georgia* (Savannah: Beehive Press, 1976). Jerusalem Church GA-242 HABS photographs, 1934 (ext.), 1936 (int.).

Page 18: Old Jail GA-264 HABS photograph, 1936. Cochran House GA-14-23 HABS photograph by L. D. Andrew, 1936; HABS drawing sheet no. 2.

Page 19: Cochran House GA-14-23 HABS drawing sheet no. 2.

Page 20: Jordan Cabin GA-164 HABS photograph by Kenneth Kay, 1972.

Page 21: Refuge Plantation GA-248 HABS photographs, 1936.

Page 23: Horton House Remains GA-2150 HABS drawing sheet no. 1.

Page 24: Gachet House GA-14-121 HABS drawing sheet no. 2.

Page 25: Travelers Rest GA-14-5 HABS drawing sheet no. 2.

Page 27: De Brahm's plan of Savannah courtesy of the University of Georgia Libraries.

Page 28: Savannah city plan, 1856, courtesy of the University of Georgia Libraries.

Page 32: Independent Presbyterian Church (GA-237) Library of Congress photograph by Frances Benjamin Johnston (LC, SCAS, Johnston). Bank of the State of Georgia engraving reprinted from *Historical Collections of Georgia* by the Rev. George White (New York:

M. A. Pudney and Russell, 1854).

Page 33: Ware-Sibley-Clark House (GA-2128) Library of Congress photograph by Frances Benjamin Johnston (LC, SCAS, Johnston).

Page 34: Ware-Sibley-Clark doorway and steps GA-2128 HABS photograph. Richmond County Courthouse GA-239 HABS photograph, 1936.

Page 35: Ware-Sibley-Clark House GA-2128 HABS drawing sheet no. 1.

Page 36: Belcher-Hunter House GA-2138 HABS photograph, 1936.

Page 37: Belcher-Hunter House GA-2138 HABS photographs, 1936.

Page 38: Houston-Screven House GA-246 HABS photograph copied in 1936.

Page 39: Mount Nebo GA-14-4 HABS drawing sheet no. 2.

Page 40: Mount Nebo GA-14-4 HABS photograph by Branan Sanders, 1934.

Page 41: Davenport House GA-14-8 HABS drawing sheet no. 3.

Page 42: Old State Capitol GA-137 HABS photograph. Harris-Pearson-Walker House (GA-14-7) photograph by Schaeffer Studio, 1980.

Page 43: Harris-Pearson-Walker House GA-14-7 HABS drawing sheet no. 5.

Page 44: Midway Congregational

Church GA-44 HABS drawing sheet no. 2.

Page 45: High Gate GA-266 HABS photograph by L. D. Andrew, 1936. Meadow Garden GA-2100 HABS photograph.

Page 46: Meadow Garden GA-2100 HABS photographs. Stage Coach Inn GA-148 HABS photograph by Ward Denis, 1936. Kolb House GA-299 HABS photograph, 1963. Rice Mill GA-2126 HABS photograph by Branan Sanders, 1934.

Page 47: Jackson House GA-278 HABS photograph by Kenneth Kay, 1972.

Page 48: Harrison House GA-2121 HABS photograph by Kenneth Kay, 1972.

Page 49: Harrison House (GA-2121) photograph by John Linley and Robbie Hattaway, 1970. Mitchell-Barron House GA-155 HABS photographs by Kenneth Kay, 1980.

Page 50: Thomas Cheely House GA-1119 HABS photograph by Kenneth Kay, 1972.

Page 51: Thomas Cheely House GA-1119 HABS photograph by Kenneth Kay, 1972; photograph of porch column and plate (not HABS) by Robbie Hattaway, 1970.

Page 52: James C. Daniel House GA-2123 HABS photograph by Kenneth Kay, 1980.

Page 53: James C. Daniel House (GA-2123) photograph of stairway from top floor by Van Jones Martin, ca. 1974, from *The Architecture of Georgia* (Savannah: Beehive Press, 1976). Carters Quarters GA-173 HABS photograph, 1934. Lufburrow House (GA-2139) photograph by Van Jones Martin, ca. 1974, from *The Architecture of Georgia* (Savannah: Beehive Press, 1976).

Page 54: Demosthenian Hall

GA-14-87 HABS photograph, 1934; HABS drawing sheet no. 2.

Page 55: College Hill GA-14-69 HABS drawing sheet no. 3.

Page 56: The Cedars GA-191 HABS photograph by L. D. Andrew, 1936.

Page 57: John Williams House GA-133 HABS photograph by L. D. Andrew, 1936.

Page 58: Boykin House GA-170 HABS photograph by Branan Sanders, 1934.

Page 59: Westover GA-14-31 HABS drawing sheet no. 5.

Page 60: Gordon-Banks House (GA-1125) photograph by William Nathaniel Banks, 1974.

Page 61: Gordon-Banks House (GA-1125) photograph by Helga Photo Studios courtesy of the magazine *Antiques*.

Page 62: Gordon-Banks House (GA-1125) photograph by Paul Beswick.

Page 63: Gordon-Banks House (GA-1125) photograph by Van Jones Martin, ca. 1974, from *The Architecture of Georgia* (Savannah: Beehive Press, 1976).

Page 64: The Homestead (GA-134) photograph by Kenneth Kay, 1972.

Page 65: Brown-Sanford House GA-136 HABS photograph by L. D. Andrew, 1936. Casulon GA-1110 HABS photograph, 1936.

Page 66: Hamilton-Johnson House GA-1123 HABS photograph by Branan Sanders, 1934.

Page 67: Thicket Sugar Mill and Rum Distillery GA-271 HABS photograph. Vann House GA-174 HABS photograph by Jack E. Boucher, 1962.

Page 68: Cowles-Sams House GA-14-27 HABS drawing sheet no. 2.

Page 69: The Magnolias GA-14-62 HABS drawing sheet no. 3.

Page 70: Boddie House GA-1143

HABS photograph by L. D. Andrew, 1936.

Page 71: Boddie House GA-1143 HABS photograph by L. D. Andrew, 1936.

Page 72: The Hermitage GA-225 HABS photograph, 1934.

Page 73: The Hermitage GA-225 HABS drawing sheet no. 3.

Page 74: Polhill-Baugh House GA-1154 HABS photograph by Kenneth Kay, 1980.

Page 76: Nathanael Greene Monument GA-1183 HABS photograph by Lewis Schwartz, 1966. First Presbyterian Church (GA-2113) engraving reprinted from *Historical Collections of Georgia* by the Rev. George White (New York: M. A. Pudney and Russell, 1854), p. 596.

Page 77: Richardson-Owens-Thomas House GA-14-9 HABS photograph.

Page 78: Richardson-Owens-Thomas House GA-14-9 HABS drawing sheet no. 6.

Page 79: Scarbrough House GA-2127 HABS photograph.

Page 80: Scarbrough House (GA-2127) photograph courtesy of the Scarbrough House Museum.

Page 81: Telfair Academy GA-217 HABS photograph, 1936.

Page 82: United States Bank (GA-291) reproduction of an 1831 steel engraving. Richardson-Owens-Thomas House GA-14-9 HABS photograph.

Page 83: Richardson-Owens-Thomas House (GA-14-9) photograph courtesy of the Owens-Thomas House Museum. Telfair Academy GA-217 HABS photograph.

Page 84: Rockwell GA-135 HABS photograph by L. D. Andrew, 1936. First African Baptist Church (GA-276) photograph courtesy of the Georgia Historical Society.

Page 85: Eldorado GA-129 HABS photographs.

Page 86: Gibbons Servants' and Carriage House GA-2137 HABS photograph by Branan Sanders, 1934. Slave Market GA-14-2 HABS drawing sheet no. 1.

Page 87: Slave Market GA-14-2 HABS photograph by Branan Sanders, 1934.

Page 88: Westover (GA-14-31) drawing based on HABS house plan and on garden plan in *Garden History of Georgia, 1733–1933*, compiled and edited by Loraine M. Cooney and H. Rainwater (Atlanta: Peachtree Garden Club, 1933). Carnes House GA-26 HABS photograph, 1936.

Page 90: Lowther Hall GA-14-59 HABS photograph.

Page 91: Richardson-Owens-Thomas House GA-14-9 HABS photograph.

Page 92: Broad Street Stores GA-273 HABS photograph by L. D. Andrew, 1936.

Page 94: Cerveaux's view of Savannah courtesy of the University of Georgia Libraries.

Page 95: William Taylor Store GA-1196 HABS photographs by Louis Schwartz, 1962.

Page 100: President's House, University of Georgia (GA-120) photograph by Kenneth Kay, ca. 1970. Johnson House GA-184 HABS photograph by L. D. Andrew, 1936. Huntley House GA-122 HABS photograph, 1936.

Page 101: Old Emory Church GA-125 HABS photograph, 1936.

Page 102: White Hall GA-161 HABS photograph, 1936. T. R. R. Cobb House GA-1116 HABS photograph by Kenneth Kay, 1980.

Page 103: Dr. Marcus A. Franklin House GA-14-66 HABS drawing sheet no. 2.

Page 104: Old Governor's Mansion (GA-156) photograph by Kenneth Kay, 1971.

Page 105: Montrose GA-227 HABS photograph by Lawrence Bradley, 1936.

Page 106: Bulloch Hall GA-14-13 HABS photograph, 1934.

Page 107: Abbot-Toombs House GA-13 HABS photographs by Branan Sanders, 1934.

Page 108: Casulon GA-1110 HABS photograph by L. D. Andrew, 1936. Few Literary Society Hall GA-198 HABS photograph, 1936.

Page 109: Maxwell House GA-1140 HABS photograph, 1936.

Page 110: Cottage behind the President's House, University of Georgia GA-1-20 HABS photograph by Kenneth Kay, 1981. White Hall GA-159 HABS photograph, 1980.

Page 111: Davis-Edwards House GA-1138 HABS photograph by Kenneth Kay, 1980.

Page 112: Nichols House GA-1146 HABS photograph by L. D. Andrew, 1936. Neal-McCormick House GA-124 HABS photograph by Branan Sanders, 1934.

Page 113: Orange Hall GA-14-16 HABS photograph, 1934. Fruitlands (GA-252) reprinted from *The House: A Pocket Manual of Rural Architecture* (New York: Fowler and Wells, 1858).

Page 114: Orange Hall GA-14-16 HABS drawing sheet no. 1.

Page 115: Clanton House GA-224 HABS photograph, 1936. Orange Hall GA-14-16 HABS photograph by Branan Sanders, 1934.

Page 116: Low House (GA-210) Library of Congress photo by Frances Benjamin Johnston (LC, CSAS, Johnston).

Page 117: Chew House GA-260 HABS photograph, 1936. Old Governor's Mansion GA-156 HABS photograph by L. D. Andrew, 1936.

Page 118: Orange Hall GA-16 HABS drawing sheet no. 6.

Page 119: The Oaks GA-14-100 HABS drawing sheet no. 2.

Page 120: Old Governor's Mansion GA-156 HABS photograph by L. D. Andrew, 1936.

Page 121: Sayre-Shivers House GA-179 HABS photograph by L. D. Andrew, 1936.

Page 122: The Parsonage GA-192 HABS photograph by L. D. Andrew, 1936. Green-Meldrim House GA-222 HABS photograph by L. D. Andrew, 1936.

Page 123: Boxwood GA-183 HABS photograph by L. D. Andrew, 1936. Old Medical College GA-14-70 HABS photograph by Branan Sanders, 1934.

Page 124: Barracks Remains GA-2146 HABS photograph by Jack E. Boucher, 1958.

Page 125: Old State Capitol GA-137 HABS photographs by L. D. Andrew, 1937.

Page 128: Zion Episcopal Church GA-1139 HABS photograph by L. D. Andrew, 1936.

Page 129: St. John's Episcopal Church GA-1192 photograph by Van Jones Martin, ca. 1970.

Page 131: Green-Meldrim House GA-222 HABS photograph by Lawrence Bradley, 1936; drawing reproduced from the Collections of the Library of Congress.

Page 132: Redd House GA-138 HABS photograph by L. D. Andrew, 1936, copied from a photograph by Don Johnson.

Page 133: Academy of Richmond County GA-229 HABS photograph by Lawrence Bradley, 1936.

Page 134: Taylor Monument GA-2105 HABS photograph by Kenneth Kay, 1980.

Page 135: First Presbyterian

Church GA-274 HABS photograph by Kenneth Kay, 1980.

Page 136: Central of Georgia Railroad Bridge GA-213 HABS photograph by Lawrence Bradley, 1936.

Page 137: Central of Georgia Train Shed GA-213 HABS photograph by Louis Schwartz, 1962.

Page 138: Central of Georgia smokestack, water tower, and privy (GA-213) photograph by Van Jones Martin, ca. 1974, from *The Architecture of Georgia* (Savannah: Beehive Press, 1976).

Page 139: Central of Georgia smokestack, water tower, and privy (GA-213) HAER drawing sheet.

Page 141: Mercer-Wilder House GA-1189 HABS photograph by Louis Schwartz, 1966.

Page 142: Johnston-Hay House GA-275 HABS photograph by Drinnon Studio courtesy of the Georgia Trust for Historic Preservation.

Page 143: Johnston-Hay House GA-275 HABS photograph by Drinnon Studio courtesy of the Georgia Trust for Historic Preservation.

Page 144: Emerson-Holmes Building GA-195 HABS photograph by L. D. Andrew, 1936.

Page 145: Dinglewood GA-293 HABS photographs by Van Jones Martin, 1980.

Page 146: Paschal-Sammons House GA-27 HABS photograph by Kenneth Kay, 1972.

Page 147: Barclay-Wetter House GA-2136 HABS photograph by Branan Sanders, 1934.

Page 148: Rankin House GA-112 HABS photograph by L. D. Andrew, 1936.

Page 149: Camak House GA-14-67 HABS drawing sheet no. 3.

Page 150: Lucy Cobb Institute

GA-1120 HABS photograph.

Page 151: James Sledge House GA-2104 HABS photograph by Dennis O'Kain, 1980.

Page 152: Gordon Row GA-2145 HABS photograph, 1958. Fountain in Forsyth Park reprinted from *Picturesque America*, edited by William Cullen Bryant (New York: D. Appleton and Co., 1874).

Page 153: Bank of Columbus GA-292 HABS photograph by Van Jones Martin, 1980.

Page 154: Ethridge House photograph by Robbie Hattaway, 1970.

Page 155: James Sledge House GA-2104 HABS photograph by Dennis O'Kain, 1980.

Page 156: John A. Cobb House GA-1166 HABS photograph by Charles E. Peterson, 1935. Lampkin-Mell House GA-1167 HABS photograph by Charles E. Peterson, 1935.

Page 157: Rossiter-Little House GA-188 HABS photograph by L. D. Andrew, 1936.

Page 158: May's Folly GA-294 HABS photograph by Van Jones Martin, 1980. Raines House GA-145 HABS photograph by L. D. Andrew, 1936.

Page 159: Raines House GA-145 HABS photograph by L. D. Andrew, 1936.

Page 160: Woodrow Wilson's Boyhood Home GA-2117 HABS photograph by Schaeffer Studio, 1980.

Page 161: Taylor-Grady House GA-1114 HABS photograph by Kenneth Kay, 1980.

Page 162: Carnes House GA-26 HABS photograph by Lawrence Bradley, 1936. Marsh House GA-15 HABS photograph by Harold Bush-Brown, 1936. Negro Cabin GA-283 HABS photograph by L. D. Andrew, 1936.

Page 163: Wormsloe GA-2126 Slave Cabin HABS photograph by Branan Sanders, 1934.

Page 164: The Hermitage GA-225 Slave Quarters HABS photograph by Charles E. Peterson, 1934.

Page 165: Timothy Bonticou Double House GA-1176 HABS photograph by Louis Schwartz, 1966.

Page 166: House, 261 Watkins Street GA-265 HABS photograph by L. D. Andrew, 1936.

Page 168: Casulon GA-1110 HABS photograph, 1936.

Page 169: Cowles-Bond House (GA-1124) gazebo photograph by Danny Gilleland, 1981.

Page 170: Boxwood garden GA-183 HABS photograph by L. D. Andrew, 1936.

Page 171: Harris-Rives Plantation plan was copied by Tim Hill from the original John Waterman drawing, which belongs to George Rives, the present owner of the plantation.

Page 174: Cox-Steward Farm GA-172 HABS photograph by L. D. Andrew, 1936.

Page 175: Peacewood GA-19 HABS photograph by L. D. Andrew, 1936.

Page 176: View of Ackworth reprinted from *Harper's Weekly*, July 9, 1864. View of Atlanta reprinted from *Harper's Weekly*, November 26, 1864.

Page 177: Augusta cotton factory reprinted from an engraving in *Confederate City* by Florence Fleming Corley (Columbia: University of South Carolina Press, 1960).

Page 178: Factor's Walk photograph by Van Jones Martin, 1982.

Page 179: View of Macon, 1857, courtesy of the University of Georgia Libraries. The engraving appeared in the *London Illustrated News* in 1863.

Page 180: Fort Pulaski GA-2158 HABS photograph by Charles E. Peterson, 1936.

Page 183: Atlanta in ruins, reprinted from an engraving in *Harper's Pictorial History of the Civil War* by A. H. Guernsey and H. M. Alden (New York: Harper Brothers, 1868).

Page 184: Confederate States Powder Works (GA-1101) drawing by C. Shaler Smith, reprinted from *Confederate City* by Florence Fleming Corley (Columbia: University of South Carolina Press, 1960).

Page 185: Confederate States Power Works Chimney GA-1101 HABS photograph by Schaeffer Studio, 1980.

Page 186: Sibley Mills GA-2116 HABS photograph by Schaeffer Studio, 1980. Muscogee Mills GA-110 HABS photograph, 1936.

Page 187: First African Baptist Church (GA-276) reprinted from *Sojourn in Savannah* by Betty Rauers, Terry Victor, and Franklin Traub (Savannah: Printcraft Press, 1973).

Page 188: Nichols-Hardman House GA-167 HABS photograph by Kenneth Kay, 1981.

Page 189: Nichols-Hardman House GA-167 HABS photograph by Kenneth Kay, 1981.

Page 190: Old Campbell County Courthouse GA-187 HABS photograph by Paul G. Beswick, 1980.

Page 191: Crescent Hill Baptist Church GA-162 HABS photograph by Kenneth Kay, 1981.

Page 192: Mickve Israel Synagogue GA-1190 HABS photograph by Louis Schwartz, 1966.

Page 193: Hancock County Courthouse GA-228 HABS photograph by Kenneth Kay, 1972.

Page 194: Zachary Daniels House GA-2112 HABS photograph by Schaeffer Studio, 1980.

Page 195: Samuel P. Hamilton House GA-1184 HABS photograph by Louis Schwartz, 1966.

Page 196: Springer Opera House GA-295 HABS photograph by Van Jones Martin, 1980.

Page 198: Parr House GA-2103 HABS photograph by Kenneth Kay, 1980. Merk House GA-2102 HABS photograph by Kenneth Kay, 1980.

Page 200: New Haywood GA-2122 HABS photograph by Kenneth Kay, 1980.

Page 201: Martin Luther King, Jr., Birth Home GA-1171 HABS photograph by Kenneth Kay, 1980.

Page 202: House, 16 West Duffy Street GA-1169-173 HABS photograph by Walter Smalling, 1980. House, 803 Whitaker Street GA-1169-223 HABS photograph by Walter Smalling, 1980.

Page 203: Seney-Stovall Chapel, Lucy Cobb Institute (GA-1120), photograph by Kenneth Kay, 1981.

Page 204: Oglethorpe County Courthouse GA-194 HABS photograph by Kenneth Kay, 1980.

Page 205: Savannah Cotton Exchange GA-1194 HABS photograph by Louis Schwartz, 1966.

Page 206: Sacred Heart Church GA-2115 HABS photograph by Schaeffer Studio, 1980.

Page 207: Equitable Building GA-2107 HABS photograph by Robert Irwin, 1970.

Page 210: Thomas-Carithers House GA-1131 HABS photograph by Kenneth Kay, 1980.

Page 211: Georgia State Capitol GA-2109 HABS photograph.

Page 216: H. C. White House GA-2106 HABS photograph by Kenneth Kay, 1980.

Page 217: Putnam County Court-

house GA-28 HABS photograph by Kenneth Kay, 1972.

Page 218: Roosevelt's Little White House GA-279 HABS photograph. Ike's Cottage GA-2114 HABS photograph by Schaeffer Studio, 1980.

Page 219: Charles Hayes House GA-2101 HABS photograph by Kenneth Kay, 1980.

Page 220: Swan House GA-2111 HABS photograph by R. Cotton Alston, 1980.

Page 221: The Fox Theater GA-2108 HABS photograph by Jonathan Hillyer Photography, Inc., 1980.

Page 222: The Fox Theater GA-2109 HABS photograph by Jonathan Hillyer Photography, Inc., 1980.

Page 224: Jimmy Carter Boyhood Home GA-245 HABS photograph by Kenneth Kay, 1979.

Page 225: Rockefeller Cottage GA-2164 HABS drawing sheet no. 4.

Page 227: Jimmy Carter House GA-244 HABS photograph by Kenneth Kay, 1979.

Page 228: Benton House photograph by Alexander Georges, ca. 1964.

Page 230: Kemp Mooney House photograph by Kemp Mooney, 1980.

Page 231: Jerry Lominack House photograph by Van Jones Martin, 1981.

Page 233: Southworth Division of the Morris-Bryan Plant photograph by Kenneth Kay, 1981.

Page 234: Procter and Gamble Plant photograph by Morgan Fitz Photographer, Inc., 1962.

Page 236: Billy Carter's Service Station GA-243 HABS photograph by Kenneth Kay, 1979.

Page 237: Hyatt-Regency Hotel photograph (ca. 1973) courtesy of John Portman and Associates.

Page 238: Jones Bridge Headquarters of the Simmons Company photograph by E. Alan McGee Photography, Inc., 1977.

Page 239: Diagrammatic drawing of the Jones Bridge Headquarters courtesy of Thompson, Hancock, Witte, and Associates, Inc.

Page 244: Georgia skyline photograph courtesy of the Georgia Department of Archives and History (large print collection 355A).

Page 245: Herndon Building GA-1170-72 HABS drawing sheet no. 6.

Page 246: Atlanta Life Insurance GA-126-256 HABS drawing sheet no. 2.

Page 247: Big Bethel Church GA-1170-72 HABS drawing sheet no. 7.

Page 248: 217 West Duffy Street GA-1169-179 HABS photograph by Walter Smalling, 1980.

Page 249: 217–225 East Bolton Street GA-1169-25 HABS photograph by Walter Smalling, 1980.

Page 253: 200 block, East Henry Street GA-1169-63 HABS photograph by Walter Smalling, 1980.

Indexes

Index of names in Part II